**"Our Country First,
Then Greenville"**

"OUR COUNTRY FIRST, THEN GREENVILLE"

A New South City during the Progressive Era and World War I

Courtney L. Tollison Hartness

THE UNIVERSITY OF SOUTH CAROLINA PRESS

© 2023 University of South Carolina

Published by the University of South Carolina Press
Columbia, South Carolina 29208

uscpress.com

Manufactured in the United States of America

32 31 30 29 28 27 26 25 24 23
10 9 8 7 6 5 4 3 2 1

Library of Congress Cataloging-in-Publication
Data can be found at http://catalog.loc.gov/.

ISBN 978-1-64336-415-5 (hardcover)
ISBN 978-1-64336-416-2 (paperback)
ISBN 978-1-64336-417-9 (ebook)

In Memory of Brittany Langley Lawson (1982–2021), Julie Marie Accetta (1980–2021), and my grandmothers, Louise Pittman Surett (1927–2020) and Louise Jones Tollison (1923–2022).

Dedicated to my children, Gladden, Catherine, and Margot.
May you leave the world a better place than you found it.

Contents

List of Illustrations ix

Acknowledgments xi

Introduction 1

CHAPTER ONE

The Politics of Race and Gender in the
"Pearl of the Piedmont" 12

CHAPTER TWO

Greenville and the Nation Respond to
War "Over There," 1914–1917 41

CHAPTER THREE

The Impact of Camp Sevier: Mobilization,
Nationalization, and Economic Boom 62

CHAPTER FOUR

"For Liberty and Humanity": Camp and
Community on the Home Front, 1917–1918 81

CHAPTER FIVE

"They Have Responded to Every Call":
Race Relations on the Home Front 104

CHAPTER SIX

"What American will have the heart or the
hardihood to say him nay?": African Americans'
Service in the Great War 123

CHAPTER SEVEN

"A University or a Training Camp": Furman University
and the Student Army Training Corps 143

viii Contents

CHAPTER EIGHT

Chaos and Confusion in 1918:
The Influenza Pandemic in Greenville 158

CHAPTER NINE

"Grow with Greenville": Progressivism in the
Postwar Era, 1919–1929 176

Epilogue: Memorialization of the Great War:
The Politics of Race and Remembrance 216

Notes 239

Bibliography 287

Index 305

Illustrations

Confederate Reunion, ca. 1915 15

African American Laundress, 1898–99 18

Soldier's Tent at Camp Wetherill 1898–99 19

Viola Neblett 24

Neblett Library 25

Gridley Ladies at Tea, ca. 1905 26

Margaret McKissick, ca. 1391 31

Children in Cotton Field, 1898–99 34

Woodside Mill, 1913 36

Dunean Mill and Village, ca. 1915 38

Stump Privy, 1916 55

Camp Sevier, 1918 64

Tents of 30th Division at Camp Sevier, 1917–18 68

Louise Mayes, 1929 95

Biggs Family 111

Biggs Family Home 112

Student Army Training Corps (SATC) at Furman, 1918 153

Nurses at Camp Sevier, ca. 1917–18 164

Rotary Club Meeting on Rooftcp, 1918 166

Furman Quarantine, ca. 1906 174

Greenville Civic and Commercial Journal cover, March 1922 186

Mary P. Gridley 187

Andrea Christensen Patterson 188

Woodside Building, 1921 191

Confederate Monument with Statue Removed, ca. 1925 194

Greenville Public Library Book Mobile, 1924–25 205

Phillis Wheatley Center, 1929 207

Phillis Wheatley Health and Hygiene Class, 1925 208

x *List of Illustrations*

Hattie Logan Duckett 211

Furman Band at Airport, 1928 214

Confederate Memorial Day, 1919 217

Elias B. Holloway with Fellow Post Workers, 1900 219

Reunion of the 30th Division, 1919 220

Spirit of the American Doughboy monument, 1921 223

Acknowledgments

Writing a book is both a solitary endeavor and one that is highly reliant on others. I'm grateful to those who encouraged me throughout this process.

This project began in the summer of 2014, when Furman undergraduate Donny Santacaterina and I began researching and writing about Greenville during World War I. He was exceptionally dedicated to this project and made the early years of it a lot of fun. Even then he was an excellent scholar, and as he nears the completion of his doctorate in history from the University of North Carolina at Chapel Hill, I am eager to see his career continue to flourish. In preparation for the centennial of American entry into the war in spring 2017, Furman undergrads Helen Mistler and Tyler Edmond joined Donny and me as curators of an exhibit for Furman's Special Collections and Archives titled "Over Here, Over There: Greenville in the Great War." After the centennial of American entry into the war, Furman students Julia Fresne, Sam Hayes, Trevor Woods, and Marlies Bronner ably assisted with research. This undertaking has been so much more rewarding because of my students' engagement with it. I'm thankful to them and for the support Furman University has invested in this project, including grants from Furman Advantage, the Furman Humanities Center, the John Block Fund, and the Research and Professional Growth Committee.

Dozens of individuals have assisted in this effort in myriad ways. I thank Julia Cowart and Jeff Makala at Furman's Special Collections and Archives; Edward Blessing and Todd Hoppock at the University of South Carolina's South Caroliniana Library; Shanna Raines and Rebecca Vannette at the South Carolina Room at the Greenville County Library; Greenville City Clerk Camilla Pitman; Darlene Parker at the Greenville County Historical Society; Jack Green, formerly of the Naval Historical Center; Carolyn Fortson at the Allendale Hampton Jasper Regional Library; Nathan Jordan at the National Archives and Records Administration in Atlanta; and Molly Silliman at the South Carolina Historical Society. I also wish to thank Anjali Carroll, Don Koonce, Kathy Redwing, and Sean Dogan.

During the first few months of COVID-19, as we negotiated our own pandemic, my students read the chapter on the Spanish influenza and provided insightful feedback and encouragement. Elizabeth Robeson read the manuscript, *xii Acknowledgments*

contributed her keen understanding of historiography, and challenged me in valuable ways. I also thank Anne Barrington, Bob Ellis, Alyssa Russell, and Caroline Moore for their editorial support. Steve Richardson, formerly of Furman's Duke Library, has been unfailingly helpful. I have benefited from his knowledge of Greenville's history and his eagerness to delve deeply into Greenville's past alongside me. I remain in awe of Judy Bainbridge's vast familiarity with Greenville's history and her unparalleled talent for sharing it with this community. She is the first person I go to when my research stalls, and I'm grateful to her for supporting me since my days as a Furman student.

I thank Richard Brown, former director of USC Press, for his interest in my research; USC Press acquisitions editor Ehren Foley for shepherding this project; and USC Press production editor Kerri Tolan for navigating its completion.

I'm blessed with a wonderfully supportive group of family and friends; your inquiries reinforced my commitment to staying the course. It isn't often that one has the pleasure and privilege of becoming colleagues and close friends with one's college mentors. I'm grateful to Marian Strobel and Diane Vecchio for inspiring and encouraging me for over twenty-five years.

My three children were born in the last four years of this undertaking. I would have never been able to complete this work without assistance from a team of trusted caregivers, especially Debbie Blake, Dahlila Coriette, Betsy Hill, Ellie and Morgan Hensarling, Heidi Ormiston, and Jamie Fletcher.

My parents, David and Linda Tollison, have always been my greatest and most steadfast cheerleaders. I remain deeply grateful to them for their encouragement and for being such dedicated and doting grandparents. My husband, Sean Hartness, has been an unfailingly patient and supportive life partner. I wouldn't want to be on this journey with anyone else.

This book is written in memory of my grandmothers, both of whom were born in the 1920s and witnessed nearly a century of change in Greenville. They have profoundly shaped me, and I'm grateful to have had them in my life for so long. It is also written in memory of my cousin Brittany Langley Lawson and dear friend Julie Accetta. Both of these beautiful women thrived in careers in which they served and uplifted others. Like many of those featured in this book, Brittany and Julie touched countless lives and made the Greenville community a better place.

With my deepest love and highest hopes, this book is dedicated to my three young children: Gladden, Catherine, and Margot. Your community's past is in these pages; I hope you will one day contribute meaningfully to its future.

Introduction

> The past that Southerners are forever talking about is not a dead past—
> it is a chapter from the legend that our kinfolks have told us, it is a living
> past, living for a reason. The past is a part of the present, it is a comfort,
> a guide, a lesson.
>
> —Ben Robertson, *Red Hills and Cotton*

In 2015, one year after European countries began their centennial commemorations of the Great War and two years before the United States began its own, historian Chad Williams wrote, "The war is arguably the central point of entry to understanding modern American history and America's place in the world."[1] Furman University undergraduate Donny Santacaterina and I had recently embarked on a research project that examined the impact of World War I on Greenville, South Carolina, and Williams's assertion resonated with us. Over the years we discovered the prevalence of this concept in the works of other scholars who have similarly argued for the war's modernizing impact on the economy, warfare, and medicine; on notions of the American citizen, civilian, and nation-state; and on African Americans and women.[2] If the war was the point of entry to modern America and all that that encompasses, we wondered, in what ways is it also a point of entry for understanding the modern era of America's communities, such as the one in which we lived?[3] It became evident that an investigation into those questions could not divorce Greenville's experiences during World War I from the civic engagement associated with the Progressive Era within which the war was embedded. A more thorough study of both the war and the era yielded an apparent conclusion: between the 1890s and 1920s, as a result of the area's industrial prowess, New South boosterism, Progressive Era civic engagement, and the Great War, Greenville evolved into a modern city.

As a historian who straddles the worlds of academia and public history, I have aspired to author a work that would contribute historiographically to conversations on the war, race relations and African American life, the expansion of women's roles, and the Progressive Era in the American South. I also hope this work will appeal to those in the general public interested in how events of the past contribute to and shape our present. World War I historian Jennifer Keene argues for the Great War's relevance in the post-9/11 world.

> The war . . . offers important cautionary tales about the diplomatic and political missteps that caused a catastrophic, and likely, unnecessary war in 1914. The cascade of events following September 11, 2001 that led to a wider war with tremendous civilian suffering and an unclear political resolution recalls the blunders of diplomacy in the summer of 1914 when expectations of a short war proved erroneous. The violent civil wars that greeted the dissolution of empires in 1918–1920 suddenly interest us anew, inviting comparisons to present-day conflicts in the Middle East. The resurgence of ethnic nationalism, the psychological trauma experienced by veterans, and the concerns over the use of chemical weapons all have parallels with the 1914–1918 tragedy.[4]

In the early twenty-first century, America's most pressing military and diplomatic challenges have included Afghanistan, Syria, and Russia, nations that were fundamentally impacted by and during the World War I era. Domestically, the COVID-19 pandemic, #MeToo movement, centennial of woman's suffrage, Black Lives Matter, and clashes over Confederate memorials have ushered in a renewed interest in the Spanish Influenza, the fight for the 19th Amendment, women and African Americans during the Progressive Era, and the Lost Cause. Keene has also noted that, "World War I shaped the world in which we live; but the reverse if also true- the world in which we live has given us reasons to examine the war experience anew." As civilization evolves, the questions we ask of the past evolve; contemporary challenges and concerns inform new modes of inquiry. The legacies of World War I and the Progressive Era are long and relevant, and contemporary events inspire fresh perspectives on the past.

Beyond its national relevance, why should this era matter specifically to Greenvillians? According to state records, Greenville County sent 4,005 men, 3,036 White and 969 African American, into the US Army, Navy, and Marine Corps. Deaths totaled 101: 68 White soldiers and 33 African Americans.[5] The emotional impact of the war on those who served and their families, and particularly those who lost loved ones, however, defies quantification. Camp Sevier increased the population, forced the expansion and modernization of municipal services, and introduced demographic diversification into the local area. The economic prosperity of the latter war years and the war's aftermath prompted extensive building on Main Street, the expansion of the downtown area, and the development of several new neighborhoods adjacent to the downtown business area. Today these areas comprise many of the city's oldest buildings and its most established

Introduction   3

neighborhoods. The patriotism prompted by the war, in conjunction with the camp and a series of beneficial collaborations with the federal government in the areas of sanitation, healthcare, and infrastructure, aided a growing nationalism and positive affiliation with the federal government. This helped heal lingering Civil War and Reconstruction-era animosities and ideologically prepared the community for the massive expansion of the federal government during the 1930s and 1940s. The efforts of White Greenvillians to memorialize the Confederacy informs the community today as it grapples with the continued presence of the city's Confederate memorial in a municipal cemetery downtown. Finally, the increased participation of men and women in civic affairs resulted in the establishment of important community amenities and organizations, many of which, such as Bon Secours St. Francis Hospital, Cleveland Park, the Greenville Chamber of Commerce, the Greenville County Library, the League of Women Voters, the National Association for the Advancement of Colored People (NCAACP), the Phillis Wheatley Community Center, Prisma Health, the Salvation Army, the United Way, the YMCA, and the Civitan, Crescent Community, Kiwanis, and Rotary clubs, continue to bring aid and vitality to the community one hundred years later.

After the war Greenville was a city of national repute and had been exposed to ideas and cultures from all over the United States and beyond, garnered from the experiences of local men returning from the fields of France who had rubbed shoulders with Australians, British, Canadians, French, and Germans. It was recognized both for its industrial might and as the birthplace of the famous Thirtieth Infantry Division, which had played an integral combat role in ending the war. The experiences of the Great War provided Greenville with a strong foundation in both improved infrastructure and the broadened attitudes of its people. The momentum of victory and economic prosperity propelled Greenville into the 1920s as a small city that boasted an active and motivated base of civic leaders. Their optimism and prosperity was not shared by all, however. It was built upon a class of mill operatives, and relied upon the preservation of racial inequality.

While this book is a micro-history of the war and the Progressive Era, it is also a local history of a community undergoing significant evolution, in part because of national and global currents and in part because of its unique local leaders, institutions, and character. The most common associations with South Carolina history tend to involve Charleston and the Civil War. Greenville and the Upcountry have been largely omitted from the historiography of both the South and the state, especially in regard to African American history. Most existing literature focuses on Charleston and Columbia (Richland County), where African American residents outnumbered White ones and organized vibrant community institutions.

In contrast, Greenville County's White residents outnumbered its African American ones three-to-one in 1910 and nearly four-to-one in 1920.[6] Thus this is a story of a small and relatively cohesive group of African American community leaders who navigated a White power structure that vastly overpowered them. I am grateful to the scholars whose work on the Upcountry I have relied upon, including but certainly not limited to Judith T. Bainbridge, Walter B. Edgar, Lacy K. Ford, Janet G. Hudson, A. V. Huff, Rachel N. Klein, and W. Scott Poole. I hope this work will help propel Greenville into a more expansive historiographic conversation and encourage scholars to include Greenville's story in future studies.

Anniversaries prompt renewed evaluation by academics, public historians, and those who blend the two roles. The centennial of World War I has inspired recent studies that range from individual biographies to transnational and world histories. Historian Jay Winter has commented that the "awareness of the significance of the local and the global will enable [a] much more sophisticated national history of the Great War to emerge."[7] Books like *Empires at War: 1911–1923* approach the war as a conflict among empires in the "long Great War era," which "expands the history of the war in both time and space."[8] In my study, the expanded chronology of the "long Great War era" is paired with a very limited geographical focus; the combination lends itself to a more sustained study of the impact of the war on a community over time.[9] With this approach the context within which the war took place can be well established, as can the actual war experience and its lingering impact on Greenville and its people throughout the following decade.

Historiographically, this study contributes to recent calls by scholars of World War I for local histories of the era. Because local history inherently illuminates the extent to which our lives are molded by the physical place in which they are conducted, such histories can confirm, complicate, and enrich established state, regional, national, and global understandings of the past. The ways that Greenville reflects, adds nuance, and defies the national narratives of the war and Progressive Era will be revealed in these pages.

Local histories are uniquely positioned to illuminate the infrapolitical relationships between individuals and their networks. They also convey the emotional impact of global events on everyday life and relay how their intricacies affect individuals, families, and communities. Letters to and from soldiers in training at Camp Sevier reveal the impact of the war experience on family relationships, with a particular emphasis on the shifting of domestic and economic responsibilities. They also offer insight into the thoughts and prayers of young men facing an uncertain future. Annual reunions for veterans of the Thirtieth and Eighty-First Divisions reveal the emotional pull these men felt toward one another, while their

Introduction   5

desire to gather in Greenville reveals a longstanding tie to the city of their training. A silent film of the Thirtieth Division's reunion in Greenville in 1919 records how boisterous these celebratory gatherings were: thousands of men, with smiles beaming under the brims of their hats, danced, hugged, and jostled each other in the streets of downtown Greenville. Furthermore, the experiences of men like William C. Hunt of the 118th Infantry, who trained at Camp Sevier and repeatedly returned to Greenville to visit friends in the decades after the war, and especially of North Carolina native Henry Bacon McKoy, who also trained at Camp Sevier and then after the war spent the rest of his life as a leading business and civic figure in Greenville, expose the prominence of the war experience in their lives decades after the fighting ended.[10] Greenvillians, like Furman's Eva Fletcher, whose memorialization efforts resulted in the first dedication and installation of Ernest Moore Viquesney's *Spirit of the American Doughboy* in the nation, demonstrate an impulse to permanently honor the war experience on Greenville's cityscape. Meanwhile community leaders such as Margaret Adger Smyth McKissick became involved in Greenville and in France with the American Legion and other organizations to aid veterans and to improve the quality of healthcare for poison gas victims and others suffering from tuberculosis.

I have endeavored to treat this time period on its own merits and not as a precursor to the war that followed it. A historian's job is to convey a place and moment in time. To that end I have relied heavily upon newspaper accounts, which captured events in their immediate aftermath. Contemporary debates effectively impart the obvious but oft-forgotten perspective that, for those living through it, the past was no more a foregone conclusion than is our present. Through debates among Furman students on whether or not the United States should join the war, the worries of parents over whether their sons would return safely from it, and the conversations that took place among Greenville couples like the Cunninghams, who negotiated the health risks of the Spanish influenza, I hope to convey to readers the extent to which tomorrow's events were as unknown to them as they are to us.[11] While newspapers have been helpful, Greenville's local papers were owned by members of the White elite. To illuminate the voices of African Americans and mill operatives, I felt compelled to engage in more expansive and creative efforts, primarily in the form of archival materials, Black-owned newspapers and oral histories, though those voices still do not appear as prominently as I would like. African American women's voices have been particularly difficult to uncover. During this time White southerners perceived African American women to be less threatening to the established racial and gender hierarchy; these women used their perceived lack of power to become effective agents of change.[12]

The effort to convey and contextualize Greenville before, during, and after the war necessitated deep investigation into the influence of the Progressive Era, a political philosophy and reform movement concentrated in the years between the 1890s and the 1920s. In few areas of American historiography is the scholarship as messy and inconclusive as it is within Progressivism, and this is particularly true of the Progressive Era in the South. Before Maureen Flanagan wrote in favor of an inclusive approach that refers to many "Progressivisms," the lack of unity among activists and absence of a singular platform prompted despair among some scholars. Peter Filene wrote an "obituary" of the period; his eulogy argued that the phrase "obscured more than it explained." Similarly Robert Harrison admitted that he had little "expectation of gluing back together the fragments of the conceptual entity that used to be called the 'Progressive movement.'"[13] Yet these terms persist. As historian Rebecca Edwards writes, "These debates, including various obituaries and requiems, have not in fact displaced usage of the terms 'progressivism' and 'Progressive Era.'"[14] Though the phrases remain a well-established and routine part of the periodization of US history, readers should not interpret everything that happened in Greenville from the 1870s through the 1920s as progressive. For most White Progressives in Greenville, racial inequality and the industrial caste system were inviolable, and local reform activity never went so far as to challenge these existing social and economic systems.

In 1912 Senator Robert La Follette of Wisconsin, a national leader of the Progressive movement, declared, "I do not know of any progressive sentiment or any progressive legislation in the South." Only 2.57 percent of South Carolinians supported the Progressive Party ticket in the 1912 presidential election, and as a result of South Carolina's "White primary," which effectively served as the election, all of Greenville's votes were cast in support of the Democratic nominee, Woodrow Wilson. Scholarly debates regarding Progressivism in the South began in 1946, when historian Arthur Link published his article "The Progressive Movement in the South, 1870–1914," in the *North Carolina Historical Review*. Ever since, scholars have debated the topic.[15] Did Progressivism exist in the South? Was it or was it not an actual movement? To what extent did it model itself after the Northeast, and to what extent did the region cultivate "its own unique brand of progressivism"?[16] To what extent does it reflect Progressivism nationally, and to what extent was it unique to the region? Did it have much influence on the national movement, and if so, what specific causes shaped that movement and how? Even among scholars who believe that Progressivism existed in the region, there are, according to William Link, "pessimistic" and "optimistic" approaches regarding the motives of leaders whose efforts could be characterized as progressive, whether in the sense of alignment with the national movement or relative to the efforts of others throughout their community.[17]

Greenville's reform activity focused on social welfare, moral reform, expanding the role of government, and efficiency. Progressive activity occurred in Greenville before the war in the form of temperance, woman's suffrage, the woman's club movement, civic beautification, and the establishment of groups such as the Rotary Club. In 1916 White Greenville business leaders fully embraced and marketed the phrase "Progressive Greenville." When the war ended, Greenville's leaders invested their time, energy, and dollars into the city with unparalleled vigor.[18] They were once again free to cultivate their aspirations for the community, which was on sound financial footing as a result of Camp Sevier and the local textile economy. Local advances associated with Progressive Era uplift included, in addition to those listed above, better roads, expanded access to electricity and clean water, inoculations from disease, improved healthcare, an awareness of the importance of literacy and libraries, improved educational opportunities, and the founding of community welfare organizations. These efforts reflect national Progressivism to the extent that many Greenvillians in the 1920s believed in the ability of community organizations and government to implement improvements and were willing to develop and financially support such efforts. Greenvillians also embraced the Progressive Era's emphasis on efficiency; their rationale for establishing the Community Fund, for example, was laden with progressive language.

Greenville's reform-minded leaders were, like many progressive activists nationally, middle and upper class and rooted in the city rather than the countryside.[19] They were motivated by a wide variety of causes, including but not limited to faith, pride, altruism, and even greed. The city's most visible White reformers included Jessie Stokely Burnett, William P. and Marie Gower Conyers, Flora Putnam Dill, Eva E. Fletcher, Eva T. Goodyear, Mary Putnam Gridley, Rhoda Livingston Haynsworth, Pete Hollis, F. Louise Mayes, J. Rion McKissick, Margaret Adger Smyth McKissick, A. Viola Neblett, Andrea Christensen Patterson, Martha Orr Patterson, George W. and Sarah "Odie" Sirrine, Nana Sirrine, and Helen E. Vaughan.[20] The city's most visible civic leaders and philanthropists included Alester G. Furman, Bennette Geer, Thomas F. Parker, John W. Norwood, Joseph "Joe" E. Sirrine, and mayors Hanny Clyde Harvley and Richard F. Watson. I have taken inspiration from Maureen Flanagan's work; though Greenville's White leaders functioned within and did not challenge a social structure that privileged themselves above both African Americans and a class of mill operatives, they were well-intentioned, dedicated, and highly engaged in growing and improving their community. As Flanagan writes, "Compassion and extending a

8 *"Our Country First, Then Greenville"*

helping hand to others—even if at times these seemed condescending attitudes—exposed a faith in a common humanity and the innate decency of people that challenged the exclusionists and overt racists. This idea also was a product of the Progressive Era."[21]

Inspired by Link's *The Paradox of Southern Progressivism,* which was one of the earliest studies to place women at the center of the Progressive Era, and subsequent works by Glenda Gilmore, this study posits women in the nucleus of Greenvillians' leadership of the home front effort and of progressive causes.[22] Certainly this study attempts "to locate new historical actors beyond the traditional focus largely on white, often male reformers, government officials, and industrialists."[23]

This study also takes the city of Greenville as its focus and does not incorporate or assess the agrarian reform aspects of this era. Nor does it include analysis of attempts to reform government regulation. It focuses primarily on the "social work wing" and on what George B. Tindall referred to as the South's "business progressivism," described as a "credo for efficiency that stressed better roads, better schools, and better public services."[24] Greenville's reformers, both White and African American, reflect the notion that the typical progressive reformer was an educated member of the elite and middle classes.

Scholars also debate the extent to which Progressivism in the South was linked to Progressivism nationally, and the extent to which regional Progressivism influenced the national movement and vice versa. Especially with temperance, woman's suffrage, and reform efforts made by Pete Hollis and African American social worker Hattie Logan Duckett, progressive Greenvillians were connected to national organizations. Historian Ann-Marie Szymanski's work suggests that scholars have underestimated the influence of the South on the national Prohibition movement. The Anti-Saloon League, Sons of Temperance, and Woman's Christian Temperance Union each studied the local option laws present in Greenville and in many other towns and cities of the South and used this information to the benefit of their national strategies. Legally Prohibition was embraced by the White South as an example of how the federal government could bring "social uplift, the purification of politics, and more orderly human relations."[25] Scholars often attribute the White South's dedication to localism as one reason why Prohibition looked different in the South and why many progressive reforms failed. Prohibition, argues Link, "convinc[ed] southerners of the need to relinquish some . . . community autonomy in exchange for a purer moral and social order." It awakened the South to "the benefits of a centralized government-based solution" and, according to Thomas Pegram, "was a doorway to a host of reforms

Introduction 9

that entailed expanded state regulation over personal liberty."[26] Support of the Prohibition Amendment reveals a willingness to move beyond localism and an acquiescence to centralized authority for the sake of a safer and more harmonious society. This acquiescence served as preparation for the increasing involvement of the federal government into citizens' lives in the 1920s, 1930s, and first half of the 1940s, and was likely of greater advantage to rural Greenvillians, who had not benefitted as much as city residents from local military camps, population growth and diversity, and other federal programs, such as road improvements and health and sanitation efforts.

Though some Greenvillians sought to "work unselfishly for the upbuilding of his community," Progressivism in Greenville wasn't a movement so much as it was, in Tindall's words, "a spirit of the age" that consisted of the efforts of a small group of community leaders.[27] In Greenville, Progressivism could largely be misconstrued as heightened volunteerism, but the sheer preponderance of new civic organizations, schools, and hospitals and clinics reveals an intensity that distinguishes it from other periods. Like the Progressive movement nationally, Progressivism in Greenville occurred in part in response to recent and significant economic growth that prompted social changes. In contrast to the industrial centers of the Northeast and Midwest, however, Greenville's population growth was due not to the massive wave of immigration that occurred in the late 1800s and early 1900s but to "internal regional migration."[28] The recent influx of rural and mountain folk into industrial jobs in villages near the nucleus of an urban community swelled the population and prompted new and increased social, cultural, educational, and municipal needs that only grew during the war years. Progressivism in Greenville focused more on advancements as opposed to reforms, and local leaders created and improved access and opportunities within established systems of race and class, as opposed to overhauling them.

Like most of the South, segregation was considered inviolable; White Progressives in Greenville worked primarily for the benefit of fellow White people and secondarily toward advancements for African Americans, particularly in regard to education and healthcare. The extent to which African Americans can be considered part of a movement of exceptional civic activism and reform has also been debated by scholars, as African Americans were perennially focused on racial uplift.[29] Thus they saw in Greenville opportunities to capitalize on increased White civic engagement, especially in the areas of community centers, education, libraries, and public health. African American leaders included A. P. Allison, Edgar W. Biggs, Charles D. and James A Brier, Hattie Logan Duckett, E. B. Holloway, Ella Mae Logan, W. E. Payne, James A. Tolbert, Hattie E. Williams, and reverends James O. Allen, Allen R. Burke, Charles F. Gandy, John F. Green, and William F. Rice.[30]

The industrial mill village system that rooted the local economy was also inviolable. Efforts to improve labor conditions and curb child labor were quickly squashed. Here progressive efforts were not oriented toward social justice but social improvements, at its best, and social control, at its worst. Most worked within the contours of the system. Mill owner Thomas F. Parker's efforts to enhance the recreational, educational, and spiritual lives of his workers were exceptional among his peers, despite his frank acknowledgment that his efforts were for the benefit of business and were in no way altruistic. Though Pete Hollis' efforts to reform the educational system for mill village children were stalwart among Progressives in Greenville, he enhanced life in mill villages in meaningful ways that did not explicitly threaten the established order.

Greenville's example supports the notion that newly industrialized southern cities may have had a slightly different experience than other southern communities, as it complicates arguments that Progressivism in the White South failed because of White southerners' suspicion of outsiders, especially northerners; as a New South city, Greenville had eagerly sought and recruited northern businesspeople since the 1870s, and some of the individuals who came to Greenville from the Northeast, such as Mary P. Gridley and Helen Vaughan, contributed very significantly to progressive advances in Greenville. Most, however, were native South Carolinians.

Certainly the impact of postbellum northern industry and the presence of training camps during the Spanish-American War and World War I had loosened the grip of localism and regionalism so prevalent in other southern communities. One of the Progressive Era's goals was the unification of North and South; Greenville's experience reveals the presence of a heightened nationalism during the war and an intentional effort, motivated by economic interests, to rejoin the national fold.

White Greenvillians of long ago pridefully promoted their high aspirations with lofty titles. From the late 1800s to the 1920s, the city's monikers evolved from the "Athens of the Upcountry" to the "Pearl of the Piedmont" to the "Textile Center of the South" and "Progressive Greenville." During the war Greenville was inspired by "Our Country First, Then Greenville," but after, it was the "Greenville Spirit" that moved them. By the end of the 1920s, with an abundance of civic organizations, municipal services, expanded infrastructure, a cityscape of new heights, and a population that had nearly tripled since 1900, Greenville's modern era had begun. The Progressive Era that both flanked and infused the war years inspired a small but active group of leaders in Greenville who attempted to both address the problems of increased industrialization and urbanization and establish a foundation of modernity that could be built upon.[31] It is my hope that this book will prompt a curiosity about and appreciation of the people and events that shaped Greenville and that its relevance will inspire continued service and civic engagement.

chapter one

The Politics of Race and Gender in the "Pearl of the Piedmont"

In 1866, when Freedman's Bureau agent John William De Forest arrived in Greenville, the officer he was replacing informed him that "you have the best station in the State." Guided by civic leadership, northern investment, and market trends that valued cotton more than corn, a heretofore unseen level of specialized industrialization revolutionized life in the upper Piedmont in the decades after the Civil War.[1] In 1867 the *Greenville Enterprise* published the following excerpt from the *Baltimore Transcript:*

> The young men of the South have it in their power to make a new South of the old. They have shown their energy and self-denial in war, and if they exhibit anything like the same qualities in peace, they will build up their section beyond the powers for mischief of their bitterest enemies. The way to do this is . . . to apply their whole souls to the work of creative industry to work in all its forms, whether the field or the sop, whether agricultural or mechanical. . . . If they were willing to perform manual drudge . . . for the sake of the South, in war, let them be willing to do the same in the ranks of peaceful industry, and the salvation of their section is secure.[2]

When De Forest concluded his fifteen-month stint in Greenville, he wrote of his experiences for *Harper's* magazine.

> There were suffering people of the better class, though not many. My district was an upland region, a country of corn rather than cotton, cultivated by small farmers and middling planters. Containing few slaves compared with the lowlands, only a moderate proportion of its capital had been destroyed by emancipation. Sherman's bummers had never crossed its borders. . . . There were few families of landed gentry so reduced as to need rations, and those few were chiefly refugees who had fled from the sea-coast during the rebellion.[3]

De Forest attended the opera and circus, enjoyed the climate and scenery, took walks of between three and eight miles daily, and, from his room at the Mansion

The Politics of Race and Gender 13

House in the heart of the town, became quite familiar with the local people. He particularly appreciated his participation in a literary club, to which he had been invited by locals. Citing the interests of this erudite group, which he noted included former governor Benjamin F. Perry and professors from Furman and the Female College, Greenville "was able to claim rank as the Athens of the up-country, thereby exciting much envy and bitterness among less pretentious communities."[4]

In the year after De Forest's departure, the South Carolina General Assembly designated Greenville as a city. The first national bank in the state opened in Greenville in 1872, and by the end of the 1870s, the new city had opened the Board of Trade and Cotton Exchange, known locally as the Chamber of Commerce. According to its first president, William Beattie, it was established to "make Greenville a big city."[5] The astute editor of the *Enterprise and Mountaineer* wrote in 1875, "Under the old system, the South could afford to devote its resources to agriculture and the raising of slaves, and grow rich and powerful. . . . But our present condition forces the necessity of manufacturing so strongly upon the judgement that no business man will deny its advantages. . . . It will bring capital, population and wealth into the country, and infuse new life and energy into our people, which they have never before experienced."[6]

At the end of the Civil War, three mills operated in the county; by the early 1880s, seven mills were operational, with its workers constituting a new social and economic class.[7] Twenty-eight percent of the state's new working class of mill operatives worked in Greenville County. They were former White tenant farmers whose lives were revolutionized by the mill village culture and dictated by mill whistles, which indicated, six days per week, when to rise, when to begin working, when to break for lunch, and when to go home at the end of the twelve-hour workday. Scholar Judith T. Bainbridge notes that 95 percent of the mill operatives were "poor, white, Protestant, and ethnically Scots-Irish," and while the city's elite often looked upon them disparagingly, they "knew that the mills and their workers were the source of growing prosperity."[8] The thriving industry was supported by a growing professional middle class of bankers, attorneys, and businesspeople who both nurtured and benefited from it; the city's population increased from 1,518 to 11,857 between 1860 and 1900.[9]

Northern investors had been introduced into this burgeoning southern industry initially in the 1870s, prompted in part when southern entrepreneurs placed orders with northern machine companies; businessmen George F. Hall, Oscar H. Sampson, George Putnam, and George C. Whitin, all of Massachusetts, became some of Greenville's earliest industrial investors. Northern firms also became the earliest sales agents and marketers for the industry, with Woodward, Baldwin, and Company of Baltimore and New York serving as the commission house for

Greenville's Piedmont Shirt Company and ultimately for more than twenty-one mills in the state.[10] The energy was infectious: in an article titled "Carolina's Mountain Queen," Ambrose Gonzales of Charleston's *Post and Courier* wrote, "With such a splendid commercial and industrial exhibit, with her magnificent location, fine climate, perfect health, powerful and intelligent press, sound financial institutions, splendid schools, colleges, and churches, there is no height in the social, industrial, and commercial world to which [Greenville's] hopeful, thrifty, and energetic people may not elevate the Pearl of the Piedmont."[11]

As revealed in the *Enterprise and Mountaineer*, Greenville's White business leaders were implementing a "New South" years before *The Atlanta Constitution* editor Henry W. Grady began writing of it in 1880, and a decade before he proclaimed it to northern industrialists J. P. Morgan, Henry Flagler, and others in New York City in 1886. Grady's vision both aligned with and ultimately reinforced those of Greenville's economic leaders; it emphasized the economic rejuvenation of the region, modeled to a degree by the northeastern Industrial Revolution, and the reconciliation of sectional animosities, motivated primarily by economic gain. The "New South Creed," as described by historian Paul Gaston, was also appealing to these White men because it relied on and strengthened a social and economic structure in which the White elite prospered from the labor of a new class of White mill hands, for whom paternalistic amenities, such as mill churches, schools, stores, and baseball stadiums, were constructed with the idea of uplifting mill village families. The New South ethos was sold on the benefits it would provide not only to elite and working-class Whites in the South, but also on the partnerships it would cultivate between northern and southern Whites. As African Americans were hired only to perform the most arduous work outside the mills, Grady's "New South Creed" was predicated upon White supremacy and economically emboldened the "redemptive" political spirit that had recently taken hold across the South. African Americans were excluded from the economic plans of both the White North and South.[12]

Alongside efforts to pursue business partnerships with northern investors and firms, native White Greenvillians joined much of the South in embracing the "Lost Cause" mentality that southern White women cultivated in the 1880s, 1890s, and beyond.[13] Based on lies, exaggerations, and calculated interpretations, the "Lost Cause" argument held that the Civil War was a noble and commendable fight that was lost only because of circumstances beyond the Confederacy's control; the objectives for which the Confederacy fought were honorable and just, despite the reality that victory in war was unattainable. It served as a "eulogy to the past that portrayed a genteel 'moonlight-and-magnolia' South where contented slaves thrived on patriarchal plantations under benevolent masters." Scholars such

Reunions of Confederate veterans continued for decades after the Civil War. In 1915, a group of veterans from Greenville attended a reunion of the South Carolina Division, United Confederate Veterans in Columbia. Events included a parade, a series of camp scenes presented at the Columbia Theatre, and a *tableau vivant*, created by 1000 Columbia schoolchildren dressed in white, red, and blue and assembled on the steps of the State House to collectively create a human Blood-Stained Banner, the third national flag of the Confederacy. Courtesy South Carolina Room, Greenville County Library.

as Karen Cox, David Blight, Adam Domby, Gaines Foster, W. Scott Poole, and Charles Reagan Wilson have explored and debunked the strategic methods by which Ladies' Memorial Associations and the United Daughters of the Confederacy (UDC), among others, defiantly crafted an insidious and false narrative designed to promote White supremacy.[14]

Upon the death of Robert E. Lee in October 1870, church bells in Greenville tolled for two hours, businesses closed, and a program featuring a choir and speeches from prominent White leaders was held at the courthouse. In 1889 White Greenvillians gathered at the opera house to similarly honor Jefferson Davis after his death.[15] Even in the years leading up to World War I, White Charlestonians chose not to fly the flag of the United States on, nor to celebrate, the Fourth of July; their resentment over federal interference in their community during the war and Reconstruction remained fierce.[16] Most White Greenvillians also preferred Confederate Memorial Day in May to the Fourth of July and participated in other Lost Cause rituals. The Fourth of July was considered by many White southerners to be a holiday for African Americans, though even African American and women's rights activist Frances "Frank" Rollin of Columbia confided in her diary, "I am no enthusiast over Patriotic Celebrations as I am counted out of the body Politic."[17]

White southerners clung to the Lost Cause interpretation in part to ensure that future generations would be educated in their interpretation of the Civil War. Across the South in the decades after the war, and particularly throughout the 1890s, the Ladies' Memorial Association and UDC earnestly promoted and memorialized the Lost Cause ethos. Statues commemorating those who served and died in the war began to decorate public land and cityscapes.[18] In 1892, amid great fanfare, the Ladies' Memorial Association of Greenville County erected a twenty-eight-foot statue depicting a Confederate soldier prominently facing south in the middle of the city's four-lane Main Street at its northern point. Sculpted by C. F. Kohlrus of Augusta, Georgia, the bronze statue was modeled from a photograph of former Greenville police chief and Civil War veteran James Blackman Ligon.[19] To promote attendance at its dedication, the local railroad company reduced its fares to Greenville for the day, which was deemed a public holiday. A crowd of several thousand, including more than a thousand public school students, three hundred Confederate veterans, a state military regiment, local law enforcement and first responders, elected officials, and members of the Ladies' Confederate Memorial Association, attended the parade and ceremony at noon on September 27, 1892.[20] After remarks from public officials, the canvas was unfurled and the statue was revealed, prompting "wild Confederate yells." The state regiment fired a salute, and as the smoke cleared, a large Confederate flag zipped along a suspended wire from atop a building across the street and stopped at the statue; according to one local newspaper, "old grizzled soldiers wept like children" at the sight of the "conquered banner" hanging above their "silent comrade." At the conclusion of the event, the crowd sang "America (My Country, 'Tis of Thee)."[21]

Words carved into the Italian marble base of the statue convey a strong Lost Cause "redemptive" spirit that suggests that a lack of success in the war did not invalidate the cause for fighting it:

> He wins the most who honor saves
> Success is not the test
> The world shall yet decide
> In truth's clear far off light
> That the soldiers

> Who wore the gray and died
> With Lee, were in the right.

White Greenville resoundingly embraced a framing of the South's efforts during the Civil War that was nostalgic and emphasized the belief that, though the cause was lost, the cause was just and right. But because Greenville had also more closely linked its economic base to northern business in the decades since the war, and Greenville's economic leadership increasingly included northerners who had come south, it more readily adopted a rational, united-front outlook that was economically beneficial to the region come April 1917.

That transition was also spurred by the presence of an army camp in Greenville during the Spanish-American War. In his book *Baptized in Blood*, Charles Reagan Wilson argues that although war in the 1860s reflected and resulted in a deeply divided sectionalism, subsequent wars helped to erode that sectionalism in favor of national reconciliation. Ironically, he argues, the Lost Cause's glorification of service to the Confederacy generated strong regional support for American entry into the Spanish-American War.[22] The editors of the *Greenville Mountaineer* and the *Gaffney Ledger* served as leading proponents of involvement in the war and in the belief that "sectional prejudice is fast becoming a thing of the past."[23] In June 1898 Greenville mayor James T. Williams, Alderman James F. Richardson, and businessman Alester G. Furman worked with state and federal officials to recruit a US Army training facility; later that summer, in a meeting with President William McKinley, the group learned that Greenville had been selected. It was one of approximately two hundred training camps established during the war; South Carolina hosted nine camps, with only those in Greenville and Summerville located outside Columbia. Named in honor of Alexander Wetherill, who died during the Battle of San Juan Hill, Greenville's Camp Wetherill was a temporary training facility for volunteer infantrymen from New Jersey, New York, Massachusetts, Missouri, and West Virginia whose regiments belonged to the Second Army Corps. In November 1898 the camp hosted six regiments that moved from Camp Meade in Pennsylvania to Greenville in anticipation of winter. With ten thousand men, the camp's population was larger than that of the city.[24] Decades later, Guy Foster and his sister, who were teenagers during the war, recalled that these men "took the town" in their blue uniforms, frequented the city's saloons, and attracted locals to their Sunday afternoon dress parades.[25] Greenville attorney and politician James M. Richardson also later recalled that Greenville's "streets were full of blue uniforms . . . and knee deep mud."[26]

The diary of nineteen-year-old Harry E. Caldabaugh, a member of Company D, Second West Virginia Volunteer Infantry, details his experiences at the

In his scrapbook, Baley described this image as "Laundry Auntie on Main Street, Greenville, SC. Hat on top [of] basket." Whites commonly used the term "Auntie" when addressing older, African American women, a practice that sparked quiet resentment. In contrast, White women were addressed as Miss, Mrs., or Ma'am. Courtesy New York Public Library.

camp. The soldiers' days lasted from 6:30 A.M. to 9:30 P.M. The men slept in tents, with wooden boards providing flooring. Inside each tent between eight to twelve men slept on muslin mattress covers filled with straw, circled around a "cone-shaped stove" that burned small pieces of wood. With no bathing facilities, the men had to take sponge baths using water and soap from the kitchen. In lieu of toilets, they dug a five-foot-deep trench, with poles and a piece of lumber placed over it. Their daily parades attracted large audiences, and the men socialized with locals and brought significant economic benefits to the community.[27] Whitehall, a majestic home built by Charlestonian Henry Middleton in 1813, was requisitioned by the government and used as either officer's quarters or a military hospital. The Mansion House hotel in the heart of Greenville's downtown housed colonels and generals and flew a thirty-foot American flag during the war.[28] New Yorker C. L. Baley, an Army photographer, frequently left the camp with his camera. He ventured downtown and was intrigued by the sight of an African American laundress and an older African American woman, whom Baley referred to as a "South Carolina Auntie," balancing baskets of laundry and food on their heads.[29] His captions and photographs, which include formerly enslaved men and women with their families at home, the former slave market,

With snow blanketing the ground, these Camp Wetherill soldiers preferred to remain inside their tent. Courtesy Hudson Area Library.

the Confederate memorial, and the stately, snow-covered homes of White southerners near the camp, reveal what he thought noteworthy and distinctive.[30] Though the army transferred the men south so they would be more comfortable throughout the winter, the weather in Greenville during those months was dismal. Young Guy Foster saw icicles on the camp's tent flaps and even one on a man's nose. The local newspaper lamented, "We fear the boys now in camp here will never look at the picture of 'Washington at Valley Forge' without thinking of Camp Wetherill. . . . It has been 87 days now and has had seventeen days of sunshine. It has had bad rain, mud, three sleets, two thunder storms, and has now brought the performance to a climax with a zeroed thermometer and a big snow."[31]

The regiments mustered out between February and April 1899, and the camp closed shortly thereafter.[32] For the six months of its duration, it had, according to Bainbridge, "jump-started the city's . . . economy, lessened residents' fear and distrust of Northerners, and renewed their sense of American identity and patriotism."[33] This profitable arrangement, which benefited both the War Department and the local community, lingered in the minds of many Greenvillians when the United States entered an even bigger conflict in 1917.

As Greenville capitalized upon its economically indomitable New South identity after the Civil War and into the early decades of the twentieth century, *de jure* and *de facto* segregation dictated relations between White people and African Americans, as they did throughout most of the country during this time. The growth of the local textile and manufacturing industry had coincided with the early decades of emancipation, and throughout the postbellum era, the textile industry shaped race and class dynamics, resulting in the creation of multitiered social strata unique to communities whose economic base was rooted in textiles and manufacturing. Race and class tensions existed between White mill operatives at the lower end of the socioeconomic scale—a group derogatorily called "lintheads"—and a relatively small population of African Americans, some of whom, such as formerly enslaved person Wilson Cooke, who paid the highest taxes of any African American in Greenville County, had more education and attained higher levels of socioeconomic success.[34] As Upcountry newspaper editor William P. Beard later wrote, the "LOWEST white man in the social scale is above the negro who stands HIGHEST by the same measurement."[35] Mill operatives clung to their Whiteness, their only tangible advantage over African Americans. Tensions between African Americans and mill workers meant that many racial conflicts in Greenville involved White people and African Americans in the same economic stratum.

According to several local newspapers, on a summer evening in August 1899, operative John R. Ellenburg of Poe Mill and members of his family were seated at their dining room table when several shots were fired into their home, which was located near a fertilizer factory that employed African Americans. The Ellenburgs' children were playing in the front yard, prompting desperate screams from their mother: "Don't shoot the children!" Ellenburg reportedly walked out his front door and challenged the African American assailants, saying, "You had better shoot again." They responded with several more shots. Very soon thereafter, a crowd of men from Poe Mill gathered and walked to the nearby fertilizer factory. One of the suspected African American assailants, a man named Tack Moore, was "captured and led to jail," which prompted a rumor among the crowd of African Americans that he was going to be lynched. A courier was sent to Mount Zion Colored Baptist Church to inform Rev. J. A. Pinson that a "negro was being lynched at Poe Mill," but Pinson refused to propagate that information without confirmation. Nevertheless the meeting at the church dispersed, with those individuals gathering weapons and joining the crowd. As one courier was dispatched to inform Reverend Pinson, another was sent to inform Sheriff Perry Gilreath, who arrived alongside police chief Robert H. Kennedy at approximately ten o'clock that evening. They found one group of about twenty White men several hundred yards away from a group of about fifty to seventy-five African Americans. Kennedy and Gilreath dispersed the group and walked closer to the fertilizer factory only to discover a group of "about 100 frenzied negroes well armed . . . [with] revolvers, shotguns, and axes, and one in the crowd brandished a reap hook," threatening to kill Kennedy if Moore was lynched. In an effort to assuage the crowd, Kennedy and Gilreath sent Reverend Pinson to the jail to confirm that Moore was indeed in prison and had not been lynched. Prior to Pinson's return, the Greenville Light Infantry was called to the scene around 2 A.M. and remained to ensure that calm prevailed for the rest of the night. Over the course of five or six hours, several shots were fired, with the newspaper reporting that most of the fighting involved clubs and hand-to-hand combat, wounding one White man and five African Americans.[36] Greenville newspapers reported that a "full fledged race riot broke out . . . between all white Poe [Mill] village residents and a neighboring settlement of black fertilizer workers" and that "at one time it looked as if wholesale slaughter of negroes would occur," though other sources indicated that "reports of a race riot in Greenville have been exaggerated."[37]

Tensions between African American and White locals, particularly textile workers, continued into the World War I era. The Poe Mill confrontation occurred in Greenville less than a year after the well-known Wilmington, North Carolina race riot, which had heightened racial tensions throughout the region.[38] In the first decade of the twentieth century, race riots continued in cities around the country, including New York (1901); Evansville, Indiana (1903); Atlanta (1906); and Springfield, Illinois (1908).

Ten days after the Poe Mill riot and just miles away from it, an "old and trusted" African American man was tied to a tree, "riddled by bullets," weighted down with stones, and thrown into the Saluda River after he allegedly slept in the same room as his employer's White children. Tom Keith lived with the family of J. B. Hawkins, who woke him the morning of August 16, 1899 by beating him with a gun. Hawkins told him to gather his belongings and leave, which he did, but soon thereafter a White mob captured and lynched him.

Between 1881 and 1899, there were three known incidents of White assailants lynching African American men in Greenville County. After Robert Williams allegedly assaulted a White woman in 1881, White vigilantes kidnapped him from jail, shot him, and hung him from a tree. In 1895 a White mob took Ira Johnson from jail after he was charged with killing a White man and shot him approximately five hundred times.

This type of "redemptive," terrorizing post-Reconstruction violence against African Americans was intended to re-entrench White hegemony in all phases of life.[39] Under Gov. "Pitchfork" Ben Tillman, a state referendum called for a constitutional convention to rewrite the state's constitution, last written during Reconstruction in 1868 when African American men held a majority in the state legislature. Tillman's objective was to overturn many of the democratic principles included in the 1868 constitution and to also ensure that African American men would not be able to exercise their Fifteenth Amendment right to vote.

Concerns about maintaining White supremacy also tainted most reform movements in South Carolina, including woman's suffrage. By holding regular "salons" at their home in Reconstruction-era Columbia, Frances Rollin and her four sisters openly advocated for woman's suffrage and African American rights. Led by Charlotte "Lottie" and Katherine Rollin, the sisters held a woman's rights convention in Columbia and established a state chapter of the American Woman Suffrage Association (AWSA), an organization that had been established in 1869 after the woman's suffrage movement split over debates regarding the Fifteenth Amendment.[40] Despite the fact that South Carolina had the highest percentage of African American lawyers of any southern state between 1880 and 1900, the end of Reconstruction suppressed, if not silenced, most African American voices, including those of the Rollin sisters.[41]

Though the woman's suffrage movement in South Carolina effectively came to a temporary end with the Rollin sisters' departure from the state, other women continued to push for the expansion of women's roles. Throughout the late 1870s and 1880s, the Woman's Christian Temperance Union (WCTU), a quasi-religious and quasi-political organization founded by Frances Willard, attracted increasing numbers of White women across the nation to their cause. In March 1881, Willard spoke at several places in South Carolina. In Greenville, she filled Buncombe Street Methodist Episcopal Church for two nights and "completely captivated" her audience. She also met with a small group of White women who soon established a local chapter. Willard's speeches must have similarly inspired students from the Greenville Baptist Female College (GBFC), who established a campus temperance society.[42] By 1882 eight cities and towns in the state had local chapters of the WCTU, and when the South Carolina WCTU was established in 1883, it became the first state chapter in the South. Their annual state conventions, including the 1885 one held in Greenville, convened women like Mary P. Gridley, A. Viola Neblett, and Sarah "Odie" Sirrine, who were eager to become involved in a cause that straddled the worlds of the personal and political.

The WCTU forged a path by which White women, and especially southern White women, could become involved in the public sphere and maintain their respectability, as it was deemed alongside church societies as the safest entrée into club activity and Progressivism. The organization introduced a reform consciousness among South Carolina women, taught its members skills that served them in this and other causes for decades, and cultivated a national solidarity with like-minded women throughout the country. Through their work with the WCTU, women were, writes historian Valeria Gennaro Lerda, "eventually accepted as agents of change in the name of womanhood and motherhood and as defenders of the moral and physical health of their society."[43]

Reform-minded students at the GBFC who established a temperance society and supported other progressive causes did so with the support of their "Lady Principal," Mary Camilla Judson, who was a steadfast advocate for the promotion of women in the public sphere. Described as "plump and erect, dressed always in a well-fitting plum or wine-colored merino wool dress with soft ruching around the neck," the well-respected and beloved Judson inspired and empowered young women at the college from the 1870s through the 1910s.[44] A native of New England, Judson joined her brother Charles C. Judson in the Upcountry in the late 1850s but returned to the Northeast during the late 1860s and early 1870s, when women's literary clubs were being established with great fervor. At the college in 1878, Judson established the first club for women in Greenville, the Judson Literary Society. The club, which was modeled after the women's clubs of the Northeast and named for her brother, sparked furious opposition from South Carolina Baptists, who rejected the practice of women speaking in public. Despite this, student members of the society held public recitations and debates and did not shy from progressive topics. In 1887, graduating senior Zulieme Skinner of Barnwell publicly read the salutatory at the closing exercises of the academic year held at Greenville's Opera House; her comments included arguments on women's education and suffrage.[45] Though Judson's position likely inhibited her from explicitly pushing beyond socially circumscribed norms, she undoubtedly passed along her aspirations to her students, many of whom became involved in reform movements, like suffrage, and went on to earn graduate degrees and work in various professions.

The women's clubs that originated in the Northeast sparked a wildfire that quickly blanketed the nation. Women, both White and African American, were hungry for the intellectual stimulation, informed conversation, and civic involvement that often resulted from club activity.

In Greenville in 1889, approximately a dozen White women, including WCTU activists Gridley, Neblett, Martha Orr Patterson, and Sirrine, gathered at the home of Frances "Fanny" Perry Beattie, daughter of Reconstruction governor Ben Perry, and collectively established the Thursday Club.[46] The club created a forum for these elite White women to engage in informed, thoughtful dialogue on various issues, such as "the Indian Question" or "the Mormon Question." Although the women agreed not to discuss controversial political topics or religion and never officially took a stance on woman's suffrage, many of its members, including Dill, Eleanor Furman, Gridley, Neblett, Andrea Christensen Patterson, Martha Orr Patterson, Ellen Perry, Putnam, Eudora Ramsay, and Sirrine, were or became leaders in the movement to gain the franchise for White women.[47] The club's earliest civic priorities were the collection of books and establishment of a

Viola Neblett was a leader in South Carolina's temperance and suffrage movements. This image of Neblett was featured in the book *A Woman of the Century*, written in 1893 by national temperance leader Frances Willard.

library; over the next several decades, they also became involved in efforts regarding industrial schools, the Young Women's Christian Association (YWCA), tuberculosis, and health and sanitation.[48] In 1898 the Thursday Club joined eighteen women's clubs throughout the state to establish and become charter members of the South Carolina Federation of Women's Clubs (SCFWC), affiliated with the national General Federation of Women's Clubs (GFWC). Referred to by the local newspaper as Greenville's "400," a Gilded Age reference to New York and Newport society, these New Women of the New South increasingly contributed their voices and energy to causes ranging from temperance to city beautification to suffrage.[49]

Historians have established the chains of social activism that link multiple nineteenth- and twentieth-century movements, including temperance, the club movement, and woman's suffrage. When the woman's suffrage movement in the state resurged, it did so among members of the SCWCTU and the Thursday Club.[50]

In April 1890 newspaperwoman and SCWCTU corresponding secretary Virginia Durant Young of Allendale traveled to Greenville to visit her "beloved friend," SCWCTU state secretary Viola Neblett. In her forties and married to a wealthy businessman, the tall, blond, curly-haired Neblett espoused a "queenly spirit" and was a genial hostess. At Neblett's home a "little knot of women" met every day during Young's visit to discuss woman's suffrage, their self-described "favorite subject."[51] The small group included fellow SCWCTU member Mary P. Gridley, who upon the death of her father, George Putnam, a founder of Camperdown Mill and owner of Batesville Mill, had within months become the first woman in the state and possibly the region to serve as president of a mill. Gridley believed that "the franchise is my right. Woman's ballot means the enforcement of social purity and better government." As early as 1888 she had written

At Neblett's home on West McBee Avenue, a small group of women and at least one man established the South Carolina Equal Rights Association in 1890. Upon her death in 1897, Neblett left funds for her home to become a library. It functioned as the Neblett Free Library from 1897–1921, and from 1922–1930, was used as a library for nearby Greenville High School. Photo from *The Nautilus* (May 1923), Greenville High School, South Carolina Room, Greenville County Library.

to the *Woman's Journal,* a national woman's suffrage periodical, to exclaim, "May the hour of woman's emancipation move more rapidly in the future than it has in the past!"[52] Over the next several decades, this four-foot-ten, tiny-and-mighty woman became involved in nearly every progressive philanthropic and civic undertaking in Greenville.[53]

Joining them were Neblett's forward-thinking neighbors and close friends, George and Sarah "Odie" Sirrine. George, a local business and civic leader, had helped lead efforts to establish the Young Men's Christian Association (YMCA) in the 1870s, and together they supported the establishment of a public school system funded by a school bond issue. Sarah "Odie" Sirrine, "whose dark eyes had a fashion of becoming starry when she talked women's rights," announced that "on the simple ground of justice I regard the ballot as my rightful heritage as a citizen of South Carolina and of the United States of America."[54] George and Sarah and their two sons were stalwarts in progressive undertakings over the next several decades.[55]

Mary Gridley's sisters and their mother, Mary Putnam, were also present at Neblett's gatherings, as were about half a dozen unknown individuals. Collectively,

In 1905, Mary Putnam Gridley was photographed having tea, likely in her stately home on West Washington Street, with her mother, Mary Putnam, and sisters. From left, Daisy P. Bailey, Flora P. Dill, Emma P. Baker, Mary P. Gridley, and Mary Putnam. Courtesy of Special Collections and Archives, Furman University.

they founded the South Carolina Equal Rights Association (SCERA) and effectively relaunched the woman's suffrage movement in the state.

Soon chapters of the SCERA dotted the state's landscape in Columbia and Charleston and even in small communities such as Frogmore (Beaufort County) and Chitty (Barnwell County). In 1892 the SCERA affiliated itself with the National American Woman Suffrage Association (NAWSA), the country's leading suffrage organization. After ascertaining that the southern states presented their most obstinate obstacle, NAWSA established a committee charged with developing a strategy to win southern votes. They engaged Virginia Young and other southern suffragists with proven records of success to help develop movements in other southern states.[56]

Per the southern strategy, in 1895 NAWSA held its annual convention in Atlanta; it was the first time the convention had ever taken place outside of Washington, DC. Gridley, Neblett, and Young attended, as did Young's friend Robert R. Hemphill, the reform-minded editor of the *Abbeville Medium*. Hemphill was a Confederate veteran, state senator, and, perhaps most significantly, the father of six daughters. During the conference Susan B. Anthony was complicit in upholding

Georgia's racial statutes, and upon the conclusion of a resounding speech by Hemphill at the convention, the former abolitionist leader instructed the band to play "Dixie."[57] The southern strategy was refined during the convention, and suffrage leaders such as Anthony, Henry B. Blackwell, Blackwell's daughter Lucy Stone Blackwell, and Laura Clay of Kentucky toured South Carolina to promote it in advance of the state's constitutional convention that fall. To assuage the concerns of White supremacists who worried that a change in suffrage laws would generate renewed interest in southern voting practices (in particular the practice of not allowing African American men to exercise their right to vote), the southern strategy argued that White supremacy could be maintained by effectively limiting the vote to White women. If southern states adopted literacy and property qualifications to woman's suffrage, most African American women would be deemed ineligible, thus ensuring more White votes. In 1895 Gridley wrote to the *Woman's Journal* and advocated for the vote for White women "in this state, so that intelligent supremacy may rule. Give an educational ballot to the women of the South, and white supremacy is assured—a very simple solution of a very intricate problem."[58] National and regional suffrage leaders joined the nearly two hundred members of the SCERA to lobby for an amendment for woman's suffrage that required that a woman own a minimum of three hundred dollars in taxable property. Each delegate to the constitutional convention received a copy of Henry B. Blackwell's pamphlet "A Solution of the Southern Question."[59]

In accordance with his desire to eliminate the possibility of African American men voting in the state, former governor Tillman chaired the committee of the constitutional convention that determined the state's new suffrage laws for all, not just women. Neblett, Young, and Clay addressed it: "Woman as an intelligent, responsible being should have a voice in law-making. Now she has indirect influence without responsibility, which is demoralizing," Neblett asserted.[60] The delegates to the convention did not adopt NAWSA's southern strategy. The new constitution raised the age of consent from ten to fourteen and improved women's property rights, yet woman's suffrage was readily defeated, and over the next several years the movement in the state began a slow decline.[61]

Around the turn of the century, in keeping with the Progressive Era nationally, Greenville's industrial and population boom created new challenges that spurred an increased commitment to civic involvement and strategic oversight of the city's growth. In 1904 the Salvation Army opened a chapter in Greenville; initially located in a tent downtown, the organization had constructed a building by 1907, which locals affectionately dubbed the "Citadel," on donated land. By the end of the decade, the Salvation Army had opened the Shelter for Homeless Women and Maternity Home and operated a Charity Aid Society.[62]

At the same time, the national City Beautiful movement, inspired by the 1893 Columbian Exposition in Chicago, was motivating cities across the US to depart from industrial, functionally driven, haphazard growth to aesthetically pleasing, strategic urban planning that inspired civic pride and engagement. The Municipal Art Society in New York City and the McMillan Plan in Washington, DC, epitomized the movement's efforts. This movement first impacted Greenville in the spring of 1904, when textile magnate and civic leader Thomas F. Parker hired Harlan P. Kelsey of Kelsey and Guild, Landscape Architects of Boston, to landscape the grounds surrounding Monaghan Mill. Parker arranged for Kelsey to meet with business and civic leaders in Greenville and Columbia, where Parker's cousin and fellow textile mill executive Lewis Wardlaw Parker lived. During his visit to South Carolina, Kelsey promoted the ideals of City Beautiful; the Civic Club of Charleston, the Civic Improvement League of Columbia, and the Municipal League of Greenville were founded after Kelsey's visit to implement this new aesthetic philosophy in their respective communities.[63] Led by Thomas Parker and Alester G. Furman and established in the spring of 1904, the Municipal League of Greenville was one of hundreds throughout the nation that developed organized, thoughtful approaches to growth. The group was guided by "Beautifying and Improving Greenville, South Carolina," a thorough study and report with recommendations written by Kelsey and Guild that had been commissioned by the league.[64] For instance, in accordance with the "Beautifying and Improving Greenville" plan, the city council established a Park and Tree Commission in 1913 that cultivated public spaces over the next several decades. Other groups, such as the Greenville Woman's Club, were also inspired by this plan; at their April meeting in 1916, under the leadership of F. Louise Mayes, the Woman's Club adopted a weeklong program, with a theme for each day. Monday was Fire Prevention Day, followed by Front Yard Day, Weed Day, Paint Day, Back Yard Day, and finally, on Saturday, Vacant Lot Day, in which the club partnered with local Boy Scouts to clean vacant lots throughout the city.[65] Although the "Beautifying and Improving Greenville" plan was deemed too costly to implement in its entirety, it offered concrete suggestions; it also reflected the racial discrimination of the era, particularly with its suggestion that White and African American communities further formalize segregation to improve sanitation. These recommendations undoubtedly influenced and bolstered Greenville's White political leaders, who passed some of the most stringent residential segregation laws in the country in 1912.

The plan was typical of Greenville and the South's brand of Progressivism; while these beautification efforts reflected national progressive efforts, the extent to which the plan encouraged further segregation reflects the extent to which progressive activity in the South was shaped by and used to codify White supremacy. When two African American businessmen attempted to build a hotel for African Americans in downtown Greenville in 1912, Greenville's city council responded by becoming one of the nation's earliest adopters (behind cities such as Baltimore, Richmond, Norfolk, Winston-Salem. and Mooresville, North Carolina) of a city-wide segregation ordinance "designed to prevent the promiscuous intermixture of the races in residential sections."[66] White city leaders in favor of strict segregation were encouraged by Kelsey's plan, which blamed "a first difficulty" on "the large negro population." The challenge, according to the report, was that the city's "negro quarters" adjoined not only the wealthiest and poorest White neighborhoods but also the city's commercial areas. Citing "administrative, economic, social, and sanitary" concerns, the report recommended the development of large, racially separate residential sections that did not encroach upon one another—and that "the line be more strictly drawn in Greenville than it is at present and the greatest precision exercised in fixing or permitting future zones of residence, if more desirable city development is to be realized in this aspect."[67]

Emboldened by the 1895 constitution and *Plessy v. Ferguson,* in which the United States Supreme Court upheld the constitutionality of separate but equal" accommodations, White citizens in South Carolina and throughout the South reinforced segregation with renewed vigor. Their efforts evolved from the more informal *de facto* segregation toward the legally prescribed *de jure* segregation, which included the adoption of residential ordinances.

On May 21, 1912, the Greenville City Council passed "An Ordinance for Preserving Peace, Preventing Conflict, and Ill Feeling between the White and Colored Races in the City of Greenville and Promoting the General Welfare of the City."[68] The legislation was based on the city of Baltimore's ordinances but was "more stringent and more far-reaching."[69] Attendance and interest in this "most interesting" legislation was strong, with "the council chamber full to its capacity with prominent citizens of the city until the ordinance was passed, showing that it was this matter which is of supreme interest in the city just now."[70] Greenville's legislation was considered more stringent because it mandated not only segregation for blocks in which all residents were either White or African American but also, going forward, segregation on blocks in which two thirds of the residents were one race or the other.[71]

Communities in Georgia, North Carolina, Kentucky, and Missouri followed.[72] Yet when compared to Baltimore; Atlanta; Ashland, Virginia; Richmond; Winston-Salem; Greensboro; and other communities in Virginia operating under the Virginia ordinance, as an article from 1914 in the *National Municipal*

Review claimed, "the Greenville ordinance goes farther than any of the others and makes it unlawful for a White person to use a house as a residence or place of abode, hotel, boarding house, restaurant, place of public amusement, store, or place of business of any kind in a colored block and has the same prohibitions as to negroes in White blocks."[73]

Regarding undeveloped land, once again the Greenville ordinance was more bureaucratic and onerous than that of the other southern communities. The *National Municipal Review* described the local laws:

> In Greenville, if the owner wishes to build upon a vacant lot in a block whereon there are no residences, he must make publication for a permit to build to the inspector of buildings, declaring whether the residences are to be used by white or colored persons. The inspector thereupon publishes the application twice a week for two successive weeks in one or more daily newspapers in the city. Unless, within five days after the date of the last publication of the notice, protest is made in writing to the inspector by a majority of the property owners in the block against the use of the proposed house as a residence by the race mentioned in the notice, the permit is issued. The permit to build the first house upon the block determines the color of the block for subsequent builders and occupiers.[74]

Penalties for violation of these ordinances varied. In Greenville the maximum fine was fifty dollars or imprisonment of no more than thirty days, whereas in Baltimore, the fines were similar, but imprisonment could last a minimum of thirty days to a maximum of twelve months. In Atlanta fines could be assessed up to one hundred dollars, or an offender might be sentenced to public works for a maximum of thirty days. Greenville's penalties were less severe than those in many southern communities, including Ashland and Richmond, and were comparable to Winston-Salem.

After the legislation had been passed, an editorial in the *Greenville Daily News* titled "Commendation" applauded the council's actions: "We hasten to commend the action of City Council in adopting without delay an ordinance looking to the segregation of races in this city. This matter is important—not because there have been clashes in Greenville, but for the reason that 'an ounce of prevention is worth a pound of cure.' The proper enforcement of the ordinance means that the races will continue to live in the same city without fear of trouble or encroachment on one another's rights."[75]

The actions of Greenville's local government and the support they received throughout the White community reveal a strong commitment to segregation and a willingness to take a national leadership role in these efforts if necessary.

Margaret Adger Smyth McKissick, the daughter of textile pioneer Ellison Adger Smyth, was photographed as a young woman in 1891. Upon her death in 1948, the *Greenville News* wrote that her "life of usefulness had touched and helped practically every strata of society in South Carolina in the last half-century." Author's Collection.

They reveal a southern White tendency to cast the separation of the races as beneficial to and respectful of each other's civil rights. As historian Janet Hudson has skillfully argued, they also reveal the belief among most White South Carolina Progressives that further racial subjugation was a desirable, if not necessary, component of "progressing" their communities, and the extent to which White South Carolinians infused White supremacy into the Progressive Era as they crafted it. "White reformers," Hudson asserts, "saw no contradiction between advocating reform for South Carolina and holding steadfastly to white supremacy."[76]

Historian Joan Marie Johnson has revealed the high degree of overlap in membership and ideals among leading suffragists, clubwomen, and members of the United Daughters of the Confederacy in South Carolina.[77] Greenvillian Martha Orr Patterson for instance, was president of the SCFWC (1902–4) and was serving as president of the South Carolina division of the UDC when she died from injuries sustained in a carriage accident in 1905.[78] Margaret Smythe McKissick of Greenwood and later, of Greenville, was a member of the UDC, president of the SCFWC (1907), and an officer in the SC League of Women Voters. Hannah Hemphill Coleman, the daughter of Robert Hemphill, organized the Abbeville chapter of the UDC and served as president of both the SCFWC and South Carolina Equal Suffrage League.[79]

The commonalities among these activist women are revealed in the pages of the *Keystone: A Monthly Journal Dedicated to Women's Work.* Two South Carolina suffragists, sisters Mary and Louisa Poppenheim, owned and edited the journal that served as the primary publication for five state women's club federations and UDC divisions for North and South Carolina and Virginia.[80] Because women's involvement in the preservation of memory and southern identity was so thoroughly lauded by White southerners, membership in the UDC provided a certain credibility with their male counterparts that protected these women when they ventured into other civic organizations. By redefining the notion of citizenship to include a reliance on women's roles as mothers and teachers and promoting their identity as Lost Cause devotees, they both created a public space for themselves as protectors of southern memory and identity that allowed many White clubwomen and suffragists in South Carolina to become more publicly and deeply involved in progressive causes as well. Johnson is careful to note, however, that these women promoted the Lost Cause "not a conscious strategy to gain authority, but because they deeply believed in its validity."[81]

Throughout the state African Americans banded together in the face of increasing restrictions. Beginning in 1907 and continuing through the war, the South Carolina Race Conference invited African Americans from across the state to convene for several days to address issues related primarily to economic advancement. It was organized by Richard Carroll, a Baptist minister based in Columbia who was employed by the Southern Baptist Convention, a White denomination, and known as "the Booker T. Washington of South Carolina." Speakers included African American and White politicians, ministers, and businessmen.[82] Carroll's particular perspective on race relations received support from mainstream White southerners, who were not threatened by his rhetoric and appreciated his nonpolitical approach. Though notices of the conferences appeared in the *Greenville Daily News,* the conferences received very little White-owned media attention other than the simple announcement of a forthcoming conference, and conference agendas featured few speakers from Greenville. African American and White Greenvillians often did not play a central role in these and other statewide efforts. According to historian Peter Lau, the locus of South Carolina's African American social and economic power was in Charleston and Columbia, "the two largest urban centers in the state and home to a well-developed class of black professionals and an organized network of racial uplift institutions."[83] In contrast, Greenville's African American residents made up a smaller percentage of a smaller population, lending even more power to its White residents and White institutions.

The same spirit which motivated Greenville's White leadership to pass some of the nation's earliest residential segregation laws prompted a heated response to an editorial that denounced segregation in the *Chicago Daily Tribune*. The editorial referenced a New York state law that had recently gone into effect prohibiting discrimination on the basis of "race, color, or religious belief" in the state's hotels, restaurants, and theaters, and stressed that it was "regrettable that it should be necessary for any State to pass a law for the enforcement of one of the fundamental principles of democracy." The author argued that while "there are signs of increase in discrimination against the negro in the north here and there, these do not indicate a tendency. Race prejudice cannot gain headway against the stream of intelligence or overcome the fusion of our common life."[84] Within days, an editorial in the *Greenville Daily News* quipped that the "few negroes" in Chicago were deemed "as well qualified to tell the South how to treat the negro, as the South is to tell California how to treat the Japanese." The author deemed that the *Tribune*'s editorial was "wrong in its conclusions as to the antidote for prejudice . . . the best way to keep down such prejudice is to keep the races as distinct and separate as possible." The editorial oddly posited that "the negro has less chance [to prosper] in the North than in the South" and that "we do not believe that the North wants him."[85] Its conclusion suggested that the status quo of race relations was based upon human nature: "And where is the higher race to be found that does not naturally revolt from amalgamation with a lower?"[86] Months later the NAACP's *Crisis* highlighted the Greenville newspaper's defense of segregation in a notice of the dueling editorials.[87]

Meanwhile Greenville looked to promote its New South identity by publicizing the city not as the "Pearl of the Piedmont" but as the "Textile Capital of the South," a moniker propagated by the Chamber of Commerce beginning in the 1910s. In the years prior, business leaders in Upcountry South Carolina had actively sought investment from northern states in South Carolina's burgeoning textile industry, which was expanding but needed capital from outside of the state to continue growth. Neighboring Spartanburg had similarly sought northern investment and ultimately earned the nickname the "Lowell of the South," while the state came to be known as the "Massachusetts of the South." By 1907 developer Alester G. Furman estimated that "it is, of course, not proper to credit the immense increase in value of real estate in Greenville altogether to our industrial plants, but in my opinion at least 60 percent of this increase in value can be traced entirely to this source." He asserted that South Carolina's cotton and knitting mills paid more than 1 million dollars per month in wages. Ranked by the production of square yards, the state's mills made fine, plain cloth, followed by sheetings

While in training at Camp Wetherill, Byron Parker, Jr. of Hudson, New York took this image of three African American children and a baby in a cotton field near the camp. Courtesy Hudson Area Library.

and shirtings, drills, coarse plain cloth, sateens, ginghams, "fancy," bags and bagging, denims, and duck.[88] Between 1900 and 1920, the number of textile mills in the state had risen from 115 to 184, and according to historian Melissa Walker, the output from the state's mills constituted one fourth of the nation's production of cotton yarn and cloth.[89]

The manufacturing of cotton in the South made sound economic sense, and it rose in tandem with the textile boom. Though in the decades before the Civil War, most Greenville farmers focused first on subsistence crops like corn and grain, with cotton production steadily increasing after 1830; after the war, between 1860 and 1890, the number of cotton bales produced in Greenville County increased more than nine times. Farmers turned the roads of Greenville County white after harvesting season with the locks of cotton taken to the town market by horse and buggy.[90] The ratio of cotton bales to bushels of corn was 1:7 in 1850 and 20:3 in 1890, with a regular cotton trade beginning in the fall of 1867. According to Huff, "an agricultural revolution had occurred," and in the two decades after the war, "with the development of cotton, the growth of the railroad, and the rise of textiles, Greenville County had catapulted into the New South."[91] By 1900 there were 203 cotton gins operating around the clock in Greenville, and many of the area's small-scale farmers relied on the production and sale of their cotton crop to purchase extra amenities, such as new shoes or meat for winter.[92] Updates on the "Cotton Situation" ran daily in the *Greenville Daily News*, with reports and speculation on prices and particular concern about embargoes and policies overseas that would affect the sale of cotton and textiles leading up to the outbreak of World War I. Despite not having the large-scale plantations of the Lowcountry, the Upcountry had a plentiful stake in the cotton market, which was inextricably linked to the textile industry.

The textile manufacturing and apparel industry was located primarily in West Greenville, where mills, bleacheries, and accompanying mill towns made up the "Textile Crescent" that fundamentally constituted Greenville's identity.[93] Judson Mill, Poinsett Mill, Roberts Mill, Dunean Mill, Mills Mill, Victor Mill, Poe Mill, Brandon Mill, Monaghan Mill, Parkers Mill, American Spinning Mill, Huguenot Mill, Camperdown Mill, Piedmont Mill, Woodside Mill, and Union Bleachery were established in the Greenville area around the turn of the century and operated through World War I and beyond.[94] In the prewar era, Greenville established its claims to textile-industry superiority with ambitious growth and additions to its mills. In September 1912 John T. Woodside announced plans to expand his mill to house 112,000 spindles, making it "the largest complete cotton Mill in the United States under one roof, and one of the largest in the world."[95] Many of the Textile Crescent mills also had their own self-contained villages, with baseball teams, churches, gardens, schools, and stores.[96] Mill operatives and their families took pride in their identities as members of those communities, and legendary rivalries existed between mill village baseball teams, which boasted impressive young talent such as "Shoeless Joe" Jackson of future Major League Baseball fame and infamy.[97] The mill communities made up a large piece of the fabric of Greenville, with the industrial ambitions of the city built upon the labor of mill operatives. The war years would dramatically affect the local textile climate—first in detrimental, then in advantageous ways.

The war infused economic stimulus into the region, which was perhaps most evident in the development of new infrastructure projects. Poor infrastructure in Greenville had been of significant concern to locals in the prewar era. The roads of the region were initially built upon Native American game trails and routes of the profitable eighteenth-century fur trade.[98] But as the fur trade grew and the population of the region evolved from groups of traders and trappers to a vibrant village life concentrated in Greenville, better routes became necessary. In 1817 state-appointed civil and military engineer John Wilson described the tortuous roads of South Carolina as "oppressive and ineffectual."[99] Travel by stagecoach was inconvenient in winter and almost impossible after heavy rain, when washed-out dirt roads, fallen trees, or roads obstructed by cows and pigs going to market prompted delays.[100] On top of this, the steep grades of the South Carolina foothills complicated wheeled travel. It was not until 1853 that Greenville was first touched by a railroad, which connected the town to the capital in Columbia and marked the end of the Upcountry pioneer period.[101] However, despite

Built between 1902 and 1912, Woodside Mill was a cornerstone of the area's economic base. The four-story, red brick behemoth was designed by J.E. Sirrine and featured a 150 foot brick smokestack. The surrounding village included approximately 400 modest mill homes. Photos from the Oscar Landing Collection, Courtesy of the Greenville County Historical Society.

investments in railroads and the birth of manufacturing in Greenville, by the turn of the century, as Greenville attorney and politician James M. Richardson wrote, "highways were in very little better condition than they were 100 years before."[102]

A national movement to improve the quality of the country's roads therefore interested those committed to civic and economic progress. As they had at midcentury, much of the South, and particularly the rural South, suffered from poor and unreliable dirt roads that were dusty at best and impassable at worst. They were particularly challenging for farmers, who had to travel into town to transport their goods, pick up mail, and conduct other business. Begun initially by cycling enthusiasts, the movement received overwhelming support from the region's farmers. According to historian Howard Lawrence Preston, "Few reform causes captured rural southerners' attention the way the good roads movement did."[103] In 1896 legislation sponsored by Georgia congressman Thomas Watson mandated rural free delivery of the mail, and within several years Congress appropriated funds to improve rural post roads. In 1901 the South Carolina Good Roads Association was founded in Greenville.

Progressive Era reformers supported "Highway Progressivism" in part because it would improve accessibility to education for the region's rural youth. In 1909 a professor from the University of South Carolina wrote that "the best and quickest way to diffuse light in dark places, is to bring the dark places within easy reach of the light. The better the highway between the two places, the nearer they are to each other. When good highways shall have been built, it will be found

that a system of good schools is at least well on the way. Good roads and good schools are all but inseparable."[104]

Progressives argued furthermore that good roads would both improve the status of women and attract tourists into the region, whose dollars could be spent improving the quality of life for the rural South. Tennessee Progressive Josephine Anderson Pearson claimed that better roads would liberate women isolated in the rural South and would be more beneficial than woman's suffrage. Progressives aimed to ameliorate regional animosities lingering from the Civil War and hoped that the presence of tourists from across the country would mitigate regional differences between the South and other areas. In 1902 the mayor of Charlotte went so far as to suggest that he did not think the Civil War would have happened if better roads had connected North and South.[105] Nearly two years into his presidency, Woodrow Wilson expressed hope that transcontinental roads and roads running from the northeastern states to Miami would, according to a news report from Washington, "be a good means of further obliterating sectional feeling between the north and the south." In a letter to the president of the Lincoln Highway Association, Wilson wrote, "I am sure the entire country is interested to see that there should no longer exist a north or a south in this absolutely united country, which we all love, and that the imaginary Mason and Dixon's line should be made once and for all a thing of the past."[106]

In addition to the Progressives, farmers and Populists hoped better roads would greatly improve their ability to take goods to market, ensuring their product was fresher and thus more valuable. Southern manufacturing would benefit from the more expeditious transfer of cotton to boxcars destined for mills throughout the region, while increased traffic through rural areas represented an unprecedented business opportunity for rural southerners. Good roads would also increase the value of farmland adjacent to such roads. They would allow for the greater enforcement of Prohibition laws and the use of chain gangs in road

Shown here circa 1915, the buff brick and black mortar Dunean Mill was completely electric and was known as the Million Dollar Mill. The mill, which manufactured fine cotton goods, was organized by Ellison Adger Smyth, widely referred to as the dean of southern textile manufacturers. Courtesy Greenville County Historical Society.

The Politics of Race and Gender 39

building and maintenance accommodated those who wished to preserve local White political control of convicts and African American labor.[107] Road improvement plans appealed to New South advocates because, like Progressives, they hoped better roads would attract tourists, but also they believed that improved infrastructure would significantly enhance the region's ability to recruit commerce and industry. The good roads movement was popular because it attracted so many different economic, political, and social factions, including farmers, the automobile and manufacturing industries, proponents of African American subjugation, and supporters of education, prohibition, and women's rights.[108]

The movement continued to gain support over the course of the first decade of the twentieth century and particularly the second, when automobiles became more widespread and were no longer an exclusive hobby of the elite. In 1910 the American Automobile Association printed its first guide to motoring in the South. That same year the southern Good Roads Tour provided a driving itinerary that navigated through Greenville on a road that eventually joined the National Highway.[109]

In a feature story on the city and its manufacturing industry in February 1900, the *New York Times* proclaimed, "Prosperity could not have marked for special favor a prettier town in South Carolina than Greenville." The article claimed that Greenville was "developing magnificently" and that the benefits were benevolently widespread: "While the owners and stockholders are getting rich, they are conferring permanent blessings upon the people." It posited Greenville as "the very best result of the industrial awakening."[110]

At the dawn of the new century, the city of Greenville boasted a population that had grown nearly eight times since 1860. Efforts to address the changes and challenges created by this population boom and rapid Upcountry industrialization were led, in large part, by women. From the beginning and continuing through the next several decades, the Upcountry dominated the leadership of the SCFWC. Johnson asserts that because the Upcountry experienced an industrial surge that introduced the challenges that accompany quick growth, Upcountry women saw and felt the problems firsthand in ways that women in other areas of the state, and particularly the Lowcountry, did not.[111] Over the course of the late 1800s and early 1900s, elite White women increasingly became involved in the Greenville community through temperance, Lost Cause education and memorialization, the club movement, and suffrage, with their efforts benefitting healthcare, education, beautification, and beyond.

On the eve of the outbreak of World War I, Greenville was ambitious and vibrant. With a robust economy, a successful record of collaboration with the federal government, and Progressive Era enthusiasm, Greenville was evolving from the Pearl of the Piedmont to the Textile Capital of the South, but despite the *Times*'s assertion, the benefits of its thriving economy were reserved for a select group of White elites and a professional class of bankers, attorneys, and businesspeople that largely supported the textile industry. For the causes of peace, prosperity, and beautification, these White elites not only adhered to but also established stringent regional standards governing racial segregation with support from the large local population of mill operatives; reform efforts often furthered the subjugation of African Americans and, in regard to the mill villages, were motivated by a desire to promote economic stability. They reveal the extent to which Progressivism in Greenville was its own unique brand.

chapter two

Greenville and the Nation Respond to War "Over There," 1914–1917

The Germans are very intolerant of any other nation aspiring to the same greatness that Prussia and Germany have fought for. They are continually "slamming" us but I've got a new defence nicely worded in German so I throw that at them and retreat (gracefully?).

—*Mary Orr, 1873*

In the early 1910s, the *Greenville Daily News* dedicated more attention to conflicts on the US-Mexico border than it did to news emanating from the Old World. The startling escalation of events that occurred in the summer of 1914 in Europe, however, quickly caught the city's attention.

On June 28, 1914, tensions in the Balkans exploded when Serbian nationalists assassinated Austrian Archduke Franz Ferdinand, the heir apparent to the Austro-Hungarian Empire. On its front page the next day, the *Greenville Daily News* ran a headline from Sarajevo, beside a large image of Mexican revolutionaries on horseback after the Battle of Zacatecas.[1] A month later, on July 29, 1914, the headline of the *Greenville Daily News* read: "Austria-Hungary Declares War Upon Servia [sic] Following Germany's Rejection of the British Proposal for Mediation." Just below it, another article reassured readers: "United States to Stay Neutral in the Balkan Crisis."[2] Due to alliances among the European nations, the crisis quickly spread beyond the Balkans. Within two weeks, the Great War had begun, with nearly all of Europe and its colonies involved.

At the outbreak of war, the United States had private and public economic interests scattered throughout Europe, with investments in both neutral and belligerent powers. The complicated nature of entangling alliances that defined the war soon disrupted this flourishing international and continental trade. As war erupted in 1914, neither side occupied the moral high ground in the eyes of the American public, and most Americans preferred neutrality when considering even remote participation in what was considered a bloody and barbaric war thousands of miles overseas. As the French and British Entente oriented themselves against the Central Powers of Germany and Austria-Hungary, and as more and more of Europe weighed in on the conflict, President Wilson initiated a campaign for "peace without victory."[3]

Whether or not Americans agreed on where to place blame for the outbreak of hostilities, there was no denying that the United States was heavily involved in the war economically. J. P. Morgan and other Wall Street bankers had invested significantly in the Entente from the start of the war, and their investments proved to be crucial to the American economy as a whole. As historian Robert Zieger writes, "Americans increasingly came to couple their horror of the European catastrophe with the appreciation of the opportunities for profit and longer-range economic benefits that the war now offered."[4] Economic interests gradually became the ultimate determinant in American involvement in the war as the shock of its outbreak passed. In Greenville the health of the cotton market was the overwhelming factor that shaped local opinion of the war.

The reaction in Greenville to the outbreak of war mirrored that of the nation as a whole, with added concerns relating to the textile industry. Despite recent conflicts in Cuba, the Philippines, and China, most Americans felt themselves morally superior to the European nations who would revert to the ferocious practice of warfare during the enlightened twentieth century. Excepting those with ethnic ties and economic interests, the location of the war across the Atlantic allowed many Americans to stay quite aloof from the news of war in Europe in 1914.

While some cities still held pro-German sentiments based on immigrant communities or economic interests, evidence does not suggest the existence of a pro-German movement within Greenville. The Midwest region of the country, especially the state of Wisconsin, with its large German population, preferred American neutrality.[5] As far south as Lexington, Kentucky, pro-German sympathies were high enough to prompt a pro-German, antiwar rally on the day after Congress declared war in April 1917. The Lowcountry of South Carolina not only boasted higher populations of immigrants and their descendants than the Upcountry, but also those immigrants and descendants yielded more influence in the economic, social, and political fabric of the community. Charleston's foreign-born White population was 2,616 in 1910, or 3 percent of the total county population, with Germans represented above all other foreign-born groups; in 1920 it was 2,455, or 2.2 percent. Greenville's foreign-born White population was 312 in 1910 and 489 in 1920, comprising 0.5 percent and 0.6 percent, respectively.[6]

By the time of the war, the German American population had thrived in South Carolina for more than 150 years. Swiss German immigrants settled in the Lowcountry and Midlands of South Carolina from the 1740s onward. During the colonial era, the residents of Orangeburgh District, which included Saxe-Gotha, were primarily of Swiss German origin.[7] Charleston was home to several German American organizations, including the German Friendly Society (1766) and the German Fusiliers Society (1775), the first German military society in the colonies and United States. German Americans made up 9 percent of the White population of Charleston in 1860 and owned significant businesses, financial institutions, and insurance companies.[8] Charlestonians of German descent were also involved in local politics; ten years before the war broke out in Europe, they represented over 20 percent of the city's aldermen.

During the early years of the conflict overseas, South Carolinians with German blood in Lexington, Orangeburg, Newberry, and Charleston Counties opposed the war. Charleston's German-language newspaper, *Deutsche Zeitung,* published accounts of their opposition and concern for family and friends in Germany. John P. Grace, former mayor of Charleston and editor of the *Charleston American,* published antiwar and pro-German editorials upon the outbreak of war, prompting threats and the loss of mailing privileges for his newspaper.[9] In contrast, the German Friendly Society celebrated their sesquicentennial in January 1916 with a sumptuous affair, during which the president of the organization, Julius H. Janhz, clearly established the society's support for their adopted homeland by highlighting the patriotism and military service of society members in the American Revolution and the Civil War and emphasizing members' involvement and investment in the Charleston community.[10]

One year later, on January 31, 1917, the crew of the *Liebenfels,* a German commercial vessel that had been detained since 1914, sank their ship in Charleston Harbor in response to news that Washington had severed diplomatic ties with Berlin, and in an attempt to block the shipping lanes emanating from the Charleston Naval Shipyard. Nine of the crewmen were convicted of blockading a navigable stream and were sentenced to one year in Atlanta's federal penitentiary. The German skipper of the *Liebenfels* and Paul Wierse, an editorial writer for *The Charleston American* newspaper who had emigrated from Berlin in 1894, were convicted of helping plot the sinking under orders from the German consul in Atlanta. In response Charleston's *Deutsche Zeitung* argued that every German American should "go about unflinchingly and serve his country patriotically and conscientiously."[11] Six days after Congress declared war, Charleston's *Evening Post* included notice that the German Rifle Club had cancelled their annual Schuetzenfest and that the festival would resume in "more auspicious times."[12] The *Deutsche Zeitung* stopped printing in 1917 when its owner, Albert Orth, was tried and imprisoned for assisting in the escape of German fugitives. The next year a new newspaper owned by Orth titled the *Southern Gazette* appeared, but it had ceased publication by 1919. Throughout 1917 and 1918, German businesses and social clubs changed their names in an effort to disguise their German affiliations. The Germania Savings Bank became the Atlantic Savings Bank, while Der Deutsche Freundschafts Bund assumed the name Arion Society, and the German Rifle Club became the Charleston Rifle Club. The German American Alliance disbanded, and fundraising for the German Red Cross ceased.[13]

Other Germans and German organizations in Charleston made their loyalty to the United States more explicit. For example, the German Artillery Hall hosted a series of patriot meetings, and young men from several notable German families served in the US military. St. Matthews German Lutheran Church hosted a ladies' sewing room, and eighty-three men from the congregation served in the armed forces.[14] The German Friendly Society hosted a "Victory Celebration Dinner" in which "Spanish Mackarel à la Clemenceau" and "Ice Cream à la Pershing" were served, and the keynote speeches were titled "Our Country," "Our State," and "Our City."[15] The society remained accepted by the Charleston power structure, though its membership declined, and it never regained the vitality it had before the war. World War I marked the end of Charleston German Americans' conspicuous pride in their Germanic identity, as it did across the country for many Americans who descended from German immigrants.

Greenville's relatively homogenous response to the outbreak of war in 1914 and in 1917 did not include the nuance that a more diverse population may have introduced. In the 1910 census, Greenville's foreign-born White population represented only 5.2 percent of the state's foreign-born White population. Most immigrants had come from, in descending order: Germany (48), England (42), Belgium (32), Russia (30), Scotland (23), Ireland (22), Assyria (22), Turkey (20), Canada (19), Austria (15), Greece (13), France (7), Hungary (7), Switzerland (6), Lebanon/Syria (4), Italy (3), China (3), West Indies (2), Panama (2), Bohemia (2), Sweden (2), and one person each from Croatia, Brazil, Denmark, India, and Egypt. Approximately 80 percent of the Germans in Greenville in 1910 had arrived by 1900.[16] The Upcountry's small Greek and Lebanese/Assyrian/Syrian populations were particularly supportive of the local Red Cross during and after the war. These immigrants had long been accepted by Greenville's White power structure because they were considered "almost" White in a state with a majority African American population. Furthermore they were civic-minded and entrepreneurial, particularly in the food industry, and chose not to work in the mills.[17] Across the country ethnic and nationalistic concerns, particularly from German, Irish, and Slavic communities, created dissension—discord of which the American government and its citizens alike became increasingly intolerant as the United States drew closer to war in the spring of 1917.

Before war erupted in the summer of 1914, Greenvillians had enjoyed an exuberant sense of anticipation, as the fields surrounding them were nurturing the most abundant cotton yield—sixteen million bales—in American history. With cotton prices at thirteen cents per pound, the bumper crop was projected to be valued around ten million dollars.[18] Furthermore South Carolina mills wove 20 percent of the nation's production of coarse cloth and, with over 4.5 million spindles, led the region in the number of spindles and trailed behind only Massachusetts nationally.[19]

However, the outbreak of war in Europe introduced great economic instability. The textile mills that were the heart of Greenville's industry felt the pressure of the war and its disruption of trade through both management and labor, and the economy of Greenville suffered as a result. While America's role in the growing conflict overseas remained ambiguous, political uncertainties led to economic uncertainties. Beginning in 1914, German *unterseeboots* terrorized Atlantic shipping routes. The cotton market became dangerously shaky in the 1914–16 period and cotton markets temporarily collapsed as a result of instability.

Speculation over cotton caused nervous tensions throughout the region. Greenvillians had good reason to be concerned: the jobs and livelihoods of thousands of residents depended on the healthy export of textiles produced from cotton.[20] On August 3, major cotton exchanges in Greenville and around the country failed to open, and they remained closed for three months because of the outbreak of war in Europe and uncertainties regarding the nation's role.[21] A headline in the August 13, 1914, *Greenville Daily Piedmont* read, "War Causes Falling Off of Revenue."[22] After the cotton market reopened in the fall of 1914, the price of cotton fell from thirteen cents to the break-even price of ten cents and ultimately to five cents, with unpicked cotton blanketing the region's fields like snow. A small but prominently placed exhortation on the front page of the *Greenville Daily News* in September 1914 read, "Buy a bale of cotton and help relieve the situation the South is now facing. Every little bit will help."[23] Locals worried the British would label cotton as contraband of war, especially after the British seized the American ship SS *Denver* for carrying cotton cargo bound for Bremen, Germany, in early January 1915.[24] Guncotton and nitrocellulose, an incendiary material several times more powerful than black powder, could be produced from raw cotton; both sides sought to import it for its explosive potential, creating a situation fraught with complexity for the neutral United States.[25]

The entire economy of Greenville reeled from the major financial loss and market confusion.[26] In early 1915 Parker Cotton Mills of Greenville went bankrupt as a result of the falling price of cotton and the interruption of imports coming from German factories, which had long supplied the mill's dyes. In response fifty-five-year-old Thomas Parker retired to devote himself to civic progress.[27] In April the *Greenville Daily News* reported that cotton was being kept out of Germany and Austria-Hungary "as if it were declared absolute contraband."[28] And months later it was: on August 22, 1915, the British Committee of Imperial Defence added raw cotton, cotton waste, and cotton yarn to their list of contraband exports. The US government respected their policy, and locally, as textile production slowed to a standstill, mill operatives throughout the Upstate declared the mills to be "overcrowded with help" making it difficult "to find sufficient work."[29] Fears regarding job security spread among thousands of Greenville textile workers. The 1915 annual report from the state's commissioner of agriculture, commerce and industries detailed the challenges: "In the year 1914 manufacturing in South Carolina surpassed agriculture in wealth-earning capacity for the first time, but it was due to the abnormal conditions caused by the cotton crisis. . . . The textile industry was hard hit by the war conditions, and so was the fertilizer industry and lumber."[30]

These anxieties led to significant disturbances, as at least two national labor unions used anxieties about the economy to capitalize on existing efforts to organize textile workers in Upcountry South Carolina. In the summer of 1914, the International Workers of the World (IWW, also known as "Wobblies") centered their southern campaign on Greenville and its environs and boasted two thousand members by May.[31] In June they organized a strike in nearby Easley, South Carolina. According to the IWW's newspaper *Solidarity*, "New Local 537 won a fight in 4 hours the previous week." In July IWW leader Joseph James Ettor encouraged and helped organize socialist demonstrations in Greenville in concert with striking workers. Considered a radical "outside agitator" by many, Ettor was credited with having organized the 1912 textile "bread and roses" strike in Lawrence, Massachusetts, which had resulted in salary increases of up to 20 percent throughout much of New England.[32] In early July 105 operatives who were members of the IWW marched through downtown Greenville carrying a red flag.[33] Seven hundred five striking workers at Lewis and Thomas Parker's Monaghan Mill caused the mill to remain partially closed for almost two months after an accumulation of "petty grievances," according to historian David Carlton.[34] Word quickly spread throughout the region and prompted communication with business leaders in Washington. On July 11, 1914, Oscar Elsas, president of the Fulton Bag and Cotton Mills in Atlanta, wrote to James A. Emery, general counsel for the National Council for Industrial Defense, that "we heard this morning that the Monaghan Mills, of Greenville, S.C., have gone on strike, and it is self-evident that this is the beginning of more trouble among the mills if such agitators as Jackson are not stopped in their unreasonable work." Elsas was referring

Greenville and the Nation Respond to War   47

to Marion Jackson, an attorney and leader of the Men and Religion Forward Movement, whose muckraking approach and support of union activity and the Social Gospel, a Christian approach to Progressive Era reforms, prompted one Fulton Mills investor to liken him to writer Upton Sinclair.[35] A week later, in correspondence exchanged between Oscar Elsas and Jacob Elsas, Oscar wrote "that under no circumstances will we hire Greenville help. We do not want to bring in any of the I.W.W. bunch. . . . We are going to exercise great caution in not bringing on new troubles."[36] Ultimately Governor Cole Blease, with support from Greenville sheriff Hendrix Rector, ordered state troopers to confront the Wobbly organizers at Monaghan. Meanwhile, according to Carlton, Parker "rapidly diffused" the situation through his willingness to meet with the strikers' workers committee, who reported the specifics of their displeasure as opposed to embracing the "one big union" concept. Furthermore they assured Parker that "there is not a man at Monaghan who would damage you at all."[37] Regardless of whether that statement was motivated by validity or appeasement, their meeting mitigated the situation.[38]

In September the IWW organized a strike in Pickens, about twenty miles from downtown Greenville. One hundred and twenty-five operatives employed by the Pickens Cotton Mill left work after some of their coworkers, who were members of the IWW, were fired for unknown reasons. When negotiations with mill authorities to reinstate the workers proved unsuccessful, the union called for a strike. According to a local newspaper report, strikers received notices to vacate their homes in the mill village within ten days, prompting all but forty-nine of them to return to work. Those who didn't return were fired and typically left town. By the fall the appeal of the IWW had peaked and was waning. Upcountry mill owners' obstinate response to the strikes discouraged most workers from continued affiliation with the IWW.[39]

Throughout 1915, another union, the United Textile Workers (UTW), guided strikers as they challenged mill leadership. Judson Mill (formerly Westervelt Mill) President Bennette E. Geer's refusal to reinstate workers who had been dismissed as a result of connections to and supposed membership in the UTW prompted two hundred of the Judson Mill employees to strike, though 654 were "directly affected," according to the Department of Labor Statistics. Judson Mill remained partially closed for weeks, with strikers picketing along surrounding fences. Two weeks after the mill reopened, in late November 1915, a conflict between workers returning to the mill and those still striking prompted one strike breaker to stab a twenty-seven-year-old striker named David Freeze. The *Greenville Daily Piedmont* described the attack: "Freeze was horribly butchered about his heart and abdomen. Three ribs, just below his heart, were severed and pulled apart. His intestines were bulging out and he was bleeding to death when he was rushed in an ambulance to City Hospital. Physicians began an operation this morning in the last hope of saving his life." Freeze died, leaving behind a wife and baby. At his funeral fellow strikers processed behind his coffin with signs that read, "The only crime this man committed was that of doing legitimate picket duty during a strike. One more innocent victim, crying to Heaven for vengeance against the brutality of the Union-hating employer." Simultaneously, in neighboring Anderson County, newly elected governor Richard Manning, known for his staunch opposition to labor unions, sent the Palmetto Guard to the town of Anderson to enforce Brogan Mill's eviction of striking workers from mill village homes.[40] The UTW had encouraged strikes among the mill's operatives throughout 1915; according to the Bureau of Labor Statistics, 575 workers were directly involved in the strike, with 1,500 workers affected. Despite the continued success of the UTW in other states, the presence of the Guard put an end to most union activity in South Carolina, and over the next several years, mill owners in South Carolina successfully convinced their employees that union support for wage increases would only result in increased unemployment.[41]

In an attempt to discredit the union in the eyes of the White mill operatives, some mill owners and managers, such as those at Monaghan Mill, introduced the one issue they knew would create problems between the union and the operatives: race. To many White southern mill operatives, the allure of working with a national organization had its limits. When mill owners accused the union of advocating for racial equality and threatened to replace White operatives with local African Americans for less pay, the strike dissipated. Efforts to work with a national organization and advocate for the rights of White workers were limited by the southern racial status quo; the racial prejudices of the White operatives hampered their own cause, as did White southerner's staunch opposition to relinquishing their autonomy to federal or national entities. As W. J. Cash later described it in his seminal work, *The Mind of the South*, White southerners thought of northern union organizers as "guerilla shock troops come South again after sixty years to renew the Reconstruction fight."[42] Bolstered by Governor Cole Blease's racist and sexualized rhetoric, which played upon White fears of African American male sexuality and the crisis of masculinity experienced by White men who left the fields to work in the factories, the South Carolina legislature passed legislation on February 16, 1915, prohibiting African Americans from employment alongside White mill workers.[43] The "Act to Compel a Separation of the Races Laboring in Textile Manufactories" read:

> Be it enacted by the General Assembly of the State of South Carolina, that it shall be unlawful for any person, firm, or corporation engaged in the business

Greenville and the Nation Respond to War 49

of cotton textile manufacturing in this State to allow or permit operatives, help, or labor of different races to labor and work together within the same room, or to use the same doors of entrance and exit at the same time, or to use and occupy the same pay ticket windows or doors for paying off its operatives and laborers at the same time, or to use the same stairways and windows and the same time, or to use at any time the same lavatories, toilets, drinking water buckets, pails, cups, dippers, or glasses: Provided, Equal accommodations shall be supplied and furnished to all persons employed by said person, firm, or corporation engaged in the business of cotton textile manufacturing as aforesaid, without distinction to race, color, or previous condition.

Penalties for violation of this act included a fine of not more than one hundred dollars. The next day the legislature amended the act to also make violation of it a misdemeanor punishable by up to thirty days of "imprisonment at hard labor."[44]

White southerners, including mill owners and operatives, took pride in the strength of the local industry that had accelerated the Piedmont region's economic strength relative to other southern communities. They knew the textile industry was the path upon which the city and its residents would thrive. Attempts from northerners that interfered with the economic stability of the industry and the segregated culture of the mill villages were typically unwelcome, and less than 5 percent of mill workers in the state belonged to a union. The most successful union in the area, the UTW, built its membership by capitalizing on worker's fears of economic vulnerability and bolstering workers' already increased bargaining position, brought on by the wartime scarcity of workers and an unusually high demand for textile goods.[45] The UTW steadily gained new members in the Piedmont of North and South Carolina and northern Georgia between 1914 and 1921, though their activity in South Carolina ceased in 1916. The UTW was successful in part due to its respect for the autonomy of local chapters. In May 1919 the *Textiles Operatives' Journal* quoted the president of the UTW, who said that the UTW "gives the greatest confidence to the rank and file of the workers, encourages and keeps organization together, is that which makes conditions liberal enough for local unions to create a substantial treasury of their own, and be in a position to give a reasonable support to the members of their own local union when emergencies arise."[46] By understanding southern suspicion of national organizations and allowing local unions to maintain some independence, the UTW was able to bring forty to fifty thousand southern textile operatives into the union by the end of the decade. Nationally its membership grew from eighteen thousand in 1914 to thirty-two thousand in 1916 and one hundred thousand by 1920, though most UTW activity that occurred in the South after 1916 occurred outside of South Carolina in Georgia, North Carolina, and Tennessee.[47]

From 1914 to 1916 in the South Carolina Piedmont, instability in the cotton market drove some workers to seek job security by joining unions, while textile mill management sought to break unions and keep wages low to combat the fluctuations in the cotton market and maintain stable prices and operations. Textile mill owners repulsed attempts at union organization by both the more radical IWW and the more moderate UTW. Greenville textile workers had an uncertain future and were at the mercy of their employers' ruthlessness in the face of unionization. The volatile cotton market was the gauge by which mill operatives could predict the stability of their families' livelihoods in the years leading up to American entry into the Great War; ironically, while speculation over joining the war brought instability, the event that undeniably returned stability to the volatile cotton market was America's entry into the war overseas.[48]

Despite the economic tribulations introduced by the war, Upcountry South Carolina remained indisputably the textile hub of the region. Throughout the late 1800s and early 1900s, Greenville and neighboring Spartanburg County vied for textile prominence. In December 1914 a committee of Greenville leaders, many of whom had ties to or were representing textile machine manufacturers based in the Northeast, began planning a trade show for the local textile industry. Joseph "Joe" E. Sirrine and James F. Richardson, who had led efforts to recruit Camp Wetherill during the Spanish-American War, served on the committee. Ten months later, in a local railroad warehouse on November 2, 1915, the committee welcomed forty thousand visitors to Greenville for the first Southern Textile Exposition.[49] The event was deemed highly successful, and almost immediately local leaders decided to build a permanent hall and host the trade show biennially. Bennette Geer chaired the committee responsible for raising funds to pay for the $130,000 red-brick building, while J. E. Sirrine and Company oversaw the exhibition space's design and construction. In December 1917 Greenville held the second Southern Textile Exposition, publicizing and celebrating the event in great fashion with the opening of the state-of-the-art "Textile Hall."[50] The grand exhibition hall showcased the latest developments in products, machinery, and equipment in the textile market for traders from around the country to view.[51] Textile Hall was the first exposition center built specifically for the textile industry in the Southeast; it placed Greenville at the forefront of the industry and was critical to the city's self-promotion as the "Textile Center of the South" and, subsequently, the "Textile Center of the World."[52]

Attracting tens of thousands of attendees at each exposition, the building itself soon also became a center for community life, hosting concerts, basketball tournaments, automobile shows, and conventions, which drew even more visitors to Greenville. Visitors to the expositions and other events relied upon the local transportation infrastructure. For some time railroads had connected Greenville directly to Atlanta, Charleston, Columbia, Knoxville, and Washington.[53] Yet nationally Americans were increasingly transporting themselves in their own automobiles. Lewis Parker had purchased the first horseless carriage sold in Greenville in 1903, and by 1910, 245 Greenvillians owned them. Greenville was the first city in the state to organize an automobile association, which crafted driving regulations regarding speeding, horn blowing, and driving on the right-hand side of the road. With 1,038 cars, Greenville County had more automobiles than any other county in South Carolina in 1914, a testament to the influx of wealth and people into the area in the early 1900s.[54] In 1915 attorney James M. Richardson purchased his first car, an Overland Roadster. Despite years of attempts from the Greenville Auto Association to mitigate problems between automobiles and horses, Richardson wrote that "horses and mules were stricken wild at the mere sight of an automobile, not to mention the swell and sound. Smashed vehicles and broken limbs littered the roadsides in their wake." To address the chaos, "legislative bodies of the State and the various municipalities rushed in to protect the public against that plaything of the rich."[55]

That same year, L. L. Stevenson, the southeastern sales manager for the Pullman Car Company, anticipated continued growth throughout the region: "I believe that the south is now entering upon a great era of prosperity. It is time for the auto salesman to prepare for the big increase in business that is sure to follow." He was right. In the next two years, automobile sales in the South skyrocketed, with sales in 1916 increasing 50 percent throughout the region from the previous year, due in large part to the sales of cotton, turpentine, and manufactured goods to the federal government and to foreign governments.[56] Yet roads had still failed to improve, to the great displeasure of automobile drivers in the county. After years of political debate and many surveys regarding which roads were most traveled, a million-dollar bond issue was approved in 1914 to be used for county road construction, with John W. Norwood, the Greenville County highway commissioner, leading the project.[57] When mill workers were laid off in the early years of the war, the city hired many of them to help pave and create roads.

Their efforts capitalized on the good roads movement that had increasingly gained momentum in recent decades. In May 1915 the Dixie Highway Association announced plans for a dual highway, which passed through Greenville on the eastern route between Asheville, North Carolina, and Augusta, Georgia, before leading to Savannah. Later that year President Wilson expressed concern for the country's "transportation problem" in his State of the Union address. Six months later he signed legislation into law after Congress voted to appropriate federal dollars to state transportation departments for the first time with the Federal Aid Road Act. This legislation required states to have governmental agencies to manage their roads. When these funds were passed, South Carolina was one of only five states, alongside Indiana, Georgia, Mississippi, and Texas, that did not have a state highway department and was thus ineligible for funds.

In *Dixie Highway: Road Building and the Modern South, 1900–1930,* Tammy Ingram has shown how the good roads movement and plans for the highway resulted in a significant shift: roads were no longer the domain of local politicians but rather that of state and federal governments.[58] For Greenvillians and their fellow South Carolinians, this shift represented yet another instance in which their progressive aspirations necessitated collaboration with the federal government.

Nearly one year after the US Senate passed the Federal Aid Road Act, five men convened in Governor Manning's office on Saturday, March 10, 1917, and created the SC State Highway Commission.[59] In April 1917 Greenville sent seven delegates, including the mayor, to Birmingham to advocate for Greenville's inclusion on the future Bankhead Highway, named in honor of John Bankhead, the US senator from Alabama considered the "Father of the Good Roads Movement." The Bankhead family had close connections with Greenville. The father of John Bankhead's wife, Tallulah, was from Greenville, and her great-great-grandfather Benjamin Kilgore was a captain of a South Carolina company during the American Revolution. John and Tallulah's eldest daughter, Louise, married US Congressman William H. Perry of Greenville, the son of South Carolina's governor during Reconstruction Benjamin F. Perry.[60] These connections were helpful; at the meeting in Birmingham, Greenville's mayor, Charles S. Webb, was appointed to the committee that selected the final path of the highway. Ultimately the Spartanburg-Gaffney-Greenville-Anderson National Highway route was selected over the capital route of Raleigh-Columbia-Atlanta to join the Bankhead Highway, though it was never named such in South Carolina as it was in other states.[61] Entrance into the war slowed progress on road development, though advocates argued that these highways ought to be a priority for the federal government since they were an important means of linking the many military camps spread throughout the South.[62]

The economic uncertainty that categorized 1914 and some of 1915 abated when the volatile cotton market improved upon the government's authorization of massive war trade and direct financing of the Allied forces from 1915 going into 1916.[63] American exports tripled from 1913 to 1916, from two billion dollars to almost six billion. Furthermore, in 1915 the Allied Powers began to borrow

Greenville and the Nation Respond to War   53

directly from US investors, which would turn the United States from a debtor nation into a creditor nation by the end of the war, based almost entirely off of these war loans.[64] The cotton market, along with the many other American industries that were heavily utilized by desperate Allied nations overseas, was instantly buoyed by Allied war dollars, despite continued terrorization of shipping on the Atlantic by German U-boats. The late 1915 and early 1916 surge in the cotton market assuaged the anxieties of many Greenvillians and brought economic hope. In the spirit of the Progressive Era, business and civic leaders organized to create the state's first Rotary Club; its weekly meetings served as a space for the city's leaders to discuss the economic, social, and cultural vitality of the community. The construction of the city's first apartment building, Davenport Apartments, was proof of the city's vibrancy; it provided downtown housing for middle-class professionals, many of whom were attracted to Greenville's thriving textile industry.[65] Several blocks away on Main Street, the cornerstone of a new Beaux Arts–style courthouse was laid in 1916 and also served as architectural evidence not only of the status quo of racial segregation, with its separate spaces for African American and White visitors, but also of increased economic stability, a shift that increased Greenvillians' general support of President Wilson.[66] As Zieger writes, the improvement in the cotton market boosted the president's popularity in most southern Democratic states: "The price of cotton—a crucial indicator of domestic health for a Democratic president reliant on Southern votes and congressional leadership—soared between the onset of fighting and the 1916 presidential election."[67] Indeed 96.7 percent of South Carolina's White male voting populace cast their support for Wilson in his reelection campaign.

Over the course of that election year, Greenvillians increasingly embraced a sense of nationalism and local pride, as Greenville increasingly warranted encouraging national attention from the federal government in the areas of public health and transportation. Prompted by a request from the State Board of Public Health, the US Public Health Service selected Greenville alongside Floyd County, Georgia; Tuscaloosa County, Alabama; Obion County, Tennessee; Clay County, Missouri; and Cumberland County, Illinois, as the six sites nationally where the US Public Health Service would conduct a sanitary survey. In Greenville the survey began on March 8 and concluded on November 1, with government officials establishing themselves in offices in the Chamber of Commerce building downtown, which the chamber provided at no cost. Throughout the spring local newspapers publicized and educated citizens about the work of the government officials, and a series of public meetings was held. Over the course of the study, 123 public lectures were given, with an estimated 24,600 Greenvillians in attendance. To encourage enthusiasm for improved sanitation, lottery tickets were issued at at least one gathering, with those holding winning numbers receiving sanitary privies as prizes.[68] Community organizations contributed significantly to this campaign as well. At the April meeting of the Greenville Woman's Club, held at the Chamber of Commerce, a representative of the US Public Health Service spoke about the sanitation efforts. The club had recently received five thousand pamphlets on sanitation, with plans to distribute them to both White and African American city residents.[69]

The federal surveyors examined 11,751 homes. Homes in cotton mill villages made up 2,241 of these, while 758 homes existed in "rural towns," and 8,752 were "strictly rural," mostly frame-construction farm homes. These federal agents kept data on how they were received in the homes of White southerners; in Greenville federal surveyors received cordial welcomes in all but 0.3 percent of those homes.[70] On average 5.1 people lived in each of the "strictly rural" farm homes, with the majority consisting of three to four rooms. Just under 60 percent of these homes had privies or water closets, while the rest had no toiletry accommodations. Based on a variety of factors, the average sanitary score for rural homes in Greenville County was 19.16 out of a possible 100. The report stated, "Thus it is evident that the farmers of Greenville County, though progressive in many respects, were backwards in the application of sanitary principles for the safeguarding of the health of their families." Out of the ninety-five rural schools inspected, students at twenty-one schools had to "resort to the woods . . . to void their excreta."[71]

With an average of four rooms and 5.5 people living in each home, the cotton mill homes were similar in size to the farm homes. Yet only 127 of these homes, or 17.65 percent, had no toilet facilities, with all other homes having water closets or privies. At 38.7, the average sanitary rating was nearly double the rating of the farm homes. Surveyors found water closets available in all the cotton mills inspected.

The report also examined four incorporated towns within the county. Surveyors gave the 758 dwellings inspected in Greer, Fountain Inn, Simpsonville, and West Greenville a combined sanitary rating of 30.9, a rating higher than the rural homes but lower than those in the mill villages.

In contrast to the rural and cotton mill village homes, the residences in the city of Greenville were in "remarkably good sanitary conditions." Every dwelling in the city limits had either a water closet that was connected to the water carriage sewer system or a well-maintained sanitary privy. The report concluded that "this city has the distinction of being the only incorporated center included in the sanitary surveys of the Public Health Service which was found on the first round of inspection to have at every place of human abode equipment for sanitary

The results of Greenville's sanitary survey were published in the US *Public Health Bulletin* No. 94 with this image, described as "A Primitive toilet, consisting of a stump of a hollow tree with a piece of canvas nailed over it, at a rural home in Greenville County, S.C."

disposal of human excreta."[72] The report credited the "energetic, intelligent, and untiring efforts" of the city health officer, Dr. Clarence E. Smith. Just eighteen months earlier, he had led a campaign to convert all the privies, or outhouses, within the city limits into sanitary privies. A sanitary privy was one that included a "water-tight galvanized iron receptacle" covered by a hinged, "fly tight" lid.[73] The report issued a rating of over 90 for homes in the city, far higher than the other types of homes in the report.

During the first ninety days of the survey, findings from the study were presented to the owners of the mill villages. The owners of sixteen of the eighteen mill villages surveyed responded immediately by installing sanitary privies in the homes that did not have approved facilities. By November 1, 73.3 percent of the homes that had either unsanitary privies or no toilet had a sanitary privy installed. However, the homes that did not receive privies were located in three mill villages. The president of Mills Mill, Walter B. Moore, installed a sewered water closet and bathtub in each of the hundred homes in the village and contracted with the Gallivan Building Company to construct a complete sewage and drainage system at a cost of forty thousand dollars. In the two remaining villages, the installation of sanitary privies was begun in the spring and completed during the summer of 1917. Due to these efforts, the sanitary rating of the mill village homes increased from 38.7 to 68.48.[74]

Nearly all the incorporated town and villages in the sanitary surveys, including West Greenville; Obion, Tennessee; Tuscaloosa, Alabama; and Excelsior Springs in Clay County, Missouri, passed ordinances requiring compliance with a set of standards for disposing of human excreta. Of the 660 homes that had been surveyed in the four incorporated towns in Greenville County, all had privies that met mandated standards by November 1916.

56   "Our Country First, Then Greenville"

The City of Greenville and Chamber of Commerce embraced the impressive rating they had received and promoted it widely. To celebrate the result, the Chamber of Commerce partnered with local organizations to plan elaborate "Health Day" celebrations, with the railroad offering discounted rates to those coming into Greenville for the celebration. An afternoon parade included a hundred health-themed floats, and after rain forced the cancellation of outdoor band performances and a pyrotechnical display, the indoor program that evening included speeches from politicians and from Assistant Secretary of the Treasury B. R. Newton and assistant surgeon general of the US Public Health Service J. W. Kerr.[75] An article in the *Greenville Daily News* proclaimed, "Today is the banner day in the history of Greenville, the fact that Greenville is one of the healthiest cities in the United States will be heralded from coast to coast."[76]

Over the course of 1916, Greenville had enjoyed several favorable experiences with the federal government, including the sanitary survey and the federal government's support of local roads, which promoted a heightened sense of nationalism among its White southern inhabitants. A committee organized by the Chamber of Commerce began to raise money for an electric sign that would display the city's patriotism and Progressivism to all who saw it. Local mill villages, schoolchildren, and hundreds of other Greenvillians donated to the cause. Throughout the spring and summer of 1916, the local newspaper ran multiple editorials that supported the fundraising efforts. "That great electric flag, hoisted high above the streets, would be inspirational, would make one conscience [*sic*] of our Nation every time it was looked upon, would be a constant reminder to the school children. . . . In the South the flag is not always applauded. . . . We should revere the flag more, should look at it more. . . . It would be an aid in The 'Americanization' movement, an impetus to sentiment for one's country."[77] One editorial, titled "Reminder of Our Nation," argued that the flag would be "a constant reminder by day and a striking reminder by night that we owe a patriotic duty to our country, that this is the first duty, and that duty to Greenville comes next."[78]

The city and chamber decided the sign would be unveiled and illuminated for the first time publicly in accordance with Health Day celebrations. The symbolic gesture of an electric American flag, with the illuminated phrase "Our Country First—Then Greenville," flying atop the Chamber of Commerce in the city's central business district, was especially significant significant during a time when electricity was an expensive novelty and many White southerners did not have positive associations with the American flag.[79] This display represented a prideful rejoining of the national fold, partnership in the city's recent and beneficial relationship with federal authority, support for the country and president during

Greenville and the Nation Respond to War   57

a time of war overseas, and satisfaction in the community's modernity and economic strength.

The sign prompted curiosity and delight. On the day it was unveiled, two electric adding machines counted the number of people who passed the intersection where the new sign was located; the local news commented that on a typical day, 35,000 people passed that intersection, while up to 150,000 passersby were expected on October 4.[80] About two weeks after it was unveiled, a representative of the Southern Public Utilities Company planned to deliver a color image of the sign to President Wilson at the American Street Railway Convention in Atlantic City.[81] An article in the *Iron Tradesman,* a publication popular among those involved in the textile industry, commented that the sign was "proof of both the progressivism and patriotism of the community."[82] Within weeks the Chamber of Commerce released the inaugural edition of a periodical they hoped would advance the community spirit and "welfare of the mountain city" and attract business to the area; they strategically named it *Progressive Greenville.*[83]

Greenville's woman's suffrage proponents were among the progressive activists who capitalized upon the city's recent and favorable relations with the federal government. Though the movement had lost momentum in the years after the 1895 constitutional convention and even more so after the death of Virginia Durant Young in 1906, it had been revived in Spartanburg in 1912, when a group of women led by Emily Plume Evans and Helen G. Howland established the New Era Club. Soon after they organized, they wired President-elect Wilson to express their support of woman's suffrage and encourage his. The next year they sponsored a special edition of the *Spartanburg Herald,* which included letters and articles from NAWSA president Anna Howard Shaw, the governors of states where women already had the franchise, suffragist Alva F. Belmont, and Hannah Hemphill Coleman, president of the SCFWC, along with other suffrage leaders. In 1914, the club "abandoned its camouflage and became the state's only avowed and admitted suffrage club."[84] After completion of the GFWC's annual convention in Spartanburg, the women of the New Era Club were joined by suffrage clubs from Columbia and Charleston and other like-minded women. They established the South Carolina Equal Suffrage League (SCESL), explicitly stated their goal of joining NAWSA, and elected as their president Emily Plume Evans, whose husband was a previous governor of the state.

The SCESL platform highlighted ten goals, which included as its first objective the passage of a measure "providing for the equal guardianship of children by mother and father." This was followed by demands for "equal pay for equal work," an eight-hour workday, the training of "sons as well as . . . daughters [in]

58   "Our Country First, Then Greenville"

regard to purity of life," raising the age of consent from fourteen to twenty-one years and the age of marriage to eighteen, the "increase of temperance sentiment," compulsory education and the abolition of child labor, and "equal educational opportunities for men and women, from the kindergarten through the university."[85]

These efforts prompted renewed interest in suffrage issues in neighboring Greenville. Ten days after the formation of the SCESL, the Equal Suffrage Club of Greenville held its first meeting at the YMCA with approximately forty women present. Elected officers included Jessie Burnett, president; Andrea Christensen Patterson, vice-president; Eudora Ramsay, secretary; and Eleanor Furman, treasurer. Burnett, an instructor in the history department at Furman, had studied at Yale and Smith Colleges and had become involved with suffrage while teaching at the University of California.[86] Ramsay, the head of the English department at Greenville Woman's College (GWC) and daughter of the college's president, had participated in a NAWSA parade in Washington, DC, in 1913. She unequivocally stated that her teaching goal was to educate "girls who are staunch advocates of women's rights." Months after the establishment of the Greenville chapter, Ramsay embarked on a speaking tour on behalf of NAWSA.[87] As a paid field director, she developed quite a following; her wit and engaging personality were as much a draw as the information she conveyed.[88] Richardson worked alongside fellow club officer Eleanor Furman, the daughter of industrialist Alester G. Furman and great-granddaughter of James C. Furman, who also became a field worker for NAWSA. Over time Mary Gridley, Ellen Perry, Helen Vaughan, and Elizabeth Perry became leaders of the local league.[89]

Over the next several years, communities large and small across the state established suffrage leagues.[90] Within two years twenty-five chapters with approximately three thousand members existed across the state.[91]

Most of these women were affiliated with NAWSA, the dominant suffrage organization nationally. A significant fissure began to develop in NAWSA, however, after Alice Paul rose to the ranks of its leadership. Paul, who had attended graduate school in England, had been influenced by the civil disobedience used by British suffragettes who belonged to the Women's Social and Political Union (WSPU). The WSPU's "Deeds not Words" motto reflected its tactics, which included spitting on members of Parliament, breaking windows, and setting post offices on fire, with one WSPU activist, Emily Davison, throwing herself in front of King George V's horse to draw attention to the cause, an action that killed her. In 1913, amid a dispute between Paul and NAWSA leaders Anna Howard Shaw and Carrie Chapman Catt, Paul left NAWSA and began the Congressional

Union (CU). She spoke throughout the country, and her message appealed to women who were becoming impatient with NAWSA.

The bitter fragmentation of the national suffrage movement reverberated very mildly in South Carolina. Real estate leader and suffragist Susan Pringle Frost of Charleston sat on the advisory board of the CU and was instrumental in inviting Paul to come to Charleston to establish a state CU chapter in 1915; thus South Carolina become only the second southern state after Virginia to have a chapter, though other southern states soon joined.[92] In 1916 the CU evolved into the National Woman's Party (NWP).

In the first two years of the war overseas, Greenville's reformers continued their volunteer efforts with little disruption, though updates of the war and its impact on the local economy remained of great interest. The fate of Greenville and America's role in the war became evident in the spring of 1917, expedited by a series of German "provocations" that incited the United States into the First World War. In January 1917 German secretary of state Arthur Zimmerman authorized the infamous "Zimmerman Telegram," which encouraged Mexico to join the German military alliance and attack the southern border of the American Southwest and Texas. The message was intercepted by British authorities and was declared an outrage of belligerence on the part of the Germans. The message to the Mexican government was sent in anticipation of the resumption of unrestricted submarine warfare, which was to begin on February 1, when German U-boats would once again terrorize ships flying flags of neutral nations as they traversed the Atlantic. On March 12, 1917, President Wilson ordered the light arming of US merchant ships in a defensive move of "armed neutrality," and four days later, between March 16 and 18, German U-boats sank three US merchant ships, two without warning and at the loss of American lives.[93] These actions, in conjunction with the substantial and increasing economic investment in the Entente powers, led Wilson to ask Congress for a declaration of war on Germany and the Central Powers on April 2, 1917.

For years Wilson had hoped he would not be forced to enter the war by German provocations. Since 1915 he had been carefully separating himself diplomatically from both the Entente and Central powers in order to project the United States as a mediating power in foreign affairs. With his PhD in political philosophy from Johns Hopkins University and a previous career in academia, which included serving as president of Princeton University, Wilson believed fervently in the power of political ideology. The president aspired to establish a world order with his proposed League of Nations that was controlled not by military might but rather with "soft" power through economic and ideological means.[94]

Upholding American democracy, he did not support the monarchial powers that characterized old Europe nor their domination of vast global empires. He specifically avoided becoming overtly involved with the Triple Entente in order to project the United States as an arbitrating, democratic force with the power to solve world conflict.[95] He saw the United States ideally as a mediator of the war and avoided aggressive acts. By refusing involvement in a war that desperately needed American military muscle in order to break a deadly stalemate in the trenches of France, Wilson aspired to position himself and his country as a morally and ideologically superior power that held the authority and legitimacy to end it. He hoped this tactic would allow the United States to restore world peace and a balanced world order, but the weight of the bloodiest and most shocking war in human history would eventually prove to make Wilson's vision unexpectedly difficult to achieve.

Upon American entry into the war, Wilson continued to use rhetoric that separated American involvement from the efforts of the Entente, keeping in line with his vision of the United States as an "arbitrator" in this conflict. Yet if Wilson wanted to take advantage of America's momentous power to establish the peaceful world order in which he so ardently believed, he would first have to flex America's military muscle to help end the war. This effort would require total mobilization on the home front and a projection of real, tangible power overseas. American entry sought to change the tide of the war and turn the United States into a premier global force. In order for these changes to occur on the national stage, they would require significant effort and a change of perspective at the local level as well. Greenville proved to be an important cog in the larger wheels of an enormous and unprecedented national mobilization machine.

Greenville's concerns on the eve of entry to the war largely reflected those of the nation. The economic impact of entry remained the nation's highest concern, with cotton the most important economic factor locally. An embargo on shipping cotton and textiles to those newly deemed enemies overseas meant a major loss in profit. Yet cotton was also a greater necessity during wartime, as "artillery shells and military uniforms alike needed cotton."[96] Furthermore, cotton was used in industrial threads for war material, as bandages and gauze, and in food products such as cottonseed oil. Once Great Britain had declared cotton a military contraband, Britain's control of the shipping lanes in the Atlantic ensured that this embargo on cotton was strictly enforced.

Even after listening to Wilson tout isolationist policies for two full years and helping elect this southern Democrat as president on an isolationist platform one year earlier, most Greenvillians understood the need for war. Dutiful support of the president combined with the heightened civic engagement of the Progressive

Greenville and the Nation Respond to War 61

Era and shortly evolved into nationally significant participation in the war effort. Over the course of the summer of 1917, major players at the federal and state levels turned Greenville into a total war machine, with the local community contributing significantly through manpower, volunteer efforts, economic means, industrial production, and the hosting of a military encampment.

chapter three

The Impact of Camp Sevier

Mobilization, Nationalization, and Economic Boom

Even before the United States entered the war, local civic and business leaders had already begun investigating the possibility of an army cantonment. From their experience with Camp Wetherill during the Spanish-American War, they knew well the benefits the camp would have on the economic landscape of their blossoming city. In March 1917 Mayor Charles Webb and community leaders John Marshall, A. L. Mills, and W. F. Robertson launched their lobbying efforts with the War Department.[1]

As soon as the US Congress declared war in April 1917, the War Department announced plans for an army encampment somewhere in South Carolina, and Charleston, Columbia, Spartanburg, Aiken, and Greenville all fought for the honor. A furious patriotic battle ensued, as all of these potential locations attempted to prove through liberty bond drives, recruitment campaigns, patriotic parades, and food donations that they were the ideal site for the new encampment.

Led by the recently established Rotary Club, the efforts of Greenville's leaders to attract the site were reliant upon widespread community support. Greenvillians strategically planned "patriotic parades" that coincided with visits from federal cantonment site inspectors and Gen. Leonard Wood of the US Army, commander of the newly created Southeastern Department headquartered in Charleston.[2] Local newspapers encouraged residents to attend the parades at all costs and to fly as many American flags as possible.[3] These parades on Main Street must have impressed federal inspectors, who were searching not only for suitable geographical locations but also for an area that would be willing to support the tens of thousands of soldiers residing in the community during their training.

On Tuesday, May 22, 1917, just over one month after the United States officially declared war on Germany, the War Department announced that not only Greenville but also Columbia and Spartanburg had been selected as locations for national army cantonment sites.[4] The next day the Greenville Chamber of Commerce submitted an offer to General Wood. The chamber worked with local landholders to provide land northeast of Paris Station and about 6 miles outside of the city of Greenville for the construction of Camp Sevier.[5]

Described by one biographer as a "military progressive," Wood was, despite his "brusque and unceremonious" and intense nature, a popular, respected, and nationally prominent figure who had been handpicked by President Teddy Roosevelt and his family as a political successor. By 1920 Wood had "emerged from the conflict as the nation's sole presidential candidate in the military-hero tradition."[6] He was a staunch advocate of preparedness in the years leading up to 1917 but had been demoted from his position as US Army chief of staff (1910–14) and passed over in consideration for the position of commander general of the national army (of which John "Blackjack" Pershing would be given command) partially because of his harsh criticism of the Wilson administration's failure to mobilize the country in advance of April 1917.[7] Wood had played a key role in organizing the volunteer officer training camps in Plattsburg, New York, which launched a national movement of military preparedness, leading to a large spike in volunteers for military service between the summer of 1915 and the Selective Service Act of May 1917.[8] When Secretary of War Newton Baker restructured the nation from four to six military districts, Wood was reassigned from the Eastern Department to the Southeastern Department. In this role he was responsible for selecting the site locations and training soldiers at the soon-to-be eleven training cantonment sites in his department.[9]

The Camp Sevier deal was brokered in negotiations beforehand but published the day after the awarding of a site to Greenville. The City and Chamber of Commerce pledged to provide the land, furnish the necessary supply of water through the Paris Mountain Water Company, assist the Southern Railway Company with building railroad sidetracks to the camp, build a highway from the campsite to the city of Greenville, and provide electric pole lines to the camp for electricity.[10] Some sources claim that General Wood's friendship with prominent Greenville civil engineer and president of the Greenville Chamber of Commerce Joe Sirrine, a son of William G. and S. "Odie" Sirrine, aided the selection.[11] Rooted in their service together in Cuba during the Spanish-American War, Henry Bacon McKoy, a veteran of Camp Sevier and an historian of the Greenville area, later described Wood and Sirrine as "fast friends."[12] Sirrine ensured that his fellow Rotarians and other leaders thoroughly feted Woods during his visit.[13]

Greenville's cantonment site was named in honor of Lt. Col. John Sevier, who served in the North Carolina militia during the American Revolution and became the first governor of Tennessee. Most cantonment sites throughout the United States were named after a historic military figure or founding father.

Camp Sevier was developed on approximately 1,900 acres southeast of Paris Mountain. Courtesy Library of Congress.

Andrew Jackson provided the namesake for Camp Jackson in Columbia, while Camp Wadsworth in Spartanburg was named after James S. Wadsworth, a Union general in the Civil War.

As plans for the camp progressed, Sirrine was given the task of designing and supervising the building of Camp Sevier.[14] In a War Department report on the construction of the sites, Sirrine was listed as the "supervising engineer" for both Camp Sevier in Greenville and Camp Wadsworth in Spartanburg; he was the only engineer responsible for the construction of more than one cantonment site.[15]

While Sirrine designed the camp layout, sewage system, waterworks, and other infrastructure, the contract for physical construction of the camp was given to Gallivan Building Company. They began work on July 16, 1917, operating under the federal Office of the Constructing Quartermaster led by Maj. Alex C. Doyle.[16] The Southern Power Company established a contract with Camp Sevier valued at $30,000 in order to construct power lines to the campsite for electric lighting. The camp was also equipped with electric lights in many of the permanent buildings by Huntington and Guerry, local electrical subcontractors. With $5,413,847.19 allotted to the project, the construction of Camp Sevier was no small undertaking.[17] Ultimately Camp Sevier construction costs totaled $6,250,500.00. Of the sixteen camps that were classified as "Tent Camp, National Guard," costs ranged from $2.5 million at Camp Fremont in Palto Alto, California, to $6.7 million at Camp McClellan in Anniston, Alabama.[18] In addition to thousands of tents, Camp Sevier included a bakery and bakery school for enlisted men, barracks, bayonet run, chapel, divisional headquarters, drill grounds, hospital, four acre lake named Jones Pond, library, multiple ranges, remount station, stockade, trenches, several YMCA buildings, and the Paris Railroad Station.

The Impact of Camp Sevier   65

The Paris School and Mountain Creek Church and Cemetery, which existed on the property before the war, remained.[19]

In his completion report, Doyle praised Sirrine, Huntington, and Guerry and James F. Gallivan, founder of the eponymous company, for their dedication and conscientiousness. Doyle wrote, "To Mr. Sirrine, the supervising engineer, (and co.) . . . much credit is due for their untiring efforts at all hours to advance the work of construction, to follow specifications, and to hold down the costs." Regarding Gallivan Construction's efforts, Doyle effused that "Mr. Gallivan (and co.) have labored night and day and without thought of personal sacrifices on this work . . . he has used every means to economize and at the same time do construction that will stand."[20] Finally, of Huntington and Guerry, Doyle wrote that they had "put their hearts into this work; it was their bit, they have considered it in service of their government."[21]

In these early days of July and August 1917, housing was not completed, and men had to find impromptu places to sleep as they arrived at the camp in great numbers via the camp's Paris Station. The desperate need for men overseas necessitated that training begin at the camp despite its unfinished state. With very few permanent wooden buildings, the camp was a "tent city," hence its description as an "encampment." The camp was connected to Greenville by either dusty or muddy roads, depending on the weather. In his memoirs McKoy, a member of the 105th Engineers, Company C, described a most inauspicious welcome; he arrived at the camp on August 20, 1917, unloaded from Paris Station, followed a "novice" lieutenant on the one-mile march in the rain from the station to the campsite, and then had to sleep in the mess hall, as "no tents had been put up and no ground cleared to put them up."[22] In his official history of the 113th Field Artillery, A. L. Fletcher writes of the early days at Camp Sevier:

> The task that lay before the regiment on that "Blue Monday" following its
> arrival in camp, was a big one, viewed from any angle. A bare start had been

made at getting the camp ready for human occupancy and that was all. Ahead of the men lay the job of clearing away a tangled forest, grubbing thousands of oak and forest pine stumps, draining acres of marshy ground and moving tons of dirt. Armed with axes, mattocks, picks, saws, shovels, ropes and other equipment the men went at it and week followed week, in dreary, monotonous grind. It was grub stumps, pile brush, rake trash all day long and the bugle called you again early the following morning to start it all over again.[23]

The 118th Infantry Regiment cleared so much land that they facetiously named themselves the "South Carolina Land and Development Company."[24]

The *Greenville Daily News* poked fun at the situation with a cartoon featuring a disappointed doughboy who states, "If this is 'Paris' I hope I'll never see London!"[25] The inexperience of the US military in training what was, at that point, the largest army in US history was reflected in the poor logistics, planning, and supplying of training camps throughout the country, not only domestically but also once the army was overseas. At Camp Sevier winter clothes were not issued until well into winter, guns that were already several years old did not arrive until Christmas, and camp conditions aided the spread of disease and, thus, death.[26] The US Army capitalized on the experience of its allies and hosted several British and French officers who already had several years of experience on the Western Front. In October 1917 Lt. Jacques Popelin of the French army arrived at Camp Sevier. He wrote of his experience,

> The situation was not, at first, very encouraging, because (and especially for the parts of instruction which needed more outdoor training than library study) we had nothing to work with. And this rendered the instruction of the enlisted men very difficult, and nearly impossible, the training of staff officers. . . . We had at first no more than four 3" guns, without equipment, for the whole brigade; we had no maps until the regiment of engineers could give us a pretty rough sketch of the camp, and then that map was drawn at the wrong scale. You had no or very few horses, and when you got some more, you had no harness to hitch them up and drill. There were no instruments, not even field glasses; no telephones except the buzzer, which was of small help because of the lack of wire; no plane tables, save the regular ones, which were unfit for artillery work, with their fixed compass and loose unsquared sheet; no signaling projectors, and no good manual on liaison, on aerial observation, on the use of meteorological elements, not even correct range tables for your 3" guns you would never fire on the front; and no description of the 75 m/m gun about which you have been told so many things, which you

The Impact of Camp Sevier   67

would use "over there" and which very few officers only saw before their landing in France.

Still, he wrote,

> I was very favorably impressed, that very first day, by the size and sturdy appearance of the men belonging to the One Hundred and Thirteenth. Mostly tall and slender, they looked robust and strong, and from that day on, I expected that we should have splendid results with so good a human material, when a few months' training would give them the soldierly appearance and military demeanor they still lacked. . . . I was glad to notice that they showed on their faces the best spirit in the world.[27]

The US Army had suffered from logistical issues, such as the feeding and transport of men and horses during the Spanish-American War; at this point it seemed little had been learned from that experience.

These challenges prompted reflections about the purpose of the conflict and the impact it might have on soldiers' long-term perspectives. From Camp Sevier in September 1917, future Pulitzer Prize winner Paul Green wrote to this father in North Carolina,

> I am liking this life as well as I could like it. Grumbling is not in my line of business, and I find that the only wise method in the army is to take whatever comes along. One must throw away his own likes and dislikes, and become a part of the big whole. . . . The only thing that keeps me sound and with a healthy point of view . . . [is] the fact that we are fighting a great fight, and for the principles of right living. I believe there is more sorrow than bitterness among the men in uniform because we are compelled to fight the Germans. . . . I often hear them, and talk, myself, talking about the chances of getting out of the melee alive. Most think we are facing certain death. . . . But despite this belief they go ahead and drill and play ball, also sing their foolish songs as if all the world was sunshine and everything was a spring morning.

Weeks later Green continued his musings on this "strangely unreal hour" in a letter to his sister Mary.

> The whirlwind of war has sucked our home in at last, but I believe each of us will live a fuller life when it's all over—say the night when we all meet again and sit down to our first meal together. If one were an atheist he almost would believe in every act of life and—beyond. On this the Christian's Heaven is built. Sometimes this whole preparation for war, the moving soldiers, the

Pyramid tents were organized in rows according to company and battery streets. Each soldier received a straw mattress cot, four issue blankets, and a kit bag, which included underwear, four pairs of socks, two pairs of shoes, two olive-drab shirts, and the issue uniform. Bath houses and latrines were located at the end of each company or battery street; large boilers provided hot water for showering in the winter, while only cold water was available in the summer. Courtesy, *The Thirtieth Division in the World War*.

> thundering trucks, and the galloping horses—all seems an unreal dream from which I soon shall wake.[28]

During the war years and after, the presence and continued influence of Camp Sevier gave the city unparalleled exposure to outside influences that served as nationalizing and modernizing forces throughout the city and county. As McKoy described in his memoirs: "They had sought and obtained an army camp, (and) had been invaded by a force of soldiers greater than their own number."[29] This invasion of different cultures, perspectives, and values into Greenville's own society was not without consequence.

In July and August, the first group of men to train at Camp Sevier arrived. These thirty thousand men made up the Thirtieth Infantry Division, nicknamed "Old Hickory" in honor of Andrew Jackson. They trained at Camp Sevier until May 1, 1918, when they left to serve with the Second Army of the British Expeditionary Force overseas. The Thirtieth included men from South Carolina, North Carolina, and Tennessee and was later bolstered by draftees from Iowa, Minnesota, Indiana, Illinois, and North and South Dakota.[30] The Twentieth Infantry

Division was formed at Camp Sevier in August 1918, and by September, 8,700 officers and men of the Twentieth were at the camp. By the end of December, their numbers had risen to 15,400.[31] In May 1918 the Eighty-First "Wildcat" Division was transferred from Camp Jackson in Columbia to Camp Sevier, where men from South Carolina, North Carolina, Florida, Alabama, and New York completed their training in July 1918 before shipping off to France. Other divisions passed through Camp Sevier or were organized at the cantonment site. The First Separate South Carolina Engineer Battalion ultimately comprised the First Battalion, 117th Engineer Regiment of the 42nd "Rainbow" Division, supposedly named for its incredible diversity of men from all over the United States, who "represented all the colors of the rainbow," according to Brig. Gen. Douglas MacArthur. The five hundred officers and men from across South Carolina spent two weeks at Camp Sevier in mid-August 1917 before being sent to Camp Mills on Long Island, New York.[32] The camp also hosted African American soldiers; 17,550 members of the 321st Labor Battalion trained at Camp Sevier between June and December 1918.[33]

The awarding of the camp and the arrival of mass numbers of young men made the public health of the Greenville community, in addition to the other communities that surrounded training camps nationally, a government priority. In September 1917 *National Geographic* published an article titled "Conserving the Nation's Man Power" to inform readers that the government was monitoring the spread of disease in communities surrounding the cantonment sites.[34] The article argued that

> when it is taken into consideration that in these locations, cities having a military population of from 40,000 to 80,000 men have been rapidly created in a few weeks; that the inhabitants of these new-raised cities have been brought from every corner of the Union, and that many of them, in spite of the utmost precautions, carry in their bodies the causal agents of disease, and that existing towns near cantonments suddenly receive a large influx of artisans, laborers, and their families, and those who inevitably follow in the train of armies, it is seen that the potentialities of the sanitary situation were very grave.[35]

Greenville was specifically listed as being under the administrative control of the Public Health Service. The concern at this time was primarily typhoid; thus the Public Health Service worked with state and local authorities, when adequate, to check "the purity of the public water supply, the efficiency of the sewage system and the scavenger service, the safety of the milk and other foods sold to the general public, the thoroughness of the prevention of communicable disease, the presence of disease-bearing insects, and the general sanitary condition of the environment in contiguity to the cantonment and those areas which troops might reasonably be expected to visit."[36] The heightened awareness of the health and sanitation of the community surrounding the camp was but one aspect of the uptick in cooperation between the federal government and the Greenville community, although later in the war, these efforts proved insufficient to combat the spread of mass disease.

For soldiers coming from rural regions throughout the South, the experience at Camp Sevier introduced them to novel amenities and aspects of modernity with which they had limited experience, such as electric lights, running water, and telegram and telephone lines.[37] In a 1917 article in *National Geographic* magazine, war correspondent Maj. Granville R. Fortescue noted that "the dragnet of draft sometimes brings to the camp men who fall below the standards of the American city or country life."[38] He described the experiences of rural men at another southern camp. The men, he wrote, "are at first bewildered by the many exactions making for cleanliness in a cantonment," including "instruction in the care of teeth, the person, and the home. . . . The men quickly come to understand the virtue of keeping themselves and their homes free from dirt, and it is certain they will carry this knowledge back to their home communities when their period of soldiering is over."[39] The same recruits were also vaccinated for smallpox and typhoid fever, which may have been their first encounter with modern medicine or even the first equivalent of a doctor's visit beyond the army physical examination.[40] Furman student Roy Farmer wrote to his college buddies, "Boys, pray for me tomorrow. Have got to be vaccinated and take one of the inoculations also. Guess both of my arms will be sore for next few days."[41] Many soldiers, like Joe Pridgen, reported these vaccines to be mildly painful, with swelling, stiffness, and scarring; one young man died from complications resulting from the vaccine.[42] For many recruits, this was their first introduction to modern medicine, and many disapproved of the suspicious practice of preventing disease by exposure to live forms of that disease.[43] Fortescue was more blunt in his assessment of what men at the training camps thought of their typhoid inoculations and vaccinations: "From personal knowledge, the writer can pronounce the typhoid inoculation, especially the second dose, a most depressing experience. Add the pain and discomfort of an infected vaccinated arm to this condition, and the morale of the soldiers fall to the vanishing point. Here is the time," according to Fortescue, that the discomfort of the shots made men "contemplate desertion."[44]

Despite these amenities, Camp Sevier, like many other training camps, did not have sanitary processes for disposing of human waste. Soldiers often used trenches and pit toilets, outhouses, and mass latrines without running water.

Much to the displeasure of residents whose wooded property bordered Camp Sevier, soldiers often disposed of human waste just outside the camp's boundaries. Landowners W. A. Edwards and a Mr. McCarter, whose first name remains unknown, filed complaints with the US Army and the US Public Health Service. In response D. J. Prather, an administrator with the Public Health Service, wrote to Lt. Col. A. M. Whaley, US Army commanding surgeon at Camp Sevier, "It would materially aid us in our efforts to sanitate the civil zone [civilian population] if you would make an effort to have this practice discontinued."[45] Such practices undermined recent efforts implemented after the 1916 sanitation survey to improve the quality of sanitary practices in the area.

In addition to electrification and sewage disposal, educational standards in the rural South lagged, and the region had lower literacy rates than other areas of the country. Though based on problematic methodologies, estimates from military intelligence testing suggested a dire reality: 14.2% of recruits tested from Minnesota were illiterate, and 16.6% of those tested from New York, with recruits from South Carolina exhibiting a distressing 49.5% illiteracy rate. In agricultural regions education was often sacrificed, as many rural families could only spare their children from working at home and in the fields during limited times of each year. Fortescue noted, "One company recruited from the hills of Virginia has 30 men in 150 who cannot read or write . . . and each night, after the drills of the day are ended, they are taught by one of their officers the rudiments of reading and writing."[46] Greenvillian John L. Plyer, who was stationed at Camp Sevier, passed down the story of one creative training solution: when some troops at Camp Sevier found marching in unison difficult because they did not know their left from their right, one company's captain allegedly had the soldiers place straw in their left boots and hay in their right; he resolved his company's marching challenges by changing his commands to "Straw! Hay!" instead of "Left! Right!"[47] Green described many of the men as "rough and brutal in regard to the delicacies of life."[48] These lackluster features became highlighted only in contrast to the more progressive northern cities from which many trainees hailed.

Greenvillians were motivated to prove themselves worthy of prestige on a national level. Low literacy rates, a predominantly rural, Protestant, and ethnically and racially static culture held southerners back in the eyes of northerners, who increasingly lived in dynamic urban environments populated by immigrants and surrounded by industrialized spaces. In 1910 nearly 18 percent of Greenvillians over the age of ten were illiterate, and even though the city population increased 46.9 percent between 1910 and 1920, 85.9 percent of Greenville County residents were classified as rural.[49] Embarrassed by literacy rates unbecoming of a city with such progressive ambitions, and with wartime business generating

72 *"Our Country First, Then Greenville"*

significant profits, civic leaders felt pressure to raise their education standards. Writing of Greenville, historian David Carlton reveals how "World War I profits financed new buildings and enlargements of old ones," particularly in terms of the schools located in the city's many mill villages. In mill schools the teacher-to-student ratio also dropped from 66.7 to 50.3 even as school attendance rose, signaling better education brought on by the economic prosperity of the textile industry during the war.[50] Adult education also improved, as the juxtaposition between literate northern men and illiterate southern men training together in cantonment camps spurred on a campaign to end illiteracy; this campaign also significantly benefited mill workers in South Carolina. Eradication of illiteracy became linked to the war effort, as better education would purportedly leave our men less prone to the threat of "German Propaganda among the ignorant classes," believed to be one weakness that attributed to the quick fall of Russia to the Germans several years earlier.[51] The SCFWC led this campaign, imploring Governor Manning to appoint an illiteracy commission; following the war this led to the creation of the nation's first state-supported adult education program.[52] Camp officers around the nation also gave weekly examinations on information presented through military lectures, and thus provided a semblance of formal education for the men there.[53] The national movement for improved education was closely linked to the war mobilization demanded by the war, particularly in Upcountry South Carolina, with improvements in education seen as both a result of and an indirect contribution to the war effort.[54]

The US Army was strategic in positioning the camps and in creating geographic diversity among the men assigned to them. The military intentionally placed the majority of training camps in the South in part due to the region's relatively mild climate, and also because it hoped to advance a sense of nationalism among White southern civilians and sodiers, who would serve alongside men from other regions of the country in such unusual and challenging circumstances over here and over there. The *Official Army Song Book,* a popular paperback book small enough to be carried by soldiers in their uniform pockets, was also used as a means to incorporate southern culture, with songs such as "Dixie," "My Old Kentucky Home," "Swanee River," and "Old Black Joe" alongside the nationalistic tunes "America, the Beautiful," "The Star Spangled Banner," and "The Stars and Stripes Forever." Fortescue, in reviewing the cantonment sites, proudly proclaimed,

> the men develop pride in their Americanism. . . . [The cantonment] turns the youth of the country into better Americans. . . . Patriotism develops through the atmosphere of the cantonment. . . . It is practical Patriotism, too, as has been proved in the way the new soldiers have bought the latest issue of liberty

bonds. That the men of the National Army give back to the government part of their pay is tangible proof of their approval of the draft and its consequences.[55]

Perhaps the single most important result of the mobilization of an army at Camp Sevier was that the soldiers and citizens of Greenville alike began to think of themselves as "Americans" and not just as Greenvillians, South Carolinians, southerners, or any other distinction.

These forms of cultural indoctrination were effective not only with southerners but also with foreign-born soldiers, 723 of whom became US citizens at Camp Sevier on June 14, 1918.[56] In *World War I: The American Soldier Experience,* historian Jennifer Keene describes how one music director from the Commission on Training Camp Activities (CTCA) noted that the common practice of using songs to teach non-English speaking troops, with them "slowly repeating the words and injecting a plea for loyalty," prompted those troops to "fully [sense] the meaning of true patriotism . . . making them true Americans through song."[57]

The federal government enthusiastically used army mobilization camps around the country as a means of "removing the hyphen" from German Americans, Italian Americans, Irish Americans, and other immigrants. During the early period of the twentieth century, some Americans felt that increasing immigration created a diverse atmosphere in the United States that threatened a collective American identity, and thus proponents of military preparedness and the passing of the Selective Service Act for universal military obligation believed the national army camps could also inculcate immigrant men with American ideals.[58] Former president Theodore Roosevelt, a zealous advocate for both the universal draft and the power of these national cantonment sites as tools of "Americanization," said, "The military tent where they will sleep side by side will rank next to the public school among the great agents of democratization."[59]

Immigrant men in the military, especially those with German-Austrian ties, suffered from a social stigma against foreigners, which encouraged them to adopt and adapt to American values. On February 13, 1918, US Marshal C. J. Lyon arrested Pvt. Heinrich Adler of the 105th Ammunition Train and Pvt. Julius Rubenstein of the Camp Sevier base hospital.[60] Rubenstein was an "unnaturalized Austrian citizen" who had been in the United States since the age of two, while the twenty-one-year-old Adler was a citizen of Germany who had been in the United States for twenty months. Rubenstein had been drafted and applied for an honorable discharge as an enemy alien. Although the honorable discharge was granted, he was simultaneously arrested. The local newspaper reported that "both men deny any hostile acts or intentions, and Rubenstein affirms his sympathy for the United States, although Adler is apparently a great admirer of the

German Emperor."[61] They were both charged with being enemy aliens and held in the county jail for at least ten days. Another article suggested that while the men were likely not spies, they were also not supportive of the American army and would probably be sent to a detention camp without a trial or opportunity to appeal.[62] Their arrests, in addition to the arrests of others charged with espionage, promoted a vigilant attitude against any foreign and suspicious activity in the Greenville and Camp Sevier communities.[63]

These attempts to undermine the military effort must have been frustrating to Camp Sevier soldiers who dutifully fortified hills, dug trenches, constructed machine-gun emplacements, and practiced rifle marksmanship and gas defense with mock gas masks. They also trained in the use of grenades, mortars, and the deadly close-combat art of the bayonet that characterized the brutal "no man's land" trench charges in France.[64] Trenches and wire entanglements were constructed on October 3, 1917, to mimic the front lines over there. Joe Pridgen described them to his mother: "Yesterday I went to walk and went over to the place where they have been digging trenches. It is really interesting although we did very near get lost going through the trenches. There are all kinds of dark tunnels and ditches. They wind around so and have so many outs and all."[65] The army also opened a school of gas defense on December 12 to prepare the men for the horrors of mustard gas.[66] Paul Green of the 105th Engineers described the discomfort of the gas masks: "I sometimes felt as [if] I'd vomit, but there was no taking it off. They drilled us hour by hour with that thing on. . . . The minute it is taken off, the gas almost suffocates you. . . . The required time to take it from satchel and place it over the face, with the mouthpiece and nose clip adjusted perfectly is 6 seconds. Very few have been able to put it on in that time."[67] During equipment inspections men were required to wear their gas masks while the inspector passed through the barracks to ensure that beds were made, shirts folded, and general military discipline and order was on show.[68] Training could be challenging and monotonous, and thus soldiers particularly enjoyed activities involving sports and athletic competitions, which the military used not only to teach useful skills but also as a form of physical conditioning. Camp Sevier served as the test site for *Suggested Athletics for Army Camps*, a manual for YMCA Athletic Directors that encouraged the use of boxing, pushball, soccer, and wrestling, in addition to semaphore code relays, and competitions, such as Tent Pitching Contest, Ambulance Loading Race, and Squad Rescue Race, designed to improve performance in the theater of operations.[69] A soldier-in-training's life included endless drills and military exercises punctuated by football and baseball games, church services, and an occasional foray into Greenville or the nearby mountains.

The Impact of Camp Sevier 75

Though the future doughboys trained and drilled several miles north of the city, their social and economic impact on the community was significant. The pace of life quickened, and benefits included "war dollars" that came into Greenville through camp trainees. The *Greenville Daily News* boasted in May 1918 that the camp had "a payroll of $1,500,000 monthly or $18,000,000 yearly," which soldiers and their families spent locally.[70] The *News* also anticipated that at least one person would visit Greenville for every two or three soldiers stationed at the camp. It was not uncommon for entire families to temporarily relocate to Greenville for days or weeks before their father, brother, or husband was shipped overseas. The social pages of Tennessee newspapers are replete with notices of relatives visiting soldiers at Camp Sevier.[71] As far away as Montgomery, Alabama, Greenville's Chick Springs Hotel purchased newspaper advertisements that noted the travel times between the hotel and camps Sevier and Wadsworth and claimed to be the "Home of Army Men and Families."[72] Friends and relatives also stayed and dined in downtown Greenville while sending best wishes to the soldiers preparing to depart for France. Local newspapers advertised tours with bird's-eye views of the bustling cantonment site so that visitors and residents could marvel at the military metropolis.[73]

At the Greenville Woman's College campus downtown, President David Ramsay halted student recruiting efforts to accommodate the enormous wave of visitors. Because so many nearby homes were already occupied to maximum capacity, he knew there would be no rooms available for students to rent off-campus and thus began to turn classrooms into bedrooms, outfitting them with furniture and bedding while also adding spare beds to already occupied rooms.[74]

Cramped housing became the norm. In December 1917 the *Greenville Daily News* declared that "practically every available room in Greenville has been put at the disposal of the families of the military men at Camp Sevier."[75] The mass phenomenon of residents offering spare rooms to visiting families was but one way that Greenvillians exhibited tolerance of the hardships and inconveniences the war imposed, with many residents financially profiting from the visitors as well. Greenville was flooded with people from out of county and out of state, with the war effort serving as a common bond.

These visitors and soldiers who flocked to Greenville for entertainment, rest, and relaxation brought huge economic gains for the city and surrounding area. In contrast to the uncertain economic situation on the eve of war, the thriving textile industry and the cantonment quickly strengthened the Upcountry economy. The *Greenville Daily News* declared in July 1917 that the "Building Boom is on in Greenville," with construction being spurred on by dollars rolling into the city from these newly established war-related sources.[76] Camp Sevier only continued to grow as the war effort pushed forward: on December 22, 1917, the *Greenville Daily News* announced construction of an aviation school of engineers to be constructed as an addendum to Camp Sevier, which would add anywhere from four to ten thousand men to the campsite.[77]

Greenvillians' pride and enthusiasm for their cantonment site continued in the form of warm welcomes and support for troops stationed there. Soldiers from all over the country regularly mingled with local civilians, buying wares from stores and eating in restaurants, with some soldiers becoming "adopted sons," as they became known around town, who ate Sunday dinners with local families.[78] The Pipers, a local couple with a baby, regularly opened their home to Joe Pridgen of Durham, North Carolina; time spent with them in their home clearly meant a great deal to Pridgen, who often included mention of them in his letters to his family. He marveled at how he "did not know them at all before I came, but now I feel . . . at home with them."[79]

The Camp Sevier Regimental Band opened the festivities at the 1917 Southern Textile Exposition at Textile Hall downtown, and such cooperation between the camp and town continued throughout the wartime years.[80] Women who volunteered with the local Red Cross knit sweaters for the soldiers at Camp Sevier at Christmas, young women dined with men stationed at the camp, locals donated foodstuffs to support the soldiers, and GWC students invited soldiers to tea dances at the Imperial Hotel downtown.[81] GWC graduates from those years remember sneaking out of windows for late-night rendezvous with Camp Sevier soldiers, prompting the need for a military policeman to be placed on the campus.[82] Naturally a mutual interest developed between Greenville and the camp, and Greenville residents routinely read newspaper columns such as "News of a Day at Camp Sevier" and "Here and There at Camp Sevier" in order to keep up with the men in whom they took great pride.[83] Greenvillians enjoyed the camp's regimental parades, lining roads with automobiles for miles around to see soldiers in a thirty-minute parade drill.[84] With several professional baseball players at the camp, such as Bill Evans, Bob Guerry, "Lefty" Allen, and Rube Eldridge, locals also loved its baseball games.[85] When officers issued a "patriotic appeal" for feline assistance in eradicating a growing rat problem in the camp warehouses, local children and their "patriotic cats" eagerly lent aid.[86]

One concern that bound Greenvillians and the soldiers in training at Camp Sevier were the frigid temperatures and dismal weather that characterized the winter of 1917–18. Climatological surveys of the southeastern United States consulted by the federal government in preparation for the establishment of training sites suggested that Greenville had relatively mild winters, with above average precipitation in the spring but no other climatological extremes.[87] The deaths of soldiers resulted not solely from the unexpected bitter temperatures but also from the lack of forward planning by the US government in its rapid mobilization of America's army. Not only were the men living in mere khaki tents at Camp Sevier, but coal and wood were in short supply, and most camp recruits had only been issued their summer khakis, leaving them with no additional winter layers.[88] Fletcher's history reveals that

> supplies of all kinds, except food, continued scarce. The rough work of clearing up forests proved to be very hard on army clothes. Men tore their uniforms into shreds. Overalls lasted only a few days. Shoes were ripped and snagged and the bottoms burned off around the brush fires. Hats lost their shape and leggings were frayed and torn. The Division Quartermaster . . . [had] not equipment enough for half the number. . . . Winter came on and there were no winter clothes. The weather was bitter cold before the men could be furnished with winter clothes and a fourth of winter was past before the first overcoats arrived.

He lamented that some "of the finest soldiers the world has ever seen lived under canvas through the worst winter the South had experienced since 1898. Mumps and measles broke out in camp and, naturally as night follows day, grippe, pneumonia and kindred ailments came and seized upon the victims, who, weakened by mumps, measles and exposure, died in great numbers."[89]

Henry Bacon McKoy protected himself from the cold after a local woman gave him an officer's wool cape left over from the Spanish-American War.[90] Soldiers' letters regularly mention the cold and difficult living conditions, with record-setting low temperatures. December 9, 1917, was particularly frigid. In letters written on that day, Ben P. Gulledge of the 118th Infantry wrote, "Kid, it is some kind of cold here," while Anne Hutchison of nearby Rock Hill, South Carolina, wrote, "Very cold today, all the water pipes frozen up. . . . Eugene wrote that he almost froze at night . . . hope I can keep the room warm."[91] In a letter home to his mother the next day, Joe Pridgen wrote, "Wish you could have seen me last night. I had on a sweater, a coat, and my bath robe and then I was almost hugging the stove. . . . We had an awfully cold night last night, this A.M. our water was frozen in the bucket in the tent. . . . Last night I had so much cover I could hardly turn over under it."[92] Realizing the dangers posed by these temperatures, women in Greenville earnestly volunteered to compensate for the lack of oversight by the army. They campaigned through the *Greenville Daily News*, which reported that almost all men at Camp Sevier would have a sweater by Christmas.[93]

By mid-December Anne Hutchison was so concerned with the well-being of her brother, Hiram, a captain stationed at Camp Sevier, that she took concerted action regarding his discomfort. On December 12 she recorded in her diary that "Mrs. Long and I went around [Rock Hill]to collect money to buy gloves for our Company at Camp Sevier. We got 200 to pay for 220 pairs of gloves. Some were very willing to give, only two stores refused to pay us a cent. . . . The snow is about four inches deep." Later Anne received reports from Camp Sevier describing men standing in waist-deep snow in mock trenches and throwing practice grenades.[94] In January 1918 Pridgen wrote, "Now believe me this weather beats anything I have ever seen. It started snowing some time before day this morning and about seven o'clock it started to hailing. Think it has stopped one minute. The worst part of it though is that it has been thundering just like summer time all the afternoon. My tent leaks a little in one or two places but I am in alto better fix than a lot of others." For these men in the new tents . . . the water was standing in some of them two or three inches deep."[95] The cold temperatures defied the expectations of young men from the North, while some soldiers from Texas saw snow for the first time. One soldier, who came to Camp Sevier from Camp Hill in Virginia, wrote, "Some large camp here. I thot [sic] we were going south, but it seems colder here than up north."[96] Charles Sellers, a native of Kings Mountain, North Carolina, kept a diary every day during his time at Camp Sevier; nearly every entry for January 1918 includes a description of the weather. On January 4 he wrote: "The roads were covered in ice, could hardly stand up." Three days later he wrote that he "almost froze," and on Friday, January 11, he wrote that "it sleeted, snowed, and rained all day. By night every thing covered in ice, large trees breaking down. Wind fierce at night."[97] Soldiers at camps Sevier and Wadsworth mailed a popular postcard drawn by C. A. David, a nationally known cartoonist who resided in Greenville, depicting a freezing soldier on guard duty with icicles formed on his rifle with the facetious caption "On Guard in the Sunny South."[98]

Mary and Gladys Green also worried about their brother Paul. In a letter to Mary, he conveyed the impact that they and women who were involved in the war effort were having. Writing that he felt like he must surrender himself to the "big whole," Paul added that

> I could not doubt that the women of the worldplay as important [a] part in this war, and will play, as the men. . . . I almost envy your position; you have such a grand opportunity to make yourself felt. Every little thing you do . . . brings the war nearer to its end. The soldiers in camp have no joys greater than receiving letters or a box from home. . . . Such a little remembrance will touch the remaining goodness in a soldier's soul.[99]

The Impact of Camp Sevier 79

A few days after Valentine's Day, Joe Pridgen wrote to this mother,

> Certainly was glad to get your letter and Valentine. The box surely did come at the right time. It came Friday 'bout supper time, and everything they had for supper had onions in it. Therefore I went up and got us a cup of coffee and came back and made supper on the box. I enjoyed all of it, the apples, jam, candy, rolls and cookies. By the way where did you get the idea of the cookies? They were about the best things I have had held in a long time. Thanks so much.[100]

By the end of the war, the social and economic impact of the more than one hundred thousand soldiers who had trained at Camp Sevier had transformed Greenville.[101] Furthermore, in the years following the war, Greenville experienced expansion and improvement in the city that came directly and indirectly from these Camp Sevier dollars. For example, Camp Sevier's enormous demand for water overtaxed the privately owned Paris Mountain Water Company, and the Greenville Water Works had to expand its operations with a million-dollar purchase of a filtering plant and pumping station on the Enoree River to satisfy the demands of its growing population.[102]

Economic gain was not the only benefit of Camp Sevier's location in Greenville. Infrastructure grew with the expansion of railways, electric lights, and water systems. Furthermore the road systems around the city improved markedly. In 1915, during the war but before American entry, city leaders saw an opportunity to improve its "oppressive and ineffectual" road system that had plagued the area with transportation issues for years.[103] The cotton scare of 1914 resulted in surplus labor, allowing Greenville's city government to hire local men to work on the roads for cheap wages. As the United States maintained its isolationism throughout 1915, Greenville passed a "road bond" program to fund the construction and improvement of roads through the sale of bonds, which cheap surplus local labor made possible.[104] By the time of America's entry into World War I, the South Carolina Highway Department had to shut down construction on road improvements to facilitate the building of military highways and other wartime necessities.[105] Rutherford Road was the first military highway in Greenville, connecting downtown to Paris Station at Camp Sevier, and provided the main artery to move troops from the army encampment into the city. Furthermore, during the war, the 105th Regiment of Engineers focused extensive effort in road building around the Camp Sevier area, improving existing roads and bridges while also creating new ones.[106] The construction of military highways was a major improvement; in 1917 the new Greenville roads system was upheld as a "monument" that was "heralded throughout all the Southland."[107]

Once the war was over, infrastructural development continued; surplus highway construction machinery remained in Greenville and was used to finish improving the roads of the area as well as to construct South Carolina's first interstate highway system.[108] The camp and its collaboration with local government and private enterprise represented an unprecedented period of cooperation between this small southern city and the federal government. The relationships between soldiers and local civilians were also unprecedented, with applications for marriage licenses from Camp Sevier soldiers setting a new record in the week before Christmas 1917. The economic and social impact of such cooperation and relationships lingered decades after the war, as "many soldiers had made friends, liked what they saw, and stayed behind."[109]

chapter four

"For Liberty and Humanity"

Camp and Community on the Home Front, 1917–1918

On the morning of Tuesday, April 3, 1917, Greenvillians awoke to a bold head-line printed in all-capital letters: "ASKS FOR A STATE OF WAR."[1] Despite the fact that a small group of civic leaders had been working quietly and proactively to recruit a cantonment site, this news was nevertheless momentous. The subhead-ings offered previews of what was to come: "Wilson Asks for an Army of 500,000 Men upon the Universal Service Plan" and "War Resolution Introduced in Con-gress."[2] Three days later Congress passed that proposed war resolution.

During the Great War, as it came to be known, the US government called upon its civilian population to contribute to the first major war mobilization effort in US history. These unprecedented domestic efforts supported the battle overseas and were collectively deemed "the home front," implying a militarized space: a "front" that needed to be reinforced, supported, and maintained just as the overseas battlefield did. In a mid-May proclamation, President Wilson warned, "It is not an army we must shape and train for war, it is a nation."[3]

Active support on the home front was encouraged by such organizations as the federal government's newly created Council on National Defense (CND) and its Woman's Committee of the Council on National Defense and by the propa-gandist Committee on Public Information (CPI). Yet the government and other home front groups insisted that it was also the responsibility of all Americans to hold themselves and their neighbors responsible for contributing to the enormous effort to win the "battle for democracy" in France. South Carolinians responded enthusiastically to the CND's request to develop a State Council on Defense and an accompanying Woman's State Council on Defense, and again when the CPI needed volunteers to disseminate information about the war effort.

Greenville's newspapers resolutely endorsed the president's request for a dec-laration of war. An editorial in the *Greenville Daily News* titled "For Liberty and Humanity" extolled American political principles and upheld the obligation to protect them. "Life is not so dear nor is peace so sweet as to be purchased by the abject surrender of our rights, our honor, our duty and our sovereignty."[4] An article in *Progressive Greenville* titled "Our Country First, Then Greenville" affirmed the Chamber of Commerce's loyalty to the country and its support of the government's efforts, both militarily and industrially. "This chamber," it asserted, "has called upon every citizen to do his bit where best he can serve, and to stand united against foreign aggression and to subordinate all selfish interests to the common good." It also contained an "important notice": "Present national conditions have thrown new burdens of responsibility on this progressive city and on its Chamber of Commerce. . . . We must stand in the forefront of American citizens in point of service to our nation and in support of our President." The notice alerted readers to a forthcoming campaign "built along military lines . . . which must be carried to success, and which will mean that Greenville will forge forward into a place of honor at the very forefront of American cities fighting for American advancement and supremacy."[5]

As men joined the military, women assumed increasingly important roles to sustain the domestic economy and the war effort. Historically the suspension of American societal norms during times of war has presented opportunities for the advancement of minorities and others outside the power structure, and in the American South, African Americans and women have eagerly pursued those opportunities. With men heading en masse to the trenches in France and an influx of soldiers into the area, women created and climbed into wartime opportunities.

For decades White women had worked as unskilled laborers in the textile mills as loom operators, weavers, and spinners. In August 1917 the Victor-Monaghan Mills promoted a woman to become an overseer of one of their cloth rooms. The local newspaper claimed it was the "first instance in the south where a woman has been made overseer of any department in the textile industry."[6] At a meeting of the Southern Textile Association in Greenville in June 1918, speakers addressed the topic of labor and the war. David Clark, a North Carolina mill executive, presented data suggesting that "the cotton mill boys of the South have gone to war in larger proportions than any other class."[7] Regardless of the veracity of these declarations, local "mill men" anticipated that "hundreds of women in this section will be replacing men in the more responsible positions leaving men free to enter the ranks" as a result of the war.[8]

Professional women also benefited. For years Anna C. Williams worked with the McCullough, Martin, and Blythe law firm in Greenville. In 1917, when the deputy clerk deputy clerk of the Federal Court for the Western District of South Carolina joined the military, she was promoted to that position. In the last month of the war, when E. M. Blythe resigned as US commissioner for Greenville County to join the military, she was further promoted to that position. The *Greenville Daily News* commented that she "is believed to be the first lady appointed to such an office in the southeast and perhaps in the United States."

"For Liberty and Humanity" 83

Despite her promotion, she retained the position of deputy clerk as well, ostensibly to return to it after the war.[9]

Meanwhile local homemaker Eugenia Duke began making sandwiches for the soldiers on a regular basis, inspired by the spirit of the city's "food pledge" campaign. Her sandwiches gained such notoriety that she established Duke's Sandwich Company in 1917. In the years before women had the right to vote in presidential elections, this woman-owned company thrived; according to company lore, Duke allegedly sold ten thousand sandwiches in one day in the spring of 1919. The most popular sandwiches included her homemade mayonnaise, prompting some soldiers to write to Duke from France requesting the recipe. After the war the popularity of her recipe led to the creation of a mayonnaise production operation in the paint shop of the former Gower, Cox, and Markley coach factory on the Reedy River.[10] Under Duke's ownership and leadership, the company grew exponentially. Large-scale production of Duke's mayonnaise, still using the 1917 recipe, continued into the twenty-first century long after C. F. Sauer Company purchased the rights to its production in 1929.[11] Historians such as Kimberly Jensen and Erika Kuhlman have argued that in the postwar era, due to propaganda, societal pressure, and redefined notions of women's responsibilities as citizens, White women were unable to maintain the gains that had been made in the workforce during the war; Duke singularly defies that assessment.[12]

The United States' entry into the war represented a crossroads for women fighting to enhance their roles politically, with the country's professed war aims providing an ideological platform that suffragists quickly capitalized upon. NAWSA leaders, such as Anna Howard Shaw and Carrie Chapman Catt, encouraged their members to support the war first and foremost and pressured the federal government to create a national women's organization for the benefit of the war. When the federal government created the WCND and appointed former NAWSA president Shaw as its chair, the federal government tacitly affirmed NAWSA's strategy to frame suffrage as both an acknowledgement and a logical progression of their wartime service to the nation.[13] Historians Elizabeth Cobbs, Lynn Dumenil, Kimberly Jensen, Joan Marie Johnson, and others have detailed the ways in which women used their service during the war as a credential for citizenship. Participation in the home front effort built upon a foundation of community engagement begun in previous decades and further expanded understandings of women's roles in and relationships to the nation. Just two months after the US joined the war, Catt established a new national journal to promote suffrage; she titled it the *Woman Citizen*.[14] These women not only redefined the notion of citizenship but also used their wartime service to propel their arguments for it.

Nationally most suffragists followed NAWSA's lead and turned their attention and efforts toward supporting the home front. In contrast Paul encouraged NWP members to continue their direct-action, confrontational tactics, which included picketing the White House with banners that used Wilson's language about democracy against him. Greenvillian Helen E. Vaughan, state chairperson of the South Carolina branch of the NWP, took great pride in having picketed President Wilson, an experience that emboldened her: "No thinking woman who has stood on the picket line with a flag, who had interviewed congressmen on suffrage, can have exactly her old relation to her government."[15] At a rally in Charleston, NWP leader Elsie Hill publicly stated that the party's wartime stance should be viewed not as disloyal but simply as the continuation of a movement that had been active for over fifty years.[16] Despite this, NWP's activism during the war was viewed as particularly radical when compared to NAWSA's stance, and in light of the Sedition Act, which forbade criticism of the government.[17]

Opponents of the movement used suffragists' continued activism during the war to level additional criticism. Soon after the US joined the war effort, Senator Tillman responded to a letter from Greenville suffragist Louise A. Jordan. "The business before the country now is to whip the Germans, not to toy with woman suffrage. There is enough time for that. After the war we can return to a discussion of minor issues. Fighting is now the main job. I am not in favor of Woman suffrage, but if the friends of the proposal press the fight now they will injure their cause."[18]

Yet even in South Carolina, described as a "reluctant state" in regards to suffrage, a small percentage of suffragists elected to follow the group whose tactics and approach were reviled even by avowed suffragists.[19] Under Vaughan's leadership of the state branch, and with encouragement from Frost and well-known national suffragist and Charleston native Anita Pollitzer, the Charleston ESL split, with some members remaining affiliated with NAWSA and others joining the NWP. The ESL in Orangeburg also split. Vaughan's leadership among her friends and fellow suffragists in Greenville was apparently persuasive and powerful; the only local league in the state to completely switch its affiliation was Greenville's.[20] In total only about one hundred of the state's suffragists were affiliated with the NWP.[21]

As head of the NWP, Paul sought a strategy to encourage support of or at least minimize the opposition to suffrage in the South, just as NAWSA had in the 1890s. Nationally opponents of woman's suffrage included those with interests in liquor and business and those who believed woman's suffrage violated biblical injunctions and was detrimental to the health of the family unit. Opponents believed that women would support a prohibition amendment and would vote for labor laws that limited child labor and the hours of a workday. The southeastern states claimed opposition to woman's suffrage in part on the grounds of states' rights, a catchphrase invoked since the 1820s for resisting the federal government and its policies. The Civil War represented the height of southern White devotion to states' rights, with Lost Cause devotees lauding that commitment. Southern politicians feared the implications that expanding the electorate would have on White hegemony.

As a politically expedient strategy, Paul encouraged southern suffragists to appeal to southern White suffrage opponents' emotional attachment to the Confederacy and its accompanying notion of states' rights. Though it was unlikely that opponents of woman's suffrage throughout the South would actually become supporters of the cause, Paul thought that if opponents could at least empathize with the suffragists' passionate commitment to a cause in the same way that Confederates served their cause, they might at least minimize their opposition. As Sid Bland has written, "Alice Paul urged southerners to sympathize with suffragists who were fighting for what was right in the same manner that Confederate soldiers fought for the cause they believed in." Paul's strategy included the hosting of afternoon tea for Confederate veterans and the Daughters of the Confederacy during the annual reunion of United Confederate Veterans in early June 1917 in Washington, an event attended by Confederate veterans from South Carolina. As head of the SCESL, Helen Vaughan served as one of the hostesses.[22]

Just as NAWSA suffragists at the constitutional convention in 1895 twenty years earlier had tailored their strategy to accommodate Ben Tillman and White supremacy, this event paired one of the nation's most progressive organizations with southern groups who fought and promoted a White supremacist agenda. It suggests the extent to which national reconciliation among White people was easier to embrace than woman's suffrage and racial progress, and the extent to which the Lost Cause had thoroughly pervaded White southern culture, even among those inclined toward progressive causes.[23]

Throughout all but the last two years of the suffrage movement in South Carolina, Tillman fought against most developments related to the Woman Question. As early as 1894, he publicly stated that suffrage among women would "rub the bloom off of the peach."[24] Over the next several decades, he steadfastly opposed the "prating of women's rights" and become one of the NWP's choice targets in the organization's letter-writing campaign. In thousands of letters— primarily from students and teachers at the state's women's colleges—these women claimed to be "the impatient young at the door of the South that is to be," or as Bland has described, "the spirit of the New South unrepresented by the old."[25] When Tillman demeaned the entire movement and remarked from the floor of the US Senate that some "pretty college girls" had asked him to support the Susan B. Anthony amendment, Vaughan openly scolded the aging congressman; her letter to him was published in the *Greenville Daily News* under the headline "Suffragist Raps Senator Tillman."[26] When the senator died months later, Vaughan successfully led a campaign to have his successor, Senator William Pollock, vote in favor of woman's suffrage.[27]

Greenville's suffragists devised ways to support the troops at Camp Sevier and to raise awareness of their cause. In June, for example, activist Eva Tarver Goodyear led a committee of the ESL that sponsored a soft drink stand during a baseball game between Camp Sevier soldiers and local citizens; the profits from the drink sales and the twenty-five-cent admission fee were donated to the local Red Cross.

Such local efforts brought greater enjoyment to the lives of soldiers in training, while others farther afield focused on the need to keep America's fighting force healthy. In the early years of American involvement in the Great War, the United States experienced threats from Pancho Villa's raiders in Mexico. Commissions that inspected the first of the camps established on the Mexican border discovered that saloons and red-light districts were almost the only options for soldiers' recreation. These young men were often exposed to lewdness and vice in the forms of drinking, gambling, and prostitution, with 30 percent of the soldiers testing positive for venereal disease. Various commission findings convinced the federal government and the military to take proactive measures.[28] When the United States entered World War I, the War Department under Secretary of War Newton Baker, himself a reform-minded politician, quickly created the CTCA. It was led by Raymond Fosdick, a social and urban progressive lawyer and reformer from New York with a proven record of fighting municipal corruption, who had organized the initial investigation of conditions along the US-Mexico border. Under his leadership the War Department charged the CTCA with enforcing sections 12 and 13 of the Selective Service Act. Section 12 authorized the president to create regulations regarding the prohibition of alcohol and deemed the sale of liquor "to any officer or member of the military forces while in uniform" a misdemeanor. Section 13 directed the secretary of war to "to suppress . . . houses of ill fame, brothels, or bawdy houses" in close proximity to military installations and made it a misdemeanor "to receive for immoral purposes" anyone within a designated distance of a military jurisdiction.[29] In order to dissuade and distract these young men from alcohol and prostitution, which had been made illegal in the five-mile "moral zones," around the camps, the CTCA worked with the War Camp Community Service (WCCS), the YMCA, the Jewish Welfare Board, and

"For Liberty and Humanity" 87

the Knights of Columbus to encourage healthy living and promote alternative forms of entertainment, such as athletics, singing programs, weekend socials at churches, dances, and soldiers' clubs. The CTCA also organized a wartime campaign to fight venereal disease, with lectures on sex education, inspirational films such as *Keeping Fit to Fight,* and posters issued by the Social Welfare Division of the Army Educational Commission. Furthermore, at the urging of New York reformer Maude Miner, the CTCA created a Committee on Protective Work for Girls, with Miner as its head. Through the late nineteenth century, rates of venereal disease during wartime were sometimes twice that of peacetime, yet recent advancements in medicine—which included a test for syphilis and the development of the drug arsphenamine—combined with extensive public health programs provided some optimism during the early days of World War I.[30]

That optimism was short-lived as conscripted soldiers were infected at nearly four times the rate of men in the regular army, with eighty thousand new cases discovered among new soldiers from September 1917 to May 1918. This prompted great concern over how to contain the spread of venereal disease.[31] "Women of ill repute" flocked to states such as South Carolina, which hosted three army camps, the Charleston Navy Yard, and the Marine installation at Parris Island, bringing venereal disease with them. Ninety percent of the women arrested near the camps in Charleston, Columbia, Greenville, and Spartanburg were infected with syphilis or gonorrhea.[32] Near Spartanburg's Camp Wadsworth, local police routinely conducted raids on local brothels. One of the nurses who had been stationed on the Mexican border during Pancho Villa's raid was Sayres Louise Milliken of Pennsylvania, who became chief nurse at the Base Hospital at Camp Sevier. Captain Milliken coordinated with the physicians to conduct routine "venereal inspections" and to treat infected soldiers. Regular reports included the patient's name, diagnosis, name of the sex partner, date and location of exposure, and whether or not any prophylactic treatment had been prescribed.[33]

On October 20 the *Greenville Daily News* reported that nine White women were tried in the city's police court as "a result of a general 'clean-up' campaign waged by the city police." Four of the women were charged with "running a bawdy house and vagrancy." The sentence for running the bawdy house was thirty days in jail or a fine of a hundred dollars, while the vagrancy charge carried a thirty-day jail sentence or a thirty-dollar fine.[34] Camp Sevier prompted the growth of a red-light district, and within three months of the camp's opening, twenty-three young White women (most of whom were under eighteen) had been arrested for vagrancy and sent to the local jail. On Thanksgiving Day fifteen young women were sent from Greenville's county jail to the National Reformatory for Wayward Girls in Washington, DC. Three of them—teenagers Marie Jones, Lois

Sarratt, and the youngest of the group, fourteen-year-old Grace Eller—escaped the reformatory, prompting a "vigorous search."[35] A federal report on the work of the CTCA's Committee on Protective Work for Girls revealed several consistencies among these young women from South Carolina: low educational attainment and low "mental age," a lack of stability in their "degenerate" families, repeated instances of "immoral relations with men," and repeated arrests.

In *Making Men Moral: Social Engineering during the Great War,* Nancy Bristow argues that fifteen-year-old Lois Sarratt typified these troubled young women. Her mother was a prostitute when she became pregnant with Lois and reared her independently. Lois was illiterate and began working in cotton mills at the age of ten. The report revealed that she had "been immoral" since the age of eleven and started work as a prostitute at thirteen. She was arrested several times while living in Greenville's red-light district, initially for selling whiskey to soldiers. She had a history of escaping from jail and a rescue home and had contracted a venereal infection by the time she was sent to Washington. Bristow writes that Lois, "according to the CTCA, was a danger to her community, to the soldiers of Camp Sevier in that community, and finally, to herself." The CTCA approved her transfer from Washington to the Sherborn Reformatory for Women in Massachusetts, alongside Pauline Richards, a married, twenty-one-year-old woman infected with syphilis and gonorrhea who authorities arrested for taking payment to live with a soldier in Greenville, and twenty-year-old Juanita Wright, also arrested for living with a soldier in nearby Spartanburg.[36] Months later, in a hearing before the Senate Military Affairs Committee on venereal disease, Training Camp Commission attorney Alan Johnstone, who was responsible for enforcing alcohol and prostitution regulations near military camps throughout the Southeast, argued that internment for the duration of the war was the only option for promiscuous women who refused treatment and rehabilitation.[37] In his testimony he highlighted South Carolina, where more than one hundred thousand soldiers were in training at any given time, as a state in particular need of support.[38] Venereal disease posed a grave threat to the strength of America's military force, and anxieties about the military's vulnerability to the spread of disease trickled down from the federal government into local communities.

Greenville's Progressive Era reformers were poised to help alleviate these illegal activities. Responding to the arrests of so many women, a group of civic leaders, including J. W. Norwood, W. E. Griffin, E. H. Howard, Marie G. Conyers, and Mary P. Gridley, organized a Juvenile Protective Bureau under the direction of social worker Rhoda Stewart.[39] Their efforts were consistent with a national response: in December 1917 Miner published an article in *Survey* magazine titled "Girls and Khaki: Some Practical Measures of Protection for Young Women in

"For Liberty and Humanity" 89

Time of War," which argued for the importance of distinguishing between detention homes and jails. The bureau established a headquarters and shelter in Greenville, located in close proximity to the red-light district, county jail, county courthouse, and Salvation Army's Citadel.[40] Locally and nationally there was cause for great concern. In a Senate Military Affairs Committee hearing in which senators discussed "the girl problem," one War Department official noted, "If the Kaiser could get these women right close to our troops and nobody would keep them away . . . he would win this war."[41] Soon after Johnstone's testimony, the federal government and the state of South Carolina each contributed forty thousand dollars for the construction of the state's first reformatory for White women. The state denied any assistance to African American women, prompting African American clubwomen to embrace the cause.[42] Ultimately, by the end of the war, ten thousand US Army active-duty soldiers had been discharged, and 6.8 million duty days lost as a result of venereal disease. Syphilis and gonorrhea trailed behind only influenza as the greatest cause of lost duty days.[43]

To help ward off the temptations of alcohol and prostitution, the Greenville community worked with the federal government's WCCS to provide healthy activities for the soldiers. "Surround the Camps with Hospitality" was the premier slogan of the WCCS, which sought to engage local volunteers, and specifically women, to improve soldier morale. A certificate from the commission stated that "the efficient training of a national American army to fight the battles of democracy requires the aid and cooperation of patriotic citizens in the war camp communities."[44] This quasi-governmental organization attempted to organize local citizens to provide information about the community, assist with transport and lodging for friends and family, and organize and promote more wholesome forms of recreation for the servicemen stationed at military installations. It served as an umbrella organization that coordinated efforts from the YMCA, Red Cross, Chamber of Commerce, and other local organizations and the disparate efforts of local citizens who wanted to contribute. In Greenville the WCCS worked with the *Greenville Daily News* to publish activities planned for the soldiers in *Trench and Camp*, a newsletter distributed at Camp Sevier. As was often the case in communities close to training camps, the Greenville WCCS also opened several soldiers' clubs downtown—one for officers, one for enlisted men, one for Jewish men—and eventually pledged money to support the opening of a club for African American men. The Poinsett Club, a private, segregated club downtown, also opened its doors to White officers. In addition to *Trench and Camp*, Greenville's WCCS produced and distributed a "Guide to Greenville" and established an information bureau in the city. These efforts were in keeping with the WCCS's objectives, detailed in "War Camp Community Service Calls," to provide information for soldiers about their new temporary home; to assist in finding rest stations, transport, and lodging for friends and family; and generally to promote and facilitate community support for the soldiers and accompanying visitors. These efforts were overwhelmingly but not exclusively oriented toward White soldiers and visitors.

The "Guide to Greenville" included a map of the city, information on entertainment and temporary accommodations for friends and relatives who accompanied a soldier to Greenville, and advertisements for three information bureaus located downtown for the soldiers-in-training. These information desks were maintained separately by the WCCS, the Greenville Chamber of Commerce, and a "Travelers Aid Agent" desk at the Southern Railway Station.[45] The locations of several "rest rooms" were also advertised in the guide. These rest rooms included a Community Club across the street from the Greenville Grand Opera House that provided free stationery, magazines, newspapers, pool tables, and pianos to White soldiers and their friends. The Community Club hosted a dance with live music on Wednesday evenings at eight o'clock, chaperoned by members of the Community Club or WCCS. The YMCA on East Coffee Street offered a similar rest room to the Community Club, as did the Neblett Free Library on West McBee Avenue. The YMCA even offered a "swim and bath" with hot water, day or night, at the charge of ten cents, while the YWCA in the Cleveland Building played music and served refreshments on Sunday afternoons.[46] The guide publicized a band concert in City Park that was held every Sunday at five o'clock and gave meeting times for local fraternal organizations, such as the Masons, Elks, and Woodsmen.[47] One noteworthy highlight, organized by the YMCA chapter located at Camp Sevier, was a visit by singer Margaret Wilson, the president's daughter, on May 23, 1918. As part of her national tour, Wilson visited Camp Wadsworth in Spartanburg and performed two concerts at Camp Sevier, with over a thousand soldiers in attendance. Afterward the YMCA held a dinner in her honor at the Hotel Imperial, where she spent the night.[48]

Faith-based opportunities made up many of the entertainment offerings in the "Guide to Greenville." Typically a Camp Sevier soldier looking at the pamphlet learned of recreation or other programs at five secular organizations and eight Greenville churches.[49] The First Baptist Church, First Presbyterian Church, Christ Church Episcopal, Buncombe Street Methodist Church, Trinity Lutheran Church, Saint Mary's Catholic Church, the local YMCA, and the Christian Science Room listed the times of their religious services as well as various other meetings, meals, and refreshments.[50] The Second Presbyterian Church once held a dinner for over one hundred soldiers, while refreshments were organized every Saturday evening at the First Presbyterian and Buncombe Street Methodist

"For Liberty and Humanity"   91

Churches.[51] A wartime committee at the First Baptist Church "threw open" the doors of their social hall to soldiers from the camp with "supper served every Saturday evening . . . by the ladies, followed by a social time," and as was the case at numerous other churches and civic organizations throughout the city, funds were authorized to provide soldiers with stationery and reading materials in a "Reading and Rest Room."[52] The Sunday service at Christ Church Episcopal was followed by "music and refreshments in the Parish House." Greenville was clearly aiming to replace vice with wholesome alternatives through worship or activities provided through religious organizations. Indeed, in the March 3, 1918, issue of *Trench and Camp,* an article listing upcoming activities for the soldiers featured only one secular event: the "weekly band concert and sing" on Sunday afternoon at the Grand Opera House.[53] The role of religion in Greenville and its influence on soldiers' lives would surely have been apparent to men arriving from all over the country. During the war the First Baptist Church even baptized approximately twenty soldiers and ordained two as ministers: Walter S. Rule from Leesville, Tennessee, and John O. Hood from North Creek in the South Carolina Lowcountry.[54]

Decades after the war, A. M. Moseley, author of a history of Buncombe Street Methodist Church, wrote, "The church would be called upon as never before to fit into the total world picture . . . [and] like all churches [Buncombe Street] was reluctant to assume its role."[55] Moseley wrote that local churches were completely unprepared and had inadequate resources to contribute to the war effort. Still the churches did what they could. First Baptist created multiple committees specifically to address soldiers' needs and considered appointing a permanent camp minister from their congregation to "extend the social, evangelistic, and pastoral ministries of this church to the men at Camp Sevier."[56] They also displayed a service flag with the names of the more than fifty young men from the congregation who were in the service. Buncombe Street Methodist appointed a committee "to look after the moral and religious life of the soldiers at Camp Sevier" and to "open our churches to them—keep it open with a reading room and furnish writing materials to make the boys feel at home."[57] Another committee was responsible for providing talent for entertainment each Saturday night to the soldiers at Camp Sevier. Churches had to learn the "rules and regulations of the army," prompting them to organize and contribute more fully to the war effort. Buncombe Street Methodist had forty-six men from their congregation serving directly in the war effort, including surgeon James E. Daniel and Rudolf Anderson, a member of a coastal artillery unit of the SC National Guard and operator of sixteen-inch "railroad guns" in France.[58]

Across the country local Red Cross, YMCA, and YWCA chapters also served as dedicated centers for the war effort and worked in conjunction with the WCCS.

Nationally Red Cross membership skyrocketed alongside America's entry into the war, with 267 local chapters in early 1917 blossoming into 2,300 chapters by the summer of 1917. One of the main functions of the Red Cross groups was fundraising, and local organizations took a lead role in collecting liberty bond pledges. In May, Eva Tarver Goodyear led a local Red Cross campaign to recruit five thousand members. On June 24, 1917, the *Greenville Daily News* printed a message that read "Give to the Red Cross at Church Today" on the front page of their Sunday morning edition.[59] Twenty thousand dollars was requested by June 26, and while only $12,900 had been collected with the help of Anderson, Spartanburg, and Laurens Counties, there was still a strong local effort to bolster donations in hopes of reaching the goal. Local ministers passed out "pledge cards" to their congregations to help raise funds. Other grassroots efforts included simply asking for money on the streets, and during the same summer, it was reported that $121.25 was collected at the intersection of Washington Street and Butler Avenue downtown.[60] In July 1917 neighboring Pickens County held an outdoor festival where volunteers served candy, refreshments, and ice cream and hosted a cakewalk to raise funds for the Red Cross. The outbreak of war had created a great deal of support for the Red Cross, even if no one could have predicted exactly why that support would be so vital by war's end. The Women's Auxiliary of the Red Cross, led locally by Eva E. Fletcher and Nana Sirrine, established their headquarters in the beautiful red-brick Marshall House downtown. They also rolled bandages, often with assistance from students at the Greenville Woman's College, knit clothing, collected and donated foodstuffs, organized ambulance companies to go overseas, and served as military aides and drivers in Army camps.[61] The women of Greenville's Crescent Avenue Red Cross Unit, for instance, made clothing, pillows, and sheets for the Coast Artillery in Charleston and for Camp Sevier.[62] The Red Cross was creative in all of these endeavors, marketing its women volunteers as versatile, flexible, and extraordinary in their efforts to serve their nation.[63] Greenville's YMCA supervised dances, while the YWCA, reinvigorated by federal funds to support women involved in the war effort, operated a Hostess House at Camp Sevier and held teas every Thursday afternoon that brought together local women with transient women living in Greenville temporarily because of the war. Greenville's Rotary Club, whose members were in large part responsible for recruiting Camp Sevier, hosted a Christmas party in 1917 for twenty thousand soldiers. In September 1918, in an effort to boost the production of gas masks for troops overseas, the United States Food Administration and American Red Cross launched a campaign to collect nutshells and the pits of apricots, cherries, olives, peaches, plums, and prunes. The burning of these culinary weapons of war produced charcoal, which effectively subdued the horrific poisonous gasses commonly used in trench warfare. Throughout Upcountry South Carolina, a fertile area for peach cultivation, and particularly in Greenville, where one local cotton mill had a government contract to produce materials for gas masks, the collection of peach pits became imbued with home front war service. Wholesale grocers, Boy Scouts, farmers, and patriotic peach consumers dutifully gathered and delivered these foodstuffs to the Red Cross Chapter House downtown on Washington Street.[64]

Greenvillians also engaged in activities and followed guidelines suggested by the South Carolina Council on Defense (SCCD), which sponsored a booklet, *The South Carolina Handbook of the War*, widely distributed across the state. The ninety-two-page booklet included three parts. Part 1 presented explanations on "how the war came to Europe" and "how the war came to America." It also described "the menace of Prussianism" and encouraged Americans to remain loyal on "the road to peace." Part 2, "The Voice of South Carolina," included writings from political and civic leaders such as Governor Manning and Senator Tillman. The third section, titled "How You Can Help Win the War," was written primarily by members of the State Council on Defense, which included E. M. Blythe, F. Louise Mayes, Joe E. Sirrine, and J. W. Wassum from Greenville. The booklet encouraged South Carolinians to eat more fish instead of beef and pork and to consume more corn while limiting wheat consumption. In sections such as "Stop Criticizing, Cheer Up, and Get Busy," authors urged state residents to exhibit unfailing support of the government, invest in Liberty Bonds, join the Red Cross, and avoid germs and stay healthy.[65] The work of the SCCD was supported locally by the War Council of Greenville, a group of "twenty-five business and professional men [who] took upon themselves the task of securing a just distribution . . . of the financial burdens of the war." When they felt that certain men had not done their part in buying Liberty Bonds, they threatened to publish the names of the "Liberty Bond Slackers" in the local paper.[66]

Families also served the war as home front "food soldiers" by implementing culinary conservation measures.[67] Under the leadership of Mary Cary, county food commission chairperson, Greenville led the state in food pledges, wherein citizens promised to donate food to the war effort by signing "food pledge cards." The local newspaper boasted that Greenville signed five thousand more food pledge cards than second-place Charleston, a testament to the proliferation of liberty gardens throughout the community.[68] Greenville hotels, restaurants, and families joined the many businesses and thirteen million other American families—more than half of all families nationally—who signed these pledge cards with the US Food Administration, led by future president Herbert Hoover, to engage in meatless Tuesdays, wheatless Wednesdays, and porkless Thursdays and Saturdays.

The Food Administration stopped short of creating "ice creamless days," a decision popular with children, and instead asked ice cream eaters to save "bacon and other fatty foods for the soldiers and their allies."[69] The state councils on defense also encouraged the cultivation of personal victory gardens and fishponds. Gasless Sundays, heatless and sometimes workless Mondays, and lightless nights were implemented by the Federal Fuel Administration in January 1918, accompanied by an order to shut down all factories east of the Mississippi River so that fuel could be quickly supplied to ships idled on the East Coast due to a shortage. On March 31, 1918, after Congress passed the Standard Time Act upon encouragement from the Federal Fuel Administration, the nation observed its first Daylight Savings Time, commonly known as War Time, in 1918. This measure followed others that had been implemented in Germany and Austria, motivated by the imperative to conserve energy and capitalize on daylight hours between April and September.

Days before War Time took effect, local merchant C. D. Stradley filled a full page in the local newspapers with advertisements for new clothing and several paragraphs encouraging fellow merchants to support the conservation war measure. On that Sunday, which also happened to be Easter, an article provided information on church services offered by various denominations, with nearly all of them extending a specific welcome to soldiers. Trinity Lutheran Church confirmed a group of soldiers from Camp Sevier, and a chorus trained by Mr. Melchers of Camp Sevier performed Franz Schubert's Mass in G. At Saint Mary's Catholic Church, the camp's chaplain, Rev. Jno. Hackett of New York, preached at the evening service, while the Associate Reformed Presbyterian Church held an evening service specifically for soldiers. The Lutheran Church, Central Baptist Church, and First Baptist Church specifically noted that services would be conducted on US War Time.[70]

The SCCD also organized a Women's State Council on Defense to organize the efforts of the county councils and other women's clubs and organizations. Mary Cary served as chairman for Greenville County, while F. Louise Mayes, also of Greenville, chaired the state council. Mayes, whose son Charles served in the US Army, resigned the presidency of the local Ladies' Auxiliary of the YMCA when she assumed her SCCD responsibilities. In her inaugural address, Mayes emphasized the importance of conserving and producing food and preaching "the gospel of economy to their neighbors."[71] In a circular letter sent in 1918, Mayes appealed for increased support from women across the state and impressed upon them the severity of the circumstances by subtly referencing the hardships of the Civil War: "There has never been a year for service to the state, and nation comparable to the present, in the past half century."[72] The SC Division of the

After her death, this commissioned portrait of Louise Mayes was on view at the Greenville County Library in October 1929 before it was taken to the DAR school in Tamassee, South Carolina, an institution she helped found during her time as State Regent. Courtesy Tamassee DAR School.

UDC pledged their full support of the SCCD, nothing that "the women of 1918 are as brave as those of the bloody sixties."[73] The SCESL and SCGFWC also publicly pledged their support. Mayes, considered one of the most prominent women in South Carolina, had previously served as head of the local Nathanael Greene Chapter of the Daughters of the American Revolution (DAR) and subsequently as State Regent for South Carolina. Her staunch and successful efforts during the war also garnered national attention; after the war ended, Mayes was granted appointment to the executive War Camp Community Service Commission in Washington, DC.[74]

Many women felt an urge to support the war because their husbands and sons were away fighting in it. For them Congress's passage of the War Risk Insurance Act was a highlight of wartime Progressive Era legislation and yet another manifestation of a benefit from the federal government. The newly created Bureau of War Risk Insurance, the forerunner of the Veterans Bureau, provided monthly payments to the wives and children of servicemen and, in some cases, servicemen's mothers. This program, which was based upon conventional notions of women and mothers as dependents of male breadwinners, was ironically instrumental in empowering women, enhancing both their "domestic authority" and expanding their relationships to the federal government. Women took advantage of conventional maternal dependence to strengthen their roles not only in the family but in their communities and their nation as well.[75]

In 1918 war songs made up 70 percent of copyrighted sheet music, and much of the responsibility for these conservation measures fell on women whose spirits were bolstered by a popular propaganda song released that year, "Heatless, Meatless, Wheatless Days."[76] In a town noted for its textile industry, Greenville women cast a nod toward their town's identity by organizing a campaign to knit sweaters and other pieces of clothing for soldiers. The campaign took on added significance since the winter of 1917–18 was one of the coldest in recent memory.[77]

Despite the patriotic fervor that permeated most communities, and the efforts of Bernard Baruch, a South Carolina native appointed by President Wilson to regulate wartime industry and pricing throughout the United States, not everyone supported the war, and many took advantage of the situation for personal benefit. With so many soldiers, visitors, and Greenvillians traveling between downtown and the camp, bus fare from Camp Sevier to the city increased dramatically to fifty cents a ticket, arousing local ire. As available lodging dwindled, the Mansion House (1824), which had closed in 1910, reopened under new ownership, and the new Imperial Hotel (1912) added a seven-story annex. Rents throughout the city skyrocketed, exasperating soldiers and their families. In editorials to the local newspaper, soldiers expressed their dismay. "It is worse than mere lip-patriotism when people who hang out the flag and sing the Star-Spangled Banner turn around and exact outrageous rentals from the very men who are offering their lives to the end that these very landlords may enjoy their property in peace instead of having it burned by the Huns. . . . For such mistreatment of the defenders of America these extortioners will answer, if not at the bar of public opinion, then before a just God. Hymn-singing and the loud mumbling of the Lord's Prayer will purchase no indemnity for such gentry."[78] To oust price gougers, Greenville mayor Hanny Clyde Harvley forced businesses and those renting housing to publish their rates daily in the newspaper.[79]

Motivated by the need to keep the government and military strong and secure, Congress passed the Espionage Act soon after the United States entered the war, and like other Americans, Upcountry South Carolinians were concerned about enemy spies and agents of foreign governments coming into the country. Accordingly in nearby Spartanburg, just days after Congress declared war, the newspaper advocated for "stricter reinforcement of the vagrancy law." The editorial stated that any such individuals "will in all probably [sic] come in as tramps, or vendors of some article to be offered the public on the streets, in their offices, or in their homes." A subsequent Greenville Daily News editorial cited the Spartanburg paper's call for increased vigilance and for the arrests of those not contributing productively.[80] That same day newspapers across the state included excerpts from Governor Manning's address to South Carolina's county and municipal authorities, urging them to emphasize vagrancy laws in the face of the state's labor and food needs.[81] In February 1918 two men and one woman arrived in Greenville from Spartanburg as purported representatives of the American Rescue Workers and solicited funds. Ensign G. E. Story of the Salvation Army became suspicious and informed the police. Several days later the three "agents" went before a local judge and were sentenced to a fifteen-dollar fine or thirty days in jail; they appealed the case and were subsequently released on a fifty-dollar cash bond.[82] In the summer of 1918, Congress passed more stringent legislation to expand the list of activities deemed threatening to the US government and military and to ensure that able-bodied men were working full time for the war effort. The Sedition Act, a set of amendments to the Espionage Act, was enacted in June, while the "work or fight" law, passed by Congress in June 1918, further enforced anti-vagrancy laws.[83]

Thirteen cases involving violation of the Espionage Act were tried in the US District Court in Greenville.[84] Most charges were levied against men, like Greenville boardinghouse keeper J. K. Hall and Judson Mill operative Howard B. Batchelor.[85] Thus, when a woman with military connections was arrested in Greenville, her story garnered national notoriety. Newspapers in at least twelve states, including California, Connecticut, Kansas, Nevada, Utah, and several southern states, published information and updates on her case. On July 23, 1918, Elsie V. Sires was arrested for violating the Espionage Act after allegedly expressing her hope that Germans would not be "run over," that the Germans had a right to sink the *Lusitania* in 1915, that the film based on James W. Gerard's *My Four Years in Germany* was a "fake," and that general accounts of German atrocities were lies.[86] Sires was a native of Germany but said she had lived in the United States for "three or four years" and was married to Edward B. Sires of the US Army, captain of the 306th Sanitary Train, 81st Division. This arrest, made on claims of casual utterances that favored her German homeland, put Sires in roiling waters despite her marriage to a US Army officer. Animosity against those of German descent and the resolve to take legal action against them were not uncommon in Greenville, particularly with propaganda from the government-organized CPI and local publications encouraging citizens to stay vigilant against agents provocateurs.

The World War I era coincided with the nation's "Golden Age of Newspapers," the dominant form of mass-media information dissemination. It was a far different field of communication from even the 1930s, when radios became more prevalent.[87] Greenvillians during this time did not have immediate access to information; letters and telegrams from family and friends in the service and a morning and an afternoon newspaper were the primary means by which locals accessed their information. News published in the morning *Greenville Daily News* and the afternoon *Greenville Piedmont* represents the limits of information available for Greenville's literate population, with the morning paper including a popular section titled "News of a Day at Camp Sevier."[88] Though literacy rates among residents of the mill villages were lower than city residents, the articles in these papers are a good indicator of what Greenville residents knew about the war on the home front.

Because commercial radio had not yet arrived, general community conversation was especially valuable as a means of securing information. George Creel, a prominent muckraking journalist and shrewd Progressive Era reformer, led the CPI. Originally commissioned by President Wilson as the means to keep the country informed about the war, the CPI transformed into a federal propaganda machine.[89] One of Creel's most innovative tactics was the idea of the Four Minute Men, nicknamed because they initially spoke to crowds in picture-show houses during four-minute reel changes. The prominent local businessmen and civic leaders who served as Four Minute Men in communities throughout the country spoke to hundreds of thousands of Americans on topics ranging from the significance of the Selective Service Act to why liberty loan drives were crucial to American success overseas. Their purpose was to promote a highly propagandist agenda.[90] Across the country Four Minute Men adapted their tactics to most effectively reach their target populations by speaking in native languages and by expanding beyond theaters into churches, pool halls, school, lodges, factories, and logging camps. In *Manipulating the Masses: Woodrow Wilson and the Birth of American Propaganda,* John Maxwell Hamilton argues that the Four Minute Men, with their creativity and reliance on the spoken word, were particularly "well-suited to conditions in the South," with its low literacy rates and rural population that lacked easy access to public infrastructure. According to Hamilton, the average adult heard approximately six speeches given by Four Minute Men throughout the war. Ultimately seventy-five thousand speakers served as Four Minute Men nationally, with two hundred in South Carolina alone.[91] Greenville's Four Minute Men included Mayor Harvley, L. P. Hollis, W. Austin Hudson, B. F. Martin, J. L. Mann, T. O. Lawton, Thomas H. Pope, W. G. Sirrine, H. K. Townes, and at least eleven additional men who were responsible for the rest of the county. Greenville's Four Minute Men included one woman, Ellen Perry, though newspaper accounts reveal that, with rare exception, women served as the organizers of the speakers' visits to schools and mills.[92]

"For Liberty and Humanity"   99

The CPI also distributed pamphlets and publications such as the *Official Bulletin*, which presented a highly subjective perspective determined by the federal government.[93] Although the Four Minute Men, CND, federal propaganda publications, and nationally syndicated articles helped foster a common national experience in regard to access to information, those who lived through the war experienced it locally far more than in subsequent wars; certainly the ubiquity of radio and the popularity of newsreels in movie theaters significantly altered the ways in which Americans experienced World War II.

Although many reformers opposed the war, they also hoped to develop a sense of national solidarity, as overcoming regional animosities was a goal shared by Progressives and government officials alike. Historian David Kennedy has written that, "it is easy to forget how vivid the Civil War seemed to Americans in the World War I era."[94] The Fourth of July, arguably the most nationalistic American holiday, had been viewed by White southerners as a holiday for "Yankees" and African Americans since the end of the Civil War. That regional trend was not arrived at collectively or easily. Historian Paul Quigley has written of the extensive discussions about the holiday that took place among Charlestonians in 1861, discussions that emanated from the "tension between their southernness and their Americanness."[95] There the '76 Association, which had organized the city's celebrations since the 1830s, voted not to celebrate the holiday in light of the outbreak of war with the North. Their "pensive ambivalence," according to Quigley, resulted from the fact that they aspired to continue to celebrate the ideals of Independence Day without celebrating the enemy nation founded on those principles. Conversely historian Drew Gilpin Faust and others have argued that, from the perspective of those who seceded, "secession represented continuity, not discontinuity; the Confederacy was the consummation, not the dissolution, of the American dream"—hence the complexity. After the Civil War, White southerners often preferred to honor Confederate Memorial Day instead on Jefferson Davis's birthday in May. When White Charlestonians neglected the holiday, African Americans took over the city's battery and adjoining park at the tip of the peninsula, a space typically off-limits to them.[96] After northern victory in the Civil War, "Americanness" became conflated with "northernness," with "the South relegated to the periphery," according to historian Carl Degler.[97] World War I, which occurred only fifty years after northerners and southerners took up arms against each other, helped renew a sense of identity rooted in the nation as opposed to a region. For that reason the US government intentionally located the majority of military training sites in the Southeast to help imbue those communities and their soldiers with a heightened sense of nationalism. Indeed months after they celebrated Confederate Memorial Day in 1917, White Greenvillians embraced and joyously marked July Fourth for the first time since before the Civil War. In addition to athletic events, Greenvillians celebrated by sinking a miniature replica of Kaiser Wilhelm's ship. Extensive effort was made to secure a German flag for this demonstration. When one could not be found, the decision was made to make one, the *Piedmont* explained, "as Greenville folk do not seem to love the flag of the Kaiser Wilhelm and therefore, have none on hand."[98]

Greenville's widespread celebration was in accordance with the CND's message to state councils that Independence Day ought to be "everywhere suitably celebrated this year on a high plane of national patriotism."[99] The editor of Greenville's morning newspaper, J. Rion McKissick, penned an editorial titled "The South and the Fourth" in which he noted the "increasing revival" of the holiday in the South as the "sentiments of discord and disunion" faded: "That slow dying resentment has in late years dwindled fast away. . . . The South now regards itself as the most important segment of the nation. . . . It is natural therefore that the Fourth of July is being restored to its former place in the Southern calendar. All over what was once the proud domain of the Confederacy the supreme national holiday is being more and more observed on a large scale." McKissick elaborated on his claim that the South was "the most important segment of the nation" by casting doubt on the "treasonable deeds that are done by groups in the North and the West," prompting the South to wonder "just how much those sections are in the Union."[100]

His sentiments reflected regional trends: historian Anthony Gaughan has argued that the South promoted its importance precisely because it believed it was "more patriotic than the rest of the country," with pacifists and German Americans in Wisconsin bearing the disdain of many southerners.[101] Even in a region known for the abundance and vitality of its religious institutions, militarism trumped Christian precepts at the Southern Baptist Convention's annual meeting in May 1917, at which members of Greenville's Baptist churches were in attendance. When J. W. Porter of Kentucky proposed a resolution pledging the "loyal and sacrificial support" of its 2,744,000 members to the war effort, some members wondered about the appropriateness of the resolution, given that it "did not bear directly on the work of the body." In response Porter invoked the Lost Cause, stating that he "could not conceive of men from the land of Lee and Jackson being opposed to such a resolution." It promptly passed.[102]

Porter's comments reflect the degree to which the South's martial tradition and Lost Cause rhetoric were rooted not only in mythology and nostalgia but also in class and rural-urban divisions; historian Jeanette Keith has detailed how many poor, rural southerners organized under the Confederate-era slogan "Rich

"For Liberty and Humanity" 101

Man's War, Poor Man's Fight" to resist and dodge the draft because they opposed federal bureaucratization and the suppression of voluntary service and felt that their service would primarily benefit the nation's urban industrial class. James Hall's study on North Carolinians reveals the extent to which the draft forced men to weigh their sense of honor and duty to the nation and to their families and communities; the same value system prompted some men to serve and some to stay. Furthermore the draft was yet another opportunity for White southerners to evaluate their relationship to the nation versus their state and region.[103] As revealed in letters, deferment requests, and questionnaires, the draft prompted not only deep reflection on issues relating to identity and responsibility but consternation as well; southerners made up nearly one-third of the nation's deserters, while South Carolina ranked eleventh nationally in the ratio of net reported desertions to total registrations.[104] Some of those convicted, like John W. Brown, spent time in the Atlanta Penitentiary after being convicted of attempted desertion and larceny at Camp Sevier.[105]

On March 23, 1918, the *Charlotte Observer* informed its readers of a drive to round up Camp Sevier deserters, reporting that "lists by counties of all deserters from their organizations, together with personal description, will be made by all commanding officers and forwarded to sheriffs. chiefs of police, postmasters, justices of the peace, and newspapers."[106] Less than two weeks later, the sheriff of Knoxville, undoubtedly incentivized by the fifty-dollar reward for each deserter, telegrammed officials at the camp to inform them that he had located deserter Robert Allen of Company D, 113th Field Artillery, 30th Division, working in Knoxville.[107] In mid-June a special agent with the Department of Justice returned thirteen deserters, in addition to nine men who had failed to report to Camp Sevier. Described as "a fine lot, independent type[s]," they had been hiding in the mountains near the new Pisgah National Forest.[108] By late June nearly all of the approximately one hundred deserters from the camp had been apprehended, and instead of being given prison sentences, the courts martial decided to immediately send them overseas to rejoin their division.[109] Like the suffragists who picketed the White House, rural White southerners and African Americans also experienced a hypocrisy between Wilsonian justifications for American involvement in the war and the ways they perceived their relationship to the government. A letter from Point Gap, North Carolina, about ninety miles north of Greenville, argued, "It is inconceivable to think that people are agoin to fight in foreign contry for and idile or principel that their own government falls far short of given them."[110] The demands of the wartime state exceeded the boundaries of what some southerners would sacrifice for the country.

Months after the Southern Baptist Convention's annual meeting, the WCCS in Greenville organized a Labor Day parade downtown, the spirit of which impressed those in attendance. Later that month *The Outlook,* a national periodical, ran a story on the event. Anderson College president John E. White's keynote address, titled "Our Common Purpose," reflected a spirit of patriotism and solidarity between not only the camp and Greenville but also the South and the rest of the nation. The article notes that the speaker was chosen in part due to his heritage as the grandson of a Confederate soldier and father of a soldier "over there." The article concluded:

> Judged from the standpoint of mass, compared with the mammoth affairs of our major cities, Greenville's celebration would be unimportant, ephemeral. But its conception, its bearing on the national purpose are noteworthy. Its unique nature in combining all the elements of the city and the camp give it significance; but its especial value may be seen in the fact that this special demonstration of National unity took place in the hill country of South Carolina, the first State to secede in '61.[111]

The consistent framing of national reconciliation within the context of the Confederacy and Civil War even by local reformers like McKissick, Mayes, and Vaughan had significant implications for African Americans in the city during the war and in subsequent decades, as White Greenvillians' postwar progress and pride in rejoining the national fold was predicated on their subjugation. The Lost Cause not only remained a source of motivation for young White men militarily but also served to inspire those on the home front to lives of service and sacrifice like their forebears did during the pedestaled years of the Confederacy.

Furthermore, McKissick's arguments for the South's exceptional loyalty to the nation were based both on an elite and nostalgic interpretation of the White southern male's sense of military duty and on the region's relative lack of diversity when compared to the immigrant-rich industrial centers of the Northeast and Midwest. His editorial effectively carved out a place of national prominence for the South by asserting that "there is more pure, undiluted American stock in the South than elsewhere. Our percentage of hyphenates and of racial admixtures is negligible as compared with the rest of the republic." Though he did not state this, McKissick's opinions reflected a belief that the homogeneous, White-controlled South held a natural leadership role in the 100 Percent Americanism movement, a nativist philosophy prompted by the massive waves of immigration in the late 1800s, White supremacy, and the hyperpatriotism of the war era. This newfound strain of nationalism was motivated not by a sense of acceptance, inclusion, and a desire to move forward in unison but rather by the lack thereof; in

"For Liberty and Humanity" *103*

McKissick's opinion the South was not only innately superior to the North and West but also essential to the nation's identity precisely because of the region's lack of diversity and intolerance of racial mixing.[112]

In 1917 and 1918, the *Greenville Daily News* consistently reported on the boosterism and Progressivism of a realtor who had recently moved to Greenville from Maine. Newton H. Fogg functioned as a one-man Chamber of Commerce; he publicized Greenville in trade journals, promoted the city along the East Coast, and had one thousand postcards with information and images of Greenville printed to distribute in Maine. Described as a "Progressive citizen," he also brought with him a host of ideas: a city market, a "Fogg Hog Plan" to support wartime food needs, improvements to the automobile association, a "Build Now" movement to address the wartime housing shortage, and a city-wide clean-up campaign designed to gather and sell waste paper in an effort to make the city a "cleaner and more healthy municipality" and to reduce the risk of fire and thus fire insurance rates. The *News* commented that "the Greenville Spirit" inspired Fogg not only to become an active civic leader but also to widely advertise "the Great Southeast and its most progressive city, Greenville."[113]

From the mid-1910s through the 1920s, an extraordinary energy, known locally as "the Greenville Spirit," invigorated the city's leadership, to the benefit of the home front and beyond.

Whether Greenvillians were or were not progressive is debatable; whether Greenville's leaders wanted to be progressive and saw themselves as such is not.

chapter five

"They Have Responded to Every Call"

Race Relations on the Home Front

When Europe went to war in the summer of 1914, the US government imposed sanctions that handcuffed the nation's economy in an effort to avoid becoming more involved in the war, and the economic impact on the United States was felt within months. Southern cotton and textile industries were hit, which particularly hurt poor White mill workers and African Americans who picked cotton and other crops. According to Janet Hudson's *Entangled by White Supremacy,* two-thirds of the state's overall labor force worked in agriculture. African Americans made up 56 percent of the state's labor force, with three-quarters of them working in agriculture. Very few African Americans held manufacturing positions.[1]

In the early decades of the twentieth century, the pervasiveness of Jim Crow kept African Americans in positions of extreme subjugation. Through disadvantaging them and supporting a prejudiced judicial system, the state's institutions assured the maintenance of White supremacy. In 1915 African Americans were tried in the court system three times as often as were White South Carolinians, with a conviction rate 4.3 times that of White convictions. In education South Carolina spent $13.98 per capita on White children but just $1.30 per African American child. Governor Tillman's goal of developing obstacles that were nearly insurmountable for African American voters at the state constitutional convention in 1895 was effective: the number of registered African American voters fell from 9,313 in 1896 to 1,645 in 1920. That constitutional convention had, according to scholar Theodore Hemmingway, created a "vast, intricate, racist machinery of oppression" in which "the typical black Carolinian of this era was poor beyond description. He lived in a weather-beaten, unpainted, poorly ventilated shack, subsisted on a thoroughly inadequate diet and was disease ridden."[2] In this environment the loss of Booker T. Washington, the nation's undisputed mainstream leader in race relations and an avowed supporter of education as a means of racial uplift, magnified an already dismal situation.

Washington's death on Saturday, November 14, 1915, in Tuskegee, Alabama, provoked widespread memorials. He had visited Greenville while on a statewide tour just six years earlier; crowds had lined the distance between the rail station

"They Have Responded to Every Call" 105

and the Opera House, where his speech had attracted a large African American and White audience.[3] On Tuesday, November 16, the Greenville chapter of the National Negro Business League, an organization established by Washington in 1900, convened in a special meeting to discuss arrangements to honor him. The next day's paper announced that the league had requested that "all negroes engaged in business [should] suspend their business for thirty minutes Wednesday from 10 to 10:30 o'clock A.M. at which time the funeral services will be conducted at Tuskegee." President W. E. Payne, the owner of several local filling stations, and acting secretary Charles D. Brier, steward of the Poinsett Club, urged all African American churches and schools to toll their bells and informed readers that a memorial service would be planned for the near future.[4]

On the day following Washington's funeral service, an editorial in the *Greenville Daily News* lauded the leader's "sane" teachings, which catapulted him to "a height which no other member of his race, so far as we know, has surpassed." The editorial praised Washington for not "mixing in with foolish and arrogant negroes of the North, nor with that class of misinformed White people who have done much evil by seeking to project their views." The writer agreed with Washington's "doctrines," that "the South and its people were the best friends the negro had; that frugality, practical education, good order, and the like were the means which would bring the negro race into a place of worth. He did not teach the impossible; he did not tear down the fruits of his own works by being antagonistic. He possessed a mind which saw clearly the relations between the two races, and he sought to make that relation more beneficial for each."[5] The same accommodation of White supremacy that made Baptist minister Richard Carroll acceptable to many White South Carolinians similarly deemed Washington not only acceptable but also, after his death, praiseworthy.

The next year Carroll visited Springfield Baptist Church, one of Greenville's oldest African American congregations, where he had served as pastor from 1873–77. Described as "the most famous colored preacher and lecturer of this section," Carroll presented a lecture titled "Good Luck and How to Get It without the Horseshoe or a Rabbit Foot." Illustrating his acceptability among White people, Carroll was "vouched for by prominent white men" as one who spread a message of "hope and cheer." The article stated that seats "will be reserved for the white people who are expected" but made no mention of any seating for African Americans.[6]

Throughout 1915 and 1916, White filmgoers became enthralled with the release of what was undisputedly the most advanced cinematic production ever created. D. W. Griffith's *The Birth of a Nation* was based on *The Clansman*, a novel and play by Thomas Dixon that glorified Ku Klux Klansmen as saviors during Reconstruction. The film's premieres were grand spectacles with theater hostesses in crinoline gowns and men dressed as Klansmen on white horses. At New York's Liberty Theatre, the film played for forty-four weeks, with patrons paying a then-exorbitant $2.20 per ticket.[7] It debuted in Greenville on February 14, 1916, in a three-day run at the Grand Opera House. The day before the local newspaper published large images from the film and an accompanying article describing the local premiere with great anticipation of not only the cinematic techniques but also the twenty-five-member orchestra that accompanied the silent film. The article argued that the film was of particular importance for Greenvillians since the plot focused on the "trying days of Reconstruction" in the South Carolina Piedmont.[8] The film returned to Greenville several times in subsequent years and remained a newsworthy item. Into the early 1920s, the film endured, according to a 1923 article in *Variety* magazine, as "the daddy of them all."[9]

Even before the film's release, it prompted widespread objection nationally from the NAACP. In Los Angeles, New York, Atlanta, and other cities throughout 1916 and 1917, local chapters protested its release and the euphoria it inspired among White audiences, to no avail. The *Atlanta Constitution* extolled the film and the response it provoked among White viewers: "Never before, perhaps, has an Atlanta audience so freely given vent of its emotions. Spasmodic at first, the plaudits of the great spectacle at length became altogether unrestrained."[10] Apparently enthusiasm for the film was so "unrestrained" that one Upcountry elected official, Congressman Samuel J. Nicholls, attacked his colleague Congressman Frederick Lehlbach of New Jersey with multiple punches to the jaw in a Washington, DC, restaurant, after Lehlbach criticized the film and the South's treatment of African Americans.[11]

Upon declaration of war against Germany in April 1917, Governor Manning created a separate commission for the state's African American population and appointed Carroll as chairman of the Negro Civic Preparedness Commission for South Carolina. In late April South Carolina newspapers, including the *Greenville Piedmont* and the *Greenville Daily News,* published a letter Carroll had written to newspaper editors, detailing how "colored county chairmen" had been appointed across the state in an effort to "plant plenty of foodstuffs, economize, and act at once." He particularly urged the state's African American ministers to preach these messages to their congregants.[12]

Several days later, in a letter published in the *Gaffney Ledger* on April 27, Chairman David R. Coker and Secretary Joe Sparks of the state campaign encouraged White preparedness councils statewide to embrace racial cooperation. "Your committee should co-operate with the negro preachers and teachers to secure the adoption of this programme. Without their help our campaign can be

"*They Have Responded to Every Call*" 107

but partially successful. Meetings should be arranged at negro churches and schoolhouses and white speakers should be furnished wherever desirable. In some counties it will be necessary for you to appoint subcommittees in different townships in order to make your campaign most effective. This should be done wherever it is necessary."[13] Communities as small as Walhalla, South Carolina, began to hold meetings with "white and colored speakers" and "resolve[d] to help in a great cause."[14]

Simultaneously many African Americans in the South were motivated to invest in the war not from their community but from new locales. The demoralizing and demeaning attitudes of White southerners, combined with wartime opportunities outside the region, inspired the exodus of nearly half a million African Americans from the South during the war years.[15] These African Americans were often recruited by labor agents from industrial centers in the Northeast and Midwest whose efforts were supported by the northern and midwestern Black press. The nation's leading African American newspaper, the *Chicago Defender,* avidly encouraged an "exodus" out of the South, touting the departure of hundreds of thousands of African Americans as a "Second Emancipation."[16] Under the leadership of editor Robert Abbott, the newspaper encouraged such defiance as a way of economically punishing the South and liberating African American families from southern White dominance and abuse.[17] Labor agents, who often advertised in African American newspapers, promised higher wages and an improved quality of life and capitalized upon the hopelessness and despondency of life in the South for many African Americans. White southerners had long deemed the agents' efforts to be highly threatening to the southern economy and their way of life, which relied heavily upon the labor of low-paid African Americans.[18] As early as the 1880s and 1890s, South Carolina and many other southern states had passed laws criminalizing the work of unlicensed "emigrant agents" and "labor agents" who attempted to coerce workers out of state.[19]

With the outbreak of war in Europe in 1914, labor agents intensified their efforts. White southerners often responded to the threat by attempting to convince African Americans that they would not want to move north and generally casting doubt on the legitimacy of the agents' promises. In August 1916 an editorial in the newspaper lamented the "Negro Labor Going North." It claimed that "[hundreds] of negro laborers are reported to be leaving North and South Carolina daily, in response to Northern industrial and railroad interests to enlist their service at high wages." The article reminded readers that "the enticement of laborers under contract, oral or written, is a criminal offense under the laws of South Carolina." The author noted the fines and imprisonment associated with violation of the law and reminded readers that anyone engaging in such activity must pay a licensing fee of two thousand dollars for each county in which he wishes to solicit. The editorial claimed:

> He may go North, but about the time persimmons get ripe and possums begin to grin and folks begin to talk about hog-killin' time, he'll be back, if he has to hoof it from Jersey City 'plum' back here. The North would not send for him if it could get anybody else, for the most vicious 'nigger-haters' in the United States live above Mason and Dixon's line. When they are through with the negro and have got all they can out of him, they'll kick him out, and then he'll come back to his white folks, back to the happy land of hoecake and hominy, back to the possum kingdom, back to the clime where chickens are not kept in safety vaults, back to the golden sunshine and the broad acres whitening what Timrod called "the snow of Southern summers."[20]

In response to increasing numbers of African Americans leaving for "the promised land," as the North and Midwest were frequently called, the *Greenville Daily News* claimed that five hundred African Americans who had emigrated from the south to Philadelphia had died, due to the winter climate, inadequate housing, and "fake promises of work" peddled by "bogus employment agents."[21]

In March 1917 the *Greenville Daily News* informed readers that "Negro emigrants are leaving [the] city" and that this was Greenville's "first exodus, although there have been a number in other parts of the State, notably from Greenwood." The article claimed that 139 African Americans had departed Greenville on three separate trains, all headed for Charlotte, which served as a common point of departure for trains north and west. In conjunction with this, Sheriff Hendrix Rector arrested suspected labor agents Will Taylor and Joe Parker, who spent the evening in the city jail.[22] The next day labor agent J. B. Maddox and his accomplice, "Fate" Crocker, were arrested in nearby Greenwood, on charges of "enticing negro labor to northern cities."[23]

African Americans also proactively sought the services of labor agents. On April 29, 1917, a gentleman from Greenville wrote in response to an ad in the *Chicago Defender*, arguably the most widely read African American newspaper of the time. His letter highlights his skills but also his willingness to engage in general labor:

> Dear Sir: I would like for you to write me and tell me how is time up there and jobs is to get. I would like for you to get me a job and my wife. She is a no. 1 good cook, maid, nurse job I am a fireing boiler, steame fitter and experiences mechenes helpe and will do laboring work if you can not get me one off those jobs above that i can do. . . . I am 27 yrs of age. If you can get me job

"They Have Responded to Every Call" 109

I would like for you to do so please and let me no and will pay for trouble. looking to hear from you wright away please if you new off any firm that needs a man give them my address please I wont to get out of the south where I can demand something for my work.

That same day an African American man living in Charleston described his desire to ameliorate his situation: "Dear Sir: I saw your add in the *Chicago Defender* where you wanted laborers and I taught that this would be a grand oppotunity for me to better my present conditions so I taught I would write you and ask you would you be kind enough as to give me a job dear sir. I am a single man and would be willing to do any kind of work. . . . There is but little down here to be gotten dear sir will you kindly grant me that favor. Hopeing to receive a favorable answer."[24]

Another man from Greenwood noted, "I wont to leave the south and go north where you get a better chance."[25] Echoing similar sentiments from Charleston, one prospective laborer wrote, "i am a hard working man i want to work and will work at any thing that pays so i rite to you . . . i dont care how soon i can get there and go to work there is no work here that pays a man to stay here so please send . . . as soon as you can. Hoping to here from you soon."[26]

In early May a "Negro mechanic" from Greenville expressed hopes of moving to offer his children better educational opportunities: "I have been impressed to the extent of writing you by having noted an article in the *Chicago Defender* regarding the good work your organization is accomplishing. I am a Negro mechanic, having served the paint trade since 1896, 30 years of age, married, no booster, a graduate of N. Y. trade school, first honor, class of 1906, wish to change location for better educational advantages for my children consequently will be glad to have you endeavor to place me. Hoping to hear from you at earliest convenience. Willing to accept position in any good north western city, with white or colored firm."[27]

In late spring 1917, after expressing his hopes of moving to Chicago or "eny where above the Mason Dixon line," an African American man living in Atlanta begged, "Please let me here from you. the peoples is leaving here by the thousands."[28]

The challenges African Americans faced in the South are abundantly clear in communications from men seeking a better way of life.[29] Deep and pervasive racism, Jim Crow segregation, and threats of violence from an unchecked White mobocracy prevailed throughout the South and, combined with a lack of political enfranchisement and legal recourse, created an untenable situation for many. These men were pushed by anguish and pulled by ambition. Their letters reveal the race consciousness that African Americans in Greenville possessed in the

1910s and a proactive commitment to improving the quality of their families' lives.

Greenville's Black population actually increased in the war years and after, though with the great White population growth the city experienced, the percentage of African Americans declined. In 1900, 19,388 African Americans lived in Greenville County. In 1910 that number climbed to 20,861, representing 30.5 percent of the total population; by 1920 the number had grown to 23,461 but made up just 26.5 percent of the overall. This percentage was significantly lower than communities of the Midlands and Lowcountry of South Carolina, such as Columbia and Charleston, and on par with Greensboro and Charlotte, North Carolina.

The exact number of African Americans from Greenville who fled north during the Great Migration is difficult to quantify, but ultimately 175,000 African Americans left South Carolina between 1900 and 1920, with 74,500 departing between 1910 and 1920. Agricultural challenges from the boll weevil, which arrived in South Carolina in 1921 and destroyed 70 percent of the state's cotton crop in two years alone, continued to prompt African American outmigration into the mid-1920s. During the decade after the war, 204,300 African Americans left the state, with the spring of 1923 accounting for a loss of 3 percent of the state's Black farm population, according to the *New York Times*.[30] In a Federal Writer's Project interview, former South Carolina farmhand Mose Austin shared his memories of that spring: "De cotton come up and started to growin', and, suh, befo' de middle of May I looks down one day and sees de boll weevil settin' up dere in de top of dem little cotton stalks waitin' for de squares to fo'm. So all dat gewano us hauled and put down in 1922 made nuttin' but a crop of boll weevils."[31]

Throughout the 1910s and 1920s, most African Americans in the South chose to remain in the state, however, and collectively during the war years, African Americans contributed significantly to the home front effort. They volunteered through segregated chapters and units of the Red Cross, SCCD, WCCS, and YMCA and contributed generously to various fundraising efforts. Like White women, African Americans served the war effort because they too hoped that their service would usher in a postwar era of greater civic and economic opportunities. Mostly, however, they were motivated to serve because the war provided greater freedom to work for the uplift of their communities and an opportunity to prove their abilities and assume a level of responsibility to the nation associated with full and realized citizenship.[32]

In Greenville, mortuary owner Edgar W. Biggs served as county chairman of the SCCD. Professor A. P. Allison led the Colored Branch of the Red Cross,

Edgar W. Biggs is shown here, with his wife, Lydia, and two children, Hopson and Edna. Courtesy South Caroliniana Library, University of South Carolina.

known as the Booker T. Washington Branch, while Hattie E. Williams, a widowed dressmaker, led the Red Cross "Colored Auxiliary" for women.[33] Scholars have long established the leadership role of churches in African American communities: in Greenville reverends James O. Allen, Allen R. Burke, Charles F. Gandy, John F. Green, and William F. Rice were particularly involved in leading home front efforts among Greenville's African American citizens, as were local businessmen, teachers, and other leaders of the local African American middle class, such as W. E. Payne, James A. Tolbert, and brothers Charles D. and James A. Brier.[34] African American women who were active during the war include Hattie Logan Duckett, Hattie Parker, Julia Gregory, and Mary J. Bates.[35]

Throughout the war local African Americans consistently and visibly displayed their support of African American soldiers and the war effort by organizing parades and mass meetings, conserving food, entertaining soldiers, creating comfort kits, knitting and sewing clothing, hosting a community club and Red Cross canteen downtown, participating in health and sanitation campaigns, and contributing financially to various war bond drives and campaigns. To African Americans the war represented opportunity; it was also a litmus test of their loyalty and abilities, both militarily and as community leaders.

Edgar W. Biggs, a prominent leader of Greenville's African American middle class, built a well-appointed home at the intersection of Brown and Elford streets near Springwood Cemetery. He was a member of Springfield Baptist and a leader in the state's Republican Party. After his death in 1932 from appendicitis, his funeral attracted hundreds of African Americans and Whites, and included eulogies from Greenville Mayor A.C. Mann, former Mayor Hanny Clyde Harvley, and US District Attorney J.A. Tolbert. Courtesy South Caroliniana Library, University of South Carolina.

In the summer of 1917, African American men led by Charles D. Brier organized community efforts to support the Red Cross campaign. Sermons, likely by Greene, Gandy, Burke, and Rice, who served as committee members, encouraged community-wide support.[36] That fall African American women organized a Colored Auxiliary of the Red Cross that attracted larger numbers of members than anticipated. Their initial effort focused on knitting clothing, blankets, and other items for the "colored troops" at Camp Sevier and Camp Jackson. They coordinated their efforts with Nana Sirrine and Eva Fletcher of the White women's auxiliary.[37]

In April 1918 two White members of Greenville's Third Liberty Loan committee, chairman J. W. Arrington and A. L. Mills, addressed a large crowd of

"They Have Responded to Every Call" 113

African Americans at Springfield Baptist Church. Those in attendance subscribed to a total of $1,150.[38]

Weeks later James A. Brier, principal of the Allen School, led a committee that planned a meeting at the new county courthouse, with speakers who informed those in attendance about the important of food production and conservation. The committee extended an invitation to all Greenville citizens, African American and White.[39] At the end of May, a parade downtown involving approximately a dozen churches, several schools, the Mutual Benevolent Society, and others benefited the Red Cross.[40]

In June 1918 Springfield Baptist Church hosted Dr. Isaac J. Lansing of New York, a well-known Methodist Episcopal minister, former president of Atlanta University, and author of *Why Christianity Did Not Prevent the War*. His lecture, titled "Perils of a Premature Peace," described the German empire's aspirations of "world domination" and what the implications of German rule in America would be. "The big crowd which heard him was aroused to a high pitch of patriotic enthusiasm." At the end of the service, the crowd sang "with spirit" the resistance hymn "Before I'd Be a Slave I'd Be Buried in My Grave."[41]

That same month local African American organizations began preparing for the arrival of significant numbers of "colored troops" at Camp Sevier. On June 13 the WCCS transported two hundred African American soldiers into the city to attend a lecture offered by a visiting professor from Oklahoma at John Wesley Methodist Church sponsored by the Red Cross Colored Auxiliary. The *Daily News* reported that this was "the first entertainment on a large scale which has been given for the colored men in uniform" and "the first of a number of similar entertainments planned for the colored men in khaki."[42]

The increase in numbers of these soldiers at Camp Sevier motivated local African Americans to increase their home front support. The Booker T. Washington Red Cross branch became very active in the summer of 1918, supporting African American soldiers at Camp Sevier and even African American soldiers passing through Greenville with comfort kits and amenities such as cigarettes, chewing gum, and postcards.[43]

In June, a parade involving local African American children and adults from the Working Benevolent Society and other organizations marched, waved flags, and rode in automobiles on the parade route from Main Street to City Park. A platoon of African American soldiers from Camp Sevier were the featured and honored guests. They marched carrying the national ensign, prompting one White Confederate veteran to remove his cap and salute in a moment of national solidarity. The parade attracted interest and support from the entire Greenville community. In a boost to the status of White citizens as the ultimate arbiters of matters concerning decorum, the *Greenville Daily News* wrote of their approval of the "spick and span" attire of the children in their best clothes and concluded that "the manifestation of their patriotism yesterday was thoroughly creditable and was accomplished in such a way as to arouse appreciation of the community for the fine cooperation they are rendering in the Nation's service. The parade and the meeting were arranged with excellent taste and all who took part reflected credit upon themselves."[44] On July 5 the WCCS pledged five hundred dollars to be used for a Community Club for Negro Soldiers until November when its next fiscal year would begin and new appropriations would be made. A fundraising drive among African Americans commenced several days later to match the donation, with twenty-four African American women sharing the responsibility for canvassing assigned areas of Greenville.[45] The *Greenville Daily News* reported that the fundraising drive had begun, with donations coming from nearby communities like Anderson, which pledged one hundred dollars. The article heartrendingly compelled local African Americans to give by printing the news that a little boy in Greenville, Le Roy Willis, had donated five dollars to the fund.[46] By the end of that month, the newspaper ran the headline "Negro Soldiers' Club Is Assured." African Americans in Greenville had raised six hundred dollars to match and exceed the amount allocated from the WCCS.

On Tuesday, August 6, months after the White enlisted soldiers' club began welcoming patrons, the Community Club for enlisted African American soldiers opened on the third floor in a large room above the People's Drug Store at 113 East Washington Street, outfitted with "comfortable chairs, reading matter, and other things to entertain the soldiers." The WCCS equipped the room with a kitchen, while the Colored Auxiliary of the local African American Red Cross hosted a canteen. Earlier accounts suggested that a "responsible colored citizen" would be placed in charge of the club.[47] The person selected was Prof. James A. Brier.[48]

In 1923, Charles H. Williams of the Hampton Institute in Virginia published the book *Sidelight on Negro Soldiers,* which offered insight into the experiences of African American servicemen and the contributions of African American home front volunteers. The Secretary of War and the Adjutant General of the Army coordinated with Williams, who spent eighteen months traveling everywhere African American soldiers served in American and in France. Williams was impressed with the African American and White women of Greenville's Red Cross, among whom he discovered a "fine spirit of cooperation," which he credited in part to Nana Sirrine, who "believed heartily in the assistance of the Negro women and finally said of them, 'They have responded to every call.'" Unlike many other

"They Have Responded to Every Call" 115

southern communities, the women of Greenville's White Red Cross Auxiliary did not object to their African American counterparts' request to also wear the Red Cross uniform. Williams highlighted Greenville as "an example of what was possible in teamwork between the races when there was hearty good will and when all were striving for a common cause." In Greenville's Red Cross auxiliaries, Williams wrote that he "found the most liberal attitude in any Southern city."[49]

According to historian Theodore Hemmingway, the war years "slowed the juggernaut of white oppression," though it seems that in actuality what may have seemed like a slowing down was actually a response to the weakening of White southerners' negotiating position, not only because of the appeal of northern and midwestern industrial and defense-sector jobs but also because service in the military offered better pay.[50] Historian Janet Hudson argues that the intervention of the federal government into state and local affairs also threatened southern White hegemony.[51]

Furthermore Hemmingway argues that the war prompted unusual feelings of solidarity, as both White and African American families said goodbye to fathers, brothers, and sons and worked on the home front to support American efforts abroad.[52] Despite this White Americans insisted on segregated efforts, often rebuffing African Americans who attempted to coordinate home front support campaigns, but balanced their disdain with encouragement of African Americans' endeavors. The country needed African Americans to help win this war, and White southerners knew that. With African Americans representing approximately 30 percent of Greenville's population, White leaders needed their engagement to meet quotas imposed by the military and by various home front organizations, especially those that raised funds for young men in the service.[53]

According to Janet Hudson, "World War I briefly gave African American reformers more leeway in their struggle for equality because whites needed their cooperation . . . and gave black reformers an authorized public forum," which "temporarily empowered African American reformers."[54] An example of how African Americans leveraged their wartime worth is revealed in the efforts of African Americans in Columbia to cancel the planned showing of *The Birth of a Nation*. Several years earlier, before the United States entered the war, the NAACP in Atlanta and several other communities unsuccessfully attempted to block the release of the film in local theaters.[55] In May 1918 thirteen African American men, all leaders in the Columbia community, met with the city council. They argued that the film, which relied on gross stereotypes and glorified racial conflict, jeopardized the sense of solidarity and cooperation that had been cultivated by the war. Richard Carroll, who chaired the African American State Council of Defense, argued that successful prosecution of the war required goodwill between

Black and White Carolinians. Fearing upset, the State Council of Defense encouraged the city council to support the cancellation of the film, which in turn convinced the manager of the Broadway Theatre to agree to the cancellation. The city council lauded the result and subsequently passed a resolution that the film not be shown, pursuant to the recommendation of the State Council of Defense.[56]

Relative to Charleston and Columbia, where African Americans outnumbered White residents, organized public attempts to challenge White hegemony were rare in Greenville. However, wartime policies created a set of conditions that emboldened and empowered a group of African Americans to organize and protest a flagrant usurpation of White supremacy.

Like all Americans, African American men and women felt the national pressure to contribute to the war, but after Secretary of War Newton Baker passed the "work or fight" rule in May 1918, which required every able-bodied man to register and also threatened to draft unemployed men, this obligation intensified. In Greenville "work or fight" illuminated intersections of race, gender, and labor when federal law inconvenienced privileged White men and women. Not only did most African American men in South Carolina earn more money through military service than in their prewar civilian jobs, but also the additional financial support provided by the Bureau of War Risk Insurance further empowered the families of those who served. In the 1910s more than 90 percent of the state's domestic work was performed by African American women, most of whom were paid between four and eight dollars per month.[57] From October 1917 through June 1918, the War Risk Insurance Act mandated that the wives of White and African American servicemen receive half of enlisted men's and noncommissioned officers' monthly pay. Beginning July 1, however, the dependents of all enlisted men, regardless of race, received $15 per month; the Bureau of War Risk Insurance changed its policy, not to promote racial equity but to promote bureaucratic efficiency.

This war benefit was a windfall to most African American families in the South. Hudson writes that "by eroding white supremacy's insularity, wartime opportunities also spawned a new and less welcomed, instability. . . . The interjection of the federal government into local issues disturbed white dominance of existing racial relationships."[58] Mayor Harvley, and Governor Manning complained of their African American cooks and servants leaving their posts during these wartime years, prompting some White Carolinians to label these women "unpatriotic loafers." Hudson has argued that "whites could not tolerate this exercise of personal autonomy in defiance of white authority" and used the derogatory slur to disguise what was, in fact, something equally or perhaps more unnerving: African American women's "breach of white supremacy."[59]

"They Have Responded to Every Call" 117

Across the South local governments responded by issuing legislation to enforce the spirit of "work or fight," targeted specifically at African American women, while cities such as Birmingham and Tampa cited "work or fight" as justification for the arrests of African American women.[60] Although the impetus behind "work or fight" laws was to maintain productivity in both agriculture and war industries, the order offered local draft boards great latitude not only to interpret the order as the White men of the local draft boards wished but also to compel the labor of certain groups of people.

On September 23, 1918, Wilson received a telegram from John R. Shillady, secretary of the NAACP, requesting that he and appropriate federal officials address the matter of forced labor among African American women throughout the South. Citing examples of local ordinances in Pine Bluff, Arkansas, and Wrightsville, Georgia, Shillady appealed to Wilson's "high sense of justice" that "will insure prompt condemnation of efforts to apply compulsory work laws to women's labor and that you will regard it as insidious and un-American to apply compulsory work principle to negro women alone."[61]

In late October 1918, assistant secretary of the NAACP Walter White wrote to Shillady, informing him of his investigative findings on "work or fight" abuses in the South.

> You will remember that when we were discussing the advisability of my making this investigation or study, that there was some doubt in both your mind and in mine as to whether the practice of conscripting Negro labor was extensive as yet. You will also remember that I said that if the condtion [sic] was not actual, at present, it was potential and might develop, if not checked at the outset. Well, since being here in the South I have learned the condition is not a potential one but rather a full grown development. . . . I will give you one example of the use of the "Work or Fight" law. In Wetumpka, Ala. a small town fourteen miles from Montgomery, the mayor had a colored cook. She quit one Saturday night, because she could get better wages elsewhere. On Sunday morning the mayor had her arrested [because she no longer had a valid employment card]. On Monday morning she came up for trial in the mayor's court before the mayor, who fined her $14.00, paid the fine himself, and then told the woman to go on out to the house and go to work and quit her foolishness. In the larger towns the Negroes have fought such practices, but they are used extensively in rural communities and in the smaller towns.[62]

Greenville was one of the "larger towns" in which "Negroes have fought such practices." In October 1918 the Greenville City Council entertained an ordinance requiring every able-bodied African American woman to carry a labor identification card proving her full-time employment. Failure to do so would result in jail time or fines. Hudson describes how African Americans organized and passionately opposed the ordinance before the city council.[63] Led by Reverend Green and Professor Brier, the group argued that African American women were heavily engaged in useful wartime occupations, had consistently supported the war effort, and should not be required by law to take jobs with such low pay. They projected that any local ordinance requiring African American women to work for low wages would, during this time of outmigration, induce these women to leave the community. City councilman and White business leader Henry T. Mills defended these Greenville women. He wanted "no humiliation for such patriotic people" and reminded the council that Greenville's African American-community had raised seven thousand dollars in the last liberty loan drive. Mayor Harvley, who had announced days earlier that the ordinance under discussion would apply to both White and African American women, told the assembled group that no serious plans were in place for such an ordinance applied exclusively to African American women and that an informal solution could be worked out.[64]

White closed his letter to Shillady by explicitly identifying the racially motivated and self-serving misuse of federal law that nearly went into effect in Greenville and operated in other southern communities. Emphatically he wrote: "A disgusting feature of these officials is that they are being successful in keeping the Negroes quiet by masking their dastardly efforts under the guise of patriotism."[65]

Pushed out of the South by agricultural challenges, Jim Crow restrictions, and violence while pulled into the industrial hubs of the northeast and mid-west by higher wages and the perception of improved civil rights, the Great Migration was one factor, along with payments to servicemen's wives and mothers from the Bureau of War Risk Insurance (BWRI), that African Americans used to increase their wartime leverage with Whites. More than at any other time in surrounding decades, Greenville's African American leadership, comprised overwhelmingly of middle class African American men, publicly resisted, and effectively defended African American women when leaders of city government attempted to use wartime policies to compel the labor of African American women.

Despite such consternation and exploitation, African Americans continued to work on behalf of the war, often in conjunction with White-led organizations. In October 1918 Greenville's WCCS appointed Hattie Logan Duckett, a local teacher, to work with "negro girls and women, with a view to bettering social conditions generally."[66] Her responsibilities mirrored those undertaken by the Juvenile Protective Bureau, which existed for White citizens, while Duckett was also responsible for improving conditions for African American soldiers at Camp

"They Have Responded to Every Call" 119

Sevier. Duckett quickly became a community leader, widely admired for her commitment to racial uplift and progressive causes.[67]

The same frustrations and pride that compelled African American leaders to protect African American women may have also propelled their home front efforts. In September 1918 the federal government announced plans for a campaign to proactively raise money to support soldiers during the military's eventual demobilization efforts. President Wilson requested that home front organizations pool their resources behind a single drive, and thus seven national organizations worked collaboratively on what they called the United War Work Campaign, a weeklong campaign set to begin on November 11. They established a Campaign Among Colored People Division whose campaign slogan was, "from the Colored people to back the Colored fighters."[68]

On October 28 a group of African American leaders convened at Thomas Parker's office and organized their committee. Chaired by Tolbert, the executive committee also included Reverend Allen, Biggs, Charles D. Brier, Reverend Burke, Reverend Gandy, Reverend Green, Prof. John C. Martin, Rev. William F. Rice, and approximately half a dozen others.[69] African Americans in Greenville proved themselves highly committed to the United War Work drive. In early November 1918, Greenville's African American leaders proposed that all of the county's organizations, including White organizations and the Liberty Boys and Girls, join them as they "go over the top" to exceed their quotas, adding that they were prepared to go "alone if necessary."[70] They created three levels of support, which they planned to publicize: the Honor Roll, the Givers, and the Slackers. The campaign aimed for all African American men and women in Greenville over the age of seventeen to contribute one dollar and rewarded those who submitted the names of "slackers" who had yet to contribute. Community pressure to not only contribute but also contribute generously was such that the *Greenville Daily News* published a letter from A.P. Allison and his wife, who requested clarification that their UWW donation was not $1.00 each, as was published, but a joint $20.00.[71] Their intense dedication was further evidenced by the fact that a teacher had been released from his position in a local African American school for not promoting the sale of Thrift and War Stamps as he should. A *Greenville Daily News* article proclaimed that, "Greenville's negroes reflect credit on Greenville County," and emphasized that Greenville's African American citizens had adopted the same wartime motto as its White citizens: "Our Country First and Then Greenville."[72]

In what would become the last fundraising drive associated with the combat phase of the war, African Americans in Greenville led the nation in per capita giving. Eight days after the armistice, the front page of the *Greenville Daily News* included the headline "G'Ville Negroes Lead Rest in U.S. in U.W.W. Drive: Far over Qutoa [*sic*], Are Driving on Hard as Ever Give $1.46 per Capita." The *Daily News* wrote that "no finer patriotic spirit has been manifested than that shown by Greenville negroes in this campaign. What they have done and are doing will stand for all time as a memorial to their loyalty and love of country." The article noted that with a population of approximately twenty-two thousand African Americans and eleven thousand over the age of seventeen, the minimum quota at sixty cents per person was $8,800 while the maximum quota was $13,200, and yet African Americans in Greenville had raised more than $14,000. The *Daily News* described the per capita giving of $1.46 per African American over the age of seventeen in Greenville as a "splendid accomplishment." Furthermore White construction companies, mills, and banks in Greenville who employed African American workers felt it was "generous and proper" to contribute another $1,800 to the $14,000 raised. The article concluded, "It is doubtful if from the Civil War to the present there has existed in any county in the United States a more mutually trustful and helpful policy between white and black races than in Greenville county and it needs no prophet to foresee that such a condition is credible and advantageous to both races and has big promise for future peace and prosperity which, apart from other matters, is a financial asset."[73] Motivated by a desire to minimize resistance and maintain subjugation and compliance for the sake of business, these myopic and exaggerated claims must have befuddled Greenville's African Americans. Throughout the war White citizens consistently channeled similar messages of racial harmony and cooperation, often embedded within Lost Cause rhetoric.

The day after the campaign ended, an editorial in the *Daily News* titled "Black Dollars" lauded the effort of local African Americans and lambasted White Greenvillians for not giving more: "Greenville is unique in many possessions, but the colored people of this country have added a distinction . . . by reason of the fact they are leading the procession . . . in the United War Work Campaign." They "have made a far better showing than white people. . . . There are very many white people who can give who have not given at all, some of them of wealth, who make a great parade of patriotism, but who will not give a cent to provide for the welfare, comfort, and happiness of our soldiers overseas." Oblivious to the differences in context, the author drew a historical parallel between enslaved people's service to the Confederacy and African American efforts in World War I by quoting from a monument in honor of "faithful negro slaves during the War Between the States," in Fort Mill, South Carolina, which memorialized the belief that the slaves "toiled for the support of the army, with matchless devotion."[74]

"They Have Responded to Every Call" 121

Based on the exemplary service African Americans in Greenville showed during the war, the author of the editorial optimistically prophesized improved postwar race relations: "This striking co-operation of the negroes with the whites will make for even better understanding and better feeling between the races in this county in the years to come." The editorial concluded with another reference to the Civil War and Reconstruction era: "The white people of Greenville county are profoundly touched by what its negroes have done of their own free will and for love of the land. They feel like that great captain of hosts and invincible leader of South Carolina in its darkest days, Wade Hampton, who said on his deathbed; 'All my people, white and black, God bless them everyone!'"[75]

This rhetoric was not unusual. Earlier in the war, an editorial in the *Greenville Daily News* titled "Black Patriots" argued that "drafted negroes have gone to the front as cheerfully as any other set of men and, if history repeats itself, they will fight with signal bravery. . . . The patriotism of these people will not be forgotten and should ever be kept in mind and taken into account for full credit in the adjustment of racial problems." The author's conclusion offers meaningful insight into the perspectives of his White readers. As if to proactively combat criticism that might be leveled at African American soldiers, he contended that "in the War Between the States they stood true to their absent masters who wore the gray . . . that in the history of the Confederacy are numerous instances where the black bodyguards went through a hell of shot and shell to rescue or bring back the bleeding bodies of the masters. Even in the dark days of Reconstruction there were many negroes who sided with the oppressed and persecuted whites and who joined with them in reestablishing white civilization."[76]

The attempt to draw historical parallels between World War I and figures of the Civil War and Reconstruction eras reveals not only the endemical nature of false, Lost Cause nostalgia but also an oblivious and patronizing perspective toward the motives and objectives of African Americans. Furthermore the "Black Patriots" editorial suggests that, for readers of *Daily News*, the only way to truly compliment African American males' military service in the war underway was to couple it with a lengthy commentary of their romanticized subservience and loyalty to White people during the Civil War and Reconstruction. Despite their "loyalty and love of country" and their "splendid accomplishment" in raising money, promoting patriotism, providing hours of robust volunteerism, and fighting overseas to defend ideals that did not apply to them, African American efforts and contributions to their community and country in support of democracy did not yield their full civil rights and economic opportunity. Scholar Rayford Logan has summarized the mood at war's end this way: "When Armistice sounded on November 11, 1918, few Negroes believed that their country appreciated their services on the battlefield, behind the lines or on the home front. . . . Negroes soon learned that the war by which the world was to be 'made safe for democracy' would not revolutionize their subordinate state in American society."[77]

Yet the war provided a platform upon which African American men and women in Greenville, such as Charles and James Brier, Hattie Logan Duckett, E. B. Holloway, and Hattie Williams, joined a small group of African American ministers, such as Rev. Charles Gandy, and became experienced community leaders; they continued to use the networks, skills, and influence they had developed in the war for the benefit of African Americans in Greenville for the next several decades. The war indelibly changed the way African Americans conceptualized themselves, and regardless of White southerners' insistence on returning as much as possible to the prewar racial status quo, African Americans' new self-image burgeoned.

chapter six

"What American will have the heart or the hardihood to say him nay?"

African Americans' Service in the Great War

In 1917 and 1918, African Americans proffered an exemplary record of support for African American troops and the war more effort more generally, despite the ambiguity and extensive prejudice that tainted the military's policies regarding African Americans. Several months before America entered the war, an editorial in the NAACP's *Crisis* posed the question: "What will President Wilson do for the colored man? What will he do against him?"[1] During his recent reelection campaign, White voters in the South had overwhelmingly supported Wilson, a fellow southerner who, by executive order just days after his inauguration in 1913, had racially segregated all offices and agencies of the federal government. As the likelihood of US entry into the war increased in the spring of 1917, the question of what Wilson would and would not do for "the colored man" loomed large, yet the war also prompted hope and anticipation. The NAACP's 1917 annual report enticed readers with its prognostication: "if thousands of black men do fight in this World War. . . then who can hold them from the freedom that should be theirs in the end?"[2]

African Americans were surprised and delighted when Secretary of War Newton D. Baker, by order of the president, called the First Separate Battalion District of Columbia Infantry of the National Guard to defend the "postal, commercial, and military channels" in Washington, DC.[3] As Emmett J. Scott, special adviser of Black affairs to the secretary of war, later reflected, "It was highly significant that their very *color* which was the *basis of discrimination in time of peace* was considered prima facie *evidence of unquestionable loyalty in time of* war [italics in the original]."[4] In the face of a common enemy and in an era of extraordinary immigration, a history of loyalty to one's country developed increased importance. It established a new standard that African Americans met and recent immigrants did not. Some newspaper editorials paternalistically defended and supported the African American desire to serve even in the weeks before the United States entered the war. When the First Separate Battalion was called to defend Washington, the *Baltimore Sun* supported African American troops at the expense of immigrants, insisting that "the Afro-American is the only hyphenate, we believe, who has not been suspected of a divided allegiance."[5] An editorial in the *Atlanta Constitution* argued that, in contrast to those who had recently immigrated to the United States, "the negro has no divided allegiance; he is plainly and entirely an American, with no blood qualms to influence his fighting against any race or nationality engaged as America's foe. He is loyal to his government, obedient to discipline, and according to military men, when he gets into the fight is full of courage."[6]

This glimpse of support did not endure long, however. Skepticism grew, and some White newspapers questioned Wilson's rationale. They speculated that he was motivated by a desire not to remove White men from their positions in industry, or perhaps a concern that the White National Guard units had significant percentages of immigrants in their ranks, including Germans. In response the *Baltimore Afro-American* asserted:

> The colored troopers are known to be loyal Americans. . . . For loyalty of this kind our country ought to be willing to pay something. It ought to be willing to pay the price of having its loyal colored men educated for commissioned officers in the very best schools in the nation; it ought to be willing to pay the price of having these citizens enjoy every right and privilege that German-Americans or any others enjoy; it even ought to be willing to have trustworthy colored officers command regiments of white men, which may not be regarded as quite so trustworthy. Our Government will do these things, if the Negro will regard his loyalty as an asset, to be sold at the price of citizenship.[7]

The opportunity to serve one's country inspired high hopes for racial uplift, and from the outset of the US entry into the war, enlisting in military service was a popular option for African American men, despite that many southern African Americans were disenfranchised, literally and figuratively, with the federal government. According to military history scholar Jami L. Bryan, African American volunteers filled the four-thousand-man quota the War Department had allotted them within one week of Congress's declaration of war.[8] The military was a lure but also an economic necessity for many desperate men. At thirty dollars per month, often supplemented by War Insurance Plans of another fifteen to thirty, the army paid better wages than most attainable jobs in cities and towns throughout the South.[9] With motivations ranging from patriotism to prudence, alongside the fact that African American men were more likely to be drafted, it is easy to

"What American will have the heart or the hardihood to say him nay?" 125

see why African American men served proportionally in greater numbers relative to their population than did White men.[10] In South Carolina, one of every seven African American men, or twenty-seven thousand, served. Approximately 900 African American men from Greenville served in the war.[11]

However, the wave of African American men who enlisted in the first week after the declaration prompted alarm among White people, whose fears of armed insurrection were rooted in the days of slave revolt and affirmed by more recent threats and conflicts, real and imagined, involving African American soldiers. During the Spanish-American War in 1898, when African American men were trained and armed, clashes between White and African American soldiers occurred in Anniston, Alabama. Near Brownsville, Texas, in 1906, White locals had accused members of the all-Black Twenty-fifth Infantry regiment of attacking a white woman, killing a White bartender, and wounding a Hispanic policeman. At the time, the Army, US Army Inspector General, and ultimately President Theodore Roosevelt upheld the dishonorable discharges of 167 servicemen, though a 1972 Congressional investigation reversed the dishonorable nature of the discharges.

Furthermore, the post-Reconstructions decades were a major era of White on Black violence designed to retrench white supremacy, with a surge in lynchings and violence inflicted against African Americans by militant groups such as the Ku Klux Klan and, in South Carolina, the Red Shirts; this transformative period is notably characterized by Rayford Logan as the "nadir" of American race relations.[12] Nationally, between the Supreme Court's decision in *Plessy v. Ferguson* in 1896 and Wilson's reelection twenty years later, 1,830 people were lynched, 86 percent of whom were African American.[13] In South Carolina 156 of the 160 people lynched from 1882 through 1968 were African American, with 71 of these lynchings occurring between 1900 and 1931.[14] South Carolina ranked tenth in the nation in the number of lynchings during this period.[15]

In 1916, White-on-Black attacks erupted in Waco, Texas, and soon after the United States joined the war, in Memphis and East St. Louis. African Americans were unsafe, and whether they expressed it, they had reason to be hostile. Inherent in southern White politicians' concerns regarding the training and arming of a critical mass of African Americans reveals a tacit understanding of the unjust nature of their own behavior. This was the racial climate in which 380,000 African American men served in the US military.[16]

Throughout the spring of 1917, the desire among so many African American men to serve triggered Governor Manning to request that African American volunteers stay on the farms of South Carolina and continue feeding the armies of the nation instead of volunteering in the armed forces.[17] Excepting a brief term during Reconstruction, African Americans had never been accepted into South Carolina's National Guard.[18] South Carolina senator "Pitchfork" Ben Tillman also opposed training and arming Black soldiers, citing his concern for regional safety.[19] Conversely, however, White government officials expressed apprehension about the safety of White southern women on the home front if only White men were sent off to war, leaving their wives and African American men at home.[20]

The military struggled to balance concerns over possible race-based civil unrest and the need to quickly raise a fighting force. Wilson, who had as president of Princeton University ceased accepting African American students, was considered by AME minister and race leader William Byrd to be "an avowed enemy of the colored people."[21] During his time in the White House, Wilson hosted a screening of *The Birth of a Nation,* a controversial film even in its day, and had repeatedly refused to support a federal anti-lynching bill, even as the number of lynchings during his tenure increased. The overwhelming response among African American volunteers forced the federal government to make decisions regarding their service in the armed forces before racial tensions in the South grew too high. While the War Department, military, and President Wilson debated how to handle African American troops in combat, African American men who volunteered were limited to service in the four existing regular army units and eight existing national guard units. With these units almost completely full around the time the United States entered the war, the government was overwhelmed, without an official policy regarding African American soldiers.[22]

On April 24, 1917, officials in Richmond, Virginia, issued a telegram on behalf of the War Department. It said, "No more negroes will be accepted for enlistment in the United States Army at present. This was the order received by Major Hardeman, officer in charge of the recruiting station [in Richmond], from the War department."[23] The explanation in the telegram for the halt to African American volunteering was "Colored Organizations filled." Although most southern states had not allowed African American men to serve in their National Guard units since Reconstruction, units elsewhere with African American troops were allowed to continue training for their use in combat roles.

Thus, with the exception of a brief time in April 1917, African American men were essentially excluded entirely from volunteering in the armed forces. Historian David M. Kennedy asserts that "further black volunteers were simply rejected, and conscription of blacks was postponed."[24] With enlistment as the only avenue into military service at that time, W. E. B. Du Bois and other prominent African American and NAACP leaders vehemently opposed this policy. According to Scott, "Up to the time of the war there had been among the colored people generally a great deal of hostility to the administration at Washington, which was regarded as unfriendly to them, and this attitude of mind is reflected in many of the editorial expressions which appeared in the colored newspapers."[25] The lukewarm response among White southerners, who volunteered in woefully inadequate numbers, particularly exasperated African Americans who wished but were prohibited from enlisting. Historian Adam Patrick Wilson argues that "while a lack of white volunteers forced Congress into conscripting soldiers, African American volunteerism was overwhelming."[26]

Weeks after the War Department ceased accepting African American volunteers, Congress passed the Selective Service Act on May 18. Though frustration over their inability to volunteer persisted, the Selective Service Act not only offered a path into the service but required males between the ages of twenty-one and thirty to register and remain subject to the draft. Through the Selective Service Act, the government could maintain control over the number of African American men who served, when they entered the service, where they would be trained, and what roles they would hold; these debates, influenced heavily by southern politicians, continued throughout the summer of 1917.[27] Special instructions applicable only to African American registrants appeared in the lower left corner of the draft card: "If person is of African descent, tear off this corner." This enabled the White men who sat on the local Selective Service Act boards to be all the more selective about who entered the service and when.[28] Local draft boards issued exemptions for White men far more frequently than for African American men, often using African American women's positions as domestics as proof of a lack of financial dependence, reinforcing not only the nation's racism but sexism as well while preserving the supremacy and comfort of the White men who employed these women.[29]

Out of frustration and in response to White southern fear about arming African American men, the June 1917 issue of the *Crisis* published an editorial directed at White southerners: "We'll fight or work. We'll fight and work. If we fight we'll learn the fighting game and cease to be so 'aisily lynched.' If we don't fight we'll learn the more lucrative trades and cease to be so easily robbed and exploited. Take your choice, gentleman."[30]

On June 5, 1917, and June 5 and September 12, 1918, the three registration days for World War I, nearly 2.3 million African American men registered representing 9.63 percent of the total of registrants.[31] While African Americans made up 10 percent of the overall national population, African American men were 14 percent of inductees.[32] By the end of the war, 367,710 were drafted to serve.[33] With African American men essentially barred from volunteering after quickly filling their quota, approximately only 4 percent of African American men who volunteered and served after Congress's declaration of war were volunteers.[34]

In some ways South Carolina was a microcosm of the South, and of the nation at large, in terms of the African American draft versus the White draft. Statistically the percentages of African American and White soldiers who were drafted from among those deemed eligible parallel one another, suggesting that the state's practices were not unusual. Statewide, African Americans were drafted at a higher rate than their White counterparts: 35 percent of the state's African American men to 26 percent of the state's White men.[35] Nationally these numbers are similar, with 34 percent of African American registrants inducted to 24 percent of White men.[36]

Scholars cite various causes for this race-based discrepancy. First, widespread prejudice toward African American draftees prompted draft boards in South Carolina to draft African American men more readily than White men and to grant exemptions to White men more readily than to African Americans. African American men may have been intimidated by the exemption application, which required literacy and a thorough understanding of Selective Service regulations. Those African American men who sought exemptions from the draft based on their roles as breadwinners for their families were also rejected at a higher rate across the nation than White men who proposed similar exemptions, generally based on one or both of two criteria: the military argued that African American men's wages were already so low that a military paycheck would improve their standard of living and that African American women's presence in the labor force identified them as more independent than nonworking White women.[37] Second, the fact that White men in South Carolina and across the nation could more easily volunteer in the army or join the navy, Marines, or Coast Guard before being drafted further skews the picture toward one of greater freedom of choice for White men. Some have argued that because White men had the option to volunteer, the quality of the White male draft pool was diminished. Finally, with only four thousand available spots in the existing African American units in April and May 1917, and with only very small numbers of African American men being accepted into the navy, 96 percent of African American men nationally essentially had no choice but to wait to be called, thus leaving a higher proportion of African Americans in the remaining draft pool.

Once the government had decided to draft African American men into the service, discussion of where and in what roles they ought to be trained soon followed and lasted throughout the summer of 1917. The promise of training camps provoked both excitement over the economic benefits of hosting a camp and concern among White southerners about how, where, in what numbers, and in what roles African American men would be trained. Governor Manning demanded strictly segregated training camps and, alongside other southern politicians,

"What American will have the heart or the hardihood to say him nay?" 129

traveled to Washington specifically to ensure that desegregated camps were not to become the norm in South Carolina. Emmett Scott recorded his visit. As special adviser of Black affairs to Secretary of War Baker, Scott, who had also served as Booker T. Washington's personal secretary, was the highest-ranking African American in Wilson's administration. Scott was tasked with handling the "negro problem" within the armed forces and later wrote that the South Carolina governor "most strongly conveyed to the War Department the feeling of the citizens of that commonwealth."[38] The language must indeed have been persuasive. While neither President Wilson nor the military considered integrating troops, they did initially plan to thoroughly utilize African American men in combat. However, pressure from southern politicians who opposed arming African American men prompted the general staff to reevaluate this approach. Ultimately the general staff agreed that arming tens of thousands of African American men alongside White men could result in "nothing short of a national calamity."[39]

The compromise reached by the general staff was that African American draftees would be segregated from their White cohort, with the maintenance of at least a two-to-one ratio of White to African American trainees to allay fears of any African American insurrection at an army training site.[40] Most important from the White perspective—and most detrimental from the African American one—African American men would be placed overwhelmingly not in combat roles but in the quartermaster and engineer corps and other services of supply, which included cement mill companies, fire trucks and hose companies, grave registration units, labor battalions, pioneer infantry units, prisoners of war escorts, salvage companies, and stevedore organizations.[41] On August 21, 1917, Army Chief of Staff Tasker H. Bliss wrote a memorandum to Secretary of War Baker, explaining that he supported this plan because it involved "the minimum of training under arms."[42] Days later, approximately 150 armed African American soldiers of the Twenty-fourth US Infantry Regiment stationed at Camp Logan in Houston clashed with White policemen and killed White civilians, affirming the fears of many southern Whites, who awaited the news of whether or not these "colored troops" would be trained in their communities.[43]

For African Americans Jim Crow subjugation was only compounded by political repression, intimidation, and the intense pressure to support the war. Few African Americans, according to historian Christopher Capozzola, publicly questioned either the obligatory registration system or the policies concerning training and placement, or the federal government's institutionalized racism, as "the stakes were too high"—though some did. In a open letter to President Wilson, titled "The Disgrace of Democracy," Winnsboro, South Carolina native and African American intellectual Kelly Miller decried the president's lack of action against lynching and his ideological hypocrisy: "Reproach is cast upon your contention for the democratization of the world, in face of its lamentable failure at home . . .The Negro, Mr. President, in this emergency, will stand by you and the nation. Will you and the nation stand by the Negro?"[44] On the night after Chief of Staff Bliss authored the memorandum to Secretary of War Baker, a biracial mob in York County, South Carolina, brutally shot, beat, and cut Rev. W. T. Sims, the African American preacher at Johns Baptist Church, allegedly "made reckless statements about the war . . . [and] endeavored to stir up opposition to the draft."[45] *The Messenger* published a letter that communicated a common desire to prioritize the welfare of African Americans over political ideals on another continent: "Let Du Bois, Kelly Miller, Pickens, Grimke, etc. volunteer to go to France, if they are so eager to make the world safe for democracy. We would rather make Georgia safe for the Negro."[46] In Greenville, the postmaster seized an anonymous and threatening letter to the Wilson administration: "You white folk are going to war to fight for your rights. You all seems to want us to go. If we was to fight for our rights, we would have a war among ourselves. The Germans has not done us any harm and they cannot treat us any meaner than you all has. Beware when you train 50,000 or 60,000 of the Negro race. It going to victory. Somewhere the Germans are fighting for they [sic] rights. You all are planning the same thing. When we get trained we are going to do the same. So Beware. Sign [sic] by the Black Nation."[47]

The day after the turmoil in Houston, Governor Manning issued a public statement: "Knowing these things and knowing the social structure of the South, stabilized and bolstered by years of trial and the southern white man's pride of position and the negro racial instincts, I hope the War Department will not offend in these things by placing negros in South Carolina camps."[48] The "social structure" and rigid maintenance of a racial hierarchy was motivated in part by self-preservation among White southerners, who had been living alongside African Americans in a way unfamiliar to the rest of the nation: in 1910, 89 percent of the nation's 9,827,763 African Americans still lived in the states of the old Confederacy.[49]

However, soon after Manning's statement and much to the chagrin of White southerners, the US military decided that African American troops would train at camps throughout the country, including the South. Camp Sevier in Greenville, Camp Wadsworth in Spartanburg, and Camp Jackson in Columbia all had African American trainees and the requisite segregated facilities. The War Department continued to adhere to the policy of sending "colored" National Guard units to camps that normally trained National Guard units, including Camp Jackson and Camp Wadsworth.[50] The majority of the African American men who

"What American will have the heart or the hardihood to say him nay?" 131

trained at these South Carolina camps were never involved directly in combat roles.

From August to December 1918, 17,550 African American troops from Washington, DC, and South Carolina served in the 321st Labor Battalion at Camp Sevier.[51] Greenville's afternoon newspaper, the *Piedmont*, argued against this waste of American manpower and advocated for widespread support of African Americans training locally, couching their rhetoric within the aims of the war.

> We are going to win this world war but cannot win it without a maximum use of our resources and maximum efficiency. There were those who did not want the Negro used as a soldier and many communities cried out against location near them of any considerable number of Negro soldiers.
>
> For some time now, there have been Negro soldiers at Camp Sevier. Their behavior has been commendable. They have been in no way offensive. Have we given enough thought to them? Have we considered their welfare as we should? A chain is no stronger than its weakest link. Likewise an army is no stronger than its weakest part. The success of our armies in Europe may depend upon the ability of our Negro troops to hold the part of the line given to them. We know what happens when any part of the line gives away. Then, let's do our part to help fit the Negro soldiers being trained at Camp Sevier for the work they will have to do in Europe.[52]

This sentiment reflects the highly patriotic and nationalistic mentality that was well developed in Greenville and other southern cities by 1918. In the 1917–18 *Negro Year Book*, contributors went so far as to describe the solidarity of 1918, in contrast to the year prior, as a "practically solid South with black and white standing shoulder to shoulder." The article highlighted the editorial, which appeared in the *Piedmont* newspaper, in addition to newspapers in Columbia, Atlanta, Memphis, and Bowling Green, Kentucky.[53]

African American soldiers at Camp Sevier often ventured into Greenville to play pushball and compete against local African American baseball teams, to march in parades, and to relax and enjoy the community center. Despite the promising cajoling of the *Piedmont*'s editorial, Camp Sevier was a hostile environment for African American soldiers. In late July 1918, the cover of the *Washington Bee,* a newspaper with a predominantly African American readership, included an editorial titled, "Appeal to Secretary of War Baker in Behalf of Men Sent South":

Dear Mr. Secretary: The Washington daily press has announced that 1,050 colored registrants are to be called in August, and sent to Camp Sevier, at

Greenville, S.C. The calling of these registrants is proper. The colored race is willing to do its bit, and valiantly, to help win this war. But please, Mr. Secretary, don't send our boys to Southern camps. To do so, with the South's well-known attitude towards our race—the South's damnable discrimination against colored men, even when they wear the uniform of an American soldier is such as to either break down an erstwhile splendid morale before they land on foreign soil to fight with every drop of their valor the Hun, or arouse a hatred which would be against the best interests of the army, the country and the race.

The Northern born and reared colored man cannot fit in with contentment into the South's scheme of un-American discrimination, segregation, and brutality to the race. Send our boys anywhere, Mr. Secretary, to the ice fields of Alaska, if you will, but for God's sake . . . don't send them South.[54]

Furthermore, in a Military Intelligence Division report dated October 1918, Camp Sevier was one of four camps in the country cited as having unusually problematic conditions for African American soldiers: they were issued worn-out, cast-off, mismatched uniforms; they had difficulty obtaining passes for town leave; and when they went into town, police harassed them mercilessly. Charles H. Williams's *Sidelight on Negro Soldiers* (1923) reports that African American soldiers consistently took a back seat to their White counterparts in regard to lodging and uniforms, turning what could have been a long-anticipated moment of pride—the donning of a US soldier's uniform—into a moment of degradation. On one occasion boxes labeled "for the current colored draft" arrived at Camp Sevier, full of "second hand, unmatched khaki suits and second hand hats."[55] An especially egregious incident occurred at Camp Hill in Newport News, Virginia, when African American draftees were given old Civil War Union uniforms and subsequently became "the laughing-stock" of the camp, prompting "humiliation" among those soldiers. It is also quite probable that African American soldiers' off-campus visits were far more limited than their White counterparts, as suggested by Lt. Col. Charles C. Ballou's "Bulletin No. 35." Reports sent to the War Department throughout the war documented that African American soldiers often reported they were kept more closely confined to the camp grounds than White soldiers and had far more difficulty obtaining passes for camp leave.[56] When African American trainees received sought-after passes to spend time in downtown Greenville, White military policemen frequently harassed them, ensuring their subordination by throwing them into the guardhouse, often without just cause, beating them, or assigning them to hard labor.

"What American will have the heart or the hardihood to say him nay?" 133

According to the October 1918 report written for the Military Intelligence Division, Maj. Walter Howard Loving, an African American officer, wrote of Greenville and Camp Sevier,

> I can safely say that a colored soldier in this city has no more show, so far as safety or justice is concerned, than a jack rabbit. The military police make it their business to interfere with every colored soldier they see on the streets, whether accompanied or unaccompanied by friends. They are cursed at and asked to show their passes, and when the proper credentials are shown they are cursed for having shown them. At night time the military police thrust revolvers into the faces of the colored soldiers and demand of them to show their passes. This is done without any cause or provocation on the part of the soldier.[57]

Major Loving's report surveyed eleven camps and highlighted particular concerns at Camps Wheeler, Jackson, Sevier, and Greene. In his report on Camp Sevier, he concluded by suggesting that actions be taken before mass violence ensued.[58]

Race-based conflict between the military and civilians had been an issue of deep concern before the United States entered the war and remained so for the duration. Race riots seemed imminent when in October 1917, just two months after the Houston incident in which African American troops killed White civilians, an incident in Spartanburg sparked tensions throughout the community. The Fifteenth New York National Guard Infantry Regiment, comprising African American volunteers, was training at Camp Wadsworth on a segregated basis per War Department orders. While on leave from the camp, Sgt. Noble Sissle attempted to purchase a newspaper at a segregated, White hotel in downtown Spartanburg and faced, according to Capozzola, an "impossible dilemma." Sissle "knew that the rules of white supremacy required him to doff his hat in the presence of a white man; he knew, too, that military regulations forbade him from ever removing Uncle Sam's cap."[59] He erred on the side of the military. The proprietor of the hotel asked him why he did not remove his hat and subsequently knocked Sissle's hat off his head. As Sissle bent to pick it up, the hotel's proprietor struck him and physically kicked him out of the hotel. Forces from Camp Wadsworth armed themselves and threatened to march on the city after hearing a rumor that two fellow soldiers had been lynched at the police station. In a display of soldierly solidarity, a group of forty soldiers, both African American and White, "rushed" the hotel but were eventually calmed down by the African American commanding officer, Lt. James R. Europe.[60]

After the turmoil Scott traveled to Spartanburg to visit members of the Fifteenth New York National Guard Infantry Regiment, to better understand and address the tense situation. In his memoir, he wrote of how the men approached him with "tears streaming down their face[s]" and voiced "how bitterly they felt in the face of the insults which had been heaped upon them from time to time as they passed through the town."[61]

Upon Scott's urging the War Department's response to the situation in Spartanburg was to move the division to Camp Mills in Long Island, New York, and overseas almost immediately. In order to get them away from the potentially volatile racial tensions that seemed ready to erupt on the home front, the Fifteenth New York unit was hastily organized into the 369th Infantry Regiment and shipped to France despite their unfinished training. After this incident at Camp Wadsworth, African American soldiers who remained on the home front were often restricted from off-camp recreational facilities to mitigate further racial tensions. When they did leave the camps, they were of course subject to the racial ordinances of the communities in which they were immersed.[62] At Camp Funston in Kansas, an official bulletin, "Bulletin No. 35," issued by Maj. Gen. Charles C. Ballou, was read to the members of the colored Ninety-second Division and subsequently circulated throughout the entire US military and into the South, where Jim Crow legislation was strongest.[63] General Ballou stated that "all colored members of his command . . . should refrain from going where their presence will be resented." Ballou recognized that African American men were "strictly within their legal rights" when entering certain establishments, but the soldier who broke the laws of Jim Crow was "guilty of the GREATER wrong in doing ANYTHING, NO MATTER HOW LEGALLY CORRECT, that will provoke race animosity."[64]

The African American soldiers from Camp Wadsworth who went to France became the first African American soldiers to be sent into combat overseas, and some of the first American soldiers to fight for democracy on French soil. But the two-to-one ratio between White and African American soldiers training in southern camps also meant that the 369th Division had never been able to train as a full unit in one location before shipping overseas, leaving them significantly handicapped in terms of teamwork, discipline, and organization as compared to other, more cohesively trained units. Despite their unfinished training stateside in Spartanburg, however, the 369th Infantry Regiment distinguished themselves overseas, accruing more than one hundred medals and awards from both the French and Americans. After arriving in Brest, France, in December, they were incorporated into the Ninety-third Division (provisional) and subsequently joined the French 161st Division. Dubbed "The Harlem Hellfighters" by the Germans, their service included a record of 191 days on the firing line; their term of service

"What American will have the heart or the hardihood to say him nay?" 135

without losing any men to capture surpassed by 5 days that of any other American regiment at the front.[65]

One instance in particular speaks to the valor of the 369th. During the early morning hours of May 14, 1918, while on night sentry duty in the Ardennes Forest in France's Champagne region, two African American soldiers, William Henry Johnson of Winston-Salem, North Carolina, and Albany, New York, and Pvt. Needham Roberts of Trenton, New Jersey, heard enemy troops cutting through barbed wire nearby. Johnson instructed Roberts to awaken and alert the French troops with whom they were serving. Johnson threw grenades at the Germans and, upon exhausting his supply, fired his rifle until it jammed when he tried to insert another cartridge. Surrounded by German troops, Johnson fought them off with his rifle until the butt splintered. When the troops tried to take Roberts prisoner, Johnson attacked them with a bolo knife, ultimately wounding between ten and twenty Germans, killing three or four, and rescuing Roberts. When French and American reinforcements arrived, Johnson was still fighting, and soon thereafter fainted from the twenty-one injuries he had sustained over the previous hour.

The next morning their White officer, Col. William Hayward, proudly invited the press and military leaders to join him in visiting the site where Johnson had saved the French regiment and fellow members of the 369th. Johnson and Roberts became the first two American soldiers to receive the Croix de Guerre, a French military decoration. Johnson also received the heightened distinction of a gold palm (Croix de Guerre avec Palme) for valor attached to his medal. He was promoted to sergeant and nicknamed "Black Death." The military lauded his valor, and he became a hero to many African Americans over there and over here.

Months later the unit suffered severely in their engagements at Chateau-Thierry and Belleau Wood, with approximately 1,500 casualties. Colonel Hayward boasted of them, "My men never retire, they go forward or they die."[66] Ultimately more than 500 men from the 369th joined Johnson and Roberts as recipients of the Croix de Guerre.

The 369th was joined overseas by another African American unit, the 371st Infantry Regiment, which also had trained in South Carolina. Established in August 1917, the renowned 371st, known as the "Red Hand," trained at Camp Jackson in Columbia and became the first drafted regiment to enter combat.[67] The regiment was deployed overseas to the Western Front in April 1918 before other American regiments due to White South Carolinians' fears that a large force of armed and trained African American men in the region could pose threats to White civilians. Once in Europe the regiment was similarly reorganized under French command, as the French needed a new supply of troops, and also out of

136 "Our Country First, Then Greenville"

fear of potential conflict between the 371st regiment and White southern regiments scheduled to arrive soon after.[68]

The Red Hand was later thrown into the great September 1918 offensive in Champagne. The regiment captured many German prisoners, shot down three German airplanes, and is remembered as one of the most forward units of the attacking army in this heralded battle.

Several South Carolinians in these units distinguished themselves in battle. James "Jim" P. McKinney, an African American soldier from Greenville who was attached to the Headquarters Company of the 371st, was wounded by shrapnel and invalided out of service once gas infection set in. After the war McKinney recorded pieces of his combat experience overseas:

> We took our positions early in the morning, and waited until our barrage had smashed the German defenses pretty well. About the time our barrage lifted, the Huns sent over a counter-barrage, but we went right through it, and over the slopes commanded by their machine guns. They turned loose everything they had to offer, and the storm of lead and steel got a lot of our men. Still, we followed our officers into the devils' trenches. A few of the Germans tried to fight with their bayonets, but we could all box pretty well, and boxing works with the bayonet. A few feints and then the death-stroke was the rule. Most of the Huns quit as soon as we got at them. Even the ones that had been on the machine guns yelled for us to spare them. I guess in the excitement some of them fared poorly. . . . While we were advancing we worked along low and took all available cover against the machine-gun fire directed against us. As soon as we came within range we opened fire with hand grenades and accounted for the machine-gun nests. I saw some of the gunners chained to their posts. Their barbed wire gave us trouble. Our artillery cut it up pretty badly, but still it was a pretty strong barrier against the advancing infantry. When we got tangled up in the wire, Fritz would play with his rifles. I've seen fellows get into a German trench with their uniforms flying in shreds.

McKinney also remembered the skill and devastation the Germans imposed. "The German artillery fire was accurate," he recounted.

> They had our ranges down to a science. . . . They were good marksmen. Why, I've seen them cut a regular ditch along a row of shell-holes to prevent our troops from using the holes for shelter. There was positively nothing they didn't do that was horrible. I've seen them cut loose at a company runner with three-inch artillery. It was a funny sight for us, but not for the runner. The Huns would drop shells all around him while he fled on wings of terror. I

"What American will have the heart or the hardihood to say him nay?" 137

never saw them get a runner with their artillery fire, but I've seen some very close shooting.[69]

Capt. A. V. R. Richey, a White officer from Laurens, South Carolina, commanded a unit of the 371st. He described the night of September 26, 1918, after receiving orders to "move forward":

> We slept that night in a French communicating trench. I say slept, but really there was no sleep, as it was raining, and the noise from the guns would not let one sleep. The French had gone over the top and were pursuing the Huns.
>
> On Sunday morning my company went over the hill. We arrived at the position the attack was to start from at 7:30, after having a deadly artillery barrage on us over the hill. At 10 o'clock Sunday morning we were ordered to advance up the valley, but in the meantime an enemy plane flew down low, discovered our position, and signalled his artillery, which opened on us, and every minute seemed to be the last one. However, by rifle fire we brought the plane down, killing the pilot and observer.
>
> Long before we reached the village we could see the cowards running up a steep hill beyond, leaving lots of machine guns to stick out, and, believe me, when we reached our objective and rounded up the machine gunners the men of the 371st made quick work of them.
>
> In all, during the two days . . . our battalion advanced about five miles without the aid of a single friendly artillery shot or any other help. We killed lots of Germans, captured lots of them, and also captured any quantity of materiel and several big guns.

Richey spoke highly of his men and their skill and perseverance. "I am proud of all my officers and all of my men," he declared. "The whole regiment fought like veterans, and with a fierceness equal to any white regiment. This was the first time any of them had been under aimed shell and machine-gun fire and they stood it like moss-covered old-timers. They never flinched or showed the least sign of fear. All that was necessary was to tell them to go and they went. Lots were killed and wounded, but they will go down in history as brave soldiers."[70] One of these brave soldiers was Freddie Stowers, born in January 1896 in Anderson County, South Carolina. He was the grandson of slaves and a farmhand in Sandy Springs prior to being drafted into the army in 1917. Described as tall and slender, with brown eyes and brown hair, Stowers was married and had a young daughter.[71] He trained with the 371st at Camp Jackson and served overseas with the regiment under French command.

Only minutes into an attack that Stowers led on a fortified position known as Hill 188 in the Ardennes region, enemy troops appeared, pretending to surrender by climbing out of their trenches with their hands up. As Stowers and his company approached, enemy forces opened fire. The company took heavy losses, but Stowers pressed onward, leading his men to the machine gun nest inflicting the bulk of the damage, despite suffering a mortal wound. He is buried in the Meuse-Argonne American Cemetery and Memorial.

The 371st regiment was later awarded the Croix de Guerre for its extraordinary contributions to the Champagne offensive. In addition, three officers of the 371st regiment were awarded the French Legion of Honor, and twenty-six men earned the Distinguished Service Cross. The entire 369th regiment and select members of the 370th, 371st, and 372nd also won the Croix de Guerre.

For some White soldiers, observation of African American combat performance mitigated the prejudices they had previously held against African American capabilities. Like Captain Richey, Lt. John B. Smith, a White officer from Greenville, took pride in the 371st division from South Carolina: "The men were all good soldiers. . . . To be frank, we were a little dubious about them. We did not know whether they would stand under fire or not. But they did . . . they were splendid fighters . . . no soldier could have behaved better under adverse circumstances."[72] Overseas experiences in World War I changed some White people's impressions of African Americans and greatly changed African Americans' perceptions of how race relations could function.

For African Americans travel overseas and contact with French colonial African soldiers expanded their view of the roles they could serve in their communities and in how they could coexist with White people. The French held far less prejudiced views of African Americans. One African American from South Carolina wrote home: "These French don't bother with no color line business. They treat us so good the only time I know I'm colored is when I look in the glass."[73] After the conclusion of the war, one officer of the regiment commented on the unique racial climate that permeated the regiment as they were under French command: "The French people could not grasp the idea of social discrimination on account of color. They said the colored men were soldiers, wearing the American uniform, and fighting in the common cause, and they could not see why they should be discriminated against. They received men in their churches and homes."[74] This relatively warm treatment elicited concern among White military leadership and prompted a memo. Believed to have been authored in part by General Pershing, the memo from the American Expeditionary Forces French liaison, Col. J. L. A. Linard, warned French officers and civilians of "the exact idea of the position occupied by Negros in the United States." Titled "Secret Information Concerning Black American Troops," the memo derided the French for exercising "familiarity" and "indulgence" with Black soldiers, behavior that was considered

"What American will have the heart or the hardihood to say him nay?" 139

to be "an affront to national policy." This was concerning because White Americans, according to the memo, were "afraid that contact with the French will inspire in black Americans aspirations which to them appear intolerable."[75] The memo, intended to assuage White American concerns and educate the French on what the US Army deemed to be appropriate interactions between French officers and civilians with African American troops, was largely ignored by the French.

White fears of postwar African American assertiveness were also echoed in popular song lyrics of the time: "How're you gonna keep 'em down on the farm after they've seen Paree?"[76] While overseas, African American soldiers also had access to African American publications such as the *Chicago Defender*, which published special editions for troops in Europe.[77] Especially for young men from the South, access to these materials and the spirit and tone in which they advocated for racial uplift would have been a novelty. Reading such publications gave African Americans from South Carolina new exposure to northern and midwestern attitudes on race relations. This recognition of what was possible prompted nervousness among White southerners, who feared what emboldened African Americans would demand of them at home after their experiences abroad. This nervousness resulted in a backlash from White people to "keep 'em down" upon their return from service overseas. Though some may have become more open to change, such as the officers who commanded Black units, many others felt threatened by this and thus more staunchly defended White supremacy after the war.

In 1919, Kelly Miller wrote that "after the negro has proved his value and worth in all of these trying ways, when after this he asks for a full measure of equal rights, what American will have the heart or the hardihood to say him nay?"[78] Yet, the commitment of African Americans to the war effort both on the home front and overseas did not lead to a widespread movement for equality after World War I as it did in the years following World War II. Substantial reward for African Americans' efforts regarding their wartime contributions did not galvanize; in fact this period was a time of extreme racial retrenchment accompanied by mass disillusionment as African American veterans returned home to a "wave of racial violence unmatched since the end of the Civil War."[79] Sociologist Rayford Logan's seminal work *The Negro of American Life and Thought: The Nadir, 1877–1901* suggested that the worst part of the African American struggle occurred during those years, while more recently, scholars such as Leon Litwack have argued for its duration through the Great Migration. John Hope Franklin wrote that the "long dark night" persisted to 1923, and George Brown Tindall referred to the 1920s as the apogee of codified race-based subjugation. Deborah Gray White argued that after the war and through the 1920s, the "New Negro faced some age-old problems."[80]

The increased incidences of racial violence support these arguments. During the summer of 1919, veterans began returning from Europe, and race riots coinciding with their return resulted in the summer of 1919 becoming vibrantly known as the Red Summer. Historian Chad L. Williams writes that "the war inflated the hopes of African Americans that a new era of democratic opportunity lay on the horizon," but upon their return these veterans confronted "a wave of racial violence unmatched since the aftermath of the Civil War."[81]

African American veterans were urged not to return to their southern homes in military regalia, and in some instances Black veterans who did so were forced to remove their military uniforms at the behest of White mobs who met them at train stations.[82] In contrast, three years after the end of World War II, President Harry S. Truman took executive action to desegregate the American armed forces with Executive Order 9981.[83] This would be the first step in significantly recognizing African Americans' contributions to a major war effort despite lingering, intense racism.

Although groups like the 369th and 371st distinguished themselves in combat, African American military service in World War I was highly restricted by White military leadership. Throughout the war African Americans were not accepted into the marines and served in very minor roles in the navy and coast guard. Most African Americans served in the US Army, but only those who served in the 92nd and 93rd Divisions experienced combat. In the whole AEF, two of every three soldiers served in combat. Over the course of the war, 1.8 million White and 200,000 African American troops served in France. Only one of five African Americans sent to France, or approximately 19 percent, saw battle, while in contrast, 57 percent of White troops sent to France were considered combatants.[84] Although special cases existed such as the renowned 371st Division, less than 9 percent of African Americans from South Carolina who served in the war served in combat roles, with fewer than 11 percent of African Americans in combat nationally, representing one-thirtieth of the army's combat forces. Over 89 percent of African Americans served, according to historian Jennifer D. Keene, in "labor battalions, pioneer infantry units, salvage companies, and stevedore organizations" and represented one-third of the army's labor units, while in comparison 56 percent of White soldiers served in noncombatant units. African Americans accounted for approximately 3 percent of combat fatalities.[85]

Furthermore African Americans who wished to pursue higher military rank encountered stiff resistance. Initially Black college graduates who aspired to serve as officers were denied the ability to train alongside White officers in already established camps. Early in the war, on May 19, 1917, however, the Wilson administration and US Army had yielded to pressure from African American leaders

"What American will have the heart or the hardihood to say him nay?" 141

and opened a segregated camp at Fort Des Moines in Iowa specifically to train 1,250 African American men, mostly graduates and faculty from Howard, Tuskegee, Harvard, and Yale Universities, as officers.[86] Wilson's conceptualization of World War I as a war to make the world safe for democracy often collided with his policies on racial inequality at home. Historian Robert Zieger has argued that "in proclaiming a democratic crusade, the Wilson administration had been forced to address, however reluctantly and episodically, the claims of disadvantaged and subordinated citizens."[87]

This segregated camp graduated only one class of Black officers in October 1917, a class of 639 men who received junior grade commissions. At least fourteen of these men were from South Carolina, all from the Midlands and Lowcountry.[88] After their commissioning the Fort Des Moines Provisional Army Officer Training School closed, and no African American officer was ever placed in charge of White soldiers. The 639 men who graduated as captains and lieutenants ultimately represented 0.03 percent of the 200,000 American officers in the US Army of the First World War.[89]

By war's end 19,909 White South Carolinians were drafted through the Selective Service Act, compared to 25,798 African American South Carolinians.[90] In Greenville County 20 percent of all adult males over the age of twenty-one were drafted, one of the highest African American draftee percentages in the state of South Carolina, with the highest percentage of 32 percent emanating from neighboring Pickens County.[91] Other counties in South Carolina drafted 8 to12 percent of all African American adult males, suggesting dubiously either that African American adult males in the Upcountry were perhaps healthier and younger (between the ages of twenty-one and thirty, per the terms of the first draft call) or that the White men who sat on local draft boards may have felt more liberty to discriminate against African Americans who applied for exemptions than their counterparts in parts of the state with better organized, populous, and vocal communities of African Americans.[92]

Throughout American history the intensity and tragedy of war has typically allowed for greater fluidity with social norms. In an era of national upheaval surrounding World War I, African American service in the US military illuminated White vulnerability to changing racial mores. Just two weeks into the war in 1917, Mississippi senator James K. Vardaman argued against the use of African American troops, claiming that if used, their service would affirm "that his political rights must be respected, even though it is necessary for him to give his life."[93] After the war Du Bois astutely reflected on the psychology behind White fears of African American physical aggression and political gains, unveiling the empathetic complexities of collective White guilt and highlighting White people's complicity. In doing so he clarified the rationale, unacceptable in mainstream White society at the time, that the very behavior White southerners feared from African Americans was justified by their own actions: "It is not so much that [White people] fear that the Negro will strike if he gets a chance, but rather that they assume with curious unanimity that he has reason to strike, that any other persons in his circumstances or treated as he is would rebel."[94]

chapter seven

"A University or a Training Camp"

Furman University and the Student Army Training Corps

With the declaration of war, many young men who were enrolled in colleges and universities across the country suddenly felt caught between competing and conflicting demands. Despite a sharp rise in enrollment at the nation's colleges and universities that began in earnest in the 1870s resulting from a national population boom and the establishment of hundreds of colleges and universities, higher education remained an elite realm. The percentage of eighteen- to twenty-four-year-olds enrolled in higher education increased from 1 to 2 percent between the 1869–70 and 1899–1900 academic years.[1] Before World War I, as historian David Levine has pointed out, students and faculty at these institutions were disconnected from mainstream Americans, who often didn't value the experience of higher education. While "few young people believed that college provided the best opportunities for economic and social mobility . . . [and] few professors were called upon to lend their knowledge to the solution of society's problems," service in the military was esteemed, particularly in the American South.[2] Through heightened discourse about the role of the nation and higher education during the Progressive Era, however, alongside the increased involvement of scholars in the service of the federal government and the development of the Student Army Training Corps (SATC), the war introduced great changes in the relationships between higher education, the federal government, and mainstream America.

This evolution built upon a progressive ethos that encouraged philanthropy, civic involvement, and professionalization. Benefactors and patrons established new colleges and universities while strengthening existing ones with endowment contributions. In the 1890s a small group of universities developed graduate research programs, and the number of earned doctoral degrees increased significantly. In 1900 fourteen leading research universities established the Association of American Universities (AAU), which aspired to raise the standards and stature of higher education and began accrediting undergraduate programs in 1914. As American universities improved the rigor of research programs, the government increasingly called on scholarly expertise. In 1916 President Wilson accepted an offer from the National Academy of Sciences, which had its roots in the Civil

War, to establish a Committee for the Organization of the Scientific Resources of the Country for National Service, whose purpose would be to "bring into cooperation government, educational, industrial, and other research organizations with the object of encouraging the . . . use of scientific research in the development of American industries, the employment of scientific methods in strengthening the national defense, and such other applications of science as will promote the national security and welfare."[3] The National Research Council, as the committee came to be known, recruited its members from the government, military, universities, private research laboratories, and corporations. Its establishment marked a significant step in both the relations between government and universities and in academia's relevance to mainstream society.

During the Great War, Furman University, an all-White male institution tied to the South Carolina Baptist Convention, was by virtue of its location an integral part of the city of Greenville's identity and culture. From 1851 through the late 1950s, the campus was located downtown on the banks of the Reedy River, blending seamlessly with the cityscape.[4] The university also hosted the Furman Fitting School, a high-school-level preparatory institution that offered military instruction. Although Furman discontinued the Fitting School in 1916, its graduates were considered "Furman Men." Less than two miles away, the university's sister institution, the Greenville Woman's College, enjoyed a similarly enmeshed relationship with the city.[5]

Six weeks before the government declared war, Furman's student newspaper, the *Hornet,* exclaimed, "We are not worried at all over any conditions as long as we have Woodrow Wilson as president. We are backing you, Mr. Wilson, do what you think is best."[6] Though the Adelphian Literary Society sponsored debates on whether or not Germany's unrestricted submarine warfare should be tolerated, articles in the *Hornet* and the *Furman Echo,* a student literary magazine, overwhelmingly supported Wilson and US involvement, which increased in fervor during the spring of 1917.[7]

On the day that Wilson asked Congress for a declaration of war, a group of students met to discuss how the war effort might impact them and what their particular roles should be. They exhibited a fiery dedication to the war cause, and their sentiments reflected the South's venerated martial tradition.[8] After a short discussion, the students drafted a letter to Wilson, proclaiming two days before the congressional declaration of war that the Montague Hall company of 55 Furman men—a significant percentage of the 235-member student body—was ready to give themselves to the service of the US military, in whatever way the president saw fit.[9] The next day, the *Hornet* advertised: "Do you belong to the Montague Hall Military Company? If not, join today."[10] The men of Montague

"A University or a Training Camp" 145

Hall immediately began to train and drill so they could more easily transition to combat readiness. The enthusiasm displayed by students at both Furman and the GWC reflected the attitudes of many Greenvillians.

Just two weeks later, the *Greenville Daily News* published mention of "compulsory" military training of the student body on Furman's campus, an apparent direct order of the administration that students must participate in calisthenics and drilling routines.[11] By May Furman students were actively readying themselves for service: a large group voluntarily hiked ten miles up nearby Paris Mountain and held a military-inspired scrimmage before hiking back to campus. The *Hornet* claimed that these men were "foot sore yet happy" and that "discipline was as good as any military school could have had."[12]

The US government, however, felt strongly that students should remain enrolled. The Selective Service Act, signed into law by Wilson in May 1918, required men twenty-one years old and older to register with the federal government.[13] While the US government realized the necessity of having educated officers to lead the AEF, they also sought a balance between the urge to send trained, learned minds into a high-casualty war and the necessity of withholding a portion of the formally educated so that future generations would not be stunted by a dearth of college-educated men. Furthermore category 5 of the Selective Service Act deemed ineligible any "student who on or before May 18, 1917, had been preparing for the ministry in a recognized theological or divinity school." Though Furman did not qualify as such, the university emphasized theological education, and many of its graduates became ministers.[14] The *Hornet* discussed the difficult decision of sending the "educated leaders of our future" into the trenches overseas and the impact that this potential loss could pose to the future of the nation.[15] University administrators endorsed the government's strategy.

On April 19, the *Hornet* reprinted an article from the University of South Carolina's student newspaper, the *Gamecock,* that included Gen. Leonard Wood's advice to students: "Tell your young men to stick to their present duties until such times as the government calls for men. . . . The most important service men can render their country now is to stay at their university and put in all the time possible under a military instructor in preparing themselves for probable service. There is no reason whatsoever for the men discontinuing college work until the government plans are definitely announced."[16] Wood's counsel reflected general government policy, which looked toward an orderly schedule of conscription that would more deliberately select men for military service without jeopardizing entire age or occupational groups. Such a strategy would not only guard against depleting the nation's brainpower but also avoid drafting too many African Americans and thereby upset the racial balance of the armed forces. Through the machinery of conscription, local draft boards would be able to curate a balance of men drafted from different ages and occupations, thus enabling certain vital industries to function without interruption. Such was the case with college men, who were already volunteering in large numbers due to the effectiveness of the Plattsburg Movement, the first volunteer officer training camp established in 1915. In April 1917 President Wilson, attempting to check the unrestrained volunteering of men, said, "Our object is a mobilization of all the productive and active forces of the nation and their development to the highest point of co-operation and efficiency . . . the volunteer system does not do this. When men choose themselves, they sometimes choose without due regard to their other responsibilities."[17] Later in May, Wilson reiterated his views that the draft should restrain the disorderly aspects of volunteerism when he called it "the virtual assigning of men to the necessary labor of the country. Its central idea was minimal disruption of the industrial and social structure."[18]

Much later in the war, the *Baptist Courier,* the official publication of the South Carolina Baptist Convention, echoed a similar sentiment. The convention, the long-standing administrative body over Furman, recognized the patriotic fervor of the university's young men but attempted to discourage them from volunteering with reassurances that remaining in college would be the best way to serve their country. On August 1, 1918, at the height of American involvement in the war, the *Baptist Courier* stated, "We have no class of citizens who are more patriotic than students." The article then detailed the policy of the federal government regarding college men volunteering for war: "In accordance with the request of the War Department all students at the age of 18 and over will be urged to enlist with the United States Army. These men will be discouraged from volunteering and will be expected to continue their college courses until they reach the draft age. This new plan enables a student to pursue his studies peacefully in the calm assurance that he is doing exactly what his country wishes him to do for he is training his mind and his muscle in order to make his future patriotic service more efficient."[19]

Inherent in these national conversations about maintaining the wartime strength of the "industrial and social structure" and the need to preserve the nation's brightest young minds for the recovery and success of the nation after the war, was an emphasis on how and why the nation needed erudite, talented, and capable young men. An editorial in the *Hornet* outlined this anticipated need: "Indeed, we shall need well trained men at the battle's front, but we shall also need well trained men in the future to direct our government and to develop our resources in order to secure our future welfare. The loss of a million of our best educated young men would cause a great swoon in our future ability as a nation."[20]

"A University or a Training Camp" 147

Months later the Furman student newspaper ran a summary of an interview with Dr. E. H. Lindley, the president of the University of Idaho, who encouraged all young men who were able to matriculate into "some good college or university" so they could prepare themselves to be more useful if called into service and, if not called, could better contribute to the "inevitable demand for well-equipped men to restore the world after the war." He expressed his belief that the young man who "makes sacrifices in order to educate himself in reality performs as patriotic a service to mankind and democracy as he would be doing in khaki" and that "it is every whit as patriotic a thing for a young man to go to college today as it is for him to go to war." Continuing, Lindley argued, "This is a scientific war and the soldier with the untrained mind is just as much a liability as an asset."[21] He and other university presidents crafted the notion that higher education was an important means of serving one's country "for war service after the war."[22] Dr. Sidney E. Bradshaw, acting president of Furman and, ironically, a professor of German at Furman and GWC, mailed a circular letter that expressed similar sentiments and encouraged parents to keep their sons in school.

Debates about the role of wartime higher education highlighted the importance of these young men to the nation's future and presented the decision to remain enrolled in college as an important and strategic means of protecting the national interest. They also effectively bolstered the gravitas associated with a university education. As Levine has argued, "In the public eye, World War I transformed the college student from a frivolous young fellow into a prospective leader of society."[23]

Despite the admonitions, some Furman men still chose to volunteer for the various branches of the US military, bypassing the system of enlistment, which only registered them for the draft and carried no guarantee of active duty. Within days of Congress's war declaration, when some National Guard units were mobilized, twelve students who had recently joined the Butler Guards, South Carolina's National Guard unit, boarded a train for Camp Moore (more commonly known as Camp Styx) in Lexington County, South Carolina. The students were but a dozen of the 147 young men who departed from Greenville for the camp, and their departure prompted a spirited show of pride from Furman's Montague Hall Military Company, who gave "yell after yell" for their former classmates. Their departure was also heralded by family, friends, and a veteran of the Civil War, who said that "it reminded him of another morning more than half a century ago when Greenville's gallant youths . . . waved farewell to home and dear ones."[24] An editorial in the local newspaper lauded the Furman students' eagerness to serve: "They will prove themselves worthy successors of the large body of the sons of Furman who heard their country's call in the War Between the States and the Spanish-American War."[25] The sense of patriotic devotion shines through in letters written back home. Furman student Carl V. Wilkes mused, "Since I first donned the uniform of my country I have longed to get nearer and nearer to the front. So you can understand that I felt a keen sense of pleasure as the Statue of Liberty gradually sank into the turbulent waters." A letter from classmate Lt. H. R. Drake revealed his perspective as a student-athlete whose closest life experience was playing football: "I don't see how any boy who is able to fight could be satisfied anywhere except in France now when we have such a big game on. Sometimes I think it amounts to more than licking Wofford on Thanksgiving, if such a thing were possible! Judging from the training that we are getting the United States must think it more important, for football training was nothing compared with this training. If we do not account for some Huns it will be our own fault and not the fault of the coach nor schedule of training. . . . I would give up almost anything to get up to the front."[26]

Colleges and universities experienced substantial decline in enrollment between 1915 and 1918, prompting great anxiety among administrators. During the 1910s most American institutions of higher education had fewer than three hundred students; the war, wrote Levine, "threatened college after college with extinction."[27] In 1917 Furman's enrollment stood at 235 students, but it dropped to 164 the following year. The president of Indiana University informed President Wilson he would close his institution if necessary, and when the University of North Carolina had nearly 1,200 students and alumni enlist by the spring of 1918, a telegram from Wilson was required to dissuade President Edward K. Graham from joining the military himself. In Chicago a group of concerned educators established the Emergency Council on Education, a wartime collaboration of fourteen national academic societies, which became the American Council on Education (ACE) and initiated the national "It's Patriotic to Go to College!" campaign.[28] These national societies, which included the AAU and the American Association of University Professors (AAUP), represented teachers and scholars who contributed significantly to the war effort, most notably, according to the AAUP, as soldiers, sailors, physicians, medical researchers, chemists, physicists, interpreters, and athletic directors. The American Library Association, Bureau of Public Information, Food and Fuel Administrations, National Council on Defense, Red Cross, State Department, War Department, and YMCA, among others, relied on the expertise provided by the faculty of America's colleges and universities.[29] Though established as wartime entities, both the National Research Council and ACE became permanent even before war's end.

Institutions that focused on agriculture and engineering were the hardest hit, while liberal arts colleges, which attracted students from higher socioeconomic

"A University or a Training Camp" 149

backgrounds, were affected the least, though this was due largely to the increase in women's matriculation at these institutions.[30] As all-male institutions, Furman and Wofford College in nearby Spartanburg did not benefit from this national trend.

The "salvation" of many colleges and universities was a program that turned college and university campuses into "military reservations." A brief experiment of the federal government that began in the fall of 1918 at 530 colleges and universities across the nation, the SATC was a department of the US Army designed to train college students to be more readily prepared to enter combat. Unlike the Reserve Officers Training Corps, which the army had begun just a few years prior, SATC members would have active, not reserve, status. The program was available to all colleges and universities, including historically Black colleges and universities, so long as at least a hundred able-bodied men over the age of eighteen were enrolled. Colleges and universities, which would "revise their curricula according to the dictates of the War Department and otherwise share their authority with military commanders," participated voluntarily, as did students.[31] An advertisement for the fall 1918 session detailed the benefits of the SATC at Furman: "Students eighteen and older become soldiers of the United States Army and will receive military training, educational instruction, housing, subsistence, uniforms, and the pay of privates—all at Government expense."[32] The program effectively boosted the numbers of students in the nation's colleges and universities, with estimates suggesting that between one-third to one-half of those enrolled would not have done so without the benefits and opportunities the SATC provided.[33] At Clemson College in nearby Pickens County, the fall semester opened with five hundred SATC students and two hundred non-SATC students. At some institutions, such as the University of Illinois, enrollments for the 1918–19 year not only recovered but also set new records, while the student body enrollment at Hampden-Sydney College in Virginia almost doubled between the winter of 1917 and the fall of 1918.[34] Thirteen colleges and universities in South Carolina coordinated with the SATC, either by hosting an Army, Navy or vocational detachment, or by sending a small group of students and faculty to an instruction camp.[35]

This cooperation between the federal government and institutions of higher education highlighted their mutual lack of commitment to equal opportunity for African Americans. In response to problems at universities in Ohio, Pennsylvania, and Nebraska, in which young African American men hoped to take part in SATC units at predominantly White colleges and universities, the War Department publicly stated that there would be "no distinctions made in race, color, or creed."[36] Col. Robert I. Rees, chairman of the War Department's Committee on Education and Special Training, which administered the SATC, declared: "No color line will be drawn in inducting men into the S. A. T. C. Colored men eligible for induction will be inducted at institutions which they attend and will not be required to transfer to other institutions."[37] Yet the agreements between the institutions and the military placed the responsibility and jurisdiction of admissions entirely in the hands of college administrators. At the Ohio State University, African American students who were already enrolled were denied admission into their campus SATC, prompting the involvement of the Cleveland and Columbus chapters of the NAACP. The War Department reaffirmed its position: "The War Department has not issued any instructions preventing Negro students from joining Student Army Training Corps at Ohio State University or any other institution. Any student mentally and physically qualified and accepted by the school officials is eligible for admittance into any Student Army organization."[38] NAACP executive secretary John R. Shillady argued that "the War Department has made no ruling requiring a separation of colored and white students in barracks or dormitory arrangements in the colleges, and that the acceptance of a student by a college under the terms and conditions usual to such colleges qualifies the student for admission to the Students' [sic] Army Training Corps provided he is able to qualify." Shillady hoped that his communication would serve as a deterrent to other universities who refused SATC admission to their African American students. So while the War Department would not "introduce the color line into those schools where it is not already drawn," according to Scott, they also "did not seek through its program to break down the color line in any institution where it was observed."[39]

Not surprisingly, southern colleges and universities maintained strict racial segregation. In his autobiography, *An Educational Odyssey,* Wofford College president Henry Nelson Snyder recalled a captain who needed to affirm to his superiors in the War Department that Wofford's SATC would make "no distinction . . . in race, color, or creed." His response to the captain offered a reminder that apparently "much relieved" him: "Certainly, Captain, but remember, all applicants must first be approved by this office."[40] Furman's status as an institution exclusively for White men was similarly protected by the power that college admissions offices retained through affiliation with the War Department.

The SATC's presence on college campuses began in late September 1918 and dramatically boosted the enrollments of participating institutions. The student bodies of Emory College in Atlanta and Alabama Polytechnic Institute (now Auburn University) increased by approximately 30 percent, with Alabama Polytechnic's SATC the largest in the South at 1,280 members.[41] This wartime aberration also significantly altered the daily routine of its members, who had previously been civilian students. The *Hornet* introduced Furman's SATC leadership on

"*A University or a Training Camp*" 151

October 4: "The Battalion is commanded by Capt. Harry Wilkins, a Citadel graduate. . . . The two cadet captains are James A. Richardson of Simpsonville commanding Company A, and M. K. Walker of Greer commanding Company B. The non-commissioned officers are about twenty in number and have had military training in various military schools throughout the state."[42]

Another *Hornet* article provides a detailed account of student life while the university was under at least partial control of the military.[43] At Furman, as with all SATC units, classes were rearranged to fit the system of military conscription as opposed to the traditional standing of freshmen through senior classes. The SATC structured classes according to "both age and standing" and issued a "prescribed course" to each student in addition to military instruction. The prescribed course was akin to a student's traditional academic major but determined by age rather than program of study.[44] Each institution retained the autonomy to determine which of its courses qualified for degreed programs. In an era in which many elementary and secondary schools canceled classes in the German language, the SATC encouraged the teaching of French and German. According to the 1917–18 and 1918–19 course catalogs, Bradshaw continued to offer such courses at Furman and GWC. Even before the official start of the SATC, director Richard Maclaurin wrote to all units, acknowledging that "the reorganization of curricula to meet the requirements of war training is obviously a problem which requires a period of constructive experimentation at educational institutions in close cooperation with the War Department."[45] Days later an article in the nearby *Keowee Courier* acknowledged that "the War Department having taken over the college and prescribing the course of instruction, the schedule committee has found it hard to adjust matters, but has organized the classes far enough to allow the college exercises to begin to-day."[46]

At the nationally prescribed time of noon on October 1, 1918, on 525 college and university campuses around the nation, the SATC simultaneously inducted 140,000–200,000 male students. A small number of colleges and universities were forced to delay their induction ceremonies; while their fellow SATC members were starting to learn to fight, others were under quarantine due to influenza, thus battling a global threat of an entirely different order.

At Rice Institute (later Rice University) in Houston, the president proclaimed, "'Go to college!' 'Return to college!' are not the mere seasonable exhortations of college president: they are governmental slogans."[47] Despite the quarantine in place at Furman and at Camp Sevier but not yet in the city, 250 Furman students took an oath of allegiance to the American flag on the library steps. The Fiftieth Infantry band from Camp Sevier played "The Star-Spangled Banner," and the local newspaper reported that the entire student body of GWC seemed present

152 "Our Country First, Then Greenville"

to support the men's commitment that, it surmised, "probably will take them to foreign fields for actual service in the cause of democracy." Acting president Bradshaw welcomed the crowd, which also included Greenvillians, before Prof. J. L. Yates and Prof. O. O. Fletcher presented comments. GWC president David Ramsay closed the ceremony with a benediction.[48]

The SATC imposed a rigid schedule. According to the *Hornet,*

> First call is at 6:30 am, then morning calisthenics, immediately into breakfast and morning classes at 8:30, then mandatory study time in the library or vacant classrooms, classes end at 12:30 and chapel is held from 12:30 until 1:00. The men then have lunch at 1:20, and drills afterwards until 3:30 in the form of squads, platoons, and companies. The drills are made up of strictly movement practice, and "no guns nor other ordnance equipment have been issued and this part of training has yet to be begun." There is leisure time from 3:30 until 5:50, when men are called for retreat and must be in their best clothes with shoes shined, etc. to the standards of the US military. They march double file into the dining room for dinner, and then have another study period from after dinner at 7:30 until 10:00pm, when taps is blown and the men go to bed.

The article continued, "We only hope the war don't get over before we get to do our share in France."[49] The writer's hopes were not granted. Even though he prepared his piece before the declaration of the armistice, it did not appear until a week after hostilities ceased.

The SATC experiment lasted only a few months but extensively, albeit temporarily, restructured American higher education. Wofford's President Snyder observed that the military officials and faculty commonly expressed the sentiment, "You won't know your college when this war is over."[50] One Furman student later noted the added complexities introduced by the influenza pandemic: "The first thirty days of the S.A.T.C at Furman were rocky ones. On the very first day the unit was organized there was a siege of the influenza epidemic, and the next day a quarantine was put upon the entire school."[51] At America's larger coeducational colleges and universities, the SATC effectively nullified fraternity life, with some fraternity houses converted to barracks, while female students were also expected to "obey military discipline as absolute duty," particularly regarding "hard work, punctuality, and curfews."[52] The chairman of the War Department's Committee on Education and Special Training, which administered the SATC, wrote that "there are no precedents to guide the colleges in this work and hence they have the finest possible opportunity for the exercise of ingenuity and creative imagination."[53]

In October 1918, Furman students marched on campus during their brief enrollment in the university's SATC. Courtesy of Special Collections and Archives, Furman University.

Such ambiguity invited conflict and consternation. At Wofford College the SATC was "markedly less popular among Wofford administrators and students than the college's own military instruction." According to Snyder, the quality of the education provided at Wofford during this wartime aberration was "reduced to its lowest terms," though he was pleased with the impact that military discipline had on reducing swearing, particularly in front of visiting mothers, and increasing chapel attendance. Twenty years later Snyder considered the balance of his authority versus that of the army captain-in-residence and conceded that throughout the war he "was never quite sure just what were [the army captain's] relationships to the whole situation."[54] Furthermore the SATC suffered from logistical challenges. At Furman the SATC outfitted members in uniforms at Camp Sevier on November 5, 1918, less than one week before the Armistice, while at Illinois College, another private and denominationally affiliated liberal arts college, guns arrived just days before November 11, and uniforms afterward.[55]

Nationally the war and global influenza pandemic intensified discomfort with both foreign enemies and illnesses. Their confluence bolstered support for nationalist movements like "100 Percent Americanism," which increasingly promoted a nativist ideology in public elementary and secondary education and the military, especially after the government's bipartisan Dillingham Commission released its report in 1911, which recommended immigration limitations from specific regions and declared that certain immigrants posed a threat to the commissioners' White, ethnocentric concept of American culture. Americanism gained greater prominence during wartime, especially since one-third of the nation's population was either foreign born or descended from parents who had immigrated to America. In this time of hyperpatriotism and with government authority increasingly seeping into the educational sector, the SATC also provoked concerns about the loss of control over their institutions. The *Furman Bulletin,* published as part of the *Hornet,* remarked that joint oversight of the SATC left it crippled and largely ineffective and that it was collaborative only in theory. Furman's Bradshaw wrote, "The weak point in the system as applied, however, was the dual control, military and academic. In the last analysis, the real control was military."[56] Indeed a headline in the *New York Times* Current History series read, "The Government Takes Over the Nation's Colleges."[57] Concerns about encroaching federal control were compounded when, just days after the *Times* declared that "three hundred and fifty-nine colleges and universities [were] taken over by the Government!," Congress passed the Smith-Towner Act, which proposed a cabinet-level Department of Education and provided the first federal funds for public education. Some, such as the National Council on Catholic War Work's Monsignor Edward A. Pace, speculated that the SATC "is the first step towards federal control of all the schools." Both Catholic and Protestant-affiliated institutions like Furman were particularly alarmed, though some state-supported institutions also felt compelled to protect their autonomy. At the University of Illinois, Vice President David Kinley grew tired of arguing to protect "the dignity and rights of the University against the encroachments of military arrogance." According to scholar Benjamin Shearer, Kinley created an "index of grievances" from the "hundreds of complaints from virtually every academic department." Just over one month after the SATC began, and less than two weeks before the Armistice on November 11, the University Council of Administration at the University of Illinois passed a resolution opposing the policies of their campus SATC military commander.[58]

With the Armistice, SATC officials in Washington informed campus units that military instruction could cease at once or at the end of the term. Soon thereafter, between December 2 and 21, SATC units across the country were demobilized. Wofford students met the end of the SATC with great celebration. An article in the *Wofford College Journal* criticized the SATC's use of discipline while lauding the ways that Robert E. Lee was able to maintain discipline among the ranks of his volunteer army.[59] At Furman, Bradshaw recalled that "the academic work accomplished in the fall term was practically nil" and that disciplinary problems arose from liberation of the "military 'lid' from repression."[60] The next month the War Department reestablished the ROTC, which had begun in 1916. Despite Wofford's challenges, President Snyder applied and received a ROTC chapter in

"A University or a Training Camp" 155

1919. It struggled in the early 1920s due to "a psychology hostile to military training" among the students but gained solid support by 1926. The University of South Carolina's ROTC unit confronted similar difficulties; administrators decided that its program was "inconsistent with the traditions of the university" and ended it on the Columbia campus in 1921.[61] Though Furman's acting president Bradshaw supported the notion of a unit at Furman, it appears that his successor, William J. McGlothlin, did not entertain the idea until the early 1930s, possibly in response to financial challenges precipitated by the stock market crash in 1929. McGlothlin's attitude reflected a postwar "anti-military sentiment" that many SATC institutions harbored, compounded by a growing national sense of isolationism due to war and pandemic, concerns about federal control over education, and the downsizing of the peacetime standing army.[62]

Nationally the SATC was largely considered a failure. The AAUP "Report of Committee on Patriotic Service" from December 1918 concluded that "the general effect of the S.A.T.C. upon the educational life of the universities was injurious. A large proportion of the institutions confess to having difficulty with the military control. . . . Fraternity life has been almost destroyed. . . . The opinion as to whether military training should be established in universities is on the whole negative."[63] Furthermore the influenza pandemic and the fact that the Armistice occurred before the SATC effectively established itself limited its contributions to the military effort. Nevertheless the young men who trained with wooden guns, drilled on the Furman baseball fields, and only occasionally visited nearby Camp Sevier were technically members of the US Army with "active" status. Thus they fall into the category of men who served militarily in WWI. Of the 190 enrolled Furman students who are credited with service in the US military, 126 contributed through their participation in the SATC.[64] There is no evidence that Furman's SATC program trained any officers who served overseas. Records suggest that sixty-four students left Furman to serve in the armed forces outside of SATC roles. Approximately 32 percent of Furman's student body actively saw non-SATC military service during the approximately eighteen months of America's participation in the war, and students on campus relished reading about their experiences, including those of students and former students like Lt. Hagood Bostick and Lt. John O. W. Donaldson, in the *Hornet*.[65]

Young men like Bostick and Donaldson who wished to serve in military aviation often sought service in either the British Royal Air Force (RAF) or the famous Lafayette Escadrille, a unit of American volunteers who served as fighter pilots under French command. Bostick, a Greenvillian who attended the Furman Fitting School, flew in the British Squadron of Rotary Motored Scouts of the RAF. Donaldson attended Furman from 1915 to 1916. He became an "ace" pilot in the RAF after shooting down seven enemy planes in two months, which won him a visit with King George V at Windsor Castle and decorations from Belgium, Great Britain, and the United States.[66] His letters home reveal multiple near-death experiences, and after the war his exploits were published in an article titled "My Capture and Escape" in *Harper's Monthly Magazine*.[67]

Overall 538 Furman men, including alumni and faculty, served in the war: 485 registered with the army, including the SATC, and fifty-three with the navy. Six Furman men perished: five died overseas, and one was killed in transport to training near Camp Jackson.[68]

After the Armistice, Furman students continued to focus on the meaning of the war. For several years they contributed opinion pieces in student publications about their war service, the victory of democracy over imperialism, the viability of the League of Nations—which they felt would succeed only if based on Christian values—and the United States' continued efforts to combat Bolshevism in the Russian Revolution. The idea that American leadership in the Allied victory over the Central Powers was the fulfillment of God's plan featured prominently in these writings. McGlothlin, Furman's new president, who had earned his master of theology at Southern Baptist Theological Seminary and his doctorate at the University of Berlin and even published a book entirely in German, *Die Berner Taufer bis 1532* (The Bernese Baptists until 1532), propagated a belief that institutions like Furman held an unusually important responsibility in the postwar era.[69]

McGlothlin derived benefit from Germany's defeat in promoting Furman, arguing that publicly supported colleges and universities were vulnerable to becoming pawns of the state. He cited the extreme nationalism that had recently "wrecked the world in the Great War" and proffered arguments that carved a special role for private institutions in the anti-German climate of the war and postwar years. In the wake of the SATC and Smith-Towner, the bill that proposed a federal Department of Education, his rationale appealed to those who criticized the Progressive Era trend toward increased governmental involvement in the nation's educational institutions as "Prussian" and even "Bolshevik." Private institutions, especially those affiliated with the Catholic Church and Protestant denominations, argued that they could ward against aggressive foreign nationalism and counteract its chaos in the world. McGlothlin was "convinced of the necessity of keeping Christianity and culture united, fearful of the neutral or secular education which was current and the apparently increasing neglect of and even hostility of Christianity in some higher educational institutions." Like many proponents of higher education nationally during the Progressive Era, he advocated for the increased relevance and involvement of American colleges and universities, especially Christian ones. McGlothlin felt that adherence to Christian values would renew humanity and civilization, proclaiming that "the supreme hour of the Christian school has come . . . it is my ambition to make Furman as good as the best."[70] His accomplishments throughout the 1920s capitalized on the area's wealth in the postwar years. Under his leadership Furman assumed a heightened stature, aided by the newly heralded role of American universities after the war.

World War I ushered in a new era for Furman and American higher education by creating and fostering pathways of collaboration between colleges and universities and the federal government, an exercise that would expand with greater success during the next world war. Furthermore the war was a watershed that propelled American colleges and universities to greater prominence; researchers and scholars collaborated with the government as never before, and as a result of a national mindset that prized university-educated young men and placed the nation's hopes for the future in their hands, a university education became a lauded and arguably necessary credential for those who wished to shape the postwar world. College and university enrollment rose 86 percent in the 1920s alone.[71]

chapter eight

Chaos and Confusion in 1918

The Influenza Pandemic in Greenville

Never a day passed that one or more funeral corteges did not wend their way down West Washington Street (where we lived) en route to the Southern depot where caskets were stacked like cord wood awaiting transportation home to loved ones.

—*Frances Marshall Withington of Greenville, South Carolina, 1918*

As the numbers of American casualties climbed due to the fighting at Cantigny, Belleau Wood, Chateau-Thierry, and Saint-Mihiel and in the US-led Meuse-Argonne offensive, one of the deadliest and most pervasive pandemics in world history infected an estimated one-third of the world's population, including American civilians and service men and women both at home and abroad. Recent epidemiological surveys estimate that the disease, known at the time as the flu, the grippe, or Spanish influenza, claimed between fifty and a hundred million lives globally in about eight months, a number much larger than the original 1927 estimate of twenty-one million.[1] The pandemic of 1918 is often cited as the greatest medical cataclysm in history; conservative estimates place the number of worldwide deaths from it at almost 5 percent of the world's population.[2] Among the most threatening and unusual aspects of this particular strain of virus was its attack more often on healthy immune systems than on weak ones. Col. Victor C. Vaughan of the Army Medical Corps, the head of the Division of Communicable Disease, described the threat: "This infection, like war, kills the young, vigorous, robust adults. . . . The husky male either made a speedy and rather abrupt recovery or was likely to die."[3] Influenza consistently infected young, healthy people, while leaving the old, weak, and infirm unaffected, and thus was exceptionally detrimental to the strength of communities and militaries the world over.[4] The devastation was compounded by several factors: in the United States, many of the nation's best doctors had been dispatched abroad; the government was slow to react to overcrowded conditions in military camps; the flu was difficult to diagnose, which often disabled swift, combative strategies; and finally the

Chaos and Confusion in 1918   159

belief that the flu was caused by a bacterium as opposed to a virus deemed efforts to develop an effective vaccine futile. Whereas the final estimated death toll from combat in World War I was twenty million, the Spanish influenza proved dramatically more lethal over a much shorter period.[5]

In November 1917 *National Geographic* magazine published an article that decisively declared that army cantonment sites were built, staffed, and adequately equipped to fight disease. It boasted that "each cantonment site has 1,000 hospital beds, and some have 1,600," and expressed confidence that there were "adequate provisions for emergencies." The Army surmised that in the camps, three hospital beds were sufficient for 100 men. The article informed readers that the hospitals had "the most modern laboratories" and "every kind of specialist." It concluded: "Disease shall not be permitted to play the role of ally to the foe."[6] Yet the next month Maj. Gen. William C. Gorgas, surgeon general of the US Army, issued a report citing 60 fatal cases of pneumonia at Camp Sevier, followed by 43 at Camp Funston and Fort Riley, Kansas, and 41 at Camp Bowie in Fort Worth, Texas. In nearly all measles cases, complications led to pneumonia, the leading cause of death in the United States until 1936.[7] At 2,900, Camp Bowie had the highest number of reported cases of measles nationally, followed by Camp Sevier with 2,000. These alarming numbers prompted a three-week-long quarantine at the camp from mid-November through the first week in December 1917.[8] From Camp Sevier, Paul Green wrote to his father, "We are quarantined for an indefinite period of time on account of measles, pneumonia, and meningitis. Many poor boys have died, as many as six in one night." He informed his papa that he had taken out an insurance policy for the benefit of his siblings, Caro and Erma. "You see there's no telling what may happen to me. This with the bonds takes nearly all my salary, but I'm wanting them to be sure of an education either way. Tell Erma and Caro I'm proud of them both."[9]

As temperatures dropped in the late fall of 1917 in Greenville, soldiers' anxieties about the spread of measles were compounded by worries about a lack of appropriate winter clothing. The soldiers at Camp Sevier were still wearing their cotton khaki uniforms and needed army-issued winter wear. On November 15, the day before the quarantine went into effect, every soldier was given an overcoat, and days later they received at least one set of winter underwear. Local volunteers with the Woman's Bureau of the Red Cross knitted sleeveless sweaters, mufflers, washcloths, bottle covers, and bed socks for them, and reports indicate that the combination of winter underwear, coats, and donated items greatly alleviated their discomfort. Still Gorgas, considered the "foremost authority on military hygiene and sanitation in the world" after his extensive experience battling yellow fever and malaria in Florida, Havana, and Panama, described his concerns

160 *"Our Country First, Then Greenville"*

about the outbreak of measles and pneumonia and the lack of winter wear at Camp Sevier in a December report.

> Sanitary conditions here are serious. Sixty men have died of pneumonia in the last month. . . . The basic unsanitary condition, however, in my opinion, is overcrowding. In the past, in this camp, the division commander has had to put eleven to twelve men in a tent, due to the shortage of tentage. At present he has to put nine men in a tent, which gives about twenty-eight square feet to the man. I urge that the division commander be directed to furnish at least fifty square feet of floor space to the man, which would give about five men to the tent. . . . There has been a good deal of discomfort and exposure on account of the men having nothing but their summer clothing. This has been in great part corrected in the last ten days by the arrival of woolen clothing and overcoats. The O.D. (olive drab) wool has not yet been issued, but the authorities are informed it is on the way. The whole command is still in khaki.[10]

In his book *The Great Influenza: The Deadliest Plague in History,* John M. Barry writes, "The winter of 1917–18 was the coldest on record east of the Rocky Mountains, barracks were jam-packed, and hundreds of thousands of men were still living in tents. Camp hospitals and other medical facilities had not yet been finished. An army report conceded failure to provide warm clothing or even heat. But most dangerous was the overcrowding." Dr. Vaughan later described the situation as "insane . . . how many lives were sacrificed I cannot estimate."[11] In an army medical report, Dr. Abraham Flexner, a pioneer in modern medical education and an experienced medical researcher, remarked that it "was as if the men had pooled their disease, each picking up the ones he had not had. . . . And greatly assisted by the faulty laying out of camps, poor administration, and lack of adequate laboratory facilities," the disease spread.[12] Dr. Vaughan attempted to warn the government of the dangers that mobilization imposed on the spread of the epidemic as thousands of men communally shared facilities in poorly sanitized camps but was rebuffed with this brusque response: "The purpose of mobilization is to convert citizens into trained soldiers as quickly as possible and not to make a demonstration in preventative medicine."[13] The *National Geographic* report had turned out to be grossly misleading, and the OD uniforms never arrived at Camp Sevier.

These conditions fostered the spread of not only measles but also the influenza virus, and like measles, pneumonia typically followed. The first mass outbreak of influenza in the United States occurred at Camp Funston near Manhattan, Kansas, where the camp hospital began receiving infected soldiers on March 4, 1918. By the end of the month, 1,100 troops required hospitalization.[14] Unsanitary camp

Chaos and Confusion in 1918 161

conditions, in which large numbers of men from different parts of the country lived and trained together, fostered the disease, making the extra-cantonment zones in the communities around these camps particularly vulnerable. Military mobilization, not only to other domestic training facilities but also overseas, provided the arteries through which the epidemic spread. Before what became known as the first wave of the influenza pandemic waned, two-thirds of the nation's army camps and over half of the country's fifty largest cities experienced alarming spikes in mortality rates caused by influenza and pneumonia.[15] In May 1918 Paul Green wrote that Camp Sevier was "under the strictest quarantine imaginable—almost. During the last few weeks not a man has been allowed to leave camp excepting married men, and they only for a short time."[16]

In mid-August newspapers around the country published reports of a renewed spike in influenza cases in Europe. Soon thereafter sailors returning from the Western Front disembarked in Boston and prompted a new and far more devastating wave throughout the United States and particularly through the military.[17] Maritime traffic channeled the virus to other ports along the Eastern Seaboard. On September 16 officials reported the first influenza cases in South Carolina at both the Naval Training Camp, located on the banks of the Cooper River in Charleston, and at Camp Jackson in Columbia. An editorial in the *Greenville Daily News* warned residents of the vicious virus by quoting Surgeon General Blue: "People are stricken on the street, while at work in factories, shipyards, offices, or elsewhere. First there is a chill, then fever, with temperature from 101 to 103; headache, backache, reddening and running of the eyes, pains and aches all over the body, a general prostration."[18] Nationally by September 23 over twenty-five camps had been infected, including Camp Sevier, which went under quarantine and reported its first cases.[19] The next day newspapers reported three thousand new cases at the camps, totaling twenty-three thousand. The Greenville chapter of the Red Cross received a telegram from division headquarters imploring all unemployed nurses to immediately enroll with the local Red Cross, and students at the Greenville Woman's College sewed more than a thousand mouth shields for Red Cross workers at Camp Sevier.[20] Eunice Mallon, whose husband was stationed at Camp Sevier, wrote in a letter on September 26 that for "the past two or three days, I have been working very hard at Red Cross Hdqgs. making face masks for the infirmary patients and attendants at Camp Sevier." She explained that they were made of "gauze[,] 5″ × 7″ or 8″, four fold, with tapes at the four corners."[21] The next day local newspapers informed readers that over 6,000 new cases of influenza had been counted at training camps nationwide, drawing the total number of those infected with either influenza or pneumonia to roughly 35,000.[22] At Camp Sevier that day officials reported 519 cases of flu. Only two

162 *"Our Country First, Then Greenville"*

days later, the report jumped to over a thousand cases; officials began to find it difficult, or perhaps fruitless, to maintain the latest count once the number of hospitalized men rose above 1,000.[23] As Major General Gorgas had observed, overcrowding in the hastily prepared tents at Camp Sevier was a serious problem, so the camp constructed new tents and drainage ditches. Camp expansion constantly sought to keep up with the medical need for personal space. In his surgeon general's report on Camp Sevier from November 1917, Gorgas had recommended a limit of five men per tent, yet in the early fall of 1918, Camp Sevier had tents that had been housing as many as eleven.[24]

Camp Sevier quickly became "an out of doors town," and soldiers took their "confinement to camp very philosophically."[25] Quarantine regulations at Camp Sevier prohibited soldiers from both leaving the camp and mass gatherings indoors. Military guards enforced these orders, as well as those that mandated that soldiers maintain a distance of at least five feet from each other when indoors.[26] Regulations did not prohibit contact outdoors, and doctors believed that proper nutrition, fresh air, and sunshine were the best remedies, as no vaccine existed for this particular strain. Chaplains held worship services outside. The YMCA hosted outdoor moving pictures. Coach W. L. Laval served as both Furman's football coach and the YMCA's physical director at Camp Sevier, where soldiers spent their afternoons playing football, baseball, volleyball, and other sports.[27] Though at least one of Furman's football games early in the season was rescheduled due to the quarantine, Furman played a team comprising members of the Forty-eighth Infantry at Camp Sevier in late October and won 26–0.[28] The 220th Field Signal Battalion traveled to play a football game against the Tigers from nearby Clemson College, and after the soldiers lost 61–0, they deployed a carrier pigeon to deliver the news back to camp.[29] In the vicinity of the camp, guards prohibited patrons from entering cafes and businesses, though they served food, drinks, and other items to customers outside.[30]

One soldier at Camp Sevier, J. C. Perrott of Company H of the Ninetieth Infantry, penned creative lyrics to the tune of the popular World War I song "Mademoiselle from Armentieres," more commonly known as "Inky Pinky Parlez-Vous." The lyrics to his version, titled "When You're Quarantined," lamented his boredom and confinement.

> Army life is not so sweet, when you're quarantined,
> To be free would be a treat, when you're quarantined,
> And you sit and ponder on, all the things you'd have done
> You're dead sure you'd have some fun, but you're quarantined.
> Every moment seems an hour, when you're quarantined,

Chaos and Confusion in 1918   163

And you wish you had the power, when you're quarantined
To take wings and fly away, where germs and Germans do not play
And right there you'd always stay, but you're quarantined.
You count the hours since it began, when you're quarantined,
And if they ever raise the ban, of the quarantine,
You vow you'll drill in rain or shine, you'll gladly make up for lost time,
You'll be the first one into line, out of quarantine.[31]

The song likely resonated with Perrott's fellow soldiers and perhaps even some local civilians.

On October 4, 1918, the *Greenville Daily News* reported that "the epidemic of Spanish influenza at Camp Sevier was believed yesterday by medical officers to have reached its crest and to have begun to decline, and it is now believed that the epidemic will very shortly play out."[32] Despite this optimism, with numbers rising every day, it was becoming evident that the epidemic had not yet crested. By October 6 nearly 50 victims had died from the disease at the camp, with 25 dying that day alone. With a bed count of 1,498, the hospital had 6,772 patients at its peak, with 66 medical officers, 692 enlisted men (assigned medical), and 142 nurses.[33] Several of the largest structures at the camp, including the Liberty Theatre and two of the YMCA unit buildings, became temporary hospitals when flu patients overwhelmed the base hospital.[34] The chief nurse at the Camp Sevier Base Hospital, Sayres Louise Milliken, described the dire situation: "At the peak of the epidemic at Camp Sevier, . . . about fifty percent of the nurses were off duty, sick, and the hospital contained about three thousand patients. . . . It became necessary to employ locally every nurse who could be secured. . . . The need was so imperative."[35]

Most of Camp Sevier's afflicted required medical attention in the late afternoons and evenings.[36] As has been affirmed by twenty-first-century chronobiology research, the natural narrowing of the bronchi that occurs at night was particularly difficult for those suffering from pneumonia. Two of Camp Sevier's victims were nurses at the base hospital, who had been "very faithful in their efforts to relieve the suffering of the sick soldiers."[37] Described as an "unusually popular woman," forty-one-year-old Alice Young of the Army Nurse Corps had received her training at the Ohio Valley General Hospital School of Nursing. Young died at 2:30 A.M. on October 4, while the next day, at 1:15 A.M., her colleague Stella E. Sanders of Nesbit, Pennsylvania, succumbed. Both of their death certificates cite bronchopneumonia, a form of pneumonia more commonly acquired in hospitals, as the cause of death. Young's body was transported to her hometown of Wheeling, West Virginia, where, in accordance with quarantine regulations, her

A group of Camp Sevier nurses was photographed outside the camp hospital. Courtesy, *Souvenir of Camp Sevier* in author's possession.

sister hosted a small, private funeral at home officiated by a local minister.[38] Young and Sanders were among the more than two hundred nurses in the ANC who died from influenza and pneumonia during the war.[39]

The stateside pandemic had serious repercussions for America's military preparedness and presence overseas. The flu hindered both the training of soldiers and the incorporation of new soldiers into the military. With numbers of sick troops climbing steeply and in anticipation of the Meuse-Argonne offensive, the largest American-led operation of the war, General Pershing beseeched President Wilson for reinforcements; his request was for 142,000 additional men between the ages of eighteen and forty-five to be drafted in early October.[40] However, as the flu continued to make its way through the camps, the dwindling number of uninfected men who would be available by the deadline was stretching the army's ability to fill this quota of new soldiers. On the evening of September 26, Wilson denied Pershing's requests. In his explanation to Pershing, Gen. Peyton March, the army's chief of staff, explained that "influenza not only stopped all draft calls in October but practically stopped all training."[41] Between September and November 1918, between 20 and 40 percent of American military personnel suffered from flu and pneumonia.[42] This shocking concession impressed the ferociousness of the flu upon the American public: France's terrifying trenches and brutal battlefields had become less deadly than America's military camps.

Beginning in late October, the US Public Health Service routinely tracked the cases of disease in the areas around the nation's cantonment sites. By October 26,

1918, the extra-cantonment zone around Camp Jackson had reported 7,656 cases, the highest number of influenza cases among the army camps in the state, followed by the zones around Camp Sevier with 3,316 and Camp Wadsworth with 1,172. After October 26 weekly statistics listed the number of cases reported over the previous seven days.[43] Greenville reaped both the economic benefits and the public health liabilities of having tens of thousands of men from all over the nation inhabiting their community, and their eagerness to support them likely fostered the pandemic. Some Greenville residents donated fruits, candies, and cigarettes that soldiers received through slits in their tents. These efforts during the quarantine supposedly "kept the donation buggy running on end for three days straight."[44] Furthermore, just a few days after officials placed a quarantine on the camp, the specifics of the mandate were amended so that the families of soldiers could go visit them. Nationally the Fourth Liberty Loan campaign began on the same day that Camp Sevier confronted over one thousand flu cases. Many cities around the nation, including Los Angeles, Nashville, Philadelphia, and Tampa, proceeded with loan kick-off parades that drew thousands despite the warnings. These gatherings soon propagated the spread of the flu. In Charleston the Board of Health considered war work "essential," so home solicitations and committee meetings continued throughout the quarantine.[45] Every day, Americans reassessed the tension created between a silent killer that necessitated stillness and solitude and the threat of a perilous enemy menace abroad that needed the nation to increase its industrial productivity and other home front aid.

The first cases of influenza among civilians in Greenville developed almost immediately after those at Camp Sevier, with the colleges affected early. Furman officials imposed a quarantine just two days into the fall semester in late September. Within days, writes Judith T. Bainbridge, thirty-five boarding students at GWC exhibited symptoms of influenza and had already overwhelmed the infirmary.[46]

South Carolina's college students and civilians were familiar with life under quarantine restrictions. Only seven months earlier, many South Carolina cities, including Charleston, Columbia, and Greenville, and colleges, including Furman, had been quarantined in response to an outbreak of meningitis. The ten-day quarantine in February 1918 closed schools, theaters, churches, and public gatherings. Furman's student newspaper reported, "We are all enjoying the light quarantine," but expressed hope that the restrictions would be lifted "so that we can rove the city streets once more."[47] Two months later Furman implemented another quarantine, this time for two weeks due to measles and mumps. At least two students were infected.[48]

Physicians believed that the Spanish Influenza could not be transmitted outdoors. In compliance with local regulations that banned indoor gatherings, the Rotary Club held its meeting on October 22, 1918, complete with lunch, on the rooftop of the Masonic Temple. Courtesy Rotary Club of Greenville.

Because of the quick spread of influenza, the South Carolina Board of Health ordered an immediate statewide general quarantine on October 7. The quarantine once again closed schools, churches, theaters, saloons, and other public places and discouraged overcrowding in businesses and public transportation. GWC and all other colleges and universities in the state followed the quarantine order.[49] An op-ed in the local newspaper acknowledged the "embarrassment and financial loss" but argued that "the public health is paramount. Such considerations are heavily outweighed by the protection and conservation of human life—the greatest wealth we have."[50] Superintendent of Greenville schools Dr. J. L. Mann issued a public statement encouraging a "backyard quarantine" for children.[51] In Greenville and Charleston, trolleys kept their windows open and limited the number of riders, though Dr. French Simpson, the US health officer for South Carolina, strongly encouraged people to walk to work.[52] Greenville County sheriff Hendrix Rector contracted influenza and described it as "the most persistent and insidious malady he had ever experienced." He encouraged Greenvillians to take the threat very seriously and lamented the loss of fifteen friends in Greenville and other counties.[53] Nationally some local health departments enforced anti-spitting laws and required citizens to wear flu masks. Surgeon General Rupert Blue also suggested that "public meetings [be] discontinued in all places where the malady becomes prevalent."[54]

The *Greenville Daily News* reported new cases each day. "Tuesday, October 8: new cases 300, new pneumonia cases 29, deaths 2; Wednesday, October 9: new cases 328, new pneumonia cases 40, deaths 7; Thursday, October 10: new cases 300, new pneumonia cases 29, deaths 5."[55] It killed quickly; victims suffered for a short as a few hours or as long as several days. Healthy individuals could wake in the morning and die by nightfall. Greenville's City Hospital was inundated.

Chaos and Confusion in 1918 167

Communities struggled to produce enough coffins, and some resorted to mass graves. Vaughan agonized over the mortality rates and surmised, "If the epidemic continues its mathematical rate of acceleration, civilization could easily disappear from the face of the earth."[56]

The vitality of communities across the nation was hit particularly hard. Pandemic fears prevailed, and anxiety and isolation stifled both home front morale and local economies. To address heightened needs, City Hospital more formally incorporated the efforts of its female supporters by creating a Woman's Board of the City Hospital, which included Flora Dill, Margaret Parker, Lou Woodside, and others.[57] At Buncombe Street Methodist Church, church leaders had a difficult time securing a volunteer willing to collect church dues during the winter of 1918 quarantine. Eventually at least one stalwart congregant, a Ms. Johnson of Lavinia Avenue, bravely began making door-to-door contact with possibly infected individuals in order to collect the monies needed to support the church. During this time the Buncombe Street church also lost their presiding elder, Rev. R. E. Turnipseed, to the Spanish flu, and Sunday school had to be suspended during the fall and winter because of the epidemic.[58] While the Spanish flu took its toll on church administration, this sort of disruption of daily lives happened all over Greenville, where shops closed for days at a time and fearful individuals, sick or not, would lock themselves in their homes to avoid exposure.[59] In addition to serving local civilians, Thomas McAfee's funeral home on South Main Street had a contract with the military to embalm the bodies of troops who had died at Camp Sevier. They and their casket makers were unable to fulfill such unprecedented demand.[60] Architect Joseph G. Cunningham, whose firm F. H. and J. G. Cunningham had designed St. Paul's Methodist Church (1909) and the Imperial Hotel (1911), contracted a mild case of the flu and was eager to return to work. In 1918 he and his brother Frank had recently built two cotton mills in Greenville, the Saluda and Okeh mills, and were serving as the treasurers of the manufacturing companies associated with the mills. Every day, to deter him from leaving, his wife, Beulah, simply pointed outside their home on East Park Avenue near Springwood Cemetery, where the daily transport of the dead passed.[61] Cunningham lived and, throughout the next several decades, built some of Greenville's most noteworthy structures.

While the government had gone to great lengths to keep the nation's best-educated men in colleges and universities, reserving their talents and capabilities for social and economic recovery after the war, it could not protect them from this virulent threat. Young adults, who generally fare better than senior citizens or children during pandemics, were ravaged by the disease.[62] Thus the primary demographic of the military camps and the backbone of civilian communities alike were devastated. Children died at twenty-two times the usual death rate, leaving behind emotionally shattered parents.[63] This disease, which could tear through populations of otherwise strong, healthy young people, shook communities to their core. Medical staff reported deaths, and though the State Board of Health in South Carolina maintained records, accurate estimates were rare. This inaccuracy stemmed from missing and incomplete population and medical records—and from the ambiguous set of symptoms through which influenza manifested itself. Influenza victims suffered from fever, severe headache, body pain, coughing up of blood, and nose bleeds. The Spanish influenza was extremely effective at drowning its victims to death in their own fluids. Lungs filled with fluid to the point where victims became "cyanotic" and turned blue-gray as a consequence of low oxygen saturation in the skin tissue. People began to doubt whether this new pandemic was just "the old Spanish grippe" or if it was a reincarnation of a far deadlier disease. Confusion and misinformation convinced many that the black and blue appearance of Spanish flu victims signaled a return of the bubonic plague. These assumed symptomatic parallels with the infamous "Black Death" heightened fear and confusion in an already war-weary Greenville. Medical professionals attributed deaths to a wide range of other afflictions, such as pneumonic flu.[64] In the twenty-first century, as epidemiological methods for disease modeling have advanced, research illuminates the full grim reality imposed by the influenza outbreak, and the number of deaths attributable to the 1918 pandemic has been revised dramatically upward.

Volunteers did what they could to help. The upsurge in Red Cross membership and volunteers that occurred nationally in the months after the United States joined the war proved critical. On October 8, 1918, Red Cross chapters across the nation received instructions on how to help combat the flu. The Red Cross issued a call for volunteers to "assume the management of the household" in homes where mothers and housekeepers were sick.[65] In response to greater needs and in the absence of medical professionals who were serving the war effort, Greenville's Red Cross joined the national effort to contribute health care workers and supplies. S. A. Darrach, field director of the American Red Cross chapter stationed at Camp Sevier, led an effort to distribute sweaters, wristlets, helmets, mufflers, socks, and other warm woolen garments knit by locals and students at GWC to more than eight thousand soldiers. The Red Cross offered classes in health care that included surgical dressing, first aid, and most important, elementary hygiene and home care of the sick.[66]

Neighbors also helped neighbors. In Brandon Mill, Jessie Lee Carter's mother frequently walked across the street to help a family with several sick members. "My mother was never afraid of the flu. . . . She said she know'd the Lord was

Chaos and Confusion in 1918   169

going to take care of her. If he wanted her to have the flu and died, that's the way for her to go."[67] The burden for care often fell on women. When Geddes E. Dodson's entire family contracted influenza, his mother continued to care for them in their home on Fifth Street in the Woodside Mill village: "We [all] had it, Mother and all of us. I remember we was all so sick, my mother just got up and went to waiting on us, giving us aspirins and hot lemon tea. I had a mattress on my bed, and I perspired so much till it went through the mattress and dripped on the floor . . . it was an awful feeling. We didn't know whether we was going to live or die. But the Lord was with us, and [H]e brought us through, every one of us. That was the rottenest sickness I ever had in my life."[68]

Misunderstandings regarding the nature of the disease spread like gossip. Chaos and confusion characterized public understanding. Rumors propagated the notion that the Germans intentionally dispersed the germ as a method of warfare. Nationally advertisements like "Warm Underwear Defies the 'Flu'" for Munsingwear undergarments; "Go to bed and stay quiet—take a laxative—eat plenty of nourishing food—keep up your strength—nature is the only cure" for Vick's VapoRub; and "Avoid Flu by sterilizing your nose" for Eucapine Salve purported remedies.[69] Physicians commonly suggested that pneumonic patients drink whiskey or brandy to fight infection. These were not legally available after the state voted to implement Prohibition in 1916, so state health officials worked with Governor Manning's office to supply Red Cross chapters across the state with limited supplies of confiscated liquor that were only available by prescription.[70] The distribution and effectiveness of alcohol as a treatment for pneumonia prompted vigorous debate among physicians in the state.[71] In an attempt to console those stricken at GWC, President David Ramsay knowingly told them that the virus attacked only the prettiest girls.[72] With a lack of strong knowledge about the disease itself, it became important to inform the public of the potential dangers of the influenza epidemic so that they could take responsibility for their own safety and protection.

People found themselves in dire need of accurate medical information—and of doctors and nurses. The war machine overseas had demanded medical personnel in huge numbers, producing a massive shortage of doctors, nurses, and other trained medical professionals on the home front.[73] Nearly 30 percent of physicians in the United States had entered into military service.[74] Particularly in Greenville, skilled medical professionals such as Dr. James E. Daniel left the city before the US declaration of war to serve in ambulance corps roles or work as physicians on the front lines in France.[75] In Greenville's Poe Mill village, thirty-one-year-old Naomi Sizemore Trammell suffered so badly she wished she would die. She recalls that an "old Doctor Walker" came to her house, since her regular doctor was serving in the military. Dr. Walker asked for some boiling hot water and a towel, and after submerging the towel, proceeded to wrap it around her head. She recalls that she "thought I'd die! He just pushed me down, he wouldn't take it off. I thought he's gon' burn me up. And he burnt that pain out of my head. That's what flu done to me."[76] No one could have anticipated that the need for doctors and nurses at home would eventually compete with the need for medical personnel abroad.

Doctors, nurses, and hospital facilities on the home front were overwhelmed. An editorial in the *Journal of the South Carolina Medical Association* opined, "At present time the physicians of South Carolina, in common with members of the profession generally throughout the country, are having their mental and physical energies taxed to the utmost through the unprecedented demands made upon them by the prevailing epidemic of influenza."[77] According to Dr. J. Decherd Guess of Greenville's City Hospital, who later wrote of his memories of the 1918 pandemic, "Doctors were worked to death."[78] When City Hospital became overwhelmed with patients from the camp and community, a home on Lawton Avenue nearby was repurposed for use as an influenza ward.[79] At least one Greenvillian resorted to placing an advertisement in the local newspaper: "Wanted—At once[.] [C]olored woman to nurse influenza patient. Phone 1347."[80]

Before World War I no African American nurse had ever served in the Army Nurse Corps, and the use of African American nurses by White organizations in any capacity during World War I was exceedingly rare. When war erupted African American nurses were effectively barred from service in the Army Nurses Corps and Navy Nurses Corps; one of the requirements was membership in a professional organization affiliated with and recognized by the recently established American Nurses Association (1896), which only permitted White members and affiliated with White organizations. Furthermore most southern states refused to grant African American nurses, even those whose training exceeded the requirements, the title of RN.[81] In this era of increasing professionalization, African American nurses developed their own organization, the National Association of Colored Graduate Nurses, in 1908. Beginning in April 1917, the organization and others persistently offered the services of African American nurses to the government. The surgeon general decided that African American nurses could join the reserve lists of the Red Cross, which served as the procurement agency for the Army Nurses Corps, but could not join the corps itself. The cause for their exclusion was the lack of segregated living quarters and mess for them at the camps.[82]

Yet African American nurses earnestly hoped to help those who were suffering and used the desperate need for medical personnel to their advantage.[83] The influenza crisis ultimately required a change in policy. In September the Red Cross placed two thousand African American nurses on active status. In *Torchbearers of Democracy,* historian Chad L. Williams argues that these women were utilized only out of necessity: "The Red Cross treated African American women particularly poorly, explicitly rejecting the volunteer services of Black nurses until the fall of 1918, when the influenza pandemic compelled a reconsideration of its policy. While Black women provided crucial assistance to Black soldiers, they did so while struggling against racism and sexism."[84]

Camp Sevier was one of very few training camps nationally to use the services of African American nurses. At Camp McClellan in Alabama, Camp Pike in Arkansas, and Camp Sevier, local African American nurses were recruited in the fall of 1918. It is not known if these nurses came from the Red Cross or if they were civilian nurses.[85] Milliken later credited a medical officer at the camp who was from the area for suggesting "that there were several good colored nurses who could be secured in the vicinity of Spartanburg, South Carolina." Approximately fifteen young African American women from the Birmingham area worked at Camp McClellan, while about one dozen Black nurses served at Camp Sevier. According to Milliken, initial discussion of the presence of Black nurses prompted opposition from the White nurses: "Fully seventy-five percent of the nurses were women of southern birth and had very positive objections to working with colored nurses." Nevertheless public health exigencies created an imperative need, and Milliken hired them. Milliken later described how the African American nurses "were assigned to the wards in the hospital in subordinate positions and with the exception of one or two who were not young enough to adapt themselves to the trying conditions under which everyone was working, these young women were found to be well-trained, quiet and dignified, and there was never at any time evidence of friction between the white and colored nurses. They served for a period of possibly three weeks."[86]

In addition to the local nurses used at these three camps, a small group of African American nurses registered with the Red Cross were sent to West Virginia to tend to the health of miners, as coal was needed for the war. Finally, due to pressure placed on the War Department from NACGN, civil rights leaders, and African American physicians and journalists, eighteen nurses were selected to join the Army Nurse Corps to ameliorate the shortage of heath care providers at Camp Sherman in Ohio and Camp Grant in Illinois, with nine nurses going to each camp. Because of delays of provisioning segregated facilities, they were not sent until after the Armistice, which also meant they would never receive any army benefits or pension.[87] The local African American nurses, Red Cross nurses, and those who were a part of the ANC were given separate quarters and utilized a mess segregated from the White nurses. Though African American nurses were also supposed to serve at Camp Dix (New Jersey), Camp Dodge (Iowa), Camp Meade (Maryland), Fort Riley (Kansas), and Camp Taylor (Kentucky), the cessation of hostilities nullified these plans.[88]

Despite historian Darlene Clark Hine's assertion that African American nurses suffered from a "triple index of inferiority" because of their race, gender, and the fact that they were not doctors, White superiors praised their work.[89] The chief nurse at Camp Grant described the nurses as "serious-minded, quiet, business-like young women, well qualified to wards, had our colored patients been segregated." Of the nurses at Camp Sevier, Milliken wrote, "Although these nurses had no opportunity to display executive ability, they did and can fill a valuable place in the nursing profession."[90] In the *Journal of the National Medical Association,* the primary publication of the African American counterpart to the all-White American Medical Association, Dr. John A. Kenney wrote more generally of African American nurses' contributions to the war, including those who served in African American hospitals during the epidemic: "In point of devotion, endurance, sympathy, tactile delicacy, unselfishness, tact, resourcefulness, willingness to undergo hardships—yea, in all that goes to make a good nurse, she has been found not one whit behind her white sister."[91] African American nurses were motivated by "the wartime experiences of African Americans [which] reinforced their determination to participate fully in both civilian life and as part of the military" and "understood their aspirations during World War I as part of a campaign for justice."[92] Although it took a medical crisis to force White leaders to concede their use, the persistent lobbying by African American nurses throughout the war yielded results that provided a foundation upon which to build in coming decades.

The pandemic dissipated by the end of October 1918. The crisis was far from over, with 4,642 cases reported in Greenville County in October alone, but the spirits of those in both the camp and community improved considerably when city, campus, and camp officials lifted quarantines.[93] The fall semester had been particularly trying at Furman, with the simultaneous implementation of the quarantine and the SATC. Furman officials lifted their quarantine on October 23 and resumed classes under the new SATC guidelines. The first issue of the student newspaper printed after the quarantine included an article that claimed, "there has been as many changes made at Furman since last session as in the entire sixty or more years preceding it."[94] After four weeks of closure, GWC administrators adjusted the academic calendar to ensure that students would receive the instruction necessary to complete the semester and that seniors would be able to graduate as planned. They added an additional day of instruction to the academic

Chaos and Confusion in 1918 173

week, postponed and shortened the exam period, and delayed and reduced the Christmas break to ten days.[95] On October 29, 1918, the mood at Camp Sevier was improved considerably by the removal of the highly restrictive quarantine. One soldier in training there, J. C. Perrot, was inspired to write a follow-up to the lyrics he penned during the quarantine. Also sung to the tune of "Mademoiselle from Armentieres," the song "Out of Quarantine" included the lines,

> Army life is gay again, we're out of quarantine,
> Just like sunshine after rain, we're out of quarantine.
> When night casts her mantle down, we're happy on our way to town,
> All are smiles, there are no frowns, we're out of quarantine.[96]

On November 3 Greenvillians were similarly ecstatic when the quarantine was lifted in the county. One week later, a soldier in the Forty-eighth Infantry stationed at Camp Sevier wrote a postcard to his family in St. Paul, Minnesota: "Last night I went to Greenville, the first time since the quarantine was lifted. We became so accustomed to staying in that one hardly desires to go away any more. But it does seem nice to be able to roam around some again. I suppose you had many flu cases up there, too?"[97] The next day spirits lifted even higher when soldiers and civilians in Greenville joined the nation in an even greater celebration.

The Armistice signaled the formal end of hostilities and coincided with the decline in influenza cases, yet the threat persisted. Lt. D. M. Wilburn, who had been a member of Furman's junior class in 1917, wrote to his former classmates that his company commander had died the past Monday and that his former "girl is in the hospital with the flu. She is not serious, but I don't like it one bit that she is in there."[98] Between November 2 and December 28, 1918, there were 1,399 cases at Camp Wadsworth, followed by 1,381 at Camp Sevier and 662 at Camp Jackson. The number of cases at South Carolina camps fell close to the median compared to other camps in the region. Camp Wheeler in Georgia had 3,060 cases during that same time frame, while McClellan in Alabama had 1,028.[99] New cases of influenza continued well into November and December. The week ending November 23 saw the highest number of new cases at 237. Over Christmas 1918 and through the last week of the year, 120 new cases developed. By the end of 1918, 7,944 cases of pneumonia and influenza had been reported in Greenville County, with 1,300 deaths, while between September 1 and the end of the war on November 11, 32,000 soldiers, both overseas and stateside, had died from influenza; nearly as many as died in combat during that same period.[100]

The camp and its base hospital remained active. Likely because of the extensive experience she gained during the pandemic, Chief Nurse Captain Milliken was promoted in December to assistant superintendent of the Army Nurse Corps

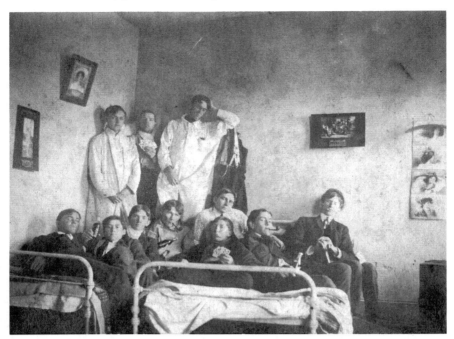

Between 1905 and 1920, Furman was quarantined six times on account of scarlet fever, measles, mumps, meningitis, and Spanish influenza. Here, Furman students under quarantine were photographed in 1906. Courtesy of Special Collections and Archives, Furman University.

in the Office of the Surgeon General in Washington, DC. Her attention shifted from the day-to-day health crises brought on by venereal disease, measles, influenza, and pneumonia to a more policy-oriented role, in which she lobbied successfully for a congressional act that granted retirement pensions for army and navy nurses. Milliken was also one of twenty-three nurses in the Army Nurse Corps to receive the Distinguished Service Medal, the highest noncombat decoration, after the war.[101]

In late January 1919, the third wave of the pandemic prompted quarantines in twelve counties throughout the state, including Greenville. The spread continued throughout that winter and spring but had subsided by that summer. It proved to be far less fatal than the second wave and was the final peak in what was arguably the worst pandemic the world has ever experienced. Smaller outbreaks persisted in subsequent years. Furman students were quarantined as part of the Greenville ordinance in January and February 1919 and again in January and February 1920, when officials placed Greenville and the university under quarantine during

Chaos and Confusion in 1918   175

yet another flu scare. In 1922 and 1924, county health officials affixed quarantine placards on specific homes, mostly in mill villages where unsanitary conditions persisted, in which residents were ill.[102]

On April 5, 1919, the hospital at Camp Sevier became US Public Health Hospital no. 26, under the auspices of the Public Health Service, and continued to serve primarily victims of influenza, tuberculosis, and severe respiratory problems brought on by exposure to poisonous gas. In May there were three hundred patients in the hospital, and by November, as a result of consolidation within the public health system, the patients numbered eight hundred.[103] The hospital operated as a tuberculosis facility until 1925.[104] Research on influenza vaccinations continued in earnest in the decades after the Spanish influenza pandemic. In the 1930s medical experts correctly identified the causative organism: influenza was a virus, not a bacterium. A 2010 study examined some of the bacterial vaccines from the 1918–19 pandemic and concluded that while none of them would have inoculated against influenza, some might have provided protection against the pneumonia that typically followed influenza and resulted in death.[105]

In reflections offered after the war and pandemic, Vaughan expressed gratitude that the death toll had not been higher since doctors "knew no more about the flu than fourteenth century Florentines had known about the Black Death."[106] These devastating times awakened a new sensibility and motivated Americans to improve access to quality medical care. In the summer after the pandemic, when local children prepared to begin the 1919–20 school year, the city enforced the vaccination record requirement as never before, and over the course of the next decade, Greenville's philanthropists, community volunteers, and businesspeople joined forces to open five hospitals and health clinics.

chapter nine

"Grow with Greenville"

Progressivism in the Postwar Era, 1919–1929

Telegrams raced across transatlantic cables by the thousands, crossing the vast ocean from Europe to the United States to deliver one of the most important messages of the century: on the eleventh hour of the eleventh day of the eleventh month of 1918, the Armistice of Compiegne ended the hostilities of World War I.

Later that day millions of Americans filled the streets of cities around the nation to celebrate the news with relief and joy. They brought to the festivities a repressed need for connection and a desperate hope for better days that had been cultivated by the October confluence of an isolating pandemic and the US offensive at Meuse-Argonne, the deadliest campaign in American history. Much of the country had just been liberated from quarantine, and many continued to wear flu masks in public. The war and pandemic had introduced uncommon fear and angst into American homes, and though many had lost loved ones, the announcement of the armistice alleviated much of the nation's distress.

New York City closed courts and schools in celebration of the news. In Los Angeles people took to the streets with "every noise-making instrument that could be secured." In the nation's capital, President Wilson "wildly cheered as he joined merrymakers." In Charleston's White Point Gardens, a segregated "victory sing" of the "Hallelujah Chorus" from Handel's *Messiah* lasted for much of the day. Charleston mayor Tristram T. Hyde encouraged "everybody in Charleston [to] lay aside all thought of business" and requested they "close their doors for the whole day [and] join wholeheartedly in the celebration."[1] Greenville greeted the news as American cities across the nation did, with a celebration that would be remembered as one of the greatest of that generation's lifetime.

Approximately thirty thousand people gathered in the streets of downtown Greenville to celebrate the momentous day. The city's afternoon newspaper, the *Piedmont,* released a special edition, with the word "Peace!" written in bold capital letters. Beneath it, revealing the area's strong Christian ethos, was a half-page image of Jesus Christ with the sun shining behind his head hovering above a city and the caption "Peace on Earth—Good Will to Men."[2] The *Greenville Daily News* reported on the thousands who "thronged streets and took part in rejoicing over "[the] peace news," including the men of Camp Sevier, who joined civilians in the festivities.[3] At Furman acting president Bradshaw granted the students' request to have the day off to celebrate but insisted on their attendance at chapel. Furman's SATC unit formed the company for a parade, marched down Augusta and Main Streets, and "with leather throated voices, made more fuss than any Furman student body ever has before. It was the greatest day of rejoicing that Furman has ever had the opportunity to engage in. . . . We were the first organization to celebrate victory on the streets of Greenville and our rejoicing was applauded by the crowds." Groups of locals joined them, with one gentleman loaning an American flag to the company. The parade continued onto the GWC campus, where the men performed marching drills in front of the cheering women, and when the parade recommenced, the women from the GWC marched at their side.

> Our course followed the route of Main Street to Washington, thence to Richardson, down to McBee Ave., back to Main, and then to the American Bank. . . . Every Furman lad had the pleasure of walking up Main St. with a girl at his side. It was probably the first time the people of Greenville had seen this stunt. . . . For the rest of the morning it was roses, roses all the way. . . . The parade finally ended at the GWC campus where we formed in a circle with the girls and all joined in singing the "Star Spangled Banner." . . . We have in the past week lived through the greatest period in history we shall probably ever experience.[4]

A few blocks off Main Street, Textile Hall served as a fitting nucleus of the celebrations. It "was jammed with celebrators, and thousands more stood in the street outside . . . waving flags, shooting fireworks, and throwing talcum powder . . . the stock of confetti having been exhausted." They made noise "with every device that human genius could devise" and embraced the end of one of the most terrible wars of all time.[5] The following Sunday local churches participated in "Peace Sunday," and several weeks later, on Thanksgiving Day, Greenvillians joined the nation in the Great National Liberty Sing.[6]

The Paris Peace Conference in January 1919 inaugurated discussions of the terms of peace, and in the spring and summer of 1919, US armed forces were demobilized. Families welcomed home their loved ones who had served, and Americans anticipated the return to the peaceful lives they had led before the war. A return to the antebellum status quo was impossible, however, as the Great War had introduced economic, political, and social changes throughout the country and particularly in Greenville.

Locally the war had aided the implementation of many advances associated with Progressive Era uplift nationally, such as Prohibition, woman's suffrage and other rights, better roads, city beautification, expanded access to electricity and clean water, inoculations from disease, improved healthcare, an awareness of the importance of literacy, improved educational opportunities, and the founding of community welfare organizations. Inspired by the local version of the Progressive Era, known as "the Greenville Spirit," the 1920s were a time of incredible growth in the city's population, infrastructure, civic organizations, and economic identity.[7] Despite the fact that the phrase "the Greenville Spirit" had been used for several years, an article in the Chamber of Commerce's new *Greenville Civic and Commercial Journal* in 1921 established its three tenets: "**Courtesy,** expressed and implied by ever individual citizen, . . . **confidence** in our city and in our people, believing both with all our hearts; and **Progressivism** in all things. Greenville's ideal? Here it is: Not only a larger city but a better city in which to live."[8] Richard Watson, who was mayor from 1923 to 1928, a graduate of Furman University, and law partner of suffrage supporter Congressman J. J. McSwain, helped shape many of these advances.[9]

Only four days after the Armistice was signed, a *Greenville Daily News* ad announced a "Greater Greenville" with the help of "every man, woman, and child." This ad was part of a series of "Grow with Greenville" campaign ads that aimed to generate pride and motivate residents to buy local goods, educate their children in Greenville, and take jobs in the flourishing city.[10] Greenville's civic leaders hoped to maintain the economic, population, and infrastructure growth that had been spurred largely by the war. From 1900 to 1910, the city of Greenville's population jumped just over 30 percent. The population doubled by 1920 and had nearly tripled by 1930. Greenville County experienced parallel growth, with a 29.4 percent jump between 1910 and 1920.[11] Its growth was similar to an increase in population statistics in nearby Columbia and Charlotte, which both increased more than 30 percent, and greater than Charleston and Atlanta, which saw a less than 20 percent increase. Though the overall population climbed in many southern cities, the war and resulting Great Migration of African Americans out of the South introduced monumental changes to the nation's racial composition.

In Greenville the percentage of African Americans as part of Greenville's total population declined steadily from 1900 onward. The actual population of African Americans in Greenville increased 12.5 percent in the ten years between 1910 and 1920, but that rate was slow when compared to the growth of the White population, which grew 37 percent and comprised 73.5 percent of the county's population in 1920.[12]

Greenville was growing quickly, yet White citizens found the community far more attractive than African Americans did. By 1930 the state switched from

"Grow with Greenville" 179

predominantly African American to predominantly White for the first time since 1810.[13] Despite the contributions of African Americans to the war effort on the home front and abroad, however, "the war in no way changed the attitude of the white man toward the social and political equality of the negro," Congressman James F. Byrnes of South Carolina later stated.[14]

Even before war's end, White southerners devised their strategy of intimidating returning African American soldiers who may have been emboldened by their experiences in the military abroad. In late October 1918, assistant secretary of the NAACP Walter White wrote to NAACP secretary John Shillady: "I have also become convinced firmly of another thing and that is that the Southern white man is totally and absolutely wrong in his idea of handling Negro Labor. He is attempting to use the old repressive methods that would have been successful forty years ago but are absolutely worse than useless today. One indication of this is the revival of the Ku Klux Klan, which white men have told me, indirectly, that is to be used to handle the Negro soldier after the war when he comes back with some 'new' idea of democracy."[15]

African American veterans were bolstered by their experiences during the war, motivated to pursue these "new" ideas, and emboldened to do so by African American leaders upon their return. According to historian Chad L. Williams, the 380,000 African American men who served became "self-conscious historical actors following the war" and assumed a distinct identity among the burgeoning Progressive Era concept of the "New Negro." In the May 1919 issue of the *Crisis,* W. E. B. Du Bois embraced the returning African Americans veterans and encouraged them to combat racism at home: "We return. We return from fighting. We return fighting."[16] Anticipating the success of the woman's suffrage movement, the *Crisis* also encouraged African American women to race to the polls and actively embrace the franchise once the federal amendment had passed, prompting Byrnes to lambaste the periodical on the floor of the US House of Representatives, in part because "it is certain that if there was a fair registration they [African Americans] would have a slight majority of voters in our state."[17] Byrnes's opposition to woman's suffrage was based in part on his desire to ensure a majority White electorate, which helped maintain the Democrats' stronghold on the region, and thus reflected the concerns of most of the White male state legislators.

White Americans' expectations of a return to the pre-war racial status quo clashed with African Americans' hopes for greater civil rights and economic opportunities. This newly emboldened African American identity threatened White hegemony across the nation and especially in the South, prompting a spike in race-based violence. "No Negro, much less the New Negro, was welcome," asserts

180 "Our Country First, Then Greenville"

historian Deborah Gray White, and "black soldiers were singled out for special brutality."[18] In 1919 nearly a dozen African American World War I veterans were lynched in uniform. Twenty-five race riots across the country between April and October left hundreds of African American and White people dead and injured.[19] Coinciding with the return of African American veterans en masse, the summer of 1919 became known as "Red Summer."

One of the first large-scale riots occurred in Charleston in May 1919 when a rumor circulated that an African American man had shot a White sailor in a pool hall at the intersection of Market and Beaufain Streets. White sailors and civilians attacked African Americans, and some returned gunfire when their businesses were attacked. The Marines detained all sailors and disarmed local African Americans. By that evening three African Americans were dead, with seventeen African American and seven White men wounded.[20]

Locally, in response to Red Summer, a small group of African American leaders, including Charles D. Brier, Reverend Rice, Reverend Burke, and E. B. Holloway, established the Negro Progressive League and began hosting biracial meetings in local African American churches for the purpose of "promoting friendship and understanding between the white and colored races." A biracial committee of five White leaders, five African American leaders, and the mayor serving as ex-officio was formed to jointly "consider questions looking to the peace and harmony of the races." These meetings often included White leaders such as Mayor Harvley, W. P. Conyers, and George W. Sirrine.[21]

Nationally the incidences of racial violence and the lack of a response from government officials prompted communication to Thomas R. Marshall, vice president of the United States, from the NAACP's Shillady, demanding due process and equal protection.[22] Issues of concern among African Americans were not on President Wilson's agenda, however, and Shillady's attempts to recruit assistance from the federal government were futile. The Ku Klux Klan had been reinvigorated in 1915 in Atlanta as an organization that supported "100 Hundred Percent Americanism" and opposed African Americans, Jews, Catholics, and immigrants. In its expanded focus, national appeal, public events, and massive membership base, it was distinctive from the Klan of Reconstruction. As scholar Kathleen Blee has written, "In areas of the United States in the 1920s, the Ku Klux Klan so dominated communities in which white Protestants were the majority that Klan life became inseparable from non-Klan life." Oral histories that Blee conducted with former members reveal that "the 1920 Klan is recalled by former members as an ordinary, normal, taken-for-granted part of the life of the white Protestant majority. . . . The mainstay of the 1920s Klan was not the pathological individual; rather the Klan effectively tapped a pathological vein of racism, intolerance, and bigotry deep within the white Protestant population."[23] Historian Linda Gordon claims that, in contrast to the earlier iteration of the KKK, "the Klan's program was embraced by millions who were not members, possibly even a majority of Americans. Far from appearing disreputable or extreme in its ideology, the 1920s Klan seemed ordinary and respectable to its contemporaries," with membership providing social and economic connections and opportunities that ushered some of its members into the middle class.[24]

Though the Klan had had a presence in Greenville and the surrounding area in the late nineteenth century, it did not reappear as part of this national resurgence locally until 1923, when one hundred men donned full regalia and marched down Trade Street in nearby Greer. Membership in Greenville's Klan increased throughout the mid-1920s and became a mainstream organization that held family picnics, coordinated with local churches and mill villages, and leased extensive space in two buildings downtown. In 1925 Dr. Hiram Wesley Evans, the Klan's imperial wizard, drew a gathering of nearly five thousand people to Greenville's City Park, where he proclaimed, "I come to South Carolina not to defend the Ku Klux Klan, for it needs no defense in a state where so many thousands of men in every walk of life are within its ranks and where it is doing great things." Later that year a large parade of Klan members paraded past the unofficial "Black Business District" downtown and burned an intimidating thirty-five-foot-high cross in the city's new Cleveland Park nearby. By the early 1930s, Greenville's klaverns were enmeshed with local law enforcement, who publicly acknowledged the Klan's efforts in investigating prostitution and Prohibition violations.[25]

Nationally many disparate groups supported a constitutional amendment for Prohibition, including the Klan, the WCTU, the Sons of Temperance, and others who favored isolationism and 100 Percent Americanism, as alcohol was closely associated with Catholicism and immigrant culture. South Carolinians had supported laws regulating and limiting the sale of alcohol since the 1870s; local option laws in the 1880s effectively paved the way for increased state and federal regulation, which was critical in a region long characterized by states' rights advocates and local autonomy.[26]

In a 1915 state referendum, White men in Greenville voted overwhelmingly to support Prohibition laws by a vote of thirty-five thousand to fifteen thousand.[27] The Eighteenth Amendment was passed in 1917 and ratified by two-thirds of the states in 1919. It went into effect nationally in January 1920 and was heralded by Greenvillians, who drank lemonade to celebrate its implementation. Though it had been supported on paper, South Carolina historian Walter Edgar argues that in practice, "prohibition was as big a failure in South Carolina as it was everywhere else."[28] Prohibitions on the manufacture and sale of alcohol gave rise to a bootlegging black market of "bathtub gin," "corn likker," "white lightning," and "moonshine" that was often speedily transported throughout the "Dark Corner" of South Carolina, giving rise to the beginnings of stock car racing as sport.[29]

While White southerners often supported the Klan and Prohibition, most decidedly opposed woman's suffrage, as the movement prompted fears about the region's ability to maintain White supremacy. After the Armistice the suffrage movement refocused and capitalized on President Wilson's recent endorsement of woman's suffrage as a war measure. The SCESL, which had canceled its 1918 convention because of the war, met in Columbia in January 1919 with twenty-two delegates. They sent a telegram to President Wilson expressing their collective support for the proposed Nineteenth Amendment and elected Eulalie Chafee Salley of Aiken as their president. Salley, a successful real estate broker, was known for her innovative tactics; she had once chartered an airplane to drop suffrage leaflets.[30] The next month more than two dozen members of the National Woman's Party who had been jailed embarked on a fifteen-city national "Prison Special" train tour in which they donned their workhouse uniforms and performed songs sung while imprisoned. The first stop on their tour was Charleston, where they attracted a crowd of three thousand at the Academy of Music on King Street. The next day the group split, with some, including Anita Pollitzer and NWP co-founder Lucy Burns, traveling to host an outdoor event on Main Street in Columbia. The Prison Special sparked the most intense divide in the movement's history in South Carolina, and NAWSA members desperately sought to distinguish between themselves and the women of the NWP. The *Bamberg Herold* wrote, "We no more believe they represent South Carolina womanhood than we believe it would snow in July."[31] Under the headline "Lunatic Women Injure Cause," the *Sumter Watchman and Southron* informed its readers that "the members of the Columbia Equal Suffrage League are about the maddest people in town today. . . . They say that much of the work they have done in months has been killed by the visit to this city yesterday of a bunch of militant suffragists."[32]

As more and more states ratified the Nineteenth Amendment, members of the state's small suffrage movement campaigned vigorously throughout the rest of that year. Unsurprisingly, in late January 1920, the men of the state legislature voted down the Anthony Amendment, with debates centering on concerns about increased federal interference in the state's voting practices and the impact that would have on the state government's ability to maintain African American subjugation. In *Entangled by White Supremacy*, historian Janet Hudson argues that "the opposition of so many white South Carolinians to woman suffrage revealed the depth and breadth of their commitment to both patriarchy and white supremacy." Politicians in South Carolina "defended the state's right to decide voting questions since such control allowed South Carolina's white men the maximum leeway in disenfranchising unwanted participants," like African American men and women.[33] US Senator Cole Blease, the former governor, later clarified his position on suffrage for women, arguing that he and most of his fellow politicians from the state "weren't voting against women's suffrage. They were voting for states' rights, that which every honest white-faced South Carolinian stands for."[34] Despite repeated efforts to appeal to White Lost Cause devotees between 1895 and 1920, which included highlighting Confederate veteran Robert Hemphill's support of suffrage at the 1895 constitutional convention and efforts by Vaughan to appeal to Confederate veterans and their descendants in the UDC, the mantle of states' rights that had been introduced in sectional debates before the Civil War continued to serve as the political justification for racial prejudice throughout World War I and for decades beyond.

The experience of woman's suffrage in South Carolina illustrates several arguments relating to southern Progressivism. First, Vaughan's criticism of state suffragists as "not well organized" supports claims that southern Progressivism was a less developed version of Progressivism nationally, especially in the Northeast. Second, Blease's comment reveals the extent to which concerns about maintaining White supremacy shrouded nearly all progressive reforms in the region. Third, it reinforces the notion that a southern tendency toward local and state autonomy conflicted with many progressive efforts. Finally, the suffrage movement in South Carolina after 1890 supports both historian C. Vann Woodward's assertion that southern Progressivism was "for whites only" and the national description of activists as urban and middle class.[35]

In early June members of the SCESL received a letter in the mail signed by Harriet Powe Lynch, Salley, and other leading suffragists. It included a clarion call: "Suffragists, hear this last call to a suffrage convention! . . . This time we are called together to rejoice over our victories and over the fact that the dreadful struggle for political freedom is over. . . . Let us tell the world of their many sacrifices . . . that we might reap the benefit and pass on the torch of political freedom to our children. . . . Then let us turn to the future and consult how we can best serve our state and nation."[36] In late June 1920, the SCESL evolved into the South Carolina League of Women Voters, which hosted a three-day Citizenship School at the University of South Carolina to educate women in voting and the rights of citizenship.[37] After ratification of the Nineteenth Amendment in August 1920, White women in South Carolina voted in their first election that November. Eight months later, on March 7, 1921, however, the state legislature rejected the notion of the emancipated "New Woman" and exerted its power to limit women's political involvement when legislators passed a bill prohibiting women from jury duty. Women's exclusion from jury duty was not unusual throughout the South at the time, though its duration until 1967 was.[38]

By 1922 Greenville's League of Women Voters chapter was an active and sizable group, with leadership from Gridley, Margaret McKissick, and "Miss Jim" Perry, the state's first female attorney, who served as president.[39] Gridley and McKissick assumed leadership positions throughout the 1920s in the state chapter. Missing from this group was Mary Camilla Judson, a mainstay among supporters of opportunities for women. She had passed away at age ninety-two, a month after she voted for the first time, a right she undoubtedly exercised "with joy," according to scholar Judith T. Bainbridge.[40] Throughout the 1920s these women advocated for a law raising the age of marriage to sixteen years with parental consent and eighteen without; an equal guardianship over children; prison reform for female convicts; a living wage for all workers and equal pay for equal work; the establishment of a Department of Child Welfare, Tuberculosis, and Venereal Disease; women's representation on the boards of schools and all other institutions that aided women and children; funding to make the licensing process for teachers more efficient; lengthening the compulsory duration of the school year; and a law requiring women to pay the poll tax, which benefited education across the state.[41] Their platform reflects many tenets of national Progressivism.

Economically the city continued to thrive throughout the Progressive Era as the presence of Camp Sevier and the wartime demands placed upon the local textile industry resulted in a financial boom. During the 1920s Greenville County represented 5.5 percent of the state's population but paid 34 percent of the total corporate state income taxes, more than any other county in the state.[42] Civic involvement was an important aspect of the progressive ethos that trickled into communities throughout the nation, and White Greenvillians possessed the funds to support the needs and advancements that interested them. Inspired by the national Community Foundation Movement, which arose during the Progressive Era, and with involvement from the Chamber of Commerce's Civics Committee, Union Bleachery executive John W. Arrington established the Greenville Community Fund in 1922 to streamline individual giving and collapse seventeen local fundraising campaigns into one. The basis of its appeal was rooted in the Progressive Era's attempt to secularize philanthropy and develop systematic processes for the benefit of efficiency. The newspaper claimed that "the drive will be a thermometer by which the temperature of Greenville's interest in welfare causes may be tested."[43] Over the course of its six-day campaign in April, it raised more than eighty thousand dollars for the benefit of the County Tuberculosis Association, Girl's Protective Bureau, Hopewell Sanitarium, Red Cross, Salvation

"Grow with Greenville" 185

Army, YMCA, and YWCA. Donations from local African Americans benefited St. Luke's Hospital and a general "Colored Community Service" fund. The board was exclusively White and included local stalwarts such as Arrington, Geer, Allen J. Graham, Gridley, Rhoda Haynsworth, Joe Sirrine, and Fred W. Symmes. In 1931 Greenville was one of seventy-four cities across the country that had a community trust.[44]

By 1924 outgoing president of the Chamber of Commerce W. P. Conyers nurtured continued civic commitment when he proclaimed, "Greenville stands upon the threshold of a new era, and the dawning of a new day, looking into a future which contains a golden promise of prosperity and happiness. This promise can be realized to the full measure, if every citizen of Greenville will continue to work unselfishly for the upbuilding of his community."[45] Greenville's financial resources enabled the efforts of motivated local leaders to develop and construct new businesses downtown, establish needed community organizations and efforts, expand educational opportunities, and implement new and improved municipal services.

Influenced by early Progressive Era activism, White Greenvillians had invested themselves in civic beautification and improvement efforts even before the war began. Motivated by the national City Beautiful movement, the Municipal League of Greenville had, since 1904, contributed to the local landscape and organized civic and political leaders to do the same. In the spirit of the Progressive Era, those committed to public service and civic-mindedness focused on the national effort during the war years but soon thereafter returned their focus to their local communities. To aid both the economy and community involvement, the Chamber of Commerce changed the name of its monthly journal from *Progressive Greenville* to the *Greenville Civic and Commercial Journal* in September 1921. Under the leadership of local businessman William "Bill" R. Timmons, who returned to Greenville after his service in the war, and in part due to its recruiting of local women and youth, chamber membership doubled between 1920 and 1923.[46]

Months after the armistice the *Ladies Home Journal* proclaimed that "the Past is dead, the world is new and whether it becomes a new heaven or hell depends largely upon you, the women who must live with and love these returned men."[47] Despite the fact that popular media encouraged the return of women to the home, women in Greenville continued to invest in their communities. The Progressive Era and the war had converged in ways that presented women opportunities to credentialize their claims to citizenship. Just as temperance, the club movement, and the UDC had opened acceptable avenues for women to become more involved outside the home, so too did the war. As evidenced by their vigorous involvement throughout the decade after the war, these women had no plans

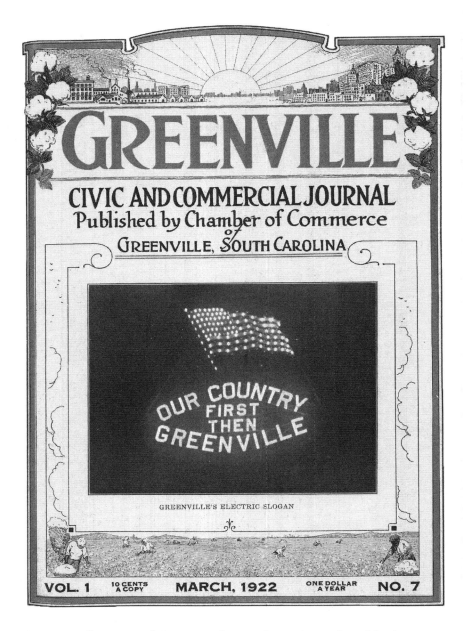

This *Greenville Civic and Commercial Journal* cover image from March 1922 reveals a rare close perspective of the electric sign in which Greenvillians took much pride. Courtesy of Special Collections and Archives, Furman University.

Mary Putnam Gridley was a leading business and philanthropic force in Greenville from the 1880s until her death in 1939. Upon her father's death in 1890, she became the first female mill president in South Carolina. As an outspoken clubwoman and civic leader, she not only represented but helped establish a new era for women in the public sphere. Image from the November 1922 *Greenville Civic and Commercial Journal*. Courtesy South Carolina Room, Greenville County Library.

to retreat from civic engagement; the war had enabled these women to see themselves as citizens who could contribute meaningfully to the welfare of the community. In 1918 women in Greenville founded a Business and Professional Women's Club; its membership was initially limited to forty, but it soon revoked that requirement, and membership rose to one hundred by early 1920.[48]

The Chamber of Commerce capitalized upon women's civic involvement and incorporated them into its efforts by establishing a Woman's Bureau in August 1921 that served as a federation of the city's White women's clubs. It was "organized for the purpose of promoting, by concerted action of the women and women's organizations, all enterprises that make for the welfare of Greenville."[49] One year into its existence, it was the only woman's bureau in the South who employed a full-time secretary, and with 230 members, it was also the largest. National periodicals expressed interest in why and how Greenville's bureau gained such prominence. Mary P. Gridley, who by the 1920s had become known as the "Dean of Women and Girls in Greenville," served as its first president and was the only woman serving on the chamber's board. Other officers throughout the 1920s included Mrs. J. W. Arrington, Anna M. Beaty, Jessie Stokely Burnett, Alice B. Cleveland, Mrs. Robert N. Daniel, Minnie Quinn Gassaway, Hessie T. Morrah, Willie Gray Martin, May Belle McGlothlin, Margaret McKissick, Mrs. E. S. McKissick, Andrea Christenson Patterson, Mary Ramsay, Nana Sirrine, and Helen Vaughan. Affiliate clubs included the Augusta Road Club, Business

Andrea Christensen Patterson was the daughter of South Carolina suffrage leader Abbie Holmes Christensen and brother of State Senator Niels Christensen, Jr., an advocate of suffrage in the state legislature. Andrea was involved in many progressive reforms, including suffrage, the club movement, and Woman's Bureau's involvement in Better Homes Week, which she led in 1926. She is pictured with her husband Lawrence Orr Patterson, a Greenville attorney and grandson of former South Carolina Governor James Lawrence Orr. Courtesy South Caroliniana Library, University of South Carolina.

and Professional Women's Club, Crescent Community Club, GWC Alumnae Club, Thursday Club, Thursday Afternoon Club, and others.[50]

In the 1920s the Woman's Bureau became involved in Better Homes, a national organization and movement designed to encourage home ownership as prudent, patriotic, and stabilizing and homemaking as a civic duty. Motivated by the housing crisis created in part by the war, the dilapidated and unsanitary conditions of private residences, and concerns about the impact of the automobile on women's lives and priorities, presidents Calvin Coolidge and Herbert Hoover served on the organization's advisory council and board, which comprised several national progressive leaders. The movement advanced the notion that "the modern twentieth-century housewife should be a trained expert, discriminating consumer, and moral arbitrator within a defined architectural setting."[51] The Better Homes movement argued that the home served as the foundation of America's social and political structure and that homes that were healthy, happy, and efficient cultivated more virtuous, patriotic citizens and consumers.

Every spring beginning in 1923, the chamber's Woman's Bureau coordinated Greenville's participation in Better Homes Week, which showcased model homes and included public programs on various progressive interests, such as public health, adult education, nutrition, and children's welfare. In 1929 Greenville was well positioned to serve as a national example of the health of the home environs; the year before, after the purchase of the Table Rock Reservoir, subsequent expansion the city's water system, and creation of a "super sewer system," the US Health Service named Greenville County the healthiest place in the nation.[52]

Over the course of Better Homes Week in April 1929, ten thousand people visited nine model homes throughout Greenville, two of which were sponsored by groups of African American women.[53] An art show at GWC and, for the first time, a community garden festival augmented the public lectures. This undertaking was executed by Greenville's clubwomen, organized through the Woman's Bureau; every White woman's club in the city participated in some way.[54] Several months later Better Homes announced that, out of the nearly six thousand cities that participated, Greenville had won first place. The celebratory luncheon in July for members of the Woman's Bureau was undoubtedly segregated; the newspaper made no mention of how African American clubwomen would celebrate.

During the early 1920s, the chamber's vigorous boosterism focused on luring potential residents and businesspeople. It also cultivated future leaders; its Junior Group, comprising young professional men, was extremely active. Early in the decade, the chamber effectively used local automobiles as advertisements of Greenville's economic identity when it arranged for new license plates that labelled Greenville as the "Textile Center of the South."[55] It continued to promote "Progressive Greenville"; advertisements for industry included references to the phrase, and during a regional convention for Rotarians in 1920, a special headline above the masthead read, "Progressive Greenville Welcomes Rotarians of Seventh District." Small towns just across the state line in North Carolina referred to "progressive Greenville citizens" and "the "spirit of progressivism trickling over the ridge" from Greenville into their towns.[56] The chamber attracted local businesses by sending "economic missionaries" via train on "acquaintance tours" along the East Coast and Canada to proclaim the "economic gospel" of the New South. It also sponsored "Open House Week," when dozens of Greenville schools, institutions, and businesses welcomed locals to become more familiar with their city.[57] Local educator and community "wheel horse" Pete Hollis chaired the chamber's "Homecoming Week" in November 1921, which was designed to attract previous residents back to Greenville. The week culminated with Armistice Day and aspired in part to recruit soldiers who had trained at Camp Sevier. By 1923 some were also calling Greenville "Convention City" as a result of the chamber's successful efforts to attract groups like the Southeastern Congress of Optometry, South Carolina Bankers Association, Southeastern Pure Food Show, and the North and South Carolina Pharmaceutical Associations, who met at Textile Hall and filled downtown hotels.[58] In early December 1926, the Retail Merchants Bureau of the chamber hosted the first Greenville Christmas parade. In advance local Boy Scouts decorated Main Street, while the Southern Public Utilities Company prepared for the "illumination that . . . will be the sensation of the South." Mayor Richard Watson met Santa Claus at the train depot on Augusta Street, where he was widely welcomed by children, and escorted him up Main Street, past Greenville's tall new buildings and thriving shops and restaurants. As Santa stood on the balcony of the Ottoray Hotel, crowds below cheered.[59] These innovative efforts boosted the city's economy, population, and vitality.

The chamber's explosion in growth and influence in the community warranted an impressive structure in the heart of downtown. In 1924 the chamber demolished famed South Carolina architect Robert Mills's Record Building, built in 1820, to build a ten-story office tower on Main Street. Nationally historic preservation remained in its nascent phase, and locally no movement existed, though at least one person, Frances Sullivan McDavid, protested the demolition of the noteworthy and historic structure.[60] The new building, which opened in November 1925, featured telephone lines and washbasins in every office. It is considered the apogee of the decades-long partnership of local architects James Douthit Beacham and Leon LeGrand, who contributed significantly to the building boom that occurred in Greenville in the 1920s, as did J. E. Sirrine and Company, who served as engineers of the structure.[61]

New construction capitalized on the addition of a new Beaux Arts–style county courthouse on Main Street and encouraged further development, resulting in a continuously expanding downtown. In 1921 John T. Woodside, owner of the largest mill under one roof in the country (and allegedly the world at the time), built a stately home at 210 Crescent Avenue that the local newspaper described as "one of the most beautiful residences in the South."[62] Downtown development attracted significant attention across the state when he constructed the Woodside Building, headquarters of the Woodside National Bank. Built at a cost of twelve million dollars and over the course of three years, the seventeen-story

The Woodside Building is shown towering over Greenville's Main Street during construction. Courtesy South Carolina Room, Greenville County Library.

structure required a special exemption by the state legislature because a state building code limited heights to fifteen stories. Once Gov. Robert A. Cooper signed the bill, it prohibited construction of any building as tall in the state for at least one year, and consequently the Woodside Building was the tallest building in South Carolina when it was opened in 1923.[63] The "Sentinel of the Carolinas," as it was pridefully nicknamed, was a symbol of the city's economic prowess and modernity, with the local news flaunting the building as a "veritable landmark of Greenville's progress" that represented "a new epoch in the business and civic history of Greenville."[64]

The building opened to the community with a lavish affair organized by the city's business leaders that lasted twelve hours. According to the *Greenville News,* "Along with the usual speeches, there was a performance of Handel's *Largo,* a 'violin obligato,' and a presentation of Godard's 'Joselyn.' . . . Elevator operators whisked thrilled patrons seventeen stories skyward to sample the 'amazing view' from the roof garden. Below, onlookers marveled at the building's architectural splendor: white marble, polished French plate mirrors, Ionic columns, bronze counter screens, and a large lobby skylight." The building aroused great pride and spurred development of other impressive structures on Main Street.[65] In 1925 the Poinsett Hotel, located beside the new county courthouse and across from the new chamber building, was built at a cost of $1.5 million. It replaced the Mansion House, a hotel that had occupied the site since the 1820s. The Poinsett was built by a corporation formed by John T. Woodside and William Goldsmith and included one hundred luxury rooms and white glove service. It was considered the most desirable place to stay for wealthy travelers coming to Greenville for the Southern Textile Exposition. Nearby the Imperial Hotel, designed by F. H. and J. G. Cunningham, who became the first architects outside New York City to design a high-rise structure in South Carolina, had been constructed in 1912 as the city's first "skyscraper" and only the third in the state. It added more rooms throughout the 1920s and became the largest hotel in Greenville by 1930.

Scholar Robert Bastion writes of how unusual it was for a small city to have more than one skyscraper, defined between 1923 and 1931 as a building with ten or more stories. His study identifies only ten cities nationally with a population of fifty thousand or less that had more than one skyscraper and reveals how exceptional Greenville's downtown was in the 1920s. Near the end of the decade, Woman's Bureau president Willie Gray Martin noted that Greenville's business district had assumed "a metropolitan flair."[66] Its skyscrapers were a testament to Greenville's economic development and modernity.[67]

Residential growth occurred in tandem with downtown development. The Prevost Apartments, the city's first downtown apartment complex, were built near the burgeoning Pettigru District during the war to help ease the city's extreme housing shortage. Neighborhoods sprouted in proximity to downtown and on and near Augusta Street, which had been paved from downtown to Grove Road in 1913 and became the new home of the Greenville Country Club in 1923. Areas of development near downtown included East Park Avenue, where architect brothers Frank and Joseph Cunningham built adjoining homes; the intersection of Hampton and Pinckney Streets; James and Earle Streets, a popular area largely built and occupied by businessmen who had benefited from the economic prosperity of the war; and Pettigru Street, the home of Boyce Lawn, where many local textile presidents, such as Lewis W. Parker, built homes. Schools such as Augusta Circle Elementary (1923), designed by Beacham and LeGrand, and Stone Avenue School (1924) followed.[68]

Greenville's population and infrastructure growth relied upon the network of recently improved and "heralded" roads, the construction of which had been prioritized by the presence of Camp Sevier.[69] After World War I ended, the SC Highway Department obtained surplus properties and its first mechanized machinery from the construction of military highways. The department used the

"Grow with Greenville" 193

equipment to create the state's first interstate highway system, continuing the wartime legacy of large-scale construction into the postwar period.[70] The first issue of the *Greenville Civic and Commercial Journal* boasted that the city had recently spent one million dollars on road development.[71]

Nationally car ownership rose significantly during the 1910s and 1920s during the age of the automobile, fostered locally by the improvement of the transportation infrastructure and evidenced by the state's decision to require license plates in 1917, the third to the last state to do so. By 1922, according to the Chamber of Commerce, Greenville had the most registered vehicles of any county in the state.[72] That year, citing increased vehicular traffic, city council voted to move the statue of a Confederate soldier that stood at the northern end of Main Street, across from the Ottoray Hotel, since its unveiling in September 1892. The city planned to place the statue in front of the county courthouse nearby. The local United Confederate Veterans and United Daughters of the Confederacy chapters objected, so much so that city council rushed to vote to remove the statue before a restraining order could be served to them. Though for months the public believed that the statue had mysteriously disappeared, city council had actually ordered the statue to be hidden. Workers had nestled the statue on a bed of hay in the back of an old wagon and whisked it away to a barn on the Gallimore farm near Paris Mountain. When word of the statue's whereabouts leaked, it was moved to yet another undisclosed location.

Meanwhile a lawsuit initiated by those who sought to keep the monument in its original location rose through the judicial ranks. In *Grady et al. v. City of Greenville et al,* the circuit court ruled against city council, who appealed the decision to the state supreme court. In June 1924 that trial reversed the lower court's decision and supported the removal of the monument to a new location. Soon thereafter Mayor Watson hosted a conference at the public library and specifically invited members of the United Confederate Veterans, surviving members of the Ladies Memorial Association, and the UDC. The conference also attracted women from UDC chapters across the state, and the women were particularly vocal. The mayor led negotiations, which ultimately resulted in the statue's relocation to grounds bordering Springwood Cemetery. A month later the same old wagon that had transported the statue into hiding two years earlier arrived at the Echols Street fire station to retrieve the soldier from its loft. By nightfall, the local newspaper reported, the "man on the monument," as he was commonly known, once again stood atop his base, "an example of fortitude and patriotism for all time."[73] Influenced by the Lost Cause, it was also an example of the confluence of many elite White Greenvillians' "patriotism" with their ancestor's treason.

From 1892 until 1922, a twenty-eight foot statue depicting a Confederate soldier stood as a memorial to Greenvillians who served in the Confederacy. It was prominently located near the Ottoray Hotel in the middle of Main Street, which became part of the Dixie highway in the 1910s. The imposing statue and its prominent location reflect white Greenvillians belief in the nostalgic, Lost Cause interpretation of the Confederacy's defeat in the Civil War. In 1922, City Council voted to move the statue, prompting two years of community negotiations and law suits. During that time, the base of the Confederate memorial remained in the center of Main Street, and most Greenvillians believed their Confederate statue had been stolen. Courtesy of the Coxe Collection, Courtesy of the Greenville County Historical Society.

Alongside economic and infrastructural development, the city also invested in improved municipal services. Established just before the war with the urging of the Municipal League of Greenville, the Park and Tree Commission, led by the "Father of Greenville's Playgrounds," John A. McPherson, created playgrounds and parks around the city throughout the 1920s with funding from a $110,000 bond referendum and the new Kiwanis Club. The commission and its efforts followed the 1907 report by landscape architects Kelsey and Associates of Boston, commissioned by the Municipal League, which included an extensive "park scheme" of large recreation areas along the Reedy River. The commission constructed playgrounds on Donaldson Street, Anderson Street, and Hudson Street and encouraged William Choice Cleveland to donate 110 acres of land for a new park adjacent to downtown Greenville in 1922. When it officially opened in 1926, Cleveland Park included two baseball fields, a horse ring, and a playground.[74] In 1924 the city used $15,000 from bond sales to purchase fifteen acres on Mayberry Street to develop a park for African American children who were not allowed to recreate in any of the city's other parks. Though Mayberry Park was surrounded by railroad tracks and was located on land prone to flooding, Sterling High School used it for baseball, football, and track, and the park quickly became a meaningful fixture in the lives of Greenville's African Americans.

Even so, White city leaders felt recreational space for African American children was dispensable. Less than ten years after the park opened, a small portion of it became a police shooting range, which created a dangerous situation for local residents on select days when the range was open to the public. In the late 1930s, the city again requisitioned over half of the park's land to lease to Baltimore businessman Joseph Cambria, who constructed Meadowbrook Park, a stadium with lights and bleachers for five thousand spectators and an adjoining parking lot. The city's recently acquired professional baseball franchise, which played in the South Atlantic League, took the same name as baseball teams that had played in Greenville between 1907 and 1912 and from 1919 to 1931. The all-White Greenville Spinners not only reflected the city's economic base but inspired pride in it.

Local African American protest against the parceling off of Mayberry Park and the creation of Meadowbrook Park was led by community leader Elias B. Holloway. Since 1890 Holloway had served as the only African American letter carrier in Greenville. He was an active member at John Wesley United Methodist Church and was among the most outspoken members of Greenville's African American middle class.[75] In 1939 Holloway publicly pressured the city for a park for African American residents in Greenville's Southernside and West Greenville neighborhoods. The city council verbally acquiesced. He was successful in eliciting from them a promise but not an actual park. Later Meadowbrook Park created a seating section for African Americans in the outfield and allowed the semiprofessional Black Spinners to play in the park on days when it was not in use by the Spinners.[76]

The population and building boom that had been sparked in part by the opening of Camp Sevier and its accompanying influx of people into town necessitated an expansion of municipal services, led by the adept Mayor Watson.[77] In

1918, by city referendum, the commissioner of public works purchased the Paris Mountain Water Company for eight hundred thousand dollars, with funding from a one million dollar bond.[78] The referendum reveals not only a willingness but also the confidence in the capabilities of local government, one of the premier tenets of Progressivism nationally. In November 1924 the city council passed a two-million-dollar bond issue to purchase the Table Rock watershed and surrounding area in northern Greenville County and build a dam to create a reservoir. Local banker W. C. Beacham served as chairman of the City Water Commission at the dam's formal dedication in May 1928.[79] Two years later, when the city began utilizing the Table Rock Reservoir, its water commission became the first system in the country to control all land surrounding a drinking water reservoir.[80] This new sewage treatment facility undoubtedly contributed to the US Health Service's assessment of Greenville city and county as "the healthiest place in the United States." Constructed by J. E. Sirrine and Company, the *Greenville News* described it as "the most modern sewage treatment plant in the world" and as a "progressive and gigantic municipal enterprise," the greatest undertaken in the South.[81]

With new buildings and neighborhoods and a growing infrastructure to support them, local leaders also invested in improvements for medical care and education. Since 1912 City Hospital had served as the primary healthcare facility for White patients in the area. In 1921, largely because of the efforts of retired textile owner and local philanthropist Thomas F. Parker, the Salvation Army's Emma Moss Booth Hospital opened, with an attached school of nursing. This facility was the first of many projects completed by Beacham and LeGrand in the 1920s.[82] The hospital's mission was to serve area mill workers and young women. After less than ten years, financial difficulties resulted in the hospital's closure and sale of the building to the Little Sisters of the Poor of Saint Francis who, in conjunction with the Catholic Diocese of Charleston, opened the St. Francis Infirmary.[83] In the mid-1920s the Shriners Hospital for children opened as a result of the efforts of several business leaders. Local Shriner leader Forest Adair, hoping to increase access to children's free hospitals nationwide, pitched the idea to W. W. Burgess of Greer, South Carolina, a promoter of the Victor and Franklin Mills; North Carolina businessman James B. Duke, founder of the Duke Endowment; and Bennette E. Geer, the president of five local textile mills. Collectively, based on funding from Burgess, they agreed to fund and equip the facility, which opened in 1927.[84]

Before and after the influenza pandemic, healthcare efforts focused largely on containing the spread of tuberculosis, which had erupted in the early 1900s. In 1915 the spread of the disease throughout South Carolina led the state to form

"*Grow with Greenville*" 197

four camps to provide treatment: Camp Alice in Sumter, Camp Pinehaven in Charleston, Marion County Camp, and Camp Hopewell in Greenville. Camp Hopewell was funded by the Hopewell Tuberculosis Association and founded and led by Rhoda Haynsworth and Gridley, with support primarily from Greenville women. Beginning in 1917, Gridley recruited assistance from Camp Sevier soldiers to sell Christmas seals as a fundraiser for the Hopewell Tuberculosis Association. It operated a small clinic inside a tent at City Hospital until 1927, when the county issued a bond to build a permanent structure. In 1930 the Hopewell Tuberculosis Hospital opened. Though it abided by segregation laws, the hospital treated White and African American patients, with White patients seen on Tuesdays by White nurses, and African American patients seen on Fridays by African American nurses. The percentage of African Americans affected by tuberculosis was much higher than it was for White people; it was the leading cause of death among African Americans in the state until 1925.[85]

Throughout the 1920s the association worked closely with African American physicians to spread awareness of causes, symptoms, and treatment. African American teachers, doctors, nurses, and other professionals were instructed by tuberculosis experts to report cases and to encourage citizens to get tested regularly so doctors could treat the patients early and prevent spreading of the disease.[86] The Over the Top Club, an African American women's group, organized efforts to sell Christmas seals, while other African American leaders established a tuberculosis committee that raised funding for sanatorium equipment.[87] Twenty-two years after Gridley began selling the Christmas seals, at the age of eighty-eight, she was still serving as the program's annual chairperson.[88]

The war had exacerbated the rates of tuberculosis. By midsummer of 1919, a tuberculosis sanitarium operating at Camp Sevier provided needed care for victims of poison gas, who, with scar tissue in their lungs, were susceptible to gas-induced tuberculosis. To encourage support during the holidays in 1922, the *American Legion Weekly,* a national periodical, noted that "South Carolina legionnaires took note of every disabled man in the State last Christmas" and featured a photo of Greenville legionnaires in "a colored ward at Hospital No. 26" after the legionnaires had decorated the ward with streamers and holiday lights.[89]

Motivated in part by the lack of quality health care for African Americans during the Spanish influenza crisis, African Americans in Greenville opened Saint Luke's Colored Hospital in a two-story building at the corner of Green Avenue and Jenkins Street in September 1920 with a formal ceremony at Springfield Baptist Church. It was described as "one of the most modern institutions in the South for colored people,"[90] and its first superintendent was Margaret H. Bright, a graduate of the nursing program at the Tuskegee Institute. The hospital had twenty-two beds in a combination of shared and private bedrooms and served patients with illnesses, those who needed surgeries, and women in childbirth. Besides the tuberculosis hospital, Saint Luke's was the only other health care facility available to African Americans, as it was difficult to receive treatment at City Hospital, where only 50 beds out of 325 were reserved for African Americans and African American doctors could not practice or operate.[91] White doctors in Greenville, like Dr. Clifton Black, supported Saint Luke's so extensively, performing surgeries and financially contributing, that he was referred to in his obituary as "the pillow" upon which the hospital depended.[92] In 1923 Dr. Matilda Evans of Columbia, president of the South Carolina State Colored Medical Association, joined Hattie Logan Duckett in raising awareness of African American public health needs in Greenville at an event well attended by African American and White Greenvillians. That same year six nurses from the new federal hospital for veterans at Tuskegee arrived in Greenville for training. Their presence was likely due to Bright's status not only as an alumna of Tuskegee but also as national secretary of the National Colored Association of Graduate Nurses.[93] Despite these efforts African Americans in the state in 1920 were three to four times more likely to die without medical attention, and the infant mortality rate was nearly twice that of White babies.[94] In 1928 the Working Benevolent State Grand Lodge assumed control of Saint Luke's. It became known as the Working Benevolent Society Hospital and began operation in the Lodge's new downtown building.

The Working Benevolent Temple and Professional Building contained office space for African American doctors, lawyers, and dentists and the first mortuary for African Americans in Greenville starting in 1922. Greenville businessman and African American leader Edgar W. Biggs chaired the project. It was designed by Beacham and LeGrand and financed by the Working Benevolent State Grand Lodge of South Carolina, an organization seeking to provide healthcare, welfare, and burial services to African Americans in need. In addition to professional offices, the building's prominent downtown location included a movie theater and space for the city's African American pharmacist and a barber.[95]

During the Progressive Era and throughout World War I, literacy and education became greater priorities nationally and locally. During the war the General Federation of Women's Clubs in South Carolina argued that literacy was the best defense against German propaganda. Their literacy campaign was inspired largely by South Carolina progressive Wil Lou Gray and by locals who were embarrassed when northern soldiers in training observed regional literacy disparities. In the year after the war's end, Central School, the city's segregated White high school,

"Grow with Greenville" 199

added the eleventh grade and was renamed Greenville High. Mill schools benefited significantly from profits generated by the war: attendance rose over the course of the war even as the student to teacher ratio dropped from 66:7 to 50:3. Yet with only elementary schools in the mill villages, parents had to pay to send their children to the city for additional schooling, though most could not afford to. Therefore many children of mill operatives began working after completion of the sixth grade.[96]

Thus, in the early 1920s, Parker led an effort among Greenville mill executives to petition the legislature for a school district for the mills. Parker had cofounded Monaghan Mill with his cousin Lewis in 1900 and engaged in pathbreaking efforts to enhance the lives of those who worked in his mills. In 1911 he addressed the faculty and students of the University of South Carolina and advocated for a greater investment in industrial and vocational education and a new state commission to oversee it; an overall improvement in mill village conditions; and a compulsory insurance program for mill operatives and mill owners, based on a German model. He argued that the current "remedy for sightless eyes, maimed bodies, and helpless widows and hungry children is long, expensive legislation" but that it could be "prompt and continuous medical service, and a regular, weekly income."[97] His efforts reflected the "business progressivism" written about by historian George Tindall, which worked to improve the lives of workers and civic services more generally for the benefit of increased efficiency and "as a means to help the South enter the American economic mainstream."[98] Bolstered by the abysmal results from literacy tests taken by the state's World War I recruits, which revealed glaring disparities between the capabilities of young White men from affluent tax districts and those from poorer areas, like the mill villages, the South Carolina legislature established a new district named for Parker in 1922 to address the lack of educational opportunity. The Parker School District, described as "the most audacious example of South Carolina's Progressive movement" in the education sector, was created by grouping together fourteen communities, of which nine were mill villages.[99] Its enrollment was the highest of any school district in the state, excepting Charleston, with a population of more than twenty-five thousand people living in the twelve square miles of the district. It became the wealthiest school district in the state with nine million dollars of taxable property.[100] In 1923, the district began printing *The Joymaker*, a newspaper published semi-monthly that sought to inform families about activities, opportunities, and news of interest relating to Parker schools. It not only unified the schools in the district but also inspired great pride in them as well.

From the beginning the school district had strong leadership from one of the leading White Progressives in the state, Lawrence Peter "Pete" Hollis. A native

South Carolinian, Hollis graduated from South Carolina College, where he led their YMCA, and had moved to Greenville after Parker hired the charismatic and innovative young man to lead his new Monaghan YMCA. The national YMCA had recently created an industrial division aimed at improving the lives of industrial workers and immigrants, and Parker had pounced on the opportunity to bring a YMCA to Monaghan. It became the first YMCA to be located in a mill village in the South, and under Hollis's leadership it offered sports, Bible study classes, film showings, a drama club, and Greenville's only "Continuation School," a night school for mill workers.[101]

In addition to the YMCA, Monaghan had a medical clinic with a staff physician and nurse, churches, and recreation facilities. When landscape designer Harlan Kelsey visited Greenville to develop his city beautification report, he was already familiar with the city. Parker had hired him to beautify Monaghan. Parker and Hollis wanted Monaghan's workers to develop a sense of pride in their village. Though "broken bottles and tin cans once disfigured the front yards," Hollis worked with residents to clean their yards, build sidewalks, and plant and maintain a community rose garden. To help them become more self-sufficient, he created a village pasture for pigs and cows, distributed seed and fertilizer, and provided backyard tilling services.[102]

Hollis had a very personal leadership style; he insisted on getting to know every family and exhibited an uncommon sensitivity to their needs.[103] His secretary said that "he never has a dime, because he is always lending money," and described how he often pledged his personal credit for a family to purchase new furniture and clothing if their home burned or if health care bills became insurmountable.[104] Monaghan employed a small group of German immigrants who were brought into the country in 1906 when Parker served as chair of the Immigration Committee of the Cotton Manufacturers' Association of South Carolina. In an oral history, Mack Duncan shared a conversation he once had with Pete Hollis: "[A] young girl died in the German community of Monaghan, and it upset everybody in the community. They didn't know why the whole community was so upset with the death of this young girl. And he [Hollis] said that he tried to find out what the problem really was, and it turned out that they didn't have a priest or pastor to go to. And so he went to town to the church—and got . . . the preacher . . . and brought him over to Monaghan, and it settled people down. They were happy; they felt right then. They were in a strange land with no religious ties."[105]

With Parker's support Hollis's efforts immeasurably enhanced the lives of Monaghan residents. In 1911 the Parkers formed the Parker Cotton Mills Company, which included sixteen mills and more than a million spindles, more than any mill in the nation, and promoted Hollis to be director of welfare activities.[106] Parker and Hollis knew the happiness of their workers correlated with economic productivity. One challenge they hoped to overcome was that mill operatives were exceptionally nomadic, as revealed in an oral history with former employee Geddes E. Dodson: "We moved to Brandon, and worked over there a while. Then I worked at Judson. I left there and went to Mills Mill and worked three nights [chuckle] all night, and then my brother got me a job back at Judson, and I went back over there. And then I went to Monaghan and stayed part of 1926 and '27, and came back to Judson and stayed a few months, and moved to Dunean the twenty-first of March in '28."[107] Parker did not want his operatives taking positions in other mills or joining a forbidden union, and despite his efforts to safeguard worker contentment and industrial stability, Monaghan was not immune to attempts by union organizers to stir workers' discontent. For decades Hollis adeptly balanced Parker's economic interests and paternalistic management ethos with those of the workers and earned the respect of both. While oral histories with mill operatives reveal an understanding that Hollis worked for the benefit and within acceptable parameters of the mill industry, they also reveal an eagerness to laud him with compliments of remarkable consistency; he is frequently described as "a good man," "a smart man," "a grand person [and] a workaholic," and "a Chamber of Commerce in one man" who "knew everybody, and everybody knew him."[108]

In his role as superintendent, Hollis became an advocate for true educational reform. He was inspired by the writings of American philosopher and educational reformer John Dewey of Columbia University, and one of his first actions as superintendent was to invite Dewey to Greenville to train teachers in "progressive education" methods. Hollis encouraged parents and teachers to employ active learning tactics, such as ridding classrooms of desks and having students sit in a circle or teaching classes outside. He also employed a full-time psychiatrist to educate parents in healthy child-rearing methods. He encouraged experiential learning in the form of science fairs and field trips, activities unusual for that time, and was widely associated with his oft-quoted "You learn by doing." Hollis believed that the most effective education took place outside the classroom and created innovative opportunities for mill residents to learn, including hiring a woman to bake biscuits inside a school mobile so women could learn how to operate electrical appliances from their front yards. Though he believed in vocational training, his efforts—perhaps inadvertently, perhaps not—enabled his students to throw off the caste system into which they had been born. Fifty percent of the children of mill village workers who graduated from Parker High School attended college.[109]

Pete Hollis embodied both sides of the historiographical debate regarding the influence of national Progressivism on the South and vice versa. He was someone who connected himself and his reform activities to national leaders and scholars but who also helped shape progressive reforms nationally. He provided seed and fertilizers to residents of mill villages and invited representatives from the US Department of Agriculture to teach mill villages how to garden. As director of the Monaghan YMCA, Hollis traveled to the YMCA Camp at Lake George, New York, where he was exposed not only to new forms of recreation but also to the progressive attitudes of many associated with the YMCA. It was at Lake George that he learned about the Boy Scouts organization and met Dr. James Naismith, the founder of basketball. Hollis learned the game and bought a rulebook and a basketball at FAO Schwartz in New York. He soon established the first Boy Scouts troop in the state and not only introduced basketball to South Carolina but also officiated the first games. It became popular among the mill villages, whose teams developed spirited rivalries. Hollis's passion and unique methods of teaching children sparked national and international attention; visitors across the country and as far as England, Germany, and New Zealand visited Parker, and in 1941 an article in *Reader's Digest* described Parker High School and Hollis's work in the Parker District as a "Mill Town Miracle."[110]

Beyond the mills Hollis was influential in the creation of the Greenville County Library, the Greenville YWCA, and the Phillis Wheatley Center, an African American community center downtown.[111] His widespread efforts brought him into contact with most of Greenville's civic, economic, and religious leaders and with many across the state. Hollis worked closely with Wil Lou Gray, for instance, a South Carolinian who was on the national forefront of shaping literacy efforts as a progressive reform.

Gray, a native of Laurens County, which adjoins Greenville, began working as a field secretary for the South Carolina Illiteracy Commission in late 1918 and also served as the state supervisor of adult schools from 1921 to 1946.[112] Gray marketed literacy as the key to economic growth in South Carolina following the end of the war because many believed it was the solution, according to her biographer, to combating "poverty, crime, lethargy, and other social blights."[113] She created state standards for adult education and improved training methods and curricula. As an experiment she organized the first Opportunity School in 1921, under the direction of the state department of education. The Opportunity School was a summer program based at the Tamassee Daughters of the American Revolution School in the Upcountry's Oconee County that included "home economics, lessons in etiquette, experiential learning, practical application of skills, Christianity, and citizenship" and was designed for White women.[114] After

"Grow with Greenville" 203

this experiment and several other weeklong programs, Gray expanded the Opportunity School from a summer program to a year-round boarding school for White women.[115] It was modeled after Dutch "folk schools" and was an "environment free from the pressures of grades, academic standing, degrees, and exams."[116] Gray, who emerged as one of the state's preeminent White progressive leaders, received support from many state leaders as she worked to empower marginalized groups by connecting literacy to democracy and economic growth.[117]

In the 1919–20 school year, the state of South Carolina dedicated 88.5 percent of its budget to White schools and 11.5 percent to "colored" institutions.[118] Greenville County spent $19.22 on each White pupil, while it dedicated $4.34 to each African American student.[119] For decades after the Civil War, the Allen School, named in 1869 for state senator James M. Allen, one of Greenville's four representatives at the 1868 constitutional convention, was the first and remained one of the few educational options for African Americans in the South Carolina Upcountry. Begun in 1866 and also known as the Freedman's School, the Allen School became part of the Greenville School District in 1886 and was the only school for African American children in the city.[120] In August 1927 the city purchased 1.6 acres, and a new school building was constructed with Works Progress Administration funds in 1936.[121]

With so few options available, support from Chicago-based philanthropist Julius Rosenwald provided a significant boost to African American children's education throughout the region. Rosenwald, president of Sears, Roebuck, and Company, began funding the education of African Americans throughout the South after being convinced to do so by Booker T. Washington. Rosenwald partnered with Washington's Tuskegee Institute to design plans for the construction of one-room, log-cabin schoolhouses. Rosenwald focused on states throughout the South, including South Carolina, because of their segregation mandates. In order to receive funds from the Rosenwald program, communities had to raise a matching sum of money, mostly coordinated through African American churches and organizations.[122]

Saint Albans School, the first Rosenwald school in Greenville County, opened in 1920.[123] Over the next ten years, the Rosenwald Fund helped construct thirty-one Rosenwald buildings in Greenville, which included twenty-six schools, three school shops, and two teachers' homes, the most buildings of any county in South Carolina. In keeping with Washington's educational philosophy of teaching technical skills, the Rosenwald schools in Greenville offered classes such as washing and greasing to prepare students for service occupations.[124] Throughout the duration of the program, it funded the construction of more than 5,300 schools across the nation. The Rosenwald Fund provided $4.7 million throughout the

South for the development of Black education, including $380,303 in South Carolina and $17,235 in Greenville County.[125] It strove to ameliorate the lives of African Americans during a time of extreme oppression by providing educational and employment opportunities for Black children and teachers and was an important contribution to the life of southern communities.

The campaign to improve literacy included not only the building and funding of schools but also library accessibility. Though A. Viola Neblett willed her home to serve as the Neblett Free Library in 1897 and Furman University had built a Carnegie Library in 1907, the community needed greater access to public libraries. Civic leaders worked collaboratively to gather support. The Thursday Club had long encouraged the development of libraries; they had supported the Neblett Library and also created their own lending libraries. In 1919 the Rotary Club hosted a dinner to increase support for the library, with an address by Justice Charles A. Woods, and in 1921, after their attempts to convert Robert Mills's building into a library were thwarted by bureaucratic challenges, Parker and his good friend Greenville banker John W. Norwood established the Greenville Public Library Association on East Coffee Street.[126] Citizens showed their support by donating books to Annie Porter, its sole librarian. Within a year of its existence, the library became publicly funded. In October 1922 Pete Hollis created a "truck library"[127] named the Parker Pathfinder that was the first bookmobile in South Carolina. Funded by Parker, once described as the "angel of the Greenville Public Library," and Norwood, this mobile library became a more accessible way to serve people who were unable to visit the public library downtown.[128] The bookmobile was especially popular among the residents of mill villages and distributed more than thirty thousand books in Parker District in its first seven months of service. The Pathfinder regularly visited Parker District schools; on those days students would be given a twenty-minute break from class or would be dismissed from classes early to borrow or return books.[129] Because of its success in the Parker District and with additional funding from Parker and Norwood, the mobile library expanded its routes to include other mills and cities.

In its first three years, the public library added ten thousand books to its collection, opened in a new building on Brown Street, and lent books to patrons more than one hundred thousand times.[130] Branches of the library later opened in nearby communities such as Greer, Simpsonville, Fountain Inn, and Tigerville. While the success of the library was of significant benefit to the White community, African Americans were excluded from its offerings and services.

Though it did not initially host a library, the Phillis Wheatley Association that Hattie Logan Duckett established on Haynie Street in 1919 quickly evolved into an indispensable institution within Greenville's African American community. In

As a joint undertaking between the Parker District and the Library, whose board was chaired by Thomas F. Parker, a Ford truck was converted into the "Parker Pathfinder." In this image from 1924, students waited in line to check out books. The Pathfinder's popularity prompted the library to build more bookmobiles and expand its reach. Courtesy South Carolina Room, Greenville County Library.

1921, Duckett purchased a home on East McBee Avenue, and in the fall of 1922, the association moved and began hosting Bible study and other classes for girls.[131] The home was intended to serve as a place to continue the work Duckett was involved in during the war with helping young African American women. Duckett, whose father was a Methodist minister, once said, "I believe in the democracy of God and the solidarity of the human family."[132] She was inspired to develop the home after a visit to Cleveland, Ohio, where Upcountry South Carolina native Jane Edna Hunter had founded the Phillis Wheatley Association, named after the first published African American female poet.[133]

In an editorial in the *Greenville Daily News*, E. B. Holloway supported the establishment of the association. He wrote that while the soldiers' clubs in the city had resulted from "community spirit," they had also prompted the need to protect and care for young African American women who did not have "the proper home environments." He also cited the need for a tuberculosis sanitarium and announced a campaign to raise money for it. He closed his letter by requesting that the city sextons increase its landscaping and maintenance efforts at African American cemeteries. Overall, Holloway wrote, "the colored people of Greenville have reached the point where they are not content."[134] His comments coincided with the closing days of Red Summer and reflect a more nuanced race consciousness that flourished spectacularly in places like New York, home of the Harlem Renaissance, and subtly in places like Greenville echoed a sentiment often expressed by African Americans after the war.

The Phillis Wheatley Association was in great demand, and four years after it opened, its expenses were overwhelming. According to Parker, two factors coalesced in 1924 that prompted the Chamber of Commerce to create a committee of White and African American leaders to develop a plan of action: first the Community Fund included the Wheatley Center as a recipient for the first time, and second, the emigration of African Americans from Greenville created great concern among Greenville's White businessmen. The local newspaper had acknowledged in recent years that "the truth might as well be faced, and the truth is that the treatment of the Negro in the South must change or the South will lose the Negro."[135] Parker and others acknowledged that "many important changes have taken place in the South and the nation in the last twenty years which concern the Negro and his relations to the white citizens of this section." They agreed that they needed to consider "how the situation could best be handled for the profit of both races."[136]

Parker helped Duckett raise sixty-five thousand dollars, and in 1924, Geer, Parker, and Graham purchased a lot on East Broad Street. The home expanded into a community center "dedicated to the educational and religious uplift of members of the colored race in Greenville." Parker, Conyers, Charles Brier, and Charles F. Gandy spoke at the dedication. The newspaper listed only the White charter members of the Phillis Wheatley Center, which included the names of several men and women known for their involvement in civic causes, like Gridley, Rhoda Haynsworth, and Hollis.[137] The new center offered a Vacation Bible School; courses in homemaking skills, nursing, and Bible study; and a home for choral groups, the Boy Scouts, sports teams, women's clubs, and the YWCA.[138] It had an extensive volunteer network, which included White women from the Woman's Bureau of the Chamber of Commerce, the Crescent Community Club, the Red Cross, YMCA, YWCA, and other organizations.

The center's by-laws mandated a biracial board, comprising five White and four African American members; the president, vice president, and treasurer were to be White, and the president appointed the secretary at his discretion. Parker served as president of the board, with E. B. Holloway as secretary. In an article in the *Southern Workman,* an African American periodical, Parker explained that "without white control of the Association being assured, it could not get either the necessary financial or moral support of the Greenville community." He continued, "The purpose of the white persons active in this movement is to create a

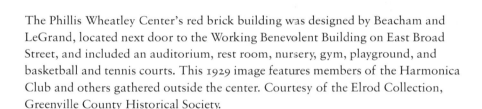

The Phillis Wheatley Center's red brick building was designed by Beacham and LeGrand, located next door to the Working Benevolent Building on East Broad Street, and included an auditorium, rest room, nursery, gym, playground, and basketball and tennis courts. This 1929 image features members of the Harmonica Club and others gathered outside the center. Courtesy of the Elrod Collection, Greenville County Historical Society.

better understanding between the races and to develop Negro consciousness and pride and a sense of responsibility along wise lines. In Greenville, where Negroes have had poor educational advantages and very limited business experience, such a movement can only hope for success when handled by local white citizens who have the confidence of both races." He concluded, "The promoters of the Center have a firm conviction that their 20,000 Negroes . . . are less beneficial and valuable to this community than the same number would be if wisely helped and guided and befriended. . . . Negro laborers are the best agricultural labor the South has ever had, or is likely to have, for they are acclimated, religious, loyal, less expensive to train, and in other ways better suited to the needs of the South than the immigrants we are apt to get from across seas."[139]

In Cleveland, Jane Edna Hunter had been "rebuked" by African Americans for approaching wealthy White donors for funding and eventually acquiescing to their insistence on oversight of her institution.[140] If African Americans in Greenville resented Parker's patronizing tone and belittling rationale, they did not allow

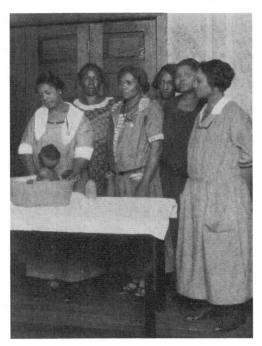

This 1925 image of a Health and Hygiene class taught by the City Nurse at Phillis Wheatley accompanied an article written by Thomas Parker in *The Southern Workman*. Collection of the Hampton University Archives, Hampton, VA.

it to affect their support and engagement with the center. In 1925, its first year of operation, 150 women, 50 men, and 250 children were active, with 40,000 visits to the center. In addition the center reached another 60,000 through extension and other programs. The center served as a critical nucleus as the first place of social welfare for African Americans in Greenville.[141]

Though it was not technically affiliated with the Phillis Wheatley Center, the Phillis Wheatley Branch of the Greenville County Library was also located in the center. The library held considerably fewer books than the main White public library. Parker was a strong proponent of self-education as a means of social and economic uplift and believed libraries were essential to achieving that aim. "Personally," he wrote, "I and other businessmen in Greenville are deeply interested in the Negro situation, to which we have already undertaken to make as worthwhile a contribution as is within our power to do so. A Negro library in this community could not expect a large circulation per capita or per volume as compared with other libraries, but . . . it may accomplish much which cannot be shown at present by statistics."[142] With his assistance the Phillis Wheatley Branch received a substantial collection of books and began to offer story hours for children.[143]

Ever since its founding in 1909, the NAACP remained at the heart of efforts aimed at racial uplift across the country. African Americans in Charleston and Columbia, where African Americans made up more than 30 percent of the local population, established chapters in 1917, but the creation of a branch in Greenville faced relentless White backlash. The process to establish a chapter began in 1927, though the application was not formally submitted until 1929. "After quite a struggle and much work," wrote Holloway to J. E. Spingarn, treasurer of the national NAACP, "I have the pleasure of forwarding a petition of fifty one names asking for a charter."[144] A few days later, Holloway received a letter informing him that the money and petition had been received, and in late October he received a branch charter and letter welcoming Greenville "into the ranks of full-fledged branches."[145] Greenville's NAACP chapter launched last among South Carolina's largest cities, and it struggled greatly to maintain membership, so much that it apparently had to renew its efforts to establish a branch. Finally in July 1938 James A. Brier helped officially charter an NAACP branch of seventy members in Greenville. At first Brier did not allow women membership, but he changed this policy in 1939 after the national chapter urged him to do so.[146] Hattie Logan Duckett was one of the first women to become a member, and the branch often met at the Phillis Wheatley Center. Through burglary, physical violence, economic intimidation, and threats, the Klan opposed the efforts of the local chapter to register voters.[147]

Under the leadership of the dynamic Rev. Charles Gandy, who began a forty-year tenure as pastor of Greenville's Springfield Baptist Church in the mid-1910s, African American church membership and facilities expanded locally, with the church serving a significant leadership role. During Gandy's leadership of the Enoree Baptist Association, he led the effort to rename the original Greenville Academy, founded in 1896, as Sterling High School and to have the city's board of education assume control of the school in 1929. Springfield significantly expanded its church facility in 1930 and served as the meeting headquarters for the local NAACP branch. Simultaneously Allen Temple AME, a mission church established in Greenville during Reconstruction, was completing its new brick, classic revival structure, designed by Cuban-born architect Juan Benito Molina.[148] Though architect William Wilson Cooke, the son of the formerly enslaved Wilson Cooke, was reared in Greenville and maintained an office in Greenville between 1905 and 1907, Molina was considered Greenville's only Black architect from the late 1920s until he killed both his girlfriend and himself in Greenville in 1940. At age forty-two Molina was prominent enough for articles regarding his death to be published in the *Chicago Defender, Pittsburgh Courier,* and *Wichita*

Negro Star and in the White-owned *Greenville News* and *Orangeburg Times and Democrat.*[149]

Though the SCFCWC was established in 1909, African American women's clubs in Greenville did not significantly develop until the 1920s. The Builder's Club at Springfield was formed in the 1920s, as was the Progressive Club at John Wesley, which included Hattie Duckett, Duckett's sister Ella Mae Logan, and Hattie Parker as members. Historian Glenda Gilmore has written, "Using women's church organizations to press for community improvement incurred less risk than preaching inflammatory sermons on civil rights," or as one African American woman in North Carolina said to an African American minister: "We can go where you can not afford to go."[150] Some women transformed their church clubs into "parapolitical" organizations, while others joined secular clubs that focused on racial uplift. Based at Phillis Wheatley, the Lend-a-Hand Club in Greenville supported efforts to raise community service funds, but their primary goal was to support the "upbuilding and maintenance of the center." Hattie Duckett, a dedicated clubwoman, later served as president of the SCFCWC. Ella Mae Logan, who taught Home Economics at Sterling, founded the Cheerful Home Circle Club, which participated in Armistice Day commemorations in the late 1920s. Hattie E. Williams, who had served as wartime head of Greenville's colored auxiliary of the Red Cross, established the Over the Top Club. In addition to fighting tuberculosis, they supported Fairwold, a home for African American young women that had been established by the SCFCWC.[151] The Will Do and the Sunshine clubs were also active during the decade. The Lend-a-Hand, Over the Top, and Cheerful Home Circle clubs were affiliated with the SCFCWC and the National Association of Colored Women, which connected these women with a statewide and national network of African American women who had dedicated themselves to the association's motto, "Lifting as we Climb."[152]

Though no renaissance occurred, African Americans in Greenville benefited from improvements in education, health care, recreation, and religious organizations. Over the next four decades, they worked persistently yet quietly toward racial uplift, developing a style of discreet, discerning progress that was effective precisely because it did not overtly threaten the White establishment. The Progressive Era, World War I, and the postwar boom opened avenues of advancement to African Americans that laid the groundwork for direct confrontation during the civil rights movement of the 1960s.[153]

As the nation had become increasingly diverse from the incredible influx of immigrants in the late 1800s, Greenville's population too began to depart from a racial and religious profile that was almost exclusively White or African American

For decades, Hattie Logan Duckett was an indefatigable community leader who improved tens of thousands of African American lives and nurtured biracial cooperation. After graduating from Claflin College, she studied social work in New York and Chicago. She remains best known as the founder of the Phillis Wheatley Center, which she developed into a vast cultural, educational, recreational, and social services center that continues today. She was also active in the South Carolina Federation of Colored Women's Clubs, the NAACP, and the Commission on Interracial Cooperation. An unknown artist painted this in 1957, the year after her death. Courtesy The Phillis Wheatley Center, Greenville.

and Protestant.[154] Greenville's first Conservative Jewish congregation, Congregation Beth Israel, was established in 1916, followed by the establishment of a Reform congregation, the Children of Israel, in 1917. Though weeks after the Armistice, one soldier from Chicago wrote in a note to his father that Camp Sevier "has some very anxious men in it, wondering just when they are to go home," many non-native soldiers who trained in Greenville returned after the war, providing a sustained boost to local social, cultural, and religious diversity.[155]

As World War I veteran Henry Bacon McKoy later wrote, "Many soldiers had made friends, liked what they saw, and stayed behind."[156] In 1916 the Census Bureau's religious census grouped Jews under the category "All Other Bodies," but by 1926 it listed 195 Jews in Greenville County.[157] In 1928 the Reform congregation commissioned a synagogue on Buist Street designed by Beacham and LeGrand, and the next year Beth Israel secured a lot less than a mile away on Townes Street to build a synagogue designed by local architect and influenza survivor Joseph G. Cunningham.[158] During this time South Carolina had among the lowest percentages of Catholics nationally, yet under the leadership of Monsignor Andrew Keene Gwynn, who led Saint Mary's Catholic Church for fifty-two years, the Catholic population in Greenville grew 68 percent between 1916 and 1926.[159] The student body of its affiliated school, which had been founded in 1900 as Sacred Heart Academy, increased steadily. It changed its name to Saint Mary's School, expanded its facilities in 1923, and promptly outgrew them by the end of the decade.[160] A new school building and Gallivan Hall, an expansion of the church's facilities, were both dedicated in 1930.[161] Two years later, when Saint Francis Infirmary opened, the school hosted its dedication service.

The city's institutions of higher education also benefited from the area's economic vitality, with new campus facilities similarly serving the needs of the greater White community. With funding from the local Rotary Club, Furman University built Manly Field, which hosted the university's football and baseball games, and during the 1920s added a dining hall and gymnasium. In 1923 the Greenville Woman's College opened its new Ramsay Fine Arts Center, designed by Beacham and LeGrand, which effectively served as Greenville's premier performing arts venue. Three years later seventy-five local men and women convened at the new Greenville Library to strategize with representatives from Columbia's Town Theatre, which had been established in 1919. Within months the group established the Greenville Artists Guild and presented its first shows at the Ramsay Fine Arts Center. Two years later the Artists Guild became the Community Little Theatre and eventually, the Greenville Little Theatre.

In addition to the expansion of Furman's campus facilities, the economic boom, combined with the lofty aspirations of university leadership, resulted in significant advancements. At his first meeting with the trustees in 1919, the newly inaugurated president of Furman, William J. McGlothlin, who used postwar fears of state-run, nationalistic education to promote Christian pedagogy, presented an ambitious course of action. In 1919 the university raised standards for admission, implemented a plan for new campus construction, announced plans to develop a law school, and established an academic Department of Education that offered specialized instruction for future teachers and school administrators.

Despite McGlothlin's concerns about the possible dangers of state-run education and increasing federal encroachment on schools and colleges, he was a strong proponent of access to education for all, not just the elite, and deemed public education vital to the functioning of democratic society.[162] His actions reflected a Progressive Era commitment to improving the quality of and access to education nationally. Shaped in large part by John Dewey and the Progressive Education Association, Progressivism, according to historian Lawrence Cremin, successfully resulted in "the transformation of the school" in American culture. In 1915 the Alabama and South Carolina state legislatures had passed compulsory school attendance laws, behind all other states excepting Georgia (1916) and Mississippi (1918).[163] With its new Department of Education, Furman aimed to educate future teachers in the latest pedagogical methods.

The university continued to improve the quality of its academic program, infrastructure, and financial strength in the 1920s. McGlothlin and his cabinet increased the number of faculty with doctorates, raised standards for faculty research and publishing, and encouraged faculty-student interaction beyond the boundaries of the classroom. A law school opened in September 1921 and, by decade's end, earned accreditation from the American Bar Association.[164] Its first class included Anna M. Beaty, its first and only female graduate, who became Greenville's third female attorney, after Jim Perry and Julia David Charles.[165] In the banner year of 1924, Furman received accreditation from the Southern Association of Colleges and Schools, while William M. Blackburn ('21) became its first alumnus to be named a Rhodes Scholar. Bennette Geer's friendship with tobacco and electric power titan James Buchanan "Buck" Duke resulted in Furman's inclusion as one of four institutions of higher education to benefit financially from the newly created Duke Endowment. When Furman celebrated the centennial of its founding in 1926, the university had never been stronger. Financial challenges throughout the 1920s and 1930s forced the GWC to rely heavily on Furman, and thanks primarily to Duke Endowment funds, the university was able to assume responsibility for providing courses for GWC juniors and seniors, which established a foundation for an eventual merger between the affectionately named Furman "hill" and GWC "zoo." Whether or not others were convinced that the "great era of the Christian school has come," as McGlothlin had announced early in his presidency, he aggressively pursued his vision of a great era for Furman.[166]

As Furman received increasing regional support and validation, Greenville's economic vitality received a significant boost with the addition of an airport. The use of aircraft during the war had inaugurated the golden age of aviation in the 1920s. Soon after war's end, city leaders began informal discussions about

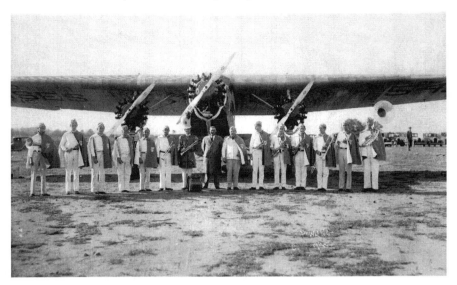

As part of the Greenville Municipal Airport's dedication festivities, members of the Furman University Band boarded the 15-passenger Ford tri-motor plane pictured behind them. Before landing, they dramatically descended with idling motors/engines so the sizable crowd below could hear their high-altitude performance. Courtesy of Special Collections and Archives, Furman University.

the need to expand the city's transportation infrastructure to include aviation. In 1926 three local businessmen established Alhayor, the state's first commercial aviation business, with airplanes based on a field outside the city. With the blessing of local government, the state legislature created the Greenville Airport Commission, which aspired to build a municipal airport by the end of the decade. It purchased a parcel of land near Laurens Road for an airport, which was formally dedicated in November 1928. Eastern Air Transport began passenger flights in December 1930, and soon the airport became a strong economic asset for area development.[167]

From the 1890s through the 1920s, the "Greenville Spirit" inspired an immense outpouring of civic engagement and boosterism among White and African American Greenvillians as they aspired to live up to their self-titled reputation as "Progressive Greenville." Greenville thrived economically and in the improvement of its civic services and cultural institutions yet struggled to adapt to the advances being made nationally by women and African Americans. Racial segregation remained a way of life in Greenville for the next forty-five years, and while the state abided by the Nineteenth Amendment for woman's suffrage beginning in 1920, the state legislature did not ratify it until 1969.

Much of the progress spawned by World War I and the advances of the Progressive Era abruptly halted with the stock market crash on Black Tuesday in October 1929. Though the resulting economic depression drastically changed life for most Americans, including the citizens of Greenville, efforts to memorialize those who had served in the world war were greatly bolstered by New Deal government programs. Rejuvenated by these funds, memorialization efforts continued through the 1930s, when another war forced a paradigm shift in how the world conceptualized the Great War. In 1939 the "World War" became World War I.

Epilogue

Memorialization of the Great War:
The Politics of Race and Remembrance

In late April 1919, leaders in Greenville announced a parade, barbeque, and dance to welcome home returning servicemen. The parade, planned for May 10, would feature "Confederate soldiers, world war veterans, and their brothers who failed to get the opportunity to 'go across,'" in addition to schoolchildren and local civic organizations.[1] On the day of the parade, twenty thousand spectators lined the streets to welcome twenty thousand returning soldiers and sailors. At the end of the parade trail, more than one hundred African American troops marched to the beat of two local African American bands, one at their front and one, led by a young African American boy, in their rear. Leading all of them was a group of military and local leaders on horseback that included Mayor Hanny Clyde Harvley, Gov. Robert Cooper, Sheriff Hendrix Rector, and E. M. Burnett, the secretary of the Chamber of Commerce, followed by a dozen automobiles "profusely decorated with Confederate flags, state flags, and the Red, White, and Blue" carrying the "white-headed heroes of the Confederacy." The day that Greenville chose to welcome back its veterans of the Great War was also Confederate Memorial Day.[2]

In City Park speeches focused more on Confederate Memorial Day than on the "Home Coming celebration," extolling the values of the Lost Cause and, in contrast, underplaying those of the Great War and its veterans. The *Greenville Daily News* reported that "the veterans in gray of the War between the States and the world war veterans in khaki were eulogized by Robert A. Cooper, governor of the State, and Major W. D. Workman, a battalion commander of the immortal Thirtieth Division." Governor Cooper expressed pride in the country but diminished the challenges the returning veterans confronted when he noted that the "veterans of the world war [are] returning to their homes" during a time when "America and the world is entering upon a new era." In contrast, "when the veterans of the Confederacy returned to their homes at the close of the war they ha[d] desolation and poverty and such conditions as will never again exist

The Confederacy continued to cast a long shadow into the World War I era, when ceremonies honoring World War I veterans, both white and African American, were often compared to the service of Civil War veterans and placed within a nostalgic, Lost Cause context. Here, Sherriff Hendrix Rector and others paused in front of the decorated Confederate statue during the parade to welcome home local servicemen from the Great War on Confederate Memorial Day. Courtesy South Carolina Room, Greenville County Library.

in this country." Of Workman's speech, the *Greenville Daily News* wrote, "Characterizing the soldiers of the Confederacy as the greatest and most fearless soldiers in the world's history of wars[,] Major William D. Workman, a returned hero of the famous Thirtieth Division, said that he appeared before the Confederate veterans as a veteran of the world war in all humility." Workman stated, "Your struggle was vastly different from the one we have just completed. You displayed in your fighting such as the world has never known[,] battling against odds that were overwhelming and which practically included the entire world. And when victory had forsaken you an[d] hope was gone you fought on and on. The deeds of the Confederacy will live forever because they are written in the hearts of a loving people." He spoke of the Confederates' "real victory," which included transforming "the devastated Southland into one of prosperity and plenty overcoming conditions and problems that would have bewildered men less resolute."[3]

Less than a year later, the *Greenville Daily News* ran a rare headline in all capital letters above its banner: "GREENVILLE IS BACKING THE AMERICAN LEGION, JOIN NOW, VETERANS." The article stated that "a large majority of the progressive men of Greenville are in line with the men of the American Legion because of the principles for which the legion, by far the strongest veteran organization in existence today, stands."[4]

In March 1919 in Paris, members of the American Expeditionary Forces convened and established the American Legion, a patriotic, service-oriented veterans' organization that Congress officially chartered months later. By mid-July legionnaires held their first state convention in Florence, South Carolina, during which the group elected officers, two of whom were Greenvillians. Attorney Guy Gullick was elected state vice commander, and attorney Major Workman—who had commanded the 1st Battalion, 188th Regiment, 30th Division and allegedly wrote the order of attack that broke the Hindenburg Line—was chosen as the state insurance officer. Though one of the earliest articles to mention the legion in the local newspaper described the organization as being "progressive" and its membership open to "any soldier, sailor, or marine who served honorably," it subsequently issued a statement in early September that clarified that "any" meant White. The national organization ceded policies regarding the racial makeup of the chapters to each state. According to scholar Steven Trout, South Carolina's legion headquarters established some of the most discriminatory policies nationwide. With a constitution that stipulated that each county must only have one post and that only White veterans could apply for charters, African American veterans in South Carolina were prohibited from establishing segregated posts.[5]

Acts of memorialization both shape and are shaped by the contemporary values of the memorialists. In Greenville a Confederate culture pervaded the memorialization of the Great War.[6] The parade's conflation of Confederate and Great War memorialization efforts perpetuated a Lost Cause ethos that subjugated African Americans, situated the Great War within the context of the legacy of the Civil War, and hampered Progressive Era efforts in Greenville and throughout the nation. The founding of the American Legion not only represents one of the earliest efforts to unite, honor, and memorialize those who had served in the war but also reflects the extent locally that segregation was de rigeur and that insistence on the racial status quo did not detract from what was deemed progressive.

Community parades and the founding of the American Legion were just two of many postwar efforts to honor those who had served and died in the Great

Greenville's postal workers were photographed in 1900. Holloway is standing on the far right, and clerk Amelia Metts, the first woman to be employed by Greenville's post office, is seated. Courtesy South Carolina Room, Greenville County Library.

War. In the decade after the war's end, there was a flurry of commemorative activity across the country in the form of statues, veterans' organizations, cemeteries, pilgrimages, holidays, murals, and living memorials such as trees, highways, buildings, community centers, and stadiums.

Greenville, too, heeded the impulse to memorialize. Col. Holmes B. Springs established and served as the first president of the Old Hickory Veterans' Association, which looked to Greenville as their "mother city." As early as April 1919, city leaders issued an official invitation to host a reunion in Greenville in late September and early October 1919 to coincide with the anniversary of their successful effort at breaking the Hindenburg Line on September 28, 1918. Community leader Henry T. Mills coordinated efforts among civic organizations to raise the monies needed to sponsor activities such as dinners, dances, airplane demonstrations, automobile rides, and street illuminations. Families, schools, and businesses volunteered to house up to 5,000 thousand men, with Greenville's mail carriers alone securing lodging for 750 servicemen.[7] In advance of the reunion, the Ottoray Hotel hosted a banquet to honor Greenville's mail carriers and their efforts. The *Greenville Daily News,* however, reported that the proprietor of the Ottoray Hotel would instead present a fruit basket to one of the carriers who had "worked just as faithfully in soliciting rooms as had the other carriers." Elias B. Holloway, the only African American mail carrier in Greenville, was prohibited from attending.[8]

The reunion was a resounding success. *The Piedmont* newspaper published a souvenir edition, which included articles on the Thirtieth Division and messages from military and local and state officials. Mayor Harvley offered the city's "heartiest welcome back home." Sixty Furman students served as guards in the various locations where the men slept.

On November 11, 1919, President Wilson proclaimed November 11 Armistice Day. The commemorations in Greenville resembled nothing like the celebrations from the year prior. Furman and Judson Mill hosted Greenville's two most significant Armistice Day programs, yet they received little media attention.[9] To encourage veterans who had trained at Camp Sevier to establish roots in the city, the Chamber of Commerce capped off Homecoming Week in 1921 with an elaborate Armistice Day celebration. Furman held annual Armistice Day commemorations in its chapel throughout the decade. Congress passed a resolution urging governors to observe the holiday in the mid-1920s, and in 1938 Armistice Day formally became a national holiday. World War II forced a revision of this holiday once more; in 1954 the name of the holiday changed to Veterans Day, though it continued to be commemorated on November 11.

Nationally, and even locally, the most newsworthy event from tthe first anniversary of Armistice Day occurred when tensions between veterans and members of the Industrial Workers of the World peaked during an Armistice Day parade in Centralia, Washington, resulting in the deaths of five American Legionnaires and subsequent lynching of one who was also a member of the IWW. Even Greenville's newspaper carried far more articles on the Centralia Tragedy than it did on the ceremonies at Furman and Judson Mill. Veterans resented the anti-capitalist rhetoric of the IWW and its "One Big Union" inclusiveness of all workers, whether African American, foreign-born, or White, and felt that they threatened to undermine the established economic, political, and social systems they had just defended in the war. The Centralia incident reinforced the trend toward 100 Percent Americanism, as it both reflected and bolstered anxieties about the growing impact of immigration, communism, and organized labor. In 1921 the American Legion announced plans to erect a national memorial in Centralia and invited submissions from across the country.

Before the war's end, sculptor Ernest Moore Viquesney anticipated the urge to memorialize. As a maker of marble headstones for Union soldiers and prisoners of war buried in the Andersonville National Cemetery in Americus, Georgia, Viquesney was familiar with war's trauma and the yearning to honor those who served and died. He was also a creative self-promotor, described by scholar Steven Trout as "more P. T. Barnum than Michelangelo."[10]

Inspired in part by the Statue of Liberty, Viquesney sculpted a soldier triumphantly raising his right fist, which holds a grenade, an explosive device ubiquitous in trench warfare. His other arm hangs at his side, clutching a rifle and attached bayonet. Viquesney often asked returning soldiers to stand in uniform for him. In 1920 he applied for a patent for his *Spirit of the American Doughboy* and subsequently began to mass market the statue using a mold he created to more efficiently produce them. In 1921 the American Legion in Centralia informed Viquesney that they had selected his *Spirit of the American Doughboy* as the winning memorial to the victims of the Centralia Massacre, which greatly enhanced Americans' awareness of the statue. Soon communities across the nation raised funds to purchase a statue to honor their own.

Just as southern women had overwhelmingly led efforts to memorialize their Confederate dead, so too did women after the Great War. In Greenville, Furman president William J. McGlothlin appointed Eva E. Fletcher, a Furman librarian, to develop a war memorial for the campus. In early 1920 Fletcher began a fundraising drive among Furman alumni and friends for a memorial bronze tablet to be placed in Alumni Hall. After the response to solicitations overwhelmed what the university had anticipated, and with suggestions from veterans that something more significant be undertaken, the university decided to erect Viquesney's doughboy. Newspapers across the nation, including Greenville's, published articles to assist statue fundraising efforts. In communities that hoped to purchase a Viquesney doughboy, these articles commonly mentioned that the American Legion had officially endorsed his sculpture and selected it for the memorial to honor the veterans who died in Centralia, though that did not come to fruition.

Thus these remembrance efforts resonated with Americans, and especially Greenvillians, who wanted both to honor those who had served the nation and to oppose the Wobblies, who "promised to undo everything the Legionnaires had fought to achieve."[11] Furman's doughboy was only the second to be manufactured. Cast in sheet bronze alloy by Friedley-Voshardt Company in Chicago, Furman's *Spirit of the American Doughboy* was placed on a five-foot-tall base of granite from Winnsboro, South Carolina, where Furman was located before its move to Greenville. Fletcher planned an elaborate unveiling ceremony for June 7.[12]

On the final afternoon of Commencement Week, as a military band played, hundreds gathered around the memorial, tightly ensconced by a vibrant American flag. The beautiful June weather, patriotic tunes, and colorful displays of the regalia worn by members of the military, Furman faculty, and graduates punctuated the feeling of anticipation. In addition to the university community, the crowd included relatives of the Furman men who died in service, the local American Legion post, and members of the public. Dr. O. O. Fletcher, Eva's husband, who was a professor of philosophy and social science at Furman, opened the ceremony with a prayer. Comments followed from President McGlothlin, Colonel Springs (representing the American Legion), and Major Workman, who paid tribute to the six Furman men who perished in the war, "expressing the hope that sadness should vanish from their memories, while pride in their service remained."

Then, as a lone bugler played "Taps," the expectant crowd grew silent. Three color sergeants in AEF uniform accompanied the mother of Pvt. Thomas J. Lyon, killed in France, to the statue. After she unfastened the Stars and Stripes, they slowly unwound it, and sunlight began to dance upon bronze. A dramatic hush fell over the crowd, followed by an emotional burst of applause at the sight of their proud, gleaming doughboy. Eva Fletcher wrote, "Tears filled the eyes of beholders, and ex-service men wept as they saw the figure, so lifelike, emerge. It shows a soldier, young and vigorous, going into battle, leggings loosely wound, shirt open at the throat, his pack awry, gas mask on chest, right hand raised, carrying a grenade, a rifle in the left hand, and his mouth open, calling to his comrades, or shouting a triumph song."[13] On the front of the granite base was inscribed the words, in capital letters: "FURMAN MEN WHO GAVE THEIR LIVES IN THE WORLD WAR," followed by the names of the six who perished. On the reverse was written, "MORE THAN FIVE HUNDRED FURMAN MEN SERVED IN THE WORLD WAR." Three young girls, dressed in white, laid a wreath of purple and white flowers and six votives, one for each of the Furman men killed.

The ceremony closed with a flag raising while the band played "To the Colors," and the crowd then removed their caps and joined in the singing of "The Star-Spangled Banner." Though Fletcher noted that Furman was "the first college

On June 7, 1921, a crowd that included hundreds of locals gathered solemnly on the campus of Furman University to honor the six Furman men who died while serving their country and unveil one of Ernest Moore Viquesney's "Spirit of the American Doughboy." Courtesy of Special Collections and Archives, Furman University.

in the land, so far as known, to erect a *statue* to her heroes," some believe that this doughboy was the first in the nation to be installed and dedicated.[14]

Doughboy statues proliferated throughout the country over the next decade, despite calls by art critics for communities to engage in more intentional reflection, consider more artful, abstract forms, and depart from the rank-and-file local soldier that typified Civil War memorials.[15] The outbreak of the Great War occurred on the heels of Civil War memorialization efforts, which emphasized local "common soldier" monuments that "represent a major turning point in the history of US commemorative art," according to scholar Jennifer Wingate.[16] The doughboy dominated Great War memorials, with the figure depicted in a more active stance. The youthful fighting soldier confidently striding forward over the barbed wire of "no man's land" was intended to honor all who served. The figure shaped domestic efforts to commemorate the war and molded popular understandings of those who served as White combat veterans, despite that less than half of those who served engaged in combat. Greenville's Civil War memorial of a soldier at parade rest (modeled after a local veteran) and its World War I memorial typify the commemorative trends of their respective wars. The several hundred "ready made stock sculpture" doughboys erected around the country, mostly in the 1920s, contributed to a "major wave of public figurative sculpture," according to Wingate. Including the Civil War monuments that preceded them, they represent "a golden age of civic sculpture" that did not resurge until the Vietnam Veterans' Memorial, dedicated on the National Mall in 1982, rekindled a new, smaller wave.[17]

In the wake of Civil War memorialization, art critics hoped to avoid the "maddening monotony," as writer and art critic Adeline Adams described in 1919, of commercialized, mass-produced monuments.[18] Yet that trend persisted as their "familiarity rather than originality" was precisely what resonated with a nationalist, xenophobic, and isolationist public overwrought from global war, pandemic, fears of communism, and the largest wave of immigration in American history. The vigorous doughboy assuaged several widespread anxieties prevalent during and after the uncertain years of the war era: apprehensions regarding the strength of White American manhood in an increasingly urbanized nation; concerns about vulnerable veterans and their assimilation back into society; and fears regarding the Red Scare, immigrants, and organized labor. According to Wingate, "For many Americans, the image of the soldier served as an antidote to radicalism, a sign of vigilance and loyalty, and a reassuring vision of American fitness and manhood."[19] The commemorative sentiment expressed by the doughboy statues was one of strength and glory, not of torment or loss, and it resonated with hundreds of communities throughout the nation.

Locally, nationally, and internationally, the American Legion continued to play a leadership role in advocating for veterans' needs and shaping memorialization efforts.[20] Of all the posts in the state, according to the *Greenville Civic and Commercial Journal,* Greenville had the "strongest post in terms of numbers."[21] Immediately after the war, the legion supported improved health care for wounded veterans, particularly for victims of poison gas. In 1927 the legion held its ninth annual convention in Paris, and at least ten Greenvillians were among the more than sixty-five South Carolinians who participated, including the vice president of the SC American Legion Auxiliary, Frances Dall; Major Hayword Mahon Jr.; and community leader Margaret McKissick.[22] In advance of the trip, *American Legion Magazine* enticed its members with claims that "the city which keeps alive the memory of its dead will extend to the Second A. E. F. a welcome that will be mellowed by remembrance of the joint sacrifice of two nations."[23]

The group of twenty thousand, joined by General Pershing, sailed from New York to France in mid-September. The French welcomed the legionnaires with extensive festivities, and the tour included battlefields, cemeteries, and sites throughout Paris. During their formal meeting, the legion unanimously resolved to create a memorial building in Paris that would also serve as a center for its activities overseas. Soon thereafter the legion took ownership of an eighteenth-century townhome in central Paris and named it Pershing Hall. For decades it assisted struggling and destitute veterans with a rehabilitation program and hosted a school for two hundred American orphans.[24]

While many of their fellow legionnaires were in France, members of Greenville's Post no. 3 were coordinating with Greer and Spartanburg to beautify and dedicate a memorial highway between Camp Sevier and Camp Wadsworth to those who perished in the Great War. With widespread community support for the living memorial, including a donation of $150 collected by children in Greenville's public schools, the post planted the first tree, an American elm, on Armistice Day and announced plans to line the highway with 3,999 more. By the end of the year, the planting on Greenville's portion of the highway, which extended to the city of Greer, was nearly complete.[25]

Greenvillians commemorated the war in other ways as well, with churches and schools establishing permanent memorials in the ten years after the Armistice. Buncombe Street Methodist, First Presbyterian, Second Presbyterian, Saint Andrews, Saint James, and Trinity Lutheran placed bronze tablets with the names of congregants who had served in the war. Greenville High School installed a bronze tablet with the names of eighty male and female alumni who served. Though they did not come to fruition, civic leaders and the city's bar association entertained ideas for a memorial library and a memorial municipal building that would straddle the Main Street Reedy River bridge.[26]

Throughout the 1920s and early 1930s, some state legislatures, including Maryland, Maine, North Dakota, Ohio, Utah, and Vermont, appropriated funds to create an official state-sponsored record of those who served in the war. In a move unusual among the southern states, the South Carolina General Assembly appropriated $6,500 in February 1929 to create "a complete roster of all South Carolina soldiers, sailors, and marines who entered the service of the United States in the War of 1917–1919 with the Central Powers of Europe."[27] The act included specific instructions for the disbursement of copies to all state offices, including the State Library, every public library and college or university in the state, and a copy to each American Legion post. *The Official Roster of South Carolina Sailors, Soldiers, and Marines in the World War, 1917–18* appeared in five hardbound books.[28] Volume 1 detailed the service records of White veterans in three parts, while volume 2 did the same for African Americans in two parts.

In the war's aftermath, local civic and veterans' groups assumed leadership of their community's memorials in part because, according to Wingate, national commemorative efforts focused on the establishment of cemeteries overseas.[29] Led by General Pershing, Congress established the American Battlefield Monuments

Commission in 1923 to create and maintain cemeteries and memorials overseas in places where American armed forces had served since April 6, 1917. According to commission records, 390 World War I veterans from South Carolina are buried in its cemeteries in Belgium, England, and France. Though the 217-feet-tall Liberty Memorial, dedicated by President Calvin Coolidge in 1926 in Kansas City, was unofficially treated as a national memorial, it was organized and funded locally, and no other memorial came close to serving as a nationally sanctioned site.

In the years that followed the end of the war, the War Department and the Graves Registration Service communicated with families who had lost loved ones. Some, like John and Victoria Rainey of Taylors, elected to repatriate their son, Pvt. Luther Rainey, who fought in the battles of Cantigny, Second Marne, and Saint-Mihiel and who died one month before the war ended during the Meuse-Argonne offensive. His body was returned, and he is buried in the Mountain Creek Baptist Cemetery, alongside soldiers who died at Camp Sevier, victims of influenza, and others.[30]

In 1929, after years of lobbying by the American Gold Star Mothers, Congress approved funding to support overseas pilgrimages for mothers and unremarried widows whose sons and former husbands were interred overseas. Between 1930 and 1933, when the project ended, approximately 6,700 of the 17,389 women deemed eligible had traveled to visit their loved one. The program was open to White and African American women, though their pilgrimages were segregated and facilities varied greatly, despite the War Department's assertion that their segregation was for the "contentment and comfort of the pilgrims" and that "no discrimination as between the various groups is contemplated."[31] White women, for instance, traveled on luxury liners, while African American women sailed on "second class" commercial steamers.[32] The news of the segregated treatment horrified poet James Weldon Johnson, who penned "Saint Peter Relates an Incident of the Resurrection Day" in 1930 in protest. Ultimately 168 African American women participated, with 7 eligible women refusing as a protest against the segregation.[33]

One of the eligible women was the mother of Pvt. Willie Wise, an African American farm hand from Prosperity, South Carolina, about seventy-five miles outside Greenville. Wise trained at Camp Jackson, sailed to Europe from Newport News, Virginia, on the *President Grant* in April 1918, and served in the 371st Division, 93rd Infantry, Company K. He survived the war but died from influenza in January 1919 and is buried in the Aisne-Marne cemetery. Had he lived, he would have sailed from Brest, France, on an eight-day journey to Hoboken, New Jersey, in February 1919 aboard the USS *Leviathan,* the same ship that later transported many of the White Gold Star women to Europe.[34] In response to the War

Epilogue   227

Department's questionnaire, mailed to all women eligible for the pilgrimage, Wise's mother wrote a letter, addressed to the War Department on the top half of a torn piece of lined notebook paper, explaining that "her financial condition" prohibited her from visiting her son. She explained, "I am trying to farm, and I can't step out of my farm that long, as that is my only way for a living." In lieu of the trip, she inquired as to whether the government might be able to provide any financial aid "for the service for my son. I would appreciate it, as I have a poor way to live."[35] The sentiment of the letter reveals both the heartache of loss and the struggles of southern, rural African Americans during the Great Depression.

With the onset of the Depression, the nation's fervor in commemorating the war waned relative to the 1920s, though New Deal programs actually enabled many projects. In 1919 Lt. Col. Wyndham M. Manning suggested the idea of a World War Memorial Building to his father, the governor of South Carolina. The idea resonated with Governor Manning; six of his sons had served in the war, and one of them, Maj. William Sinkler Manning, died of combat wounds in the final week of the war during the Meuse-Argonne offensive. Governor Manning formally proposed a World War Memorial Building, and soon thereafter the general assembly appropriated one hundred thousand dollars for a memorial to South Carolina's White service members on the campus of the University of South Carolina and another hundred thousand for a memorial to African American service members on the campus of the State Agricultural and Mechanical College in Orangeburg. A World War Memorial Commission, with two representatives appointed by Manning from each congressional district, raised private funds from 1919 to 1935. Greenville's Alester G. Furman served as one of the commissioners, representing the Fourth District.[36] However, the assembly's funding was withdrawn as a result of the Depression, and building plans were scaled in half. Several years later, the New Deal's Public Works Administration provided approximately thirty-three thousand dollars for the project, and construction began.

On Memorial Day in 1935, Wyndham Manning laid the cornerstone for the structure in a ceremony that included the governor, the members of the memorial commission, presidents of the state's colleges, and the Richland Post Drum and Bugle Corps. The keynote speaker, former Senator Roach S. Stewart, used the forum not only to express his hope that "generations to come would gaze upon this building, and remembering why it was erected, would preserve the ideals for which it stood," but also to frame the war and those who served in it within the greater Lost Cause interpretation of the Civil War. Though his comments lauded the service of South Carolina's veterans in the Great War, they also reminded the audience that "no land could boast soldiers greater than those men who followed Lee and Jackson." The veterans of the Great War were, in Roach's perspective and in the perspective of many White southerners, penultimate to those who wore Confederate gray. He also presented a divine reframing of the purpose behind Confederate defeat when he surmised, "As one looks back on history, one cannot but believe the Lord let the southern cause go down in defeat that a united America might save the world from the imperialism of the Kaiser."[37] The thirty-minute program was significantly shorter than the dedication programs of the 1920s and closed with a prayer from Rev. R. C. Betts, chaplain of the state senate, that also linked these memorialization efforts to the Civil War: "Oh Lord of hosts, be with us, lest we forget." Taken from Rudyard Kipling's 1897 poem "Recessional," the concluding phrase of his prayer had become closely associated with the memorialization of the Civil War and subsequently the Great War, and connoted a Lost Cause nostalgia for many White South Carolinians.

Completed in 1937, the limestone temple memorial building features a facade of columns, with inscriptions and dedications throughout its interior and exterior. The most prominent is above the front entrance: "Dedicated to the Men and Women of South Carolina Who Offered Their Lives in the Winning of the War." The office building served as home to the Department of Archives and History on its bottom floor, with a chapel and office space for the American Legion upstairs. The building represents one of several dozen memorials to the Great War constructed in part by New Deal programs.

Commemorative events continued in Greenville throughout the 1930s as well. In Greenville the Rotary Club hosted an Armistice Day celebration in 1933 in which its twenty-seven members were asked to attend in uniform. The *Greenville News* reported that "sandbags, barbed wire entanglements and other reminders of the battlefield formed a realistic setting for the program."[38] The next year around Memorial Day, the women of the American Legion Auxiliary placed a small bronze plate embedded within a Greenville County granite tablet near one of the main entrances of the old Camp Sevier site. The inscription read, "In memory of the men who trained here and those that made the supreme sacrifice in the great world war." They dedicated it in a ceremony attended by 750 that was described as "brief, without ostentation, but it carried many of those gathered there back to the days when the note of bugle sounded almost unceasingly over the hills and valleys of Camp Sevier."[39] In 1937 the Thirtieth "Old Hickory" Division once again held a reunion in Greenville in which it celebrated in rousing fashion its contributions to the war effort, which included breaking through the supposedly impregnable Hindenburg Line in France. Newspaper articles once more posited these Great War veterans as descendants in a mythic Confederate lineage: "The sons and grandsons of those heroes in a lost cause that ended at Appomattox had cut a gate through the greatest defensive line in military history

and from that moment on it was realized by all that the end of the cruel conflict
. . . was but a matter of time."[40] Greenvillians lauded their return. Festivities
included a parade, a dance and show at Textile Hall, a "Golden Gloves boxing
exposition," and a visit to a "beer and weiner roast" at the Camp Sevier site.
Greenville Country Club and the public golf course at Hillandale waived green
fees for the veterans. Nearly two decades after war's end, the local newspaper
captured the sense of anticipation: "Men of Old Hickory, Greenville bids you
welcome again. You were loved then; you are loved now."[41] In 1938 the American
Legion Armistice Day program included a parade down Main Street preceding
a football game between Greenville High School and Easley High in Sirrine Stadium. A state historical marker honoring Camp Sevier and sponsored by the
American Legion in Greenville was fabricated and intended to be dedicated on
Armistice Day but was delayed, as the legion hoped to acquire land for a park
surrounding the marker. The marker was later placed at the corner of Wade
Hampton Boulevard (US Route 29) and Artillery Road.[42]

The outbreak of World War II in Europe in 1939 bluntly and brutally dis-
abused the world of the notion that the Great War was the war to end all wars.
The twenty-fifth anniversary of the World War I armistice on November 11, 1943,
was heavily overshadowed by news of the current war and was summarized in this
article that appeared on the cover page of the *Greenville News* the next day:
"The roar of production machinery at home and the thunder of modern warfare
abroad all but drowned out yesterday the usual commemoration of the Armistice
day that 25 years ago ended the bloody slaughter of the First World war."[43] In
contrast to World War I, efforts to memorialize the service of World War II veterans were conspicuously lacking. Scholar James Loewen reasons that the country,
from a memorialization standpoint, was still coming to grips with the legacy of
the bronzed, stone-inscribed, lofty commemorative rhetoric of the Great War
memorials in light of the more recent conflict and, with the onset of the Cold
War so soon after the end of World War II, lacked the confidence to inscribe
proclamations of war's end.[44] Often communities simply added names to memorials they had erected in the previous decades. In Greenville in the late 1940s,
Furman added a plaque with the names of fifty-five Furman men who died in
World War II to the doughboy. Many of the World War I divisions maintained
the practice of annual reunions, and those divisions that were reactivated during
World War II often invited those veterans to join them. On a weekend in October
1956, the Eighty-First "Wildcat" Division held their annual reunion in Greenville,
with veterans from both world wars in attendance. The Hotel Greenville served
as the headquarters for the 500 men, representing thirty-two states, and about
150 of their wives. Reunion activities included a banquet and ball, a trip to Camp

Sevier, and the dedication of a marker, placed between City Hall and the Masonic Temple, to the Wildcats that trained at Camp Sevier.[45]

Renewed interest in World War I arose in the 1960s as a result of several factors. In 1962 Barbara Tuchman published her seminal work on World War I, *The Guns of August*, a Pulitzer Prize winner and *New York Times* bestseller. President John F. Kennedy had read the book and made several references to it during the harrowing days of the Cuban Missile Crisis, prompting some scholars to credit her arguments about the misunderstandings and miscalculations of World War I as an influence on his actions and reactions during that crisis.[46] The Great War's legacy influenced other cultural forms as well. In 1966, less than a year before the fiftieth anniversary of American entry into the war, the *Greenville News* included an article on "military touches in feminine clothes," with a contemporary take on the "doughboy pants suit," in "red Shetland wool with long jacket and epaulette shoulders" being fabricated by Junior Sophisticates of New York.[47]

Acts of memorialization often reveal more about the memorialists than they do those being memorialized. The fiftieth anniversary of World War I, for example, was extensively shaped by the fighting in Southeast Asia. In 1967, months after the centennial of American entry, the *Greenville News* featured the centennial of World War I on a full, interior page with a brief article and large images and biographies of notable men from Greenville who had served in the war. In the midst of the civil rights movement, African American veterans were excluded. The article claimed that "the American people in 1917–18 for the most part knew little about Ypres, Chateau-Thierry and Belleau Wood as Americans today know of Da Nang, Hanoi, Bien Hoa and other battlefields. The scenes of war have changed but the purpose seems to have remained the same some 50 years later. Since 1917, when America entered World War I, the nation has continued to find itself involved in world conflict: Latin America in the 1920s; China in the 1930s; global war in the 1940s; Korea in the 1950s; and Vietnam in the 1960s."[48] The article estimated that fewer than seven thousand veterans of the Great War lived in the state at the time. In anticipation of the anniversary of the end of the war in 1968, the local newspaper ran a United Press International story on the "lush" Argonne. "Fifty years have gone by since the cold, windy September days of 1918 when American armies unleased their great Meuse-Argonne offensive against reputedly impregnable German positions northwest of Verdun. The war ended 50 years ago Monday."[49] On Veterans Day the *Greenville News* began its most prominent editorial that day with the words, "On the 50th anniversary of the armistice which ended the fighting in World War I, it is sobering to note that the 'war to end war' did not do so; that more war veterans are being produced on this Veterans Day 1968; and that war will continue indefinitely into the future." The editorial encouraged readers to welcome home the "new veterans" who "have fought together without regard to race, creed, or color" in the spirit of the South Carolina Human Relations Council's Operation Gratitude, a program designed to assist African American and White veterans of Vietnam with educational opportunities, employment, and housing. "Doing that is perhaps the best way to contribute toward the peace at home and the eventual peace of the world so ardently desired by all Americans—to keep alive the unrealized hope that arose throughout the world 50 years ago."[50] In its summer 1970 issue, the *Furman Magazine* also contextualized the forthcoming fiftieth anniversary of its doughboy within the context of the Vietnam War. In an introduction to a reprint of Fletcher's 1921 article, "Lest We Forget," the magazine offered reflections that characterize the human impulse to assume the past was somehow less complex than the present. "Good was Good and Bad was Bad, and it was taken for granted that every man who could would fight for his country. But fifty years and three wars later the issues are not so clear."[51]

The civil rights movement awakened American society to its deep racial inequalities, and slowly, in subsequent decades, the nation began to address the legacy of that inequality. In the South Carolina Upcountry, the legacy of race and its impact on the politics of remembrance are pointedly revealed in the legacy of Cpl. Freddie Stowers and the community of Greenwood's memorialization challenges.

In the years during and soon after the Great War, White soldiers received the nation's highest medals of distinction, with South Carolinians receiving more medals of honor than any other state, excepting New York and Illinois. African American soldiers were recipients of the Medal of Honor in conflicts from the Civil War, when the medal originated, to the Spanish-American War. Yet military decorations awarded to African American soldiers in and after World War I were fewer in number and of less distinction. In the decades after war's end, dozens of White soldiers received the Medal of Honor, while not one African American did.[52] As decades passed, and institutional racism in the military and society gradually decreased, African American veterans of other US conflicts were once again awarded this honor, beginning with the conflict in Korea. In 1990 Congress asked the army to review Medal of Honor records, whereupon they discovered paperwork recommending Corporal Stowers of the 371st for a Medal of Honor. After a team traveled to France to investigate, the Army Decorations Board approved the honor. Seventy-three years after he was killed in action, at a White House ceremony on April 24, 1991, Freddie Stowers of Sandy Springs, South Carolina, became the first African American recipient of the Medal of Honor for

World War I. Stowers's two surviving sisters, Georgina and Mary, accepted the award from President George H. W. Bush. At Fort Benning in Georgia, an elementary school honors Stowers, as does the Single Soldier Complex at Fort Jackson, formerly Camp Jackson. On Veterans Day, 2015, Anderson University erected a statue of Stowers on their campus, not far from where he grew up, and a scholarship for Anderson high schoolers bears his name.

Stowers's case prompted a similar study that scrutinized Medal of Honor nominations from World War II, which revealed that several African American servicemen who had been awarded the Distinguished Service Cross should have received the Medal of Honor, and thus their medals were upgraded during President Bill Clinton's administration.[53]

The investigation that resulted in Stowers's Medal of Honor sparked further studies, which revealed that Jewish Americans, Hispanic Americans, and Japanese Americans had also been subject to racial and ethnic discrimination and had not received the medals for which they qualified. Consequently the legacy of Freddie Stowers includes restitution to other minority groups as well. Furthermore the centennial of World War I, commemorated between 2014 and 2018, prompted renewed interest in honoring veterans from the war. During President Barack Obama's administration in 2015, Sgt. William Henry Johnson became the second African American Medal of Honor recipient from World War I.[54] At that same ceremony, Obama similarly awarded it to World War I soldier Sgt. William Shemin of the Fourth Infantry Division, whose Jewish faith was believed to have similarly influenced the commendation process. From 1991 to 2015, presidents Bush, Clinton, George W. Bush, and Obama awarded more than fifty minority men the Medal of Honor for service in World War I, World War II, Korea, and Vietnam.

About fifty miles away from Stowers's hometown, the city of Greenwood also aspired to reconcile a history of racial discrimination in the way it honored and memorialized its servicemen from the world wars. On Armistice Day in 1929, thousands gathered to dedicate a world war memorial, funded collectively by the American Legion Post no. 20, the Legion Auxiliary, and public donations. The nearly thirty-thousand-pound Winnsboro granite monument was erected in downtown Greenwood to the soldiers who had died in the Great War. In 1948 the community added a plaque with the names of those who had died in World War II. Sometime soon thereafter it created a new plaque for the soldiers from the Great War, identifying them instead as veterans of "World War I." The names on both the new plaques were organized separately by race.

For decades journalists and visitors to Greenwood pointed to its war memorial at the heart of Main Street as evidence of small-town southern racism. According

Epilogue 233

to one Greenwood resident, the monument regrettably suggested that Greenwood was "a backwoods racist town . . . not the Greenwood I grew up in."[55] In 2011 Greenwood mayor Welborn Adams suggested to the local American Legion that the plaques ought to be changed, but the idea received no support. Three years later, however, its executive committee voted unanimously to change the memorial. In 2014 Mayor Adams and the local American Legion chapter led efforts to raise private funds needed to remove the existing markers and create new ones that integrated the listing of Greenwood's war dead. Forty-three donors, forty-one of them White, donated fifteen thousand dollars. They planned to unveil the new markers in a ceremony that the mayor described as a "celebration of togetherness" on Martin Luther King Day in 2015, but just weeks before Adams was "stunned" to learn that he would be breaking the law. The Heritage Act, a legislative compromise passed by the SC General Assembly in 2000 when the Confederate Battle Flag was removed from atop the State House dome, prohibits the addition, removal, or altering of war monuments and memorials without a two-thirds vote by the general assembly. It has granted select exemptions, the most high-profile being the removal of the Confederate battle flag from the state house grounds in 2015 in the wake of the killing of nine African American churchgoers at Charleston's Mother Emanuel African Methodist Episcopal (AME) Church.[56]

State senators filed a bill to legitimize the removal of Greenwood's plaques, but it did not gain further support, likely because it also included changing the name of Clemson's Tillman Hall, named for "Pitchfork" Ben Tillman. Undeterred, Adams and members of the American Legion recommitted themselves to finding a way to proceed and filed a legal challenge to the Heritage Act. To help bolster their suit, Greenwood's city council passed a resolution in support of replacing the plaques. In May 2018 circuit judge Frank Addey ruled that Greenwood could modify its monument, because while it sat on publicly owned land, the memorial itself was privately owned. In June, Greenwood resident Trey Ward, owner of a local painting company and former member of a band named the New Dixie Storm, felt a "moral imperative" to act. Quietly and without warning, he switched the plaques. Though he publicly said, "All I really did was turn some screws on a plate," the plaintiff's attorney, Armand Derfner of Charleston, described the court decision as "the first nail in the coffin of the Heritage Act."[57]

The years-long fight to alter and protest Greenwood's memorial sparked intense debate among not only politicians but also the public, journalists, and scholars, who weighed the attributes and drawbacks of various options: leaving the plaques as they were; leaving the plaques but adding one that contextualized the history of racism in the American military and in Greenwood; and lastly removing the old and adding the new plaques. This multiyear battle attracted

234 "Our Country First, Then Greenville"

attention from the *Los Angeles Times, Military Times, New York Times, Philadelphia Tribune, Seattle Times,* and CBS and NBC News. In Greenwood and elsewhere, memorials that involve race, reconciliation, repair, and remembrance have far-ranging implications for the many groups they affect.

The centennial commemoration of World War I, which began in 2014 in Europe, was conspicuously absent from the Greenwood debates. Globally the centennial of the outbreak of the war shed light on competing interpretations of the war's origins. The anniversary offers an excellent historiographical case study of the criticality of perspective, and how the questions we ask about the past evolve as society's experiences evolve. In 2014 competing public memories opened old wounds in the former Yugoslav countries. Was Gavrilo Princip, the assassin of Archduke Franz Ferdinand, "a terrorist or a freedom fighter"?[58] As anticipated in a roundtable discussion with some of the world's leading scholars of the war, the centennial highlighted significant disparities in not only the existence of a public memory of World War I but also public understandings of the war's relevance to our world today. According to scholar Jennifer Keene, the war is most relevant in countries in which it occupies a critical place in their national identity and in places where it continues to provide valuable political lessons.[59]

In 2013 American historian Adam Hochschild described World War I as "a cataclysm that changed our world forever but that remains curiously forgotten here."[60] Scholars of the war have long questioned why "Americans have such a historical blind spot to World War I."[61] They have lamented the lack of attention that the American public has given to the war in recent decades, despite its legacy and relevance to global challenges facing the United States in the early and mid-twenty-first century, such as relations with Russia and the Middle East, in addition to countless domestic issues. Even years after the centennial, journalist Michael Peck opened an article about the commemoration of World War I with the enticing question, "Why does the First World War get no respect in America?"[62]

While the Great War was memorialized locally in its aftermath, the national domestic response was lacking. In comparison the Vietnam Veterans Memorial on the National Mall was dedicated in 1982, just seven years after American withdrawal from South Vietnam. Though begun in 1986, the Korean War Veterans Memorial was dedicated on the forty-second anniversary of that war's armistice in 1995. Congress passed legislation for a World War II memorial in 1993, less than fifty years after that war's end. Prominently situated between the US Capitol and the Lincoln Memorial, the National World War II Memorial was dedicated in 2004.

Proponents of a national memorial to World War I persisted. Also in 2004, Congress designated the Liberty Memorial and a new, expanded museum in

Kansas City as the nation's official World War I Museum. In advance of the war's centennial, the World War One Centennial Commission, created by President Obama in 2013, proposed another national memorial, to be located in the nation's capital. On Veterans Day, 2017, the commission ceremoniously broke ground on the National World War I Memorial in Pershing Park on Pennsylvania Avenue. The US Commission on Fine Arts and the National Capital Planning Commission approved final designs for the memorial and its sculpture, created by artist Sabin Howard, in 2019. On April 16, 2021, President Joseph Biden spoke at the dedication ceremony, held virtually during the global COVID-19 pandemic.

In Greenville the centennial of World War I prompted a widespread, year-long grassroots effort known as Remembering Old Hickory that honored the Thirtieth Division. Members of the community, including police officers and sheriff's deputies, wore poppy pins and placed "Remember Old Hickory" decals on their vehicles. Greenville's city and county councils proclaimed September 29, 2018, the hundred-year anniversary of the day the Thirtieth broke the German defensive line, as "Remember Old Hickory Day" and commemorated their service with a ceremony at McPherson Park. In addition to this effort, an exhibit at Furman University that coincided with the centennial of American entry into the war examined how Greenville and Furman both contributed to and were affected by the war. Titled "Over Here, Over There: Greenville in the Great War," the exhibit included artifacts and images from various museums and historical societies in the community. For its duration the original Viquesney doughboy, whose home since 2004 has been downtown Greenville's Upcountry History Museum, returned to Furman's campus and was prominently displayed in the entrance to the James B. Duke Library. In 2018 the Upcountry History Museum hosted the exhibit "Answering the Call: From Recruit to the Front Lines." Programs hosted by civic organizations, from rotary clubs to the Daughters of the American Revolution, focused on the anniversary. In 2018 and 2019, at least half a dozen public programs in the South Carolina Upcountry concentrated on the service of African American soldiers from South Carolina and of African Americans who trained there, like Freddie Stowers and the Harlem Hellfighters. Certainly, with the benefit of more than half a century of scholarship on social and cultural history, the centennial commemorations of World War I have been the war's most inclusive thus far.[63]

At the dedication of the War Memorial Building in Columbia in 1937, assistant US secretary of commerce Col. J. Monroe Johnson, a Furman alumnus and veteran of World War I, astutely observed that "civilizations of people can be accurately judged by their monuments."[64] Loewen has succinctly described acts of memorialization as a "tale of two eras"; these sites honor the event or person being memorialized but also reveal the values of the people, place, and time in which the memorial was created. This concept is applicable to both those who support and those who oppose any given memorial. Despite the increased emphasis on inclusivity exhibited in the centennial commemoration of World War I and the racial awakening that has occurred in the wake of the killing of African Americans like George Floyd, a reluctance to honor the accomplishments of African Americans persists. Since 2007 the 371st Infantry Regiment Memorial Monument Association has worked to honor the 371st, a unit of African American soldiers from the South, and largely from South Carolina, who valiantly served with the French and were decorated by the French and the Americans. The group's effort to place a memorial to the 371st Infantry Regiment on the grounds of the State House in Columbia, however, has been obstructed by South Carolina's Heritage Act, which gives the state legislature power not only over what memorials are removed from public land but also what is added.[65] After more than a decade of unsuccessful lobbying, the association announced in 2019 that the memorial would be placed in Centennial Park at Fort Jackson, where the 371st was formed, trained, and deactivated.[66] The world war memorials in Greenwood offer insight into debates on how we remember, while the struggle to honor the 371st sheds light on debates about who deserves to be remembered.

In his novel *1984*, George Orwell famously wrote, "Who controls the past controls the future: who controls the present controls the past."[67] Between the 1890s and 1920s, a Confederate culture, shaped largely by the United Daughters of the Confederacy, sought to inculcate White southerners and especially White southern youth with a belief that the Old South was idyllic and Reconstruction, in great contrast, was a cruel, tragic period of African American rule. The textbook issued to South Carolina public school children in 1940 included a chapter titled "Reconstruction—the State's Darkest Day," which claimed that "most of the negroes were ignorant and some of them were almost savages."[68] A chapter in a 1964 state textbook was titled "The Ordeal of Reconstruction" and began with the following quote: "The federal bayonets removed, the power of the thieves destroyed, the so called government fell to pieces of its own imbecility, came to nought of its own all-pervading corruption." It argued that the state was "governed by a ruthless band of thieves . . . more dangerous than ordinary gangs of robbers" and that White men, "feeling that their lives and property were in danger . . . began to form a secret organization."[69] Inherent in this self-serving, southern White interpretation, according to historian Eric Foner, was a warning: "Any effort to restore the rights of Southern blacks . . . would lead to a repeat of the alleged horrors of Reconstruction."[70]

The southern White men who used terror to "redeem" themselves and their region and reimplement White domination were portrayed as the heroes of these stories; they have long served as the source of inspiration for those who feel threatened by the expansion of civil liberties and economic opportunity. Throughout the twentieth century, this calculated narrative organically evolved and was invoked by those who opposed communism, civil rights, and decolonization. In the early twenty-first century, it erupted tragically in South Carolina at Charleston's Mother Emanuel AME Church in 2015, and in Charlottesville, Virginia, in 2017. The racially motivated mass murders at a grocery store in Buffalo, New York, in 2022 were inspired in part by the killings at Mother Emanuel and serve as yet another tragic reminder that "the Lost Cause's lies still have deadly consequences."[71]

As the beginning of the sesquicentennial commemoration of Reconstruction approached, the *New York Times* lamented that while the National Park Service had "overhauled" its Civil War sites during the 150th anniversary of the conflict, the service's 408 properties nationwide "still do not include a single site dedicated to the postwar struggle to build a racially equal democracy."[72] Two years later, in Beaufort, South Carolina, the National Park Service opened its first site that concentrates on the Reconstruction period, now known as the Reconstruction Era National Historical Park.[73] Its website acknowledges that "despite the importance of Reconstruction, many Americans know very little about it. And what they do know is often outdated or inaccurate. Historians once portrayed the period as a failure. . . . Now they see its broad triumphs and also its long reach." Historian Gregory P. Downs has claimed that "there may not be any field of history where the gap between what historians know and what people believe is as vast."[74] Sites such as the Reconstruction park will continue to dispel the Lost Cause's dangerous notion that the period was so "tragic" that White southerners needed to quash, at any cost, its promise and potential for African Americans, and will explore the complex notions involved in America's "Second Founding."

From the erection of Greenville's Confederate memorial in 1892 to the city's decision to welcome home Great War veterans on Confederate Memorial Day and beyond, the Lost Cause has loomed large.

In 2022 the city of Greenville fulfilled a master plan that had been developed as an early twentieth-century City Beautiful reform and hoped to reconcile a racial wrong committed nearly a century earlier, when the city chiseled away Mayberry Park. By developing a large public park on land that borders the Reedy River, it implemented the third and final park suggested by Harlan Kelsey in his 1907 report, *Beautifying and Improving, Greenville, South Carolina*. By naming it Unity Park, developing it on land that formerly encompassed the Mayberry site, and creating spaces that honor E. B. Holloway and other local African American leaders, Mayor Knox White has acknowledged that "Unity Park is not just about a park. . . . It's a much more profound message than that. . . . The history is so deep, so rich. . . . This park has always been about the names, the faces, the people and the voices . . . that for too long in Greenville's history have been ignored." Unity Park, he asserted, "is about Greenville, South Carolina. It's about our children. It's about our future."[75]

Yet one mile away the memorial to Greenville's Confederate dead stands, where it has since 1924. The legacy of the Lost Cause lingers, and the perplexing politics of race and remembrance persist.

Notes

Introduction

1. Robertson, *Red Hills and Cotton*, 28; Capozzola et al., "Interchange: World War I," 499.

2. Black, *Great War and the Making of the Modern World*; Budreau, *Bodies of War*; Capozzola, *Uncle Sam Wants You*; Conwill, *We Return Fighting*; Dumenil, *Second Line of Defense*; Helling, *Great War and the Birth of Modern Medicine*; McCartin, *Labor's Great War*; Neiberg, *Path to War*; Proctor, *Civilians in a World at War, 1914–1918*. Resolved. All appear in new Bib.

3. Donny Santacaterina graduated from Furman University in 2015 and is currently enrolled in a doctoral program in history at the University of North Carolina at Chapel Hill. His keen research skills and exceptional dedication to this project were invaluable in the early years of it. He also contributed a lot of fun to this process, and I wish to acknowledge the debt of gratitude I owe to him.

4. Das et al., "Global Perspectives on World War I," 113. See also Capozzola et al., "Interchange: World War I," 477.

5. Megginson, "Black South Carolinians in World War I," 153, 156; "91 Local Soldiers Died during War," *Greenville Daily News*, February 23, 1920, 8; Herbermann, *Catholic Encyclopedia*, 699. Differing accounts place Greenville County war deaths between 91 and 101. One source indicates that 12 of the men who died were in the navy. South Carolina lost 50 officers in the American Expeditionary Forces (AEF), with an additional 1,088 deaths during the war. Two officers and 14 men were prisoners; 162 officers and 2,063 additional men were wounded. The state provided 53,482 soldiers, or 1.42 percent of the US Army. In 1920 the state began offering free tuition at state institutions to former soldiers. Statewide, including all the branches of the military, 64,739 South Carolinians served, and 2,085 perished during the war.

6. 1910 Census, 589, 598–9, 640; Huff, *Greenville*, 420. This data is based on census information for Charleston, Greenville, and Richland counties.

7. Das et al., "Global Perspectives on World War I," 96.

8. Gerwarth and Manela, *Empires at War: 1911–1923*, x.

9. Capozzola, "United States Empire." Capozzola's chapter treats American military involvement in World War I within the context of US imperial pursuits in Cuba, the Dominican Republic, Haiti, Mexico, the Philippines, Puerto Rico, and elsewhere.

10. "Have You Heard That . . . ?" *Greenville News*, July 13, 1933, 7.

11. See Andrew Huebner's contributions in Capozzola et al., "Interchange: World War I," 468.

12. Gilmore, *Gender and Jim Crow*, 227.

13. Filene, "Obituary for 'the Progressive Movement,'" 20–34; Harrison, *Congress, Progressive Reform, and the New American State, 11*; Johnson, "One . . . Two . . . Many Progressivisms"; Zonderman, "Yet Another Look at the Progressives."

14. Edwards, "Politics, Social Movements, and the Periodization of U.S. History," 471.

15. Some of the scholars whose works have influenced my thoughts on Progressivism include Dewey Grantham, Glenda Gilmore, Janet Hudson, Valeria Genraro Lerda, James Leloudis, Arthur and William Link, Ann Firor Scott, Ann Marie Szymanski, George B. Tindall, and C. Vann Woodward.

240   *Notes to Pages 6–12*

16. Lerda, "Southern Progressivism in Historical Perspective," 73. Lerda references one of Woodward's conclusions from *Origins of the New South*.

17. Link, *Paradox of Southern Progressivism*, 73–74.

18. In Greenville most reformers also assumed leadership roles in the home front effort. I do not wish to suggest, however, that Progressive efforts ceased completely during the war; in fact, many of them either incorporated the war into their cause or used the war to propel it.

19. Szymanski, "Beyond Parochialism," 135–36. Elizabeth Sanders's work argues that farmers were the primary force behind the Progressive movement, though most other scholars of the era identify activists as urban and middle class. Others have suggested that the urban identity of the reformers was a primary reason why southern progressivism failed. More recently, however, scholars such as Maureen Flanagan, Kenneth Finegold, and James J. Connolly have demonstrated the fluidity of the southern progressive rural-urban spectrum.

20. I made a decision early in this project to attempt to uncover the actual names of women who are relevant to this history and not simply their husbands', which is how most written materials from this period represent them. This has not been possible in all cases, but where it has, I hope to restore a sense of identity rooted in these women's accomplishments and not exclusively their marital status. This list is not exhaustive and includes only those men and women who appear in leadership positions in at least two areas of the home front effort and/or reform.

21. Flanagan, *America Reformed*, 112.

22. Perry, "Men Are from the Gilded Age, Women Are from the Progressive Era," 31, 33. In a discussion of Link's *Paradox of Southern Progressivism*, Perry notes that woman's suffrage and the causes women became involved in were central to southern progressive efforts for change.

23. Adam Quinn, "Reforming History," The H-Net Book Channel. April 26, 2017, https://networks .h-net.org/node/14542/discussions/179611/.

24. Tindall quoted in Lerda, "Southern Progressivism in Historical Perspective," 74. As Lerda writes, historian Richard Hofstadter asserted that the "ferment of the Progressive era was urban."

25. Szymanski, "Beyond Parochialism," 109.

26. Link and Pegrem quoted in Szymanski, "Beyond Parochialism," 109, 113.

27. Lerda, "Southern Progressivism in Historical Perspective," 75; Conyers, "Personal Word from the Retiring President," 1. Scholars have also debated the cohesiveness and disunity of progressivism nationally and especially in the South.

28. Doyle, *New Men, New Cities, New South*, 11.

29. In *Origins of the New South, 1877–1913*, Woodward argues that progressivism in the South was "Progressivism for whites only."

30. Both Charles D. Brier and his brother James A. Brier used the spellings *Brier* and *Briar*. The preponderance of primary sources I have incorporated uses *Brier*, and thus I have too. James A. Tolbert was African American and is not to be confused with Joseph Augustus Tolbert, a White Greenville attorney and politician who served as US District Attorney. He and his family were active in the state's Republican Party.

31. Lerda, "Southern Progressivism in Historical Perspective," 77.

Chapter 1: The Politics of Race and Gender in the "Pearl of the Piedmont"

1. Huff, *Greenville*, 178. According to Huff, the Upcountry "underwent a series of major economic shifts in the twenty-five years after the Civil War that basically altered life in the Southern Piedmont and set the region on a new course."

2. "Southern Young Men," *Greenville Enterprise*, February 7, 1867.

3. John William De Forest, "Drawing Bureau Rations," *Harper's* 36, no.216 (May 1868), 792, 798; Huff, *Greenville*, 151. De Forest's official title was "Acting Assistant Commissioner of the Bureau, Sub-District of Greenville, South Carolina."

Notes to Pages 13–19 241

4. De Forest, "Bureau Major's Business and Pleasures," 774; Laura Ebaugh, "Nineteenth Century Diary of Greenville, South Carolina," 2. Laura Ebaugh Papers, Greenville County Historical Society. DeForest was likely referring to the Literary Club of Greenville, established in January 1867.

5. Huff, *Greenville*, 193.

6. Huff, 190, quoting *Enterprise and Mountaineer,* June 2, 1875.

7. Huff, 189.

8. Bainbridge, *Historic Greenville,* 42.

9. Huff, *Greenville*, 192.

10. Huff, 186–88.

11. Huff, 210; Ambrose Gonzales, "Carolina's Mountain Queen," *Charleston News and Courier,* July 8, 1889.

12. For more on this, see Gaston, *New South Creed.*

13. C. R. Wilson, *Baptized in Blood,* 162.

14. Blight, *Race and Reunion*; Cox, *Dixie's Daughters*; Huff, *Greenville,* 207–8; C. R. Wilson, *Baptized in Blood,* 11, 18, 34, 37, 58, 161; Budreau, *Bodies of War,* 91–94; Domby, *False Cause,* x; Foster, *Ghosts of the Confederacy*; Poole, *Never Surrender.*

15. Huff, *Greenville,* 208.

16. Kytle and Roberts, *Denmark Vesey's Garden,* 59, 76, 89–91, 152–54.

17. Columbia: City of Women, "The Rollin Sisters." Accessed December 17, 2022. https://www.columbiacityofwomen.com/. Rollin sometimes wrote under the pen name Frank A. Rollin, including in her 1868 biography of Martin Delany, published as *Life and Public Services of Martin R. Delany.*

18. For more information on Confederate monuments, see Mills and Simpson, *Monuments to the Lost Cause;* Gallagher, McPherson, and Nolan, *Myth of the Lost Cause.*

19. Huff, *Greenville,* 208. Ligon was the first to enlist in the Saluda Volunteers, Company G, Fourth SC Volunteer Regiment. He attained the rank of sergeant before war's end.

20. Huff, *Greenville,* 208; Siegler, *Guide to Confederate Monuments,* 359–61.

21. "Greenville's Great Day," *Pickens Sentinel,* October 5, 1892.

22. C. R. Wilson, *Baptized in Blood,* 162; Poole, *Never Surrender,* 190–91.

23. *Gaffney Ledger,* quoted in Poole, *Never Surrender,* 191.

24. "Greenville Had Military Camp during Spanish-American War," *Greenville News,* October 15, 1965, 38.

25. Oral History with Guy Foster and Mrs. Arsinoe Foster Geiger, September 21, 1964, (9) Camp Wetherill Materials, Greenville County Historical Society.

26. James M. Richardson, "Scion of the Flatwoods," unpublished manuscript, 1941. Special Collections and University Archives, James B. Duke Library, Furman University.

27. "Lone Surviving Soldier Wishes to See Greenville," *Greenville News,* December 15, 1968; "Greenville Had Troops in 1898–99," *Greenville News,* February 26, 1974.

28. "Visiting Dignitaries Stayed at Mansion House," *Greenville News,* March 12, 2003.

29. For more on the use of *Aunt* as a term intended respectfully by Whites but often received with resentment by African Americans, see Tucker, *Telling Memories among Southern Women,* 94–95, 209–10.

30. "Sc Photo CL Baley Collection," Schomburg Center, Photographs and Prints, New York Public Library; Megginson, *African American Life in South Carolina's Upper Piedmont,* 32.

31. News item quoting the *Greenville Daily News* in the *Watchman and Southron,* February 22, 1899.

32. Huff, *Greenville,* 254–56; Judith Bainbridge, "Alester Furman was a Community Builder and Businessman," *Greenville News,* July 28, 2017; Willis and the Greenville County Historical Society, *Remembering Greenville,* 132.

33. Judith Bainbridge, "Camp Wetherill Opened Greenville to the Larger World," *Greenville News,* February 15, 2018.

242 Notes to Pages 20–23

34. *Fourteenth Census of the United States Taken in the Year 1920:* Vol. 3, *Composition and Characteristics of the Population by States.* (Washington, DC: Government Printing Office, 1922), 930–33. In 1910 and 1920, Greenville ranked fourth in the state behind Horry, Oconee, and Pickens counties in the highest percentages of White inhabitants by county. In 1940 Greenville had moved up to third behind Pickens and Oconee County. Hale, *Making Whiteness,* 20–24; Simon, *Fabric of Defeat,* 7, 31, 32–35, 51, 83, 173–74, 235.

35. Beard quotation in *Abbeville Scimitar,* February 1, 1917, cited in Hudson, *Entangled by White Supremacy,* 162.

36. "Race Riot in Greenville," *Watchman and Southron,* August 16, 1899. A bullet cut the suspenders of the one White man, J. C. Couch, who also had three other gunshots rip his clothing while he was trying to save Ben Odam, the one White casualty. A gunshot wounded Odam in his jaw. The most serious injury among the African American men was inflicted upon John McCutcheon, who was shot in the wrist. The Ellenburgs' home near the fertilizer factory was located on Buncombe Road.

37. "Race Riot in Greenville," *Anderson Intelligencer,* August 9, 1899; "Serious Race Riot," *Abbeville Press and Banner,* August 9, 1899.

38. "Race Riot in Greenville," *Anderson Intelligencer.*

39. Equal Justice Initiative, "Greenville, South Carolina, Dedicates Historical Marker Recognizing Lynching." Accessed December 17, 2022. https://eji.org/news/; Angelia L. Davis, "Greenville Lynching to Be Memorialized in Virtual Community Event," *Greenville News,* March 22, 2021; Angelia L. Davis, "Black History Month: A Look at Greenville Lynching Victim Ira Johnson," *Greenville News,* February 14, 2021; Angelia L. Davis, "Black History Month: A Look at Greenville Lynching Victim Robert Williams," *Greenville News,* February 15, 2021. For more information on Greenville's Community Remembrance Project and its affiliation with the Equal Justice Institute in Montgomery, visit the websites of these organizations.

40. For more on the Rollin sisters, see Terborg-Penn, *African American Women in the Struggle for the Vote,* 42–45. Terborg-Penn cites Benjamin Quarles's dissertation from the 1930s, which claimed that African American women in South Carolina were voting in certain districts in 1870 (ibid., 24).

41. Burke, *All for Civil Rights,* 2.

42. Bainbridge, *Academy and College,* 82–85; West, "'A Hot Municipal Contest,'" 535; "Miss Willard's Address Last Night," *Greenville Daily News,* March 31, 1881, 4; "Plans and Purposes of the Womens' Temperance Christian Union of Greenville, S.C.," *Greenville Daily News,* May 8, 1881, 1.

43. Lerda, "Southern Progressivism in Historical Perspective," 77, 82; A. F. Scott, "After Suffrage," 300. For more on the WCTU and its role in the cultivation of national solidarity, see Blum, *Reforging the White Republic,* 14–15.

44. Owens, *Thursday Club,* 11; Thursday Club (Greenville, SC) Records, Duke Library, Furman University Special Collections and Archives; Bainbridge, *Academy and College,* 76, 82–85.

45. "Greenville Woman's College Catalog, 1886–1887," Furman University Course Catalogs, Furman University, Greenville, SC.

46. Owens, *Thursday Club,* 119–24. Charter members included Frances McCall Perry Beattie, Mary P. Gridley, Flora P. Dill, Constance Furman, Mrs. Abraham Issacs, Vashti Burriss Keys (Mrs. W. W. Keys), Mrs. Sarah McPherson, Viola Neblett, Martha Orr Patterson, Mary Putnam, Sarah Odie Sirrine, and Kate Sloan (Mrs. C. H. Sloan). Other women with World War I and Progressive Era connections who later joined them included Daisy P. Bailey, Laura Ebaugh, Margaret Smythe McKissick, Margaret Smith Parker (Mrs. Lewis Parker), Annie Porter, Andrea Christensen Patterson, Mary Ramsay (Mrs. David Ramsay), and Susan E. Turnipseed.

47. Judith Bainbridge, "Thursday Club Active in Greenville for 128 Years." *Greenville News,* A4. One controversial topic that was forbidden was the discussion of anything relating to the North versus the South. Another early club for White women in South Carolina was the Seneca Once-a-Week Club, founded on September 24, 1896. In 1898 that club's president, Ludia Merriam Coleman (Mrs.

Notes to Pages 23–29 243

M. W. Coleman), organized the South Carolina Federation of Women's Clubs. The other Greenville club that was included as a charter member of the organization was the West End Club. See Johnson, "Louisa B. Poppenheim and Marion B. Wilkinson," 109, 125.

48. Owens, *Thursday Club,* 34–37.

49. "Women and Society: Events of the Past Week among Greenville's '400' Women's Clubs," *Greenville Daily News*, October 14, 1900, 5. Over the course of one year, membership in the SCFWC skyrocketed to approximately one thousand women.

50. Ulmer, "Virginia Durant Young: New South Suffragist," 14–20; untitled article, *Anderson Intelligencer,* October 22, 1885. Barbara Bellows Ulmer, "Virginia Durant Young: New South Suffragist" (MA, University of South Carolina, 1979): 14–20.

51. "State Correspondence: Straws against the Current," *The Woman's Journal*, July 24, 1897, 238–39; "Thought Seeds in Lotus Land," *Woman's Journal*, June 15, 1895, 186.

52. "Two Martyrs for Woman's Rights," *Woman's Journal*, July 14, 1888, 359.

53. Adams, "Four Sisters from Boston," 24; McLeod, "Home/Economics," 225–32.

54. "State Correspondence: Straws against the Current," *Woman's Journal*, July 24, 1897, 238–39; Henry, "New Women of the New South," *Arena,* Vol. 11, 359–60.

55. Judith Bainbridge, "Now Almost Forgotten, W. G. 'Bill' Sirrine was Once One of Greenville's Most Powerful Men," *Greenville News*, August 13, 2020; Trotter, "Like Father, like Sons: A Look inside the Sirrine Family," *Greenville Journal*, September 24, 2020.

56. Letter from Virginia Durant Young to the editor, *Woman's Journal,* July 9, 1897; "State Correspondence: Straws against the Current," 238–39. For more on Young, see Ulmer, "Virginia Durant Young: New South Suffragist"; Herndon, "Woman Suffrage in South Carolina"; Terry Walters "Woman of Vision—Mary Putnam Gridley," Thursday Club Centennial Luncheon, Greenville, March 1989 Centennial Luncheon, address transcript, Special Collections and Archives, Furman University.

57. Bellows, "Virginia Durant Young," 45.

58. Mary P. Gridley, "Why Southern Women Desire the Ballot," *Woman's Journal*, February 2, 1895, 34.

59. Judith Bainbridge, "Viola Neblett Was Women's Rights Pioneer," *Greenville News*, Sep 15, 2010; Henry B. Blackwell, "A Solution of the Southern Question," Woman Suffrage Leaflet 3, no.2 (October 1890): 2, Suffrage Collection, Sophia Smith Collection Stevenson, *Woman as Slave in Nineteenth-Century American Social Movements,* 249.

60. Henry, "New Woman of the New South," *The Arena*, Vol.11.

61. Harper, *History of Woman Suffrage,* 925; Kantrowitz, *Ben Tillman and the Politics of White Supremacy,* 232–38. During this period of relative inactivity in Greenville, after the constitutional convention and Viola Neblett's death and before the establishment of the New Era Club in Spartanburg, Elizabeth Cady Stanton's death made the front page of the *Greenville Daily News* on October 28, 1902.

62. Salvation Army, "History in Greenville." Accessed December 17, 2022. https://www.salvation armycarolinas.org/. The tent was located at the corner of Brown and Washington Streets. Mr. C. E. Graham donated the land to the Salvation Army for its building. The Charity Aid Society was established by Mrs. W. G. Sirrine and Mrs. W. W. Burgiss.

63. W. H. Wilson, *City Beautiful Movement,* 75–95; Thacker, "Working for the City Beautiful," 27–50.

64. Kelsey and Guild, "Beautifying and Improving Greenville, South Carolina: Report to the Municipal League, Greenville, South Carolina" (Boston: Kelsey & Guild, 1907). South Carolina Room, Greenville County Library; Thacker, "Working for the City Beautiful," 27–50.

65. "Meeting of Greenville Woman's Club," *Greenville Daily News*, April 16, 1916, 3.

66. "We Can't Ignore Facts," *Greenville News*, May 19, 1926, 4. Nearby Anderson adopted a segregation ordinance in 1913. W. E. B. Du Bois, "Opinion," *The Crisis* 7 no. 2 (December 1913): 64.

244 *Notes to Pages 29–32*

67. Kelsey and Guild, "Beautifying and Improving Greenville," 12.

68. Greenville City Council Minutes, May 21, 1912, Office of the City Clerk, Greenville; Ordinances 570A-K, 1912, Greenville City Code, Office of the City Clerk, Greenville.

69. Stephenson, "Segregation of the White and Negro Races in Cities by Legislation," 497; "Council Meeting Was an Interesting One," *Greenville Daily News,* May 22, 1912; Formal Minutes for Regular Meeting of Council of the City of Greenville, SC, Tuesday, May 21, 1912.

70. "Council Meeting Was an Interesting One."

71. Stephenson, "Segregation of the White and Negro Races in Cities by Legislation," 497, 499, 500.

72. Power, "Apartheid Baltimore Style," 310; Silver, "Racial Origins of Zoning in American Cities," 26.

73. Stephenson, "Segregation of the White and Negro Races in Cities by Legislation," *Municipal Review*, 499.

74. Stephenson, 499.

75. "Commendation," *Greenville Daily News,* May 24, 1912.

76. Hudson, *Entangled by White Supremacy,* 7.

77. Johnson, Southern Ladies, New Women, 31–32.

78. Huff, *Greenville,* 199; "Suffragists Here Join Woman Party," *Greenville Daily News,* February 11, 1918. Martha Orr Patterson was the daughter of James L. Orr, who served as a US congressman, Speaker of the US House of Representatives, governor of South Carolina, and minister to Russia. She was the founding secretary of the Thursday Club and president of Industrial School. It is likely that she would have become involved in the suffrage movement had she lived longer. Her son married Andrea Christensen, the daughter of well-known suffragists Abbie and Niels Christensen of Beaufort. Andrea Christensen Patterson helped establish the South Carolina Equal Suffrage League in 1914 and later became an officer in the Greenville Equal Suffrage Party when it joined the National Woman's Party. For more on the Christensens, see Tetzlaff, *Cultivating a New South.*

79. Gergel, "Irene Goldsmith Kohn," 203; "Women Keeping Pace with Forward March," *The State*, February 18, 1916. In this article that Coleman authored, she wrote that the UDC, SCFW, and DAR were "made up of practically the same women, numbers of women holding membership in all three." Other South Carolina women with leadership roles in these organizations include Harriet Powe Lynch, Margaret Smyth McKissick, the Poppenheim sisters, and the Pollitzer sisters.

80. Johnson, *Southern Ladies, New Women,* 10; "Official Announcement," *Columbia State,* November 30, 1913, 26. When the *Keystone* discontinued publication in 1913, Hannah Hemphill Coleman worked with the *State* to assume, at least until May 1914, responsibility for publicizing clubwomen's news in the Sunday editions of the newspaper.

81. Johnson, *Southern Ladies, New Women,* 5. As Terborg-Penn writes, "Feminist history must face reality: although most suffragists were feminists, most of the white ones were also racists." Terborg-Penn, *African American Women in the Struggle for the Vote,* 166.

82. Hudson, *Entangled by White Supremacy,* 38, 157. It seems unlikely that Booker T. Washington would have appreciated this comparison. According to Janet Hudson, Washington once privately said to Oswald Garrison Villard of the NAACP that "Carroll had 'many qualities that neither you nor I would admire, but at the same time there is no discounting the fact that he has tremendous influence with the white people of South Carolina." According to the *History of the American Negro, South Carolina Edition*, edited by A. B. Caldwell, Senator Ben Tillman said of Carroll, "Reverend Richard Carroll is a colored man highly thought of by the white people of South Carolina. He has always borne a good reputation and has a great deal of sense." Caldwell, *History of the American Negro,* 312.

83. Hudson, *Entangled by White Supremacy,* 38, 157. To further this point, the NAACP chapters in Columbia and Charleston were founded in 1917, with the first Upcountry branch formed in

Notes to Pages 32–42 245

Anderson County in 1919. Greenville's NAACP chapter did not obtain a charter until 1938. Judith Bainbridge, "Bravery and Defiance: NAACP Beginnings," *Greenville News,* May 4, 2016, http://www.greenvilleonline.com/.

84. "Fighting Race Prejudice," *Chicago Daily Tribune,* September 8, 1913, 6.

85. "Fighting Race Prejudice," *Greenville Daily News,* September 11, 1913, 4.

86. "Fighting Race Prejudice," *Greenville Daily News,* September 11, 1913, 4.

87. Du Bois, "Opinion," *The Crisis* Vol. 7, No. 2, December 1913, 75.

88. Kohn, *Cotton Mills of South Carolina,* 187, 193.

89. Simon, *Fabric of Defeat,* 15; Walker, *All We Knew Was to Farm,* 15.

90. Batson, *History of the Upper Part of Greenville County,* 347.

91. Huff, *Greenville,* 178, 189.

92. Batson, *History of the Upper Part of Greenville County,* 347–48.

93. Willis and the Greenville County Historical Society, *Remembering Greenville,* 103.

94. Ibid., 103–13; Huff, *Greenville,* 235–39.

95. Huff, *Greenville,* 237.

96. Ibid., 242–44. The turnover of mill ownership poses challenges for scholars interested in the mills' archival records. Furthermore, many mill records were destroyed or lost when northern investors purchased many of the Upcountry mills after World War II.

97. Ibid., 299–300. Jackson, a Greenville native, began playing baseball for Greenville's Brandon Mill textile mill baseball team. He earned more playing for the baseball team than he did from his job in the mill and was eventually recruited by the local Greenville Spinners baseball team, where he received his nickname after taking off a pair of ill-fitting baseball spikes and finishing a game without his shoes. Later Jackson advanced to the major leagues and became famous as an outfielder for the Chicago White Sox. His part in the 1919 World Series conspiracy to intentionally throw the series in exchange for five thousand dollars branded him in infamy, and he was banned from Major League Baseball in 1921. In 1929 he returned to Greenville and lived there until his death in 1951.

98. Batson, *Early Travel and Accommodations,* 1–3.

99. Batson, 30.

100. Batson, 29–30.

101. Batson, 104.

102. Richardson, *History of Greenville County,* 105.

103. Preston, *Dirt Roads to Dixie,* 14.

104. Quoted in Preston, 17.

105. Preston, 12, 14–17, 36–38, 40.

106. Quoted in "Forget Forever the Mason and Dixon Line," *Greenville Daily News,* June 23, 1914.

107. Ingram, *Dixie Highway,* 154.

108. For more on the good roads movement, see Ingram, *Dixie Highway.*

109. Preston, *Dirt Roads to Dixie,* 39, 47.

110. "South Carolina's Mill," *New York Times,* February 4, 1900.

111. Johnson, *Southern Ladies, New Women,* 8.

Chapter 2: "Over There"

1. "Heir to Austrian Throne and Wife Are Assassinated," *Greenville Daily News,* June 29, 1914.

2. "Austria-Hungary Declares War Upon Servia Following Germany's Rejection of the British Proposal for Mediation" *Greenville Daily News,* July 29, 1914, 1.

3. Tooze, *The Deluge,* 63–66. For the Allies, the Triple Entente consisted of France, the Russian Empire, and the United Kingdom. For the Central Powers, the Triple Alliance consisted of Germany, Austria-Hungary, and Italy. Soon nations of Europe and beyond, from Bulgaria to Australia, declared for a side and fought in the Great War.

246 Notes to Pages 42–46

4. Zieger, foreword, *America's Great War*.

5. N. G. Ford, *Americans All!*, 17–18.

6. Fourteenth Census of the United States Taken in the Year 1920: Vol. 3, Composition and Characteristics of the Population by States. (Washington, DC: Government Printing Office, 1922): 930–33.

7. Saxe-Gotha changed its name to Lexington in 1775 to honor the patriots of Lexington, Massachusetts. Orangeburgh dropped the *h* in the years after the Civil War.

8. Acts and Joint Resolutions of the General Assembly of the State of South Carolina, Passed at the Regular Session of 1915, 79, 80, 704–6; Strickland, "How the Germans Became White Southerners," 53. Other Charleston organizations included the Der Deutsche Freundschafts Bund (the German Friendship Alliance, 1830s), Der Deutsche Bruderlicker Bund (German Brotherly Alliance), and the Deutsche Schuetzen Gessellschaft (German Rifle Club, 1856). German-American businesses included the Germania Savings Bank (1874), Germania Life Insurance Company (1891), Germania Mutual Fire Insurance Company (1891), Kaiser Fire and Marine Insurance Company (1891), Germania Brewing Company (1896), and approximately half a dozen bakeries throughout the city.

9. Edgar, *South Carolina in the Modern Age*, 44.

10. Herbert Sanborn, "Our Founders and Their Fatherland." Papers of the German Friendly Society, South Carolina Historical Society, Addlestone Library, College of Charleston.

11. Kuntz, "German-American Identity in Charleston during World War I," 30.

12. Kuntz, 34; "No Scuetzenfest This Spring," *Charleston Evening Post,* April 12, 1917.

13. Wieters, "Ethnicity, Politics, and Society in the New South," 60–61.

14. Wieters, 60–61.

15. William Knobeloch, d. ca. 1887, Papers, 1856–1919 (1055.00), Papers of the German Friendly Society 1909–1919, South Carolina Historical Society, College of Charleston, Addlestone Library.

16. *Fourteenth Census of the United States Taken in the Year 1920:* Vol. 3, *Composition and Characteristics of the Population by States.* (Washington, DC: Government Printing Office, 1922) 930–933. In 1910 there were 6,054 foreign-born White people living in the state, with approximately 340 of them, or about 5.2 percent, living in Greenville. In 1910 there were 48 Germans living in Greenville; all but 10 of them had been there since 1900 or before.

17. Stathakis, "Almost White," 171–72.

18. Huff, *Greenville,* 279.

19. Cox, "Cotton Chaotic Home Front: The First World War and the Southern Textile Industry," 181–206.

20. Belcher and Hiatt, *Greer,* 87. For more on how the war impacted the cotton market in Alabama and other southern states, see Floyd, "'A Diarrhea of Plans and Constipation of Action': The Influence of Alabama Cotton Farmers, Merchants, and Brokers on Angle-American Diplomacy during the First World War, 1914–1915," 13–40.

21. Huff, *Greenville,* 279.

22. "War Causes Falling Off of Revenue," *Greenville Daily Piedmont,* August 13, 1917.

23. "Buy a Bale of Cotton . . . ," *Greenville Daily News,* September 15, 1914.

24. Belcher, *Greenville County,* 64.

25. Belcher, 64.

26. Huff, *Greenville,* 279.

27. Bainbridge, *Greenville Communities,* 4.

28. "Keeping Cotton Out of Germany as If Contraband," *Greenville Daily News,* April 19, 1915.

29. Carlton, *Mill and Town in South Carolina,* 206.

30. South Carolina Commissioner of Agriculture, "Labor Division Cotton Report," 455.

31. Carlton, *Mill and Town in South Carolina,* 251.

Notes to Pages 46–51   247

32. Leatherwood, *Quest for Streetcar Unionism in the Carolina Piedmont,* 14; Kuhn, *Contesting the New South Order,* 99.

33. "Mill Shut Down: Weavers of Monaghan Mill Refuse to Make Up Time—Parade under Flag," *Newberry Weekly Herald,* July 14, 1914. It appears that Ettor arrived in Greenville on July 16 and that the parade took place on July 9.

34. Mitchell, *Textile Unionism and the South,* 35.

35. Between 1914 and 1916, Jackson remained subdued after a group of textile leaders seized upon some anti-Semitic comments he had offered publicly and developed a strategy that included soliciting the support of Julius Rosenwald, who had expressed concerns about anti-Semitism in Atlanta ever since the Leo Frank case in 1912.

36. Fulton Bag and Cotton Mills Records, box 6, folder 11, Correspondence, July 1914, Georgia Tech Special Collections. By 1916 Fulton Mills had developed a card system for every mill employee, assessing the employee's abilities and making note of whether or not the employee had ever been involved with any union activity.

37. Carlton, *Mill and Town in South Carolina,* 251, 252.

38. Dunlap, "Victims of Neglect," 87; "Labor Leader at Greenville," *Newberry Weekly Herald,* July 21, 1914.

39. "Strike at Pickens Mill," *Pickens Sentinel,* September 3, 1914; Carlton, *Mill and Town in South Carolina,* 251.

40. Brogan is sometimes listed as Brogon. "Strike at Brogan Mill," *Textile Worker* 4, no. 7 (December 1915): 4–5; "Strike at Judson Mill, *Textile Worker* 4, no. 7 (December 1915): 4–5. Bainbridge, *Greenville Communities,* 6; *Monthly Review of the US Bureau of Labor Statistics* 3, no. 1 (July 1916): 24, 27. A report titled "Conciliation Work of the Department of Labor" tracked the department's activities from its inception on March 4, 1913, onward. YES Between March 4, 1913, and June 6, 1916, the report states that 234 "controversies" took place involving 250,000 employees directly and more than 300,000 indirectly. The only two South Carolina mills listed during this date span are Judson Cotton Mills and Brogon Mills.

41. Leatherwood, *Quest for Streetcar Unionism in the Carolina Piedmont,* 15; *Monthly Review of the U.S. Bureau of Labor Statistics,* 27.

42. Cash, *Mind of the South,* 353; Langston, "Greenville, Unionism, and the General Strike"; Langston, "Anti-unionism in Greenville Textiles," 27–31.

43. For more on the fierce independence of mountain and Upcountry White farmers contextualized in broader constructions of White southern male masculinity, see works by historians Bertram Wyatt-Brown, Stephanie McCurry, W. J. Cash, and Lacy K. Ford.

44. SC General Assembly, Acts and Joint Resolutions 1915, 79, 80, 704–6; Bass and Poole, *Palmetto State,* 72; Simon, *Fabric of Defeat,* 15, 41.

45. Simon, *Fabric of Defeat,* 15, 41, 101; Clark, "United Textile Workers," 1457.

46. Mitchell quotes from the journal in Mitchell, *Textile Unionism and the South,* 11.

47. Mitchell, *Textile Unionism and the South,* 11.

48. Simon, *Fabric of Defeat,* 40.

49. Judtih T. Bainbridge, "Textile Hall," in Edgar, *South Carolina Encyclopedia.*954.

50. "185 Exhibits at Mammoth Textile Show Next Week," *Greenville Daily News,* December 8, 1917. Textile Hall was located on West Washington Street at the current site of St. Mary's Catholic Church.

51. Cooper, Greenville, 129.

52. "Weekly Report on the Cotton Situation," *Greenville Daily News,* July 7, 1917.

53. Showalter, "America's New Soldier Cities," 469; "Textile Hall."

54. Richardson, *History of Greenville County,* 105; "Annual Meeting Auto Association," *Greenville Daily News,* April 8, 1911; "If You Own an Auto, Come Out Tonight," *Greenville Daily News,*

248 Notes to Pages 51–56

February 7, 1910; Judith Bainbridge, "Greenville's 'Motor Mile' Stretches Back to 1903," *Greenville News,* August 21, 2021.

55. James M. Richardson, "Scion of the Flatwoods." unpublished manuscript, 1941. Special Collections and University Archives, James B. Duke Library, Furman University.

56. Preston, *Dirt Roads to Dixie,* 56, 57, 60, 163–64.

57. The actual amount of the bond was $950,000, but locals affectionately referred to it as "the million dollar bond."

58. Ingram, *Dixie Highway,* 2.

59. "No Federal Aid for This State," *Greenville Daily News,* March 30, 1916.

60. Louise Perry was thus a sister-in-law of Frances "Fannie" Perry Beattie, the first president of Greenville's Thursday Club.

61. Preston, *Dirt Roads to Dixie,* 45–47, 57, 60–61, 89; "Greenville GeBankhead [*sic*] Road," *Greenville Daily News,* April 21, 1917.

62. Preston, *Dirt Roads to Dixie,* 61.

63. Zieger, *America's Great War,* 16.

64. Kennedy, *Over Here,* 337–38.

65. The Davenport Apartments were developed by Greenville businessman G. D. Davenport at a cost of fifty-seven thousand dollars. They were designed by Greenville architect Joseph L. Lawrence, and Davenport's friend Eugene Gilphalian oversaw the construction between 1915 and 1916. Filled with modern amenities, the building welcomed its first resident in January 1916. National Register of Historic Places, Davenport Apartments, Greenville, Greenville County, South Carolina, 17/372423/ 3857010; "Davenport Apartments Soon Be Ready for Occupancy; Not a Finer Building of Its Kind in the State; Twenty-Nine Complete Apartments in Building," *Greenville Daily News,* August 24, 1915; Judith Bainbridge, "Apartment Building Was Height of Style in 1918," *Greenville News,* February 12, 2003; Judith Bainbridge, "Davenport Apartments Retain Their Style," *Greenville News,* April 19, 2006.

66. For information on how this courthouse was built to preserve Jim Crow segregation, see Weyeneth, "Architecture of Racial Segregation"; National Register of Historic Places, Greenville County Courthouse, Greenville, South Carolina, National Register #10817723044.

67. Zieger, *America's Great War,* 16; "Four New Store Fronts to Be Put on Main Street," *Greenville Daily News,* July 31, 1917; "Greenville Receives Noteworthy Mention in Iron Tradesman," *Greenville Daily News,* September 11, 1917. In 1917 and after, downtown Greenville continued to benefit from the area's economic vitality. The articles argue that "within two years the installation of modern storefronts has completely changed the appearance of the business section of Greenville into one of the most exquisite of any small city in the country" and describe Greenville as "among the most progressive cities of the south."

68. US Office of the Surgeon General, *Public Health Bulletin No.94,* fig. 52.

69. "Important Meeting of the Greenville Woman's Club," *Greenville Daily News,* April 16, 1916.

70. US Office of the Surgeon General, *Public Health Bulletin No. 994,* 209–10.

71. *Public Health Bulletin No. 94,* 211.

72. *Public Health Bulletin No. 94,* 214.

73. *Public Health Bulletin No. 94,* 315.

74. *Public Health Bulletin No. 94,* 207–26; "Build a Large Disposal Plant," *Greenville Daily News,* May 14, 1916; "Sanitation at Conestee Mills," *Greenville Daily News,* July 14, 1916.

75. US Office of the Surgeon General, *Public Health Bulletin No. 90–94,* 222; "Formation of Health Day Parade Announced; Prizes Offered for Best Floats," *Greenville Daily News,* October 1, 1916.

76. "To Count People Passing Corner," *Greenville Daily News,* October 4, 1916.

Notes to Pages 56–62   249

77. "The 'Electric Flag,'" *Greenville Daily News,* May 26, 1916.

78. "Reminder of Our Nation," *Greenville Daily News,* June 14, 1916.

79. "Erecting Electric Flag: Will Be in Readiness for Big Health Day Celebration," *Greenville Daily News,* September 30, 1916.

80. "To Count People Passing Corner," *Greenville Daily News,* October 4, 1916.

81. "Photograph of Local Flag for President," *Greenville Daily News,* October 17, 1916.

82. Huff, *Greenville,* 253, 280; "Greenville Receives Noteworthy Mention in Iron Tradesman," *Greenville Daily News,* September 11, 1917.

83. "New Publication for Greenville," *Greenville Daily News,* December 22, 1916.

84. Taylor, "South Carolina and the Enfranchisement of Women," 299.

85. Platform adopted by the Equal Suffrage League of South Carolina, 1914. Ida Salley Reamer Papers, Manuscripts Division, South Carolina Library, University of South Carolina, Columbia.

86. "The Equal Suffrage Club Meets to Plan for Coming Battle," *Greenville Daily News,* May 26, 1914; Link, *Paradox of Southern Progressivism,* 185. The YMCA was located at the corner of East Coffee and Brown Streets downtown. Jessie Stokely Burrett was married to Dr. W. M. Burnett, a Greenville physician. They lived on East Park Avenue. In the 1920s she became involved with the local chapter of the American Association of University Women.

87. "In and around the College," 69. For information on President David Ramsay's feeling about his daughter's activism, see Ramsay, David Marshall. "An Old Man Answers His Daughter." North American Review 235 (February 1933): 172–177. Ramsay also served as publicity chairman for the SCESL.

88. Strobel, Marian Elizabeth. "Eudora Ramsay Richardson." In *101 Women Who Shaped South Carolina,* edited by Valinda Littlefield, 113. Columbia: University of South Carolina Press, 2020; Huff, *Greenville,* 263.

89. Elizabeth Perry (Mrs. L. R. Collins) Newspaper Clippings, Women's Suffrage, Maggie's Letters and Clips, D2#40 (1), Greenville County Historical Society; Oral History with Ellen Perry, by Verena Bryson and Gretchen Robinson, Greenville County Foundation and Greenville County Library, November 30, 1979, Ellen Perry Folder, South Carolina Room, Greenville County Library. Ellen Perry taught at the school at Poe Mill, and in April 1916 became supervisor of Mill Schools for Greenville County. She was instrumental in creating the Parker School District, and in the 1920s she became a librarian at the Greenville Library.

90. Huff, *Greenville,* 263.

91. Taylor, "South Carolina and the Enfranchisement of Women," 301; Monica Maria Tetzlaff, "South Carolina Equal Suffrage League," in Edgar, *South Carolina Encyclopedia,* 896.

92. Bland, "Fighting the Odds," 36; Green, *Southern Strategies,* 27–28.

93. Zieger, *America's Great War,* 51.

94. Tooze, *Deluge,* 16.

95. Tooze, 16.

96. Hamer, *Forward Together,* 14.

Chapter 3: The Impact of Camp Sevier

1. "Greenville Campaigned for Camp Sevier," *Greenville News City People,* August 20, 2000.

2. "Impressive Parade on Memorial Day," *Greenville Daily News,* May 8, 1917.

3. "With Prospects of Armed Camps Dotting the Country Let the Flag Wave in the City," *Greenville Daily News,* April 20, 1917.

4. A Camp Sevier historic marker near the site of the old camp names May 21, 1917, as the date the camp was approved. Other sources say May 22, which may have been the day that the government announced the approval. Coordinates of the marker are N 34° 53.989 W 082° 20.269.

250 *Notes to Pages 63–67*

5. Chamber of Commerce to General Leonard Wood, May 23, 1917, file 8(C) Camp Sevier, Henry Bacon McKoy Papers, Greenville County Historical Society; Moore, "Charleston in World War I," 39–40.

6. Lane, *Armed Progressive*, xv.

7. McCallum, *Leonard Wood*, 267–68; Wood, *Leonard Wood*, 303.

8. McCallum, 293–95. Wood's participation in the so-called Plattsburg Movement is also noted in Lane, *Armed Progressive*, 193.

9. Lane, *Armed Progressive*, 212–15. Also see McCallum, *Leonard Wood*, 267–68.

10. Chamber of Commerce to General Leonard Wood, Minutes of the Special Meeting of Council of the City of Greenville, June 28, 1918. Office of the City Clerk, City of Greenville.

11. McKoy, "The Spanish American War in Greenville: Remember the Maine!" unpublished paper, file 9(D) Camp Wetherill Notes 1964–1968, Henry Bacon McKoy Papers, Greenville County Historical Society. Joseph E. Sirrine was the son of civic leaders Sarah and George W. Sirrine and brother of William G. Sirrine.

12. Henry Bacon McKoy to Frances Withington, October 18, 1969, Camp Sevier File, Henry Bacon McKoy Papers, Greenville County Historical Society. McKoy went out of his way to write a letter to Frances Withington, who was writing a paper on Camp Sevier, to "call to [her] attention something that might otherwise be missed in regards to [Camp Sevier]," that "Mr. Sirrine brought General Wood to Greenville, and because of this visit, Camp Sevier was established here."

13. "Gen. Woods Spent Busy Forenoon in Greenville Today," *Greenville Piedmont,* June 21, 1917.

14. "Copy of the original lease that was arranged by the Greenville Chamber of Commerce" for the land where Camp Sevier was to be located, file 8(C) Camp Sevier, Henry Bacon McKoy Papers, Greenville County Historical Society. This document mentions J. E. Sirrine as the president of the Greenville Chamber of Commerce at the time.

15. US War Department, *Annual Reports: 1918,* 1329–31. While the documents do not specify Sirrine's compensation, the publication mentions that supervising engineers should be paid "$2,500 to $4,000."

16. US War Department, *Annual Reports: 1918,* 1329–31. The first contractor fee was $60,000 for the initial construction, with a second contract signed in July 1918 worth $128,250 for additional construction.

17. "Construct Line to Camp at Cost of $30,000," *Greenville Daily News,* July 13, 1917. All figures are in 1917 dollars.

18. US Army Center of Military History, *Organizations and Activities of the War Department,* 172.

19. US Army Center of Military History, *Organizations and Activities of the War Department,* 172. 429.

20. "Completion Report of Camp Sevier," Alex C. Doyle, Major QMC, Constructing Quartermaster, 19, file 8(C), Camp Sevier, Henry Bacon McKoy Papers, Greenville County Historical Society; "Jas. F. Gallivan Dies Here After Illness of Week," *Greenville News,* February 9, 1936.

21. "Completion Report of Camp Sevier," 19.

22. "If This Is Paris I Hope I'll Never See London!," postcard with annotations by Henry Bacon McKoy, Camp Sevier File, Henry Bacon McKoy Papers, Greenville County Historical Society.

23. Fletcher, *History of the 113th Field Artillery,* 21

24. Murphy and Thomas, *The Thirtieth Division in the World War.*

25. "If This Is Paris I Hope I'll Never See London!"

26. Fletcher, History of the 113th Field Artillery, 24.

27. Popelin quoted in Fletcher, 181–82. See also Rogers, *History of the 119th Infantry, 60th Brigade, 30th Division* (Wilmington: Wilmington Chamber of Commerce, 1920): 2.

Notes to Pages 68–72 251

28. Paul Green to William Archibald Green, September 18, 1917, and Paul Green to Mary Green, October 1917, Paul Eliot Green Papers (#3693), Selected Letters, 1917–1919, Southern Historical Collection, University of North Carolina at Chapel Hill.

29. McKoy, *Greenville, S.C.*, 35.

30. "Greetings From Camp Sevier," Vertical Military File, South Carolina Room, Greenville County Library; Helsley, *Hidden History of Greenville County*, 95.

31. US Army Center of Military History, *Territorial Departments Tactical Division Organized in 1918*, 660–61. The Twentieth was demobilized at Camp Sevier in February 1919.

32. Snead, "South Carolina Engineers in the 42nd (Rainbow) Division in World War I," 49.

33. Sutherland, *African Americans at War*, 731.

34. Blue, "Conserving the Nation's Man Power," 255.

35. Blue, "Conserving the Nation's Man Power," 261.

36. Blue, 261.

37. "Construct Line to Camp at Cost of $30,000," *Greenville Daily News*, July 13, 1917; Charles G. Sellers, "War Diary of Charles G. Sellers, Jr." entry from January 25, 1918. Accessed December 17, 2022. https://nature.berkeley.edu/. Many of the Camp Sevier recruits from the two largest divisions that trained there, the Thirtieth and the Eighty-First, hailed from national guard units organized in North Carolina, South Carolina, Virginia, and Tennessee. Fortescue, "Training the New Armies of Liberty," 435.

38. Fortescue, "Training the New Armies of Liberty," 435.

39. Fortescue, 435.

40. Fortescue, 435.

41. Roy Farmer, letter published in the *Furman Hornet*, March 28, 1918.

42. "Dickson County Boy Dies in Camp," *Leaf-Chronicle*, November 19, 1917; letter from Joseph Davis Pridgen to "Mama," August 19, 1917, box 1, Folder Letters August 1917, Joseph Davis Pridgen Papers, 1917–1984, Archives and Manuscripts, Rubenstein Library, Duke University, Durham, NC.

43. Fortescue, "Training the New Armies of Liberty," 434–35.

44. Fortescue, 435–36.

45. "Disposal of excreta" folder, Military Organizations Collection, WWI Papers, Military Collection, State Archives of North Carolina; North Carolina Department of Natural and Cultural Resources, "30th Division Sanitation Practices at Camp Sevier 1917."

46. Fortescue, "Training the New Armies of Liberty," 435.

47. John L. Plyer Jr., interview with Donny Santacaterina, Greenville, SC, 2014. Plyler's father, John Laney Plyler of Travelers Rest, South Carolina, was a second lieutenant of the Quartermaster Corps at Camp Sevier and shared these stories regarding the cultural differences between the soldiers at Camp Sevier.

48. Paul Green to William Archibald Green, September 18, 1917. Green also noted, however, that "even tho' such is the case they deserve the respect and admiration of the rest of the world. I know when I am mustered out I shall not be so refined nor so easy going as once I was." For more information on Paul Green, see Davis, *World War I and Southern Modernism*.

49. Guy Gullick, "Greenville County: Economic and Social," *Bulletin University of South Carolina*, no. 102 (September 1921): 45–46, South Carolina Historical Society, College of Charleston, Addlestone Library.

50. Carlton, *Mill and Town in South Carolina*, 261.

51. Carlton, 263.

52. Carlton, 264.

53. Farmer letter, *Furman Hornet*. Roy Farmer was stationed in Urbana-Champaign, Illinois, for military training at the time.

252 Notes to Pages 72–76

54. Carlton, *Mill and Town in South Carolina*, 265.

55. Fortescue, "Training the New Armies of Liberty," 436.

56. Sawyer, *Greetings from Camp Sevier*, 11.

57. Keene, *World War I*, 74.

58. Kennedy, *Over Here*, 16–17.

59. Kennedy, 17.

60. Sawyer, *Greetings from Camp Sevier*, 11.

61. "Arrests at Camp Sevier of German and Austrian," *Gaffney Ledger*, February 26, 1918.

62. "Enemies Still in County Jail," *Greenville Daily News*, February 23, 1918.

63. Sawyer, *Greetings from Camp Sevier*, 11.

64. Helsley, *Hidden History of Greenville County*, 87; Letters from Paul Green, September 18, 1917, through May 13, 1918, Paul Eliot Green Papers (#3693), Selected Letters, 1917–1919, Southern Historical Collection, University of North Carolina at Chapel Hill.

65. Letter from Joseph Davis Pridgen to "Mama," November 13, 1917, box 1, Folder Letters August 1917- December 1917, Joseph Davis Pridgen Papers, 1917–1984, Archives and Manuscripts, Rubenstein Library, Duke University, Durham, North Carolina.

66. Sawyer, *Greetings from Camp Sevier*, 6, 10.

67. Paul Greene to William Archibald Green, November 22, 1917, Paul Eliot Green Papers.

68. "Layout for Equipment Instruction," Camp Sevier file, Henry Bacon McKoy Papers, Greenville County Historical Society.

69. Marriott, *Suggested Athletics for Army Camps*, 1–6, 35–37, 43–44, 52–53, 61, 84–92.

70. "What the Cantonment Means to Greenville," *Greenville Daily News*, May 22, 1917.

71. See, for example, "Bristol People Visit Camp Sevier," *Bristol Herald Courier*, October 26, 1917; "Personal Mention," *Sunday Journal and Tribune*, November 25, 1917; and "Ground Glass Found in Candy," *Chattanooga News*, February 15, 1918.

72. Chick Springs Hotel advertisement, *Montgomery Advertiser*, July 5, 1918.

73. Advertisement, *Greenville Daily News*, October 3, 1917.

74. Bainbridge, *Academy and College*, 154.

75. "Boys of 30th Division Boost the City Population," *Greenville Daily News*, December 9, 1917.

76. "Building Boom is on in Greenville," *Greenville Daily News*, July 27, 1917.

77. "Greenville Gets Aviation School of Signal Corps," *Greenville Daily News*, December 22, 1917.

78. "Boys of 30th Division Boost the City Population."

79. Letter from Joseph Davis Pridgen to "Mama," December 27, 1917, box 1, folder Letters August 1917, Joseph Davis Pridgen Papers, 1917–1984, Archives and Manuscripts, Rubenstein Library, Duke University, Durham, NC.

80. Cooper, *Greenville*, 129.

81. "Every Soldier to Have a Sweater," *Greenville Daily News*, January 8, 1918; "Lovely Women Ask Soldiers to Dine," *Greenville Daily News*, October 6, 1917; "Will You Help Give Men at Camp Sevier a Joyous Christmas?" *Greenville Daily News*, December 11, 1917; Bainbridge, *Academy and College*, 155.

82. Bainbridge, *Academy and College*, 155.

83. "News of a Day at Camp Sevier," *Greenville Daily News*, July 2, 1918; "Here and There at Camp Sevier," *Greenville Daily News*, October 7, 1917.

84. "Sevier Lost to Kenilworth Inn," *Greenville Daily News*, September 17, 1918; "Thousands Attend Parade at Camp," *Greenville Daily News*, August 6, 1917.

85. "Major League Team among Sevier Soldiers," *Greenville Daily News*, October 7, 1918.

86. Cooper, *Greenville*, 139.

Notes to Pages 77–81   253

87. Sullivan, "Climatological Data: South Carolina Section," *US Department of Agriculture,* March 1917, in Camp Sevier File, Henry Bacon McKoy Papers, Greenville County Historical Society.

88. Helsley, *Hidden History of Greenville County,* 89.

89. Fletcher, *History of the 113th Field Artillery,* 23–24.

90. Untitled annotation, Camp Sevier Files, Henry Bacon McKoy Papers, Greenville County Historical Society; McKoy, *Greenville, S.C.,* 34–35; Period Materials, 9(E) Camp Wetherill, 1898, Greenville County Historical Society. That woman was Kate Wier (Wynne), who lived on North Main Street. Cpl. Hugh Dunn had given the cape to her during his time at Camp Wetherill. Wier similarly befriended soldiers from Camp Sevier who patrolled in front of her home, providing them with hot food and drinks to sustain them during that unusually cold winter.

91. Ben P. Gulledge to Minnie Jones, December 9, 1917. Ben P. Gulledge Papers, Southern Historical Collection, University of North Carolina Historical Collection; journal entry, December 9, 1917, Hutchison Family Papers, South Caroliniana Collection, University of South Carolina; "The City Shivers in Bitter Cold," *Greenville Daily News,* December 10, 1917.

92. Letter from Joe Pridgen to "Mama," box 1, December 10, 1917, folder Letters, August 1917–December 1918, Joseph Davis Pridgen Papers, 1917–1984, Archives and Manuscripts, Rubenstein Library, Duke University, Durham, NC.

93. "Will You Help Give Men at Camp Sevier a Joyous Christmas?"

94. Journal entry, January 25, 1918, Hutchison Family Papers, South Caroliniana Library, University of South Carolina. "Our Company" was likely Hiram's Company H of the 118th Infantry.

95. Letter from Joe Pridgen to "Mama," January (date illegible) 1918, box 1, folder Letters, August 1917–December 1918, Folder January 1918, Joseph Davis Pridgen Papers, 1917–1984, Archives and Manuscripts, Rubenstein Library, Duke University, Durham, NC.

96. Erwin [last name unknown] to Benjamin Draeger, September 11, 1918, in the author's possession.

97. Sellers, "War Diary of Charles G. Sellers, Sr." Sellers was part of Battery F, Second Battalion, 113th Field Artillery Regiment, and the 55th Field Artillery Brigade, which was assigned to the 30th Infantry Division.

98. "Camp Sevier Lament," cartoon, *Greenville News,* June 26, 1962.

99. Paul Greene to Mary Green, October 1917, Paul Eliot Green Papers (#3693).

100. Letter from Joe Pridgen to his "Mama," February 18, 1918, box 1, Folder Letters, August 1917–December 1918, Folder February 1918, Joseph Davis Pridgen Papers, 1917–1984, Archives and Manuscripts, Rubenstein Library, Duke University, Durham, NC.

101. Huff, *Greenville,* 285.

102. Cooper, *Greenville,* 140.

103. Batson, *Early Travel and Accommodations,* 1–3.

104. Richardson, *History of Greenville County,* 106.

105. John Hammond Moore, "Roads and Highways," in *South Carolina Encyclopedia,* 809.

106. Sawyer, *Greetings from Camp Sevier,* 18.

107. "Greenville Roads Attract Everyone," *Greenville Daily News,* September 14, 1917. 9

108. "Roads and Highways."

109. McKoy, *Greenville, S.C.,* 35.

Chapter 4: "For Liberty and Humanity"

1. "For Liberty and Humanity," *Greenville Daily News,* April 3, 1917; Huff, *Greenville,* 280.

2. "Asks for a State of War," *Greenville Daily News,* April 3, 1917.

3. "May 19, 1917: Message Regarding Military Draft," Presidential Speeches, Woodrow Wilson Presidency, Miller Center, University of Virginia

254   *Notes to Pages 81–84*

4. "For Liberty and Humanity."

5. "Our Country First, Then Greenville," *Progressive Greenville* 1, no. 5 (April 1917): 3.

6. "Women to Replace Absent Men," *Greenville Daily News*, August 6, 1917.

7. Belcher, *Greenville County, South Carolina*, 65–66.

8. Belcher, 65.

9. "Mrs. Williams U.S. Commissioner," *Greenville Daily News*, October 2, 1918; untitled article, *Woman Citizen*, December 7, 1918, 568.

10. "Over Here: The Homefront during World War I," *Carolina Stories*, South Carolina Educational Television, May 4, 2007; Tollison Hartness, "Sandwich Lady: Eugenia Duke's Popular Spread Remains a Household Name," *Town*, March 29, 2016, 62; Rebecca Kilby, "'The Finest Work': At Greenville Coach Factory, Ebenezer Gower and Thomas M. Cox Laid the Foundation for the Upstate's Manufacturing Success," *Upstate Business Journal*, May 22, 2015. https://upstatebusinessjournal.com /management-2/. Also known by locals as "The Firm," Gower, Cox, and Markley was founded in 1835 and was regarded as the largest coach factory south of Washington, DC. They sold their paint shop to Duke's Mayonnaise in the automobile era. The coach factory's paint shop was later purchased by Greenville's Peace Center and is utilized as an outdoor event space on the banks of the Reedy River downtown.

11. Duke's Mayonnaise, "Our History." https://dukesmayo.com/pages/history. Nearly one hundred years after its founding, Duke's was the third largest mayonnaise brand in the United States, behind Hellman's and Kraft. Certainly, its success was aided by the out-of-town soldiers stationed at Camp Sevier who returned from the war and lived the rest of their lives, more often than not, in places far from South Carolina. Duke's Sandwich Company celebrated its centennial in 2017.

12. Jensen, *Mobilizing Minerva*, 153–56; Kuhlman, *Reconstructing Patriarchy after the Great War*, 7–8, 144.

13. Dumenil, *Second Line of Defense*, 33–43.

14. *Woman Citizen*, December 1, 1917. Catt received a bequest to begin a new journal, and merged the *Woman's Journal*, the *Woman Voter*, and the *National Suffrage News* to create the *Woman Citizen*, which began publication on June 2, 1917.

15. Quoted in Bland, "Fighting the Odds," 39. A letter from Vaughan was published in the July 21, 1917, issue of the *Suffragist*. She wrote, "How I wish I could be with you helping at headquarters and going forth with the banners! You are all so magnificent in your persistent loyalty and courage. I am more proud every day that I, too, have picketed."

16. Bland, "Fighting the Odds," 38.

17. Dumenil, *Second Line of Defense*, 37–43. In an oral history conducted decades later, Alice Paul admitted that the NWP's continued activism spurred suspicion and repeated calls to investigate the organization's finances. "After 1917 they were always charging that we were being financed by the Germans, because the war was on, and all these women in the National American [Woman's Suffrage Association] and all these people who were for the war said we were interfering with American defense and therefore it was perfectly clear that the Germans were financing it." Alice Paul, interview with Amelia R. Fry, July 10, 1977, b11235867, Suffragists Oral History Project, Regional Oral History Office, Bancroft Library, University of California, Berkeley.

18. Letter from Sen. Benjamin R. Tillman to Louise A. Jordan (Mrs. Fletcher Jordan), May 17, 1917, Women's Suffrage, Maggie's Letters, Mrs. O. Perry Earle, Jr. (2), D2#41, Greenville County Historical Society.

19. Taylor, "South Carolina and the Enfranchisement of Women," 302.

20. Elected officers included Elizabeth F. Perry, chairperson; Martha Orr Patterson, Mary P. Gridley, and Eva Tarver Goodyear (Mrs. Chester Goodyear), vice-chairpersons; Louise Jordan, recording secretary; R. P. Webster, corresponding secretary; and Marie Richardson, treasurer. Vaughan had also served as head of the Greenville chapter and the SCESL.

Notes to Pages 84–89   255

21. Bland, "Fighting the Odds," 42; "Gergel, "Irene Goldsmith Kohn," 177.

22. Bland, "Fighting the Odds," 39. For more on how political expediency during the suffrage movement often trumped efforts aimed at sisterhood between the races, see Terborg-Penn, *African American Women and the Struggle for the Vote*.

23. I would like to acknowledge the influence of Janet Hudson's *Entangled by White Supremacy* on my interpretations of the distinctiveness of southern Progressivism, particularly in the ways that progressivism existed alongside and even reinforced White supremacy

24. Kantrowitz, *Ben Tillman and the Reconstruction of White Supremacy*, 232. Tillman offered these remarks in his "laying of the Cornerstone at Winthrop" speech at Winthrop University on May 12, 1894.

25. Bland, "Fighting the Odds," 38.

26. "Suffragist Raps Senator Tillman," *Greenville Daily News*, March 22, 1918; Bland, "Fighting the Odds," 38. At the same time, Greenvillian Psyche Webster, who served in various leadership capacities in the South Carolina branch of the NWP, also engaged in a public exchange of terse letters with Senator Tillman.

27. Pollock was Tillman's elected replacement. Vaughan spearheaded the "Helping Pollock to Declare" statewide campaign, which included a multipronged strategy to influence Pollock to declare himself in favor of woman's suffrage. As part of this campaign, the *Greenville Piedmont* and *Charleston Evening Post* published editorials in support of suffrage, and hundreds of people, including Mayor Harvley and Mary P. Gridley, wrote letters encouraging Pollock to publicly proclaim his support. Bland, "Fighting the Odds," 41–42; Huff, *Greenville*, 263; Helen E. Vaughan, "South Carolina Demands Suffrage Amendment," *Suffragist*, February 8, 1919, 5, 10.

28. Vuic, *Girls Next Door*, 12–14; "War Camp Community Service," articles from Camp Sevier box, South Carolina Room, Greenville County Library.

29. Buchanan, "War Legislation against Alcoholic Liquor and Prostitution," 521, 525.

30. Keene, *World War I*, 71–81; Bristow, *Making Men Moral*, 114–19; Beardsley, "Allied against Sin," 189.

31. Beardsley, "Allied against Sin," 193.

32. Hudson, *Entangled by White Supremacy*, 107–8. Hudson cites Alan Johnstone of the CTCA's testimony before the US Senate Military Affairs Committee on June 18, 1918.

33. US Public Health Service to the Commanding Surgeon, Camp Sevier, January 21, 1918, regarding Thirtieth Division soldiers, Military Organizations collection, WWI Papers, Military Collection, State Archives of North Carolina; Helsley, *Hidden History of Greenville County*, 95.

34. "Nine White Women in Police Court," *Greenville Daily News*, October 20, 1917.

35. "3 Wouldn't Stay at Reformatory," *Greenville Daily News*, December 23, 1917.

36. Bristow, *Making Men Moral*, 118–19.

37. Beardsley, "Allied against Sin," 196.

38. Hudson, *Entangled by White Supremacy*, 107.

39. Judith T. Bainbridge, "Greenacres: Operating on a Loving Shoestring," *Greenville News*, December 5, 2016. According to Bainbridge, the bureau's headquarters on the corner of Falls and Broad Streets was located in close proximity to the red-light district on East Court Street, the county jail and county courthouse, and the Salvation Army's Citadel. In the 1920s the home, Greenacres, shifted its focus to more generally support young women in need.

40. Shah, "Against Their Own Weakness," 469.

41. Beardsley, "Allied against Sin," 193.

42. Hudson, *Entangled by White Supremacy*, 107–8. The South Carolina Federation of Colored Women's Clubs helped establish Fairwold, a reformatory for young African American women approximately ten miles north of Columbia. For more information see Johnson, *Southern Ladies, New Women*, 175–94.

256 Notes to Pages 89–92

43. Korzeniewski, "Sexually Transmitted Infections among Army Personnel in the Military Environment," 166.

44. "War Camp Community Service," South Carolina Room, Greenville County Library.

45. Both the WCCS and Chamber of Commerce's bureaus were located at the intersection of Main and Washington Streets, with the WCCS located above Gapen's Cigar store.

46. Nan E. Birnie (Mrs. James Birnie) led the Ladies Auxiliary of the YMCA after Mayes assumed leadership of the Women's State Defense Council.

47. "Guide to Greenville," War Camp Community Service, Greenville County Historical Society.

48. "Miss Wilson Gets Ovation at Camp," *Greenville Daily News,* May 24, 1918; Helsley, *Hidden History of Greenville County,* 90.

49. The secular organizations included three information bureaus, one community club, and one public library.

50. "Guide to Greenville," War Camp Community Service, Greenville County Historical Society.

51. Sawyer, *Greetings from Camp Sevier,* 11–13.

52. Daniel, *Century of Progress,* 83–87. The YMCA on East Coffee Street, the First Baptist Church on West McBee Avenue, the Knights of Columbus on West Washington Street, Christ Episcopal Church on East Coffee Street, the First Presbyterian Church on West Washington Street, the Neblett Free Library on West McBee Avenue, the Jewish Welfare Rooms on McBee Avenue, and the Colored Soldiers Club at 113 East Washington Street all advertised reading and rest rooms for the men of Camp Sevier in *Trench and Camp.* Listings found in the Camp Sevier box, South Carolina Room. The First Baptist committee included the names of many prominent White Greenvillians. Those who served included A. A. Bristow, A. G. Furman, J. M. Geer, H. J. Haynsworth, Edwin Howard, T. H. Pope, W. D. Workman, H. P. McGee, J. H. Morgan, Mrs. C. M. Landrum, Mrs. G. W. Quick, and Mrs. W. C. Williams.

53. "For the Soldiers When in the City," *Trench and Camp,* March 3, 1918.

54. Daniel, *Century of Progress,* 83–87.

55. Moseley, *Buncombe Street Methodist Story,* 78.

56. Daniel, *Century of Progress,* 85.

57. Moseley, *Buncombe Street Methodist Story,* 78.

58. "Time Fails to Dim Their Memories," *Greenville News,* July 30, 1967. Less than ten years after the war ended, Anderson became the father of Rudolf Anderson, who was one of the nation's earliest U-2 pilots and was the sole combat fatality of the Cuban Missile Crisis when he was shot down and killed in action over Cuba in 1962.

59. "5,000 Members to be C'ville's Goal," *Greenville Daily News,* May 24, 1917; "Give to the Red Cross at Church Today," *Greenville Daily News,* June 24, 1917.

60. "Nearby Towns Help to Swell Red Cross Fund—$7000 Needed," *Greenville Daily News,* June 24, 1917.

61. "Marshall House Now Being Razed," *Greenville News,* August 17, 1930. Eva Fletcher (Mrs. O. O. Fletcher) had also served as president of the Women's Missionary Union at First Baptist Greenville in 1914–16 and led Furman and Greenville's efforts to raise funds for a doughboy statue. Nana Louise McLeod Sirrine was Mrs. W. G. Sirrine. Prior to her marriage, she worked as a nurse in Asheville. She later served as the treasurer for the Salvation Army's Bruner Home for Children and as the director of woman's work for the local Red Cross. After the war she taught a nursing class at the YWCA. The Marshall House was the home of Greenville mayor John B. Marshall and was also used as the headquarters for the Poinsett Club. Located at the corner of Butler and West Washington Streets, the home was razed in 1930.

62. Eleanor Keese Barton, History of the Crescent Music Club (Greenville, South Carolina), n.d., South Carolina Room, S.C. Pph. Box 26, Greenville County Library; "Community Club Pays Tribute to Founders," *Greenville Piedmont,* April 10, 1936. The Crescent Avenue Red Cross Unit was the

Notes to Pages 92–97   257

forerunner of the Crescent Community Club and Crescent Music Club. Some of its members included Mrs. Mary Cary, Mrs. Davis Furman, Mrs. J. W. Norwood, Nana Sirrine, and Mrs. A. B. Wardlaw. The organization began in 1916 when more than twenty women from the Crescent Avenue and McDaniel Avenue neighborhood convened to discuss how best to protect their children during a meningitis outbreak. In 1921 the group of clubwomen changed their name to the Crescent Community Club.

63. "They Knit and Play Tennis Equally Well," advertisement, *Greenville Daily News*, September 4, 1917; "Patriotic Greenville Subscribed $200,000 More than Her Quota," *Greenville Daily News*, June 16, 1917; "Women Urged to Show Patriotism," *Greenville Piedmont*, March 26, 1917; "Many Applicants for Ambulance Co.," *Greenville Piedmont*, June 5, 1917; Bainbridge, *Academy and College*, 155.

64. "How Wholesale Grocers Can Help," *Greenville Daily News*, September 13, 1918; "Save Your Peach Stones and Nut Shells," *Greenville Daily News*, October 4, 1918; "Greenville Answers," *Outlook*, September 25, 1918, 123.

65. South Carolina State Council of Defense, *South Carolina Handbook of the War*. The chairman of the State Council of Defense for Greenville was J. B. Bruce.

66. "War Council Hereafter Will Print Names of Liberty Bond Slackers," *Greenville Daily News*, October 20, 1918. For more on the heavy-handed and politically driven agenda that Governor Manning and David Coker had for the SCCD, see Hamer, "World War I and South Carolina's Council on Defense," 61–88.

67. Cooley, "Food Soldiers," 89–115.

68. "Greenville Led South Carolina in Food Pledges," *Greenville Daily News*, November 18, 1917.

69. "Eat Ice Cream and Help Win the War," *Greenville Daily News*, February 13, 1918.

70. "Observe War-Time, Dr. Quick Urges," *Greenville Daily News*, March 28, 1918; "In Greenville Churches," *Greenville Daily News*, March 24, 1918; "In Greenville Churches," *Greenville Daily News*, March 31, 1918.

71. "Mrs. Mayes Presides at Woman's Council Defense," *Greenville Daily News*, August 2, 1917.

72. "Mrs. Mayes Sends Appealing Letter," *Greenville Daily News*, February 13, 1918.

73. "Woman's Division Council on Defense," *Greenville Daily News*, July 28, 1918.

74. "Mrs. F. L. Mayes Died Yesterday," *Greenville News*, March 17, 1923; "Signal Honor for Mrs. F. Louise Mayes," *Greenville Daily News*, November 15, 1913; "Mrs. Mayes Sends Appealing Letter," *Greenville Daily News*, February 13, 1918.

75. For more see Hickel, "War, Religion, and Social Welfare."

76. Wingate, "Over the Top," 32.

77. Helsley, *Hidden History of Greenville County*, 89.

78. "A Soldier's Editorial," *Greenville Daily News*, June 28, 1918; "The Rent Hold Up," *Greenville Daily News*, June 22, 1918.

79. Huff, *Greenville*, 261.

80. "Enforce the Vagrancy Law," *Greenville Daily News*, April 19, 1917.

81. "Arrest Vagrants Urges Governor," *Greenville Daily News*, April 19, 1917.

82. "Rescue Workers Were Convicted," *Greenville Daily News*, February 16, 1918. The two men convicted by Judge John M. Daniel were Clarence Ellis and Cleo Whitt. The woman convicted was Ellis's wife. They were represented by attorney B. F. Martin. James H. Price represented Ensign Story.

83. "Loafers Beware Says Chief Noe," *Greenville Daily News*, June 28, 1918.

84. Paperwork from these cases is archived at the National Archives and Records Administration, Atlanta, Georgia.

85. "Faces Federal Jury," *Columbia State*, June 13, 1918 "Re-try Espionage Case at Anderson," *Greenville Daily News*, May 21, 1919; "JK Hall Charged with Disloyalty," *Greenville Daily News*, June 12, 1918; Atlanta Federal Penitentiary Case Files, JK Hall Folder, National Archives and Records

258   *Notes to Pages 97–101*

Administration, Atlanta; Criminal Dockets for the U.S. District Court, Greenville, SC, #702 J.K. Hall File, National Archives and Records Administration, Atlanta; Howard B. Batchelor Registration Card, U.S., World War I Draft Registration Cards, 1917–1918, Ancestry.com; Criminal Dockets for the U.S. District Court, Greenville, SC, #583 H.B. Batchelor File, National Archives and Records Administration, Atlanta. J. K. Hall, fifty-eight, was a brother of former police commissioner J. C. Hall. He allegedly criticized the constitutionality of the draft law, President Wilson and his policies, and the sale of Liberty Bonds. He was convicted and served time in the US penitentiary in Atlanta. Howard B. Batchelor, forty, was an operative in the card room at Judson Mill, where his wife also worked. In May 1918 Batchelor was convicted after five men testified against him, providing statements he had made about how the "damned President had shoved the price of everything up so high" and how the Red Cross "wasn't for nothing but to keep up a bunch of damned whores and thieves." He was convicted and sentenced to two months. Interestingly it seems that Batchelor registered for the draft on September 12, 1918.

86. "Charge Army Captain's Wife with Violation of the Espionage Act," *Greenville Daily News*, July 24, 1918.

87. For further discussion on the influence of print journalism before 1930, see Douglas, *Golden Age of the Newspaper*.

88. This section of the newspaper was initially titled "The Camp Sevier News." It appears to have begun in June 1917 and changed names approximately one year later.

89. Kennedy, *Over Here*, 58–59.

90. Zieger, *America's Great War*, 78–79; Hamilton, *Manipulating the Masses*, 136–54. Hamilton asserts that Four Minute Men spoke to audiences totaling nearly 315 million nationally.

91. Tindall, *The Emergence of the New South*, 49.

92. "Four Minute Men Organize County for War Savings," *Greenville Daily News*, March 18, 1918; "Drive for Funds to Beat Huns Going Good in Greenville County," *Greenville Daily News*, March 22, 1918. Additional Four Minute Men included D. L. Bramlett, F. M. Burnett, W. C. Cleveland, E. Y. Hillhouse, W. J. Thackston, J. D. Lanford, James M. Richardson, and T. D. Wood. In Greenville, Four Minute Men frequently spoke at Liberty Theater and Textile Hall.

93. Kennedy, *Over Here*, 60–61.

94. Kennedy, *Over Here*, 178.

95. Quigley, "Independence Day Dilemmas in the American South," 263.

96. Ibid., 237; Weyeneth, "Architecture of Racial Segregation," 18; Stokes, *Myrtle Beach*, 48–49; Chafe, Gavins, and Korstad, *Remembering Jim Crow*, 59.

97. Degler, "Thesis, Antithesis, Synthesis"; Quigley, "Independence Day Dilemmas in the American South," 238.

98. "Entire Piedmont to Celebrate the 4th," *Greenville Piedmont*, July 3, 1917.

99. Stokes, *Myrtle Beach*, 48–49.

100. "The South and the Fourth," *Greenville Daily News*, July 5, 1917.

101. Gaughan, "Woodrow Wilson and the Rise of Militant Interventionism in the South," 804.

102. Southern Baptist Convention, *Annual*, 32; Laurence M. Vance, "Joseph Judson Taylor, Man of Peace," March 18, 2015. https://libertarianchristians.com/2015/03/18/man-of-peace/; Sumners, "Joseph Judson Taylor," 12; *Baptist World*, May 31, 1917, 7–8.

103. Keith, *Rich Man's War, Poor Man's Fight*, 2; Hall, "Manhood, Duty, and Service," 41–60.

104. Hamer, "World War I and South Carolina's Council on Defense," 61–88; US War Department, *Final Report of the Provost Marshall General to the Secretary of War on the Operations of the Selective Service Systems to July 15, 1919*, 52–53, 271South Carolina had 5,630 net reported desertions, 1.83 percent of the total of those registered, above the national average of 1.41 percent. Of these 2,516 were apprehended or dismissed, with 3,114 desertions outstanding. South Carolina ranked eleventh nationally in the ratio of net reported desertions to total registration and in the ratio of

Notes to Pages 101–106 259

outstanding desertions to total registration (1.01) at the end of the war. The national average of outstanding desertions to total registration was 0.72.

105. Department of Justice, Office of the Superintendent of Prisons, U.S. Penitentiary, Atlanta, 1910–1930, Record Group 129: Records of the Bureau of Prisons, 1870–2009, Inmate Case Files, 1902–1922, John W. Brown #8211, National Archives and Records Administration, Atlanta. Brown, a native of Goldsboro, NC, was initially sentenced to ten years.

106. "Drive to Round Up Camp Sevier Deserters," *Charlotte Observer,* March 23, 1918.

107. Telegram regarding Robert Allen, box 7, Military Organizations, WWI Papers, State Archives of North Carolina.

108. "Mountain Delinquents Who Fled Camp Sevier Returned Voluntarily," *Greenville Daily News,* June 18, 1918.

109. "Camp Sevier Deserters Are Rushed Overseas," *Greenville Daily News,* June 28, 1918.

110. Keith, *Rich Man's War, Poor Man's Fight,* 56, 85; J. A. Parrott to Congressman Edwin Y. Webb, May 2, 1917, file 256, box 28, Webb Papers, Southern Historical Collection, University of North Carolina at Chapel Hill.

111. "Greenville Answers," *Outlook,* September 25, 1918, 123.

112. Huff, *Greenville,* 283–84; "The South and the Fourth" and assorted articles from the *Greenville Daily News,* July 1–5, 1917.

113. "Insurance Organ on Clean Up Idea," *Greenville Daily News,* March 6, 1918; "N. H. Fogg to Be Field Secretary," *Greenville Daily News,* March 19, 1918; "North Will Hear of Sunny South," *Greenville Daily News,* January 13, 1918; "Working to Lower Insurance Rates," February 11, 1918; "Chamber Adopts Fogg Hog Plane," *Greenville Daily News,* March 22, 1918; "Some Building Operations," *Greenville Daily News,* December 16, 1917.

Chapter 5: "They Have Responded to Every Call"

1. Hudson, *Entangled by White Supremacy,* 20–21.

2. Hemmingway, "Prelude to Change," 212–13.

3. Jackson, "Booker T. Washington in South Carolina, March 1909," 218.

4. "Negroes of City Show Respect for Late Booker Washington," *Greenville Daily News,* November 17, 1915.

5. "Booker T. Washington," *Greenville Daily News,* November 17, 1915.

6. "Richard Carroll Speaks Here Tonight: Well Known Negro Lecturer and Minister Will Be at Springfield Baptist Church," *Greenville Daily News,* May 9, 1916.

7. This amount is just over fifty dollars in 2021 terms; Thomas Doherty, "'The Birth of a Nation' at 100: 'Important, Innovative and Despicable,'" *Hollywood Reporter,* http://www.hollywoodreporter.com/race/.

8. "Scenes from *The Birth of a Nation,*" *Greenville Daily News,* February 13, 1916; "For the Benefit of Thousands Turned Away before the Masterpiece of Modern Art D. W. Griffith's 8th Wonder of the World: *The Birth of a Nation,*" *Greenville Daily News,* May 25, 1916.

9. "'Still the daddy of 'em all!' crowed *Variety* trumpeting a re-release in 1923. 'No matter how often seen, there's always that 'kick' or thrill involved that no other special feature or general release has held." Doherty, "'Birth of a Nation' at 100."

10. Ned McIntosh, "'Birth of a Nation' Thrills Tremendous Atlanta Audience," *Atlanta Constitution,* December 7, 1915; Hunter, *To 'Joy My Freedom,* 220.

11. "'Birth of a Nation' Caused the Fight," *Greenville Daily News,* May 13, 1916.

12. "Calls upon Negroes to Enter Patriotic Move," *Greenville Piedmont,* April 21, 1917; Richard Carroll, letters to the editor, *Newberry Weekly Herald* (April 24, 1917), *Newberry Weekly Herald* (April 27, 1917), and *Edgefield Advertiser,* April 25, 1917; "Richard Carroll Urges Colored Leaders to Preach Preparedness," *Greenville Daily News,* April 22, 1917.

260 Notes to Pages 107–111

13. "Civic Preparedness Campaign: South Carolina's Agricultural, Industrial and Economic Resources Must Be Mobilized to Meet War Conditions: 'Service for All,'" *Gaffney Ledger* (supplement), May 1, 1917.

14. "Meeting for Colored Citizens," *Keowee Courier,* May 2, 1917.

15. Lau, *Democracy Rising,* 21. For more on the Great Migration in South Carolina, see Hudson, *Entangled by White Supremacy,* 148–75.

16. Robert S. Abbott, "Exodus," *Chicago Defender,* September 2, 1916.

17. Ethan Michaeli, "Bound for the Promised Land," *Atlantic, January 11, 2016.*

18. Lau, *Democracy Rising,* 60.

19. Bernstein, *Only One Place of Redress,* 8–27.

20. "Negro Labor Going North," *Greenville Daily News,* August 19, 1916.

21. "Many Negroes Caught in 'Job-Net' in Philadelphia; 500 Die in Three Months," *Greenville Daily News,* March 29, 1917.

22. "Negro Emigrants Are Leaving City," *Greenville Daily News,* March 27, 1917.

23. "Agent Is Held for Enticing Negroes," *Atlanta Georgian,* March 28, 1917.

24. Anonymous letter from Greenville, April 29, 1917, in E. J. Scott, "More Letters of Negro Migrants," 416; Anonymous letter from Charleston, April 29, 1917, in E. J. Scott, "More Letters of Negro Migrants," 418.

25. Anonymous letter from Greenwood, May 8, 1917, in E. J. Scott, 418.

26. Anonymous letter from Charleston, April 27, 1917, in E. J. Scott, "More Letters of Negro Migrants," 421.

27. Anonymous letter from Greenville, May 2, 1917, in E. J. Scott, 436.

28. E. J. Scott, *Scott's Official History of the American Negro in the World War,* 447.

29. One letter, in particular, reveals the depths of some African Americans' struggle. Approximately two weeks after war was declared, a man from Daphne, Alabama, pled for relief from dire circumstances: "Sir: I am writing you to let you know that there is 15 or 20 familys wants to come up there at once but cant come on account of money to come with and we cant phone you here we will be killed they dont want us to leave here & say if we dont go to war and fight for our country they are going to kill us. . . . We work but cant get scarcely any thing for it & they dont want us to go away & there is not much of anything here to do & nothing for it Please find some one that need this kind of a people & send at once for us. We dont want anything but our wareing and bed clothes & have not got no money to get away from here with & beging to get away before we are killed and hope to here from you at once." E. J. Scott, 451.

30. Hudson, *Entangled by White Supremacy,* 151; Lau, *Democracy Rising,* 25–26; South Carolina Cotton Museum, "Boll Weevils." http://www.sccotton.org/6701.html.

31. Mose Austin, interview by John L. Dove, January 24, 1939, Federal Writers Project, Library of Congress.

32. Salem, *To Better Our World,* 205–30.

33. Hattie E. Williams was an important leader in Greenville in the 1910s and 1920s. Official records list her as a "mulatto." Her husband, Henry, died sometime between 1903 and 1910 and is buried in Richland Cemetery in Greenville. They had three children and lived at 113 Washington Street, where a servant, Allen Berry, also resided with them. After Henry's death Williams was listed as a dressmaker and moved to Brown Street. In the late 1920s, she served on the board of her church, Allen Temple AME. She died on October 2, 1936, and is buried in Richland Cemetery. Her daughter, Carrie Thompson of Greenville, was a district president of the SCFCWC in the 1950s. "79th Anniversary of Allen Temple A.M.E. Church, June 1954 program," Churches G AME/CME, Allen Temple (AME) Folder, South Carolina Room, Greenville County Library.

34. The ministers' church affiliations are as follows: Rev. Allen R. Burke of Tabernacle Baptist, Rev. Charles F. Gandy of Springfield Baptist Church, and Rev. John F. Green of John Wesley United

Methodist Episcopal Church, Fred W. Bostic Jr., "The History of John Wesley United Methodist Church" (no info, 2006) 6, Churches G Methodist File, John Wesley United aka Silver Hill Methodist/Episcopal (East Court St), South Carolina Room, Greenville County Library; "Dedication and Open House, Springfield Baptist Church, December 5, 1976," program, South Carolina Room, Greenville County Library.

35. Julia Gregory was a local schoolteacher, and Mary Bates served as superintendent of St. Luke's Hospital in the 1920s.

36. "Nearby Towns Help to Swell Red Cross Fund," *Greenville Daily News*, June 24, 1917.

37. "Knitting for Colored Troops," *Greenville Daily News*, November 12, 1917.

38. "Colored People to Aid in Drive," *Greenville Daily News*, April 24, 1918.

39. "Colored People Meet Saturday," *Greenville Daily News*, April 25, 1918. James A. Tolbert, E. W. Biggs, Charles D. Brier, Dr. A. E. Boyd, and A. P. Allison also served on the planning committee.

40. "Colored People Sanction Parade," *Greenville Daily News*, May 26, 1918.

41. "Dr. Lansing Spoke to Colored People," *Greenville Daily News*, June 13, 1918.

42. "Entertainment for 200 Negro Soldiers," *Greenville Daily News*, June 13, 1918; "200 Colored Soldiers Entertained in City," *Greenville Daily News*, June 14, 1918.

43. "Colored Red Cross Branch Looks After the Colored Soldier," *Greenville Daily News*, June 21, 1918.

44. "Colored People Did Themselves Proud in Patriotic Spectacle," *Greenville Daily News*, June 27, 1918. Prof. James A. Brier "presided over the exercises," and the secretary of the Chamber of Commerce, F. M. Burnett, was one of the speakers.

45. "Community Club for Negro Troops," *Greenville Daily News*, July 6, 1918.

46. "Funds for Negro Club Growing," *Greenville Daily News*, July 10, 1918.

47. "Community Club for Negro Troops."

48. "Negro Soldiers' Club Is Assured," *Greenville Daily News*, July 30, 1918.

49. Williams, Sidelight on Negro Soldiers, 124–26.

50. Hemmingway, "Prelude to Change," 213.

51. Hudson, *Entangled by White Supremacy*, 148–49.

52. Hemmingway, "Prelude to Change," 213.

53. Hudson, *Entangled by White Supremacy*, 147.

54. Hudson, *Entangled by White Supremacy*, 101–2.

55. Hunter, *To 'Joy My Freedom*, 220.

56. Hudson, *Entangled by White Supremacy*, 111–13.

57. Hudson, 21.

58. Hudson, 148.

59. Hudson, 114.

60. Oscar W. Adams, "What Negros Are Doing," *Birmingham (AL) News*, October 6, 1918; Ortiz, *Emancipation Betrayed*, 151.

61. John R. Shillady to Woodrow Wilson, September 23, 1918, National Archives, General Records of the Department of Justice.

62. Walter White to John Shillady, October 26, 1918, Work or Fight file, Series I, NAACP Papers, Library of Congress, Washington, DC.

63. Hudson, *Entangled by White Supremacy*, 101–19.

64. "Negro Women to Be Put to Work," *Greenville Daily News*, October 2, 1918; "Labor Ordinance to Include Both Races," *Greenville Daily News*, October 4, 1918; Greenville, SC City Council Minutes, October 8, 1918, Office of the City Clerk, Greenville; Gallivan, "Henry Thompson Mills"; "Henry T. Mills," *Greenville News*, March 9, 1960. Described as "warm," with a "patrician appearance and manner," Mills was active in the First Presbyterian Church, and was known for his empathy

262   Notes to Pages 118–125

and advocacy of others. After his death, the *Greenville News* wrote of him, "Such men comprise the real heart of a community, and all who knew him will treasure his memory."

65. Walter White to John Shillady, October 26, 1918.

66. "Worker Among Negro Girls is Appointed," *Greenville Daily News*, October 17, 1918.

67. Lau, *Democracy Rising*, 90, 251.

68. United War Work Campaign, "Campaign Among Colored People." *Bulletin XV*, November 11–18, 1918. https://hdl.handle.net/2027/nnc2.ark:/13960/t06x1zj8z.

69. "Colored Citizens behind Big Drive," *Greenville Daily News*, October 29, 1918.

70. "Greenville Negroes to Go Over the Top First United War Work Drive," *Greenville Daily News*, November 8, 1918.

71. "Allison Gave Twenty Dollars to Colored United War Work," *Greenville Daily News*, December 17, 1918. From the article it is clear that Professor Allison was concerned that the balance of his donation may have been stolen.

72. "Greenville Negroes to Go Over the Top First United War Work Drive."

73. "Greenville Negros Lead Rest in US in U.W.W. Drive," *Greenville Daily News*, November 19, 1918.

74. "Black Dollars," *Greenville Daily News*, November 19, 1918.

75. "Black Dollars."

76. "Black Patriots," *Greenville Daily News*, October 25, 1917.

77. Logan, *Betrayal of the Negro*, 371–72; Ortiz, *Emancipation Betrayed*, 169.

Chapter 6: African Americans' Service in the Great War

1. W. E. B. Du Bois, "Editorial," *Crisis* 13, no. 3 (January 1917): 111.

2. NAACP, *Freeing America*, 1; Litwack, *How Free is Free?*, 41.

3. E. J. Scott, *Scott's Official History of the American Negro in the World War*, 35–36.

4. Scott, 36.

5. E. J. Scott, 37.

6. "The Negro in War," *Atlanta Constitution*, July 12, 1917; C. L. Williams, *Torchbearers of Democracy*, 32.

7. E. J. Scott, *Scott's Official History of the American Negro in the World War*, 37–38; "Why This Particular Honor?," *Afro-American*, March 31, 1917.

8. Bryan, "Fighting for Respect," 11; Kennedy, *Over Here*, 159, 162–63; A. P. Wilson, *African American Army Officers of World War I*, 26–27.

9. Keene, "Comparative Study of White and Black American Soldiers during the First World War," 72.

10. For the number of African American volunteers in April and May 1917, see Keene, "Comparative Study of White and Black American Soldiers during the First World War," 75, and Megginson, "Black South Carolinians in World War I," 153, 162.

11. Megginson, 153.

12. Logan, *Negro in American Life and Thought*.

13. Rubin, *Last of the Doughboys*, 261.

14. American Map Company. *Lynchings by States and Counties in the United States, 1900–1931: (data from Research Department, Tuskegee Institute); cleartype county outline map of the United States*. New York: American Map Company, [1931?]. https://www.loc.gov/item/2006636636/.

15. D. T. Williams, "Amid the Gathering Multitude"; Tolnay and Beck, *Festival of Violence*, 259.

16. Rubin, *Last of the Doughboys*, 26. Rubin cites 350,000 as the total of African American men who served. More recent sources, including Chad L. Williams's *Torchbearers of Democracy*, references 380,000 as the number of African Americans who served in the war, with 367,000 of those drafted. The remainder either enlisted or were already serving when the United States joined the war.

Notes to Pages 125–131   263

17. For the number of South Carolina African American volunteers in April and May 1917, see Megginson, "Black South Carolinians in World War I," 162. For the call by Richard Manning for African Americans to stop enlisting, see Hamer, *Forward Together,* 17.

18. The South Carolina National Guard, and all other states who had not accepted African Americans, were required to do so after President Harry Truman signed Executive Order 9981 desegregating the US Armed Forces in 1948. Hamer, *Forward Together,* 17.

19. C. L. Williams, *Torchbearers of Democracy,* 53.

20. Williams, 53.

21. Lentz-Smith, *Freedom Struggles,* 31.

22. Keene, "Comparative Study of White and Black American Soldiers during the First World War," 75; Megginson, "Black South Carolinians in World War I," 162. Twenty thousand had volunteered, leaving only four thousand open slots available given the limited units in which African Americans were allowed to serve.

23. E. J. Scott, *Scott's Official History of the American Negro in the World War,* 35.

24. Megginson, "Black South Carolinians in World War I," 162; Kennedy, *Over Here,* 159.

25. E. J. Scott, *Scott's Official History of the American Negro in the World War,* 35.

26. A. P. Wilson, *African American Army Officers of World War I,* 26.

27. Memorandum for the chief of staff, August 21, 1917, mentioned in Keene, "Comparative Study of White and Black American Soldiers during the First World War," 75.

28. Keith, "Politics of Southern Draft Resistance," 1338.

29. Keith, *Rich Man's War, Poor Man's Fight,* 73; Keith, "Politics of Southern Draft Resistance," 1350.

30. Quoted in Johnson, "Learning the Fighting Game," 30.

31. C. L. Williams, *Torchbearers of Democracy,* 53.

32. Bryan, "Fighting for Respect"; C. L. Williams, *Torchbearers of Democracy,* 55.

33. C. L. Williams, *Torchbearers of Democracy,* 6; Capozzola, *Uncle Sam Wants You,* 33.

34. Keene, "Comparative Study of White and Black American Soldiers during the First World War," 75.

35. Megginson, *Black Soldiers in World War I,* 5–7.

36. Megginson, "Black South Carolinians in World War I," 161. *Scott's Official History of the American Negro in the World War,* 67–68, has slightly different numbers.

37. Megginson, "Black South Carolinians in World War I," 161–62; Kennedy, *Over Here,* 163.

38. E. J. Scott, *Scott's Official History of the American Negro in the World War,* 75–76.

39. Keene, *Doughboys, the Great War, and the Remaking of America,* 22.

40. Kennedy, *Over Here,* 160.

41. Keene, *Doughboys, the Great War, and the Remaking of America,* 23.

42. Keene, 23.

43. Hudson, Entangled by White Supremacy, 95.

44. Miller, "The Disgrace of Democracy," 9–10.

45. Capozzola, Uncle Sam Wants You, 33; "Negro Preacher Meets Death at Mob's Hands," *Concord Times,* August 27, 1917; "Death of Sims Yet a Mystery," *Charlotte News,* August 26, 1917.

46. "Messages From the Messenger," *The Messenger,* November 1917, 31.

47. Litwack, How Free is Free?, 40; Ellis, "W. E. B. Du Bois and the Formation of Black Opinion in World War I: A Commentary on 'The Damnable Dilemma,'" 1585.

48. Hudson, 97.

49. Donald, "Determining If the Actions of African American Combat Forces during World War I Positively Affected the Employment of African American Combat Soldiers during World War II," 8.

50. E. J. Scott, *Scott's Official History of the American Negro in the World War,* 76.

51. Smith and Zeidler, *Historic Context for the African American Military Experience,* 293.

264 Notes to Pages 131–139

52. Quoted in Work, "In 1918 Southern White Paper Unstinted in Praise of Negro Troops," *Negro Year Book,* (1919) 84.

53. "In 1918 Southern White Paper Unstinted in Praise of Negro Troops."

54. William C. Chase, "An Appeal to Secretary of War Baker," *Washington Bee,* July 27, 1918.

55. C. H. Williams, *Sidelights on Negro Soldiers,* 26.

56. E. J. Scott, *Scott's Official History of the American Negro in the World War,* 103.

57. Major W. H. Loving to Chief, Military Morale Division, October 13, 1918, Subject: Conditions among Negro Troops in Camp Sevier, doc. 5, subfile 10218-280, Microfilm Publication M1440: Correspondence of the Military Intelligence Division Relating to "Negro Subversion" 1917–1941, National Archives; Bristow, *Making Men Moral,* 163; Ewing, *Age of Garvey,* 63.

58. Bristow, *Making Men Moral,* 274.

59. Capozzola, *Uncle Sam Wants You,* 34.

60. E. J. Scott, *Scott's Official History of the American Negro in the World War,* 79–80; Mjagkij, *Loyalty in Time of Trial,* 89; Ellis, *Race, War, and Surveillance,* 85; Hudson, *Entangled by White Supremacy,* 94. Some reports identify a local White man, and not the hotel's proprietor, as the one who kicked Sissle.

61. E. J. Scott, *Scott's Official History of the American Negro in the World War,* 81.

62. Zieger, *America's Great War,* 103–4.

63. Charles C. Ballou was promoted to brigadier general in August 1917 and major general on November 28, 1917.

64. E. J. Scott, *Scott's Official History of the American Negro in the World War,* 98. Capitalization is included in Scott's publication of "Bulletin No. 35."

65. Scott, 259; Barbeau and Henri, *Unknown Soldiers,* 71–72.

66. National Archives, "Photographs of the 369th Infantry and African Americans during World War I." https://www.archives.gov/.

67. Hudson, *Entangled by White Supremacy,* 13.

68. Jeff Wilkinson, "African-American World War I Unit from SC Fought with Honor," *Columbia State,* November 11, 2015, http://www.thestate.com/.

69. E. J. Scott, *Scott's Official History of the American Negro in the World War,* 236.

70. Scott, 237.

71. Freddie Stowers World War I Draft Registration Card, Anderson County, South Carolina. Ancestry.com. *U.S., World War I Draft Registration Cards, 1917–1918* [database on-line]. Provo, UT, USA: Ancestry.com Operations Inc, 2005. For his family's perspective on their involvement in memorializing Stowers, see Jackson, *Corporal Freddie Stowers.*

72. Hamer, *Forward Together,* 17.

73. Hamer, *Forward Together,* 13.

74. E. J. Scott, *Scott's Official History of the American Negro in the World War,* 238.

75. "A French Directive," *Crisis* 18, no. 1 (May 1919): 16–18.

76. Hamer, *Forward Together,* 13; full lyrics to "How You Gonna Keep 'Em Down on the Farm?" in "Songs the Soldiers and Sailors Sang, 1917–1918," Henry Bacon McKoy Scrapbook Collection, Camp Sevier, Special Collections and Archives, Furman University: "How ya' gonna keep 'em down on the farm, / After they've seen Paree? / How ya' gonna keep 'em away from Broadway, / Jazzin' around, paintin' the town? / How ya' gonna keep 'em away from harm— /That's the mystery! / They'll never want to see a rake or plow, and who the heck can parlez-vous a cow? / How ya' gonna keep 'em down on the farm, / After they've seen Paree?"

77. Hamer, *Forward Together,* 14.

78. Miller, *History of the World War for Human Rights,* 554.

79. Marc Parry, "Roots of Freedom: Historians Reveal African Americans' Roles in the Great War and How It Influenced Later Civil Rights Struggles," *Chronicle of Higher Education,* May 19, 2014.

Notes to Pages 139–144   265

80. Logan, *Negro in American Life and Thought*, 52; John Hope Franklin, "Federal Enforcement of Civil Rights," Sidney Hillman Lecture Series, Howard University (December 1961), 1891–2010, box W25, John Hope Franklin Papers, Rubenstein Library, Duke University, Durham, NC; Tindall, *Emergence of the New South*, 160; White, *Too Heavy a Load*, 115. See also Conyers, *Charles H. Houston*, 146; Litwack, *Trouble in Mind*, 481–596; Field, "Introduction," 421, 425. According to Kendra Field, Franklin specifically identified 1923 in the Sidney Hillman Lectures at Howard University in 1961.

81. Parry, "Roots of Freedom"; C. L. Williams, *Torchbearers of Democracy*, 224.

82. Parry, "Roots of Freedom."

83. Harry S. Truman, Executive Order 9981, Establishing the President's Committee on Equality and of Treatment and Opportunity in the Armed Forces.

84. Keene, "Comparative Study of White and Black American Soldiers during the First World War," 74–75; Kennedy, *Over Here*, 162. Keene writes, "These percentages are extrapolated from the figures of 2,057,675 cumulative arrivals in Europe of American military personal and 1,078,222 actual combat strength of the American Expeditionary Forces (AEF) by November 11, 1918, provided by the American Battle Monuments Commission, 1938," 502" (p. 36, n9). Kennedy quotes from "Disposal of the Colored Drafted Men," report of Col. E. D. Anderson, chairmen of the Operations Branch, General Staff, May 16, 1918, found in Barbeau and Henri, *Unknown Soldiers*, 191–201.

85. Keene, "Comparative Study of White and Black American Soldiers during the First World War," 74.

86. Megginson, *Black Soldiers in World War I*, 5–7; Iowa Public Television, "Black Officers at Fort Des Moines in World War I," 2003. https://www.iowapbs.org/iowapathways/mypath/2514/.

87. Zieger, *America's Great War*, 151.

88. Zieger, 103; Megginson, *Black Soldiers in World War I*, 167.

89. Zieger, *America's Great War*, 103; Jeff Morgan, "First Black Officers Trained for World War I at Fort Des Moines 100 Years Ago" October 23, 1917. https://medium.com/iowa-history/.

90. E. J. Scott, *Scott's Official History of the American Negro in the World War*, 68; Newby, *Black Carolinians*, 188.

91. Megginson, *Black Soldiers in World War I*, 6.

92. Megginson, "Black South Carolinians in World War I," 162–63.

93. Lentz-Smith, *Freedom Struggles*, 37.

94. Keene cites Sundquist, *Oxford W. E. B. Du Bois Reader*, 602, in *Doughboys, the Great War, and the Remaking of America*, 22; Keene, *United States and the First World War*, 62.

Chapter 7: "A University or a Training Camp"

1. Snyder, *120 Years of American Education*, 64–65. The number of institutions of higher education nearly doubled between 1869 and 1889. Brickman, "American Higher Education in Historical Perspective."

2. Levine, *American College and the Culture of Aspiration*, 23.

3. National Academy of Sciences, "History." https://www.nasonline.org/about-nas/history/.

4. The campus was located on today's Falls Park and County Square.

5. The land of the former campus is now known as Heritage Green.

6. Editorial, *Furman Hornet*, February 15, 1917.

7. Although their work is no longer accessible on the web, I wish to acknowledge the work of former Furman University undergraduates Eddie Marjan and Miranda Flowers, completed as part of our freshman seminar "Furman in the World." Eddie Marjan, "Student Perceptions and Understandings, World War I," and Miranda Flowers, "William Joseph McGlothlin: An Administration of Accomplishments," Furmaniana, World War I, Special Collections and University Archives, Duke Library, Furman University.

266 Notes to Pages 144–149

8. Scholars such as Charles Reagan Wilson and W. J. Cash have written about the southern military tradition and its role in southern White male identity.

9. "Military Company Formed at Furman," *Greenville Daily News*, April 4, 1917.

10. Editorial, *Furman Hornet*, April 5, 1917.

11. "Compulsory Military Training at Furman," *Greenville Daily News*, April 18, 1917.

12. "Furman Soldiers Take Long Hike," *Furman Hornet*, May 17, 1917.

13. This was later changed, and a national registration requiring men age eighteen to forty-five was held on September 12, 1918, less than two months before the end of combat.

14. Furman University, "Furman History and Traditions"; McGlothlin, *Baptist Beginnings in Education*, 126. Furman had been loosely affiliated with The Southern Baptist Theological Seminary from the 1850s through the 1870s. With support from Furman administrators, the seminary acquired Furman's theological library and a twenty-six-thousand-dollar endowment originally raised for a theological school at Furman.

15. Editorial, *Furman Hornet*, April 5, 1917.

16. "Gen. Wood's Answer to Students' Query," *Furman Hornet*, April 19, 1917.

17. Kennedy, *Over Here*, 147.

18. Ibid., 148.

19. "College Students and the War," *Baptist Courier*, August 1, 1918.

20. Editorial, *Furman Hornet*, April 5, 1917.

21. "The College Man's Hour," editorial, *Furman Hornet*, October 4, 1917.

22. "The College Man's Hour," *Furman Hornet*, October 4, 1917, 2.

23. Levine, *American College and the Culture of Aspiration*, 24.

24. "Young Manhood of Greenville Depart," *Greenville Daily News*, April 17, 1917.

25. "Good for Furman!," *Greenville Daily News*, April 17, 1917.

26. "Furman Soldiers in First World War Conflict Stood Out," *Greenville News*, November 10, 1940. "Huns" was a derogatory name for German soldiers in both world wars.

27. Levine, *American College and the Culture of Aspiration*, 24.

28. Levine, 28.

29. "Report of Committee U on Patriotic Service," *Bulletin of the American Association of University Professors* 5, no. 3 (March 1919): 31–34.

30. "Report of Committee U on Patriotic Service," 25.

31. Shearer, "Experiment in Military and Civilian Education," 214.

32. "S.A.T.C.," advertisement, *Greenville Daily News*, September 12, 1918. Privates received thirty dollars per month.

33. "Report of Committee U on Patriotic Service."

34. "Clemson College Opened," *Keowee Courier*, September 25, 1918; Shearer, "Experiment in Military and Civilian Education," 215; Patrick Kelly and Branch Vincent, "HS-C, Influenza, and WWI," Hampden-Sydney College, Accessed 2017: http://blogs.hsc.edu/hsc1918/.

35. *Student Army Training Corps: Descriptive Circular*, October 14, 1918, 20, 28, 32; E. J. Scott, *Scott's official history of the American Negro in the World War*, 334–41; North Carolina Department of Natural and Cultural Resources "An Army of Students." The Citadel, Clemson, the College of Charleston, Erskine, Furman, Newberry, Presbyterian, South Carolina Medical College, the University of South Carolina, and Wofford hosted Army detachments. Only Clemson hosted a naval detachment. Clemson, South Carolina A and M (now South Carolina State University) and the University of South Carolina hosted vocational detachments. Allen and Benedict sent small groups of students and faculty to an instructional camp for HBCU's held at Howard University in August and September 1918. In comparison, twelve colleges and universities in North Carolina, including three HBCUs, coordinated with the military to develop SATC units.

Notes to Pages 149–156 267

36. Snyder, *Educational Odyssey,* 264; E. J. Scott, *Scott's Official History of the American Negro in the World War,* 102.

37. Scott, 338.

38. Scott, 339.

39. Scott, 339.

40. Snyder, *Educational Odyssey,* 264.

41. Levine, *American College and the Culture of Aspiration,* 28.

42. "Military Training Instituted at Furman," *Furman Hornet,* October 4, 1918.

43. "A Tale about Swan White and What She Might See Nowadays," *Furman Hornet,* November 8, 1918.

44. "A Tale about Swan White and What She Might See Nowadays."

45. Shearer, "Experiment in Military and Civilian Education," 216.

46. "Clemson College Opened."

47. Levine, *American College and the Culture of Aspiration,* 28.

48. "S.A.T.C. Formally Opened at Furman," *Greenville Daily News,* October 2, 1918. The ceremony at Furman began at eleven in the morning and concluded at the nationally prescribed time of twelve o'clock.

49. "Tale about Swan White."

50. Snyder, *Educational Odyssey,* 264.

51. "Tale about Swan White."

52. Shearer, "Experiment in Military and Civilian Education," 218.

53. Shearer, 218; Levine, *American College and the Culture of Aspiration,* 28.

54. Barker, "Sane Sense of Loyalty to Nation in Peace and War," 26–32.

55. "All Have Uniforms," *Furman Hornet,* November 8, 1918; Rammelkamp, *Illinois College,* 498.

56. "Furman University and Army Training," *Furman Bulletin* 1, no. 1 (1918): 1; Sidney E. Bradshaw, "Military Feature Suggested," *Furman Bulletin* 1, no. 2 (1919): 4.

57. "The Government Takes Over the Nation's Colleges," reprinted in *The European War* (New York: New York Times Co., 1919), 17, 265–68.

58. Shearer, "Experiment in Military and Civilian Education," 219.

59. Barker, "Sane Sense of Loyalty to Nation in Peace and War," 28; "Lee and His Army," 19.

60. Bradshaw, *History of Furman University,* 8.

61. West, "University of South Carolina in the Great War," 85.

62. Barker, "Sane Sense of Loyalty to Nation in Peace and War," 40–42. Though the ROTC program was established nationally in 1916, Furman did not have a unit on campus until May 4, 1950. Interim president Sidney E. Bradshaw supported it, and President William J. McGlothlin applied for a unit soon before he died from injuries sustained in a car accident in May 1933. His successor, Bennette E. Geer, discussed the issue with trustees at their May 1935 meeting. He noted that he had no opinion on the matter and suggested that it should be discussed by the Executive Committee of the Board of Trustees.

63. "Report of Committee U on Patriotic Service."

64. "Compulsory Military Training at Furman."

65. This percentage represents the sixty-four who experienced active, non-SATC service of an average of 199 Furman students enrolled during 1917 and 1918. This 32 percent is also more accurate in gauging Furman students' direct participation in the war effort than the statement that "190 Furman men" served in the military as reported by most secondary sources.

66. Image label, Furman University Special Collections and University Archives exhibit, "Over Here, Over There: Greenville in the Great War" (February–May 2017), Greenville. Curated by Helen Mistler, Donald Santacaterina, and Courtney Tollison. Joan O. W. Donaldson, a native of North

268   Notes to Pages 156–159

Dakota and distant relative of Furman's first president, James C. Furman, attended Central School (now Greenville High School) and Furman from 1915 to 1916 before matriculating at Cornell University. After the war Donaldson authored an article, published in *Harper's* magazine, that chronicled his wartime experiences. During his final flight, he was shot down, captured by German forces, and placed in a German prison camp. The next day he and a fellow American lieutenant made their first escape attempt by climbing out of a second-story window. The men escaped and continued to trudge through Belgium and Holland back to the Allied camps after two additional captures and subsequent escapes. Donaldson reached England a few days before the end of the war and was received alongside other flyers by King George V. For his service he earned the British Distinguished Flying Cross, the US Distinguished Service Cross, and the Belgian Croix de Guerre. Once Donaldson returned home after the armistice was signed, he wrote that the United States is a country "which no one can appreciate so well as those who have been away from it." He was killed in 1930 while performing a stunt during an air show. In 1951 the Greenville Air Force Base was renamed Donaldson Air Force Base. Today the SC Technology and Aviation Center occupies the former base, while their airport remains known as Donaldson Field. For more information see John O. W. Donaldson, "My Capture and Escape," *Harper's Monthly,* July 1919, 244–55; US Congress, "Donaldson Air Force Base," A1742.

67. John O. Donaldson to Nannie Donaldson Furman, October 31, 1918, Furman University and the Great War, Special Collection and University Archives, Duke Library, Furman University; Donaldson, "My Capture and Escape."

68. These men include Pvt. Otis Baggott Brodie, killed when two train cars overturned soon after leaving Camp Jackson for Camp Sevier on May 10, 1918; Lt. John Hodges David, the first officer from South Carolina to die in the war; Lt. Charles Turner Gardner, who was injured during the Battle of Chateau-Thierry, died during the Battle of Soissons, and is buried in the Oise-Aisne American Cemetery in France; Cpl. Talmadge W. Gerrald, who died during the Battle of Cantigny; Pvt. Thomas "Tommie" Jefferson Lyon Jr., a member of the "Lost Battalion" killed in the Ardennes Forest; and Sgt. Charles E. Timmons Jr., who was killed in Bellicourt, France, and is included in the Tablets of the Missing at Somme American Cemetery.

69. Duren, *Lasting Legacy to the Carolinas,* 119.

70. McGlothlin, "The Christian School, the War, and the Future," 5–12; McGlothlin, *Baptist Beginnings in Education;* Wilkinson, "The Life and Work of William J. McGlothlin."

71. Snyder, *120 Years of American Education,* 64–65.

Chapter 8: Chaos and Confusion in 1918

1. Barry, *Great Influenza,* 396–97.

2. Ibid., 397.

3. Wright, *Get Well Soon,* 186.

4. Barry, *Great Influenza,* 397–98.

5. National Archives and Records Administration, "The Deadly Virus: The Influenza Epidemic of 1918." https://www.archives.gov/.

6. Showalter, "America's New Soldier Cities." 446.

7. Barry, *Great Influenza,* 152.

8. Letter from Joseph Davis Pridgen to "Mama," November 13, 1917, box 1, folder Letters August 1917, Joseph Davis Pridgen Papers, 1917–1984, Archives and Manuscripts, Rubenstein Library, Duke University, Durham, NC. On November 13, 1917, days before the quarantine went into effect at Camp Sevier, Pridgen wrote to this mother: "My cold is lots better now, and I haven't caught the measles yet. We have about twelve in the hospital now with the measles. We have a measle inspection twice a day now. I thought sure he was going to accuse me of having them today, but he did not. I had been sitting by a hot fire most all day so when the doctor came around my face was red. He looked at

Notes to Pages 159–164   269

my chest then my eyes, then my throat, then he asked if I had ever had the measles. I told him I sure had so he passed on by. Believe me I sure would hate to have to go to the hospital for about twenty one days."

9. Paul Green to Papa (William Archibald Green), November 22, 1917, Paul Eliot Green Papers (#3693), Selected Letters, 1917–1919, Southern Historical Collection, University of North Carolina at Chapel Hill.

10. "Testing the War Machinery of a Nation: A Review of the Investigation in Congress," *Outlook* (December 26,1917): 677. December 26, 1917.

11. Barry, *Great Influenza*, 148.

12. Barry, 148.

13. Barry, 148.

14. Barry, 169.

15. Barry, 169.

16. Paul Green to Papa, November 22, 1917.

17. Opdycke, *Flu Epidemic of 1918*, 46.

18. "The 'Flu,'" *Greenville Daily News*, September 21, 1918.

19. "Quarantine Camp to Prevent Flu," *Greenville Daily News*, September 24, 1918.

20. "Call for Nurses to Combat 'Flu,' *Greenville Daily News*, September 27, 1918.

21. The Historical Marker Database, "Camp Sevier." Eunice Marion Mallon (1890–1962) was married to US Army major Francis Bernard Mallon (1886–1983). After the war he was stationed in Coblentz, Germany, where the couple's son Richard was born. Eunice is sometimes listed as Eunice Casey Mallon. The Mallons are buried in Arlington National Cemetery.

22. "Rescind Draft Call Account Flu," *Greenville Daily News*, September 27, 1918.

23. Sawyer, *Greetings from Camp Sevier*, 11.

24. "Testing the War Machinery of a Nation: A Review of the Investigation in Congress," *Outlook* (December 26, 1917): 677; Helsley, *Hidden History of Greenville County*, 97.

25. "Influenza Epidemic at Camp Sevier Now Rapidly Being Checked," *Greenville Daily News*, September 27, 1918; "Crest Is Passed in 'Flu' Epidemic," *Greenville Daily News*, October 4, 1918.

26. "Quarantine Camp to Prevent Flu."

27. "Have Football at Furman This Year," *Greenville Daily News*, September 26, 1918.

28. "Furman Wins," *Charlotte Observer*, October 27, 1918; "Furman Ends Season Saturday with Game with Presbyterians," *Greenville Daily News*, December 6, 1918.

29. Helsley, *Hidden History of Greenville County*, 93.

30. "Influenza Epidemic at Camp Sevier Now Rapidly Being Checked," *Greenville Daily News*, September 27, 1918.

31. "When You're Quarantined," *Greenville Daily News*, November 22, 1918.

32. "Crest Is Passed in 'Flu' Epidemic."

33. *Order of Battle of the United States Land Forces in the World War, Zone of the Interior: Organizations and Activities of the War Department*, Volume 3, Part 1 (Washington, DC: U.S. Government Printing Office, 1988), 280–82.

34. "Lift Quarantine within the Camp," *Greenville Daily News*, October 29, 1918.

35. Carnegie, *Path We Tread*, 172; Thoms, *Pathfinders*, 166–67; Jones and Saines, "Eighteen of 1918–1919," 880.

36. "New Cases of Flu at Camp Decrease," *Greenville Daily News*, October 8, 1918.

37. "Getting the Best of 'Flu' at Camp," *Greenville Daily News*, October 6, 1918.

38. "Funeral for Miss Alice M. Young," *Wheeling (WV) Daily Intelligencer*, October 7, 1918.

39. Gavin, *American Women in World War I*, 252–55; Feller and Moore, *Highlights in the History of the Army Nurse Corps*, 10. Six nurses died at Camp Jackson and one at Camp Wadsworth.

270 *Notes to Pages 164–169*

40. Opdycke, *Flu Epidemic of 1918,* 51.

41. Opdycke, 51; Bollet, *Plagues and Poxes,* 107–8. By early October there were 35,146 influenza cases and 3,036 pneumonia cases at all training camps.

42. Byerley, "U.S. Military and the Influenza Pandemic."

43. United States National Library of Medicine, National Institutes of Health, "Epidemic Influenza," *Public Health Reports,* January 3, 1919, 1–2.

44. Camp Sevier Box, Misc. Documents, South Carolina Room, Greenville County Library.

45. Nic Butler, "Pandemic and Panic: Influenza in 1918 Charleston," March 20, 2020. https://www.ccpl.org/.

46. Bainbridge, *Academy and College,* 156.

47. Editorial, *Furman Hornet,* February 21, 1918.

48. "Locals," *Furman Hornet,* April 25, 1918.

49. United States Department of Health and Human Services, "South Carolina," in "The Great Pandemic: The United States in 1918–1919." https://cybercemetery.unt.edu/.

50. "The City Quarantine," *Greenville Daily News,* October 5, 1918.

51. "State Board Put Quarantine on City and County," *Greenville Daily News,* October 8, 1918.

52. "State Board Put Quarantine on City and County"; "Individuals Can Stop Influenza," *Columbia State,* October 2, 1918; "Pandemic and Panic: Influenza in 1918 Charleston."

53. "Sheriff's Warning," *Greenville Daily News,* October 8, 1918.

54. "State Board Put Quarantine on City and County."

55. Huff, *Greenville,* 286.

56. Katie Vloet, "'This Infection, Like War, Kills the Young,'" Medicine at Michigan, Fall 2018. https://www.medicineatmichigan.org/.

57. "Hospital Woman's Board," *Greenville Daily News,* December 12, 1917. Lou Woodside was Mrs. John T. Woodside.

58. Moseley, *Buncombe Street Methodist Story,* 82.

59. Barry, *Great Influenza,* 348.

60. Partridge and Towell, *Transformation,* 39. The authors cite their 2010 interview with Thomas McAfee III, Thomas McAfee IV, and John McAfee.

61. Huff, *Greenville,* 286; Chamber of Commerce advertisement, *Greenville Daily News,* November 6, 1918.

62. Opdycke, *Flu Epidemic of 1918,* 47.

63. Opdycke, 47.

64. Barry, 180, 350.

65. Examples of information from the Red Cross published in newspapers include the following: "U.S. Red Cross Declares War on Influenza," *San Francisco Chronicle,* October 8, 1918; "Rush of Calls for Doctors and Nurses," *Boston Globe,* October 8, 1918; "Red Cross Turns Its Attitude to War on Influenza," *Newport News (VA) Daily Press,* October 8, 1918.

66. "Every Soldier to Have a Sweater," *Greenville Daily News,* January 8, 1918.

67. Jessie Lee Carter interview with Allen Tullos, May 5, 1980, H-0237 Southern Oral History Program Collection #4007, Wilson Library, Southern Historical Collection, University of North Carolina at Chapel Hill.

68. Geddes Elam Dodson interview with Allen Tullos, May 26, 1980, H-0239, Southern Oral History Program Collection #4007, Wilson Library, Southern Historical Collection, University of North Carolina at Chapel Hill.

69. "Warm Underwear Defies the 'Flu,'" *Greenville Daily News,* October 17, 1918; "Spanish Influenza—What It Is and How It Should Be Treated," *Greenville Daily News,* October 12, 1918; "Avoid 'Flu' by Sterilizing Your Nose," *Greenville Daily News,* October 24, 1918.

70. "To Use Liquor Only for Pneumonia Cases," *Greenville Daily News,* October 21, 1918.

Notes to Pages 169–174   271

71. "Whiskey in Influenza and Pneumonia," editorial, *Journal of the South Carolina Medical Association* 14, no. 10 (1918): 277–80.

72. Bainbridge, *Academy and College,* 156.

73. Barry, *Great Influenza,* 143.

74. Byerley, "U.S. Military and the Influenza Pandemic."

75. "Dr. Daniel Will Leave on Tuesday," *Greenville Daily News,* April 9, 1915.

76. Naomi Sizemore Trammell interview with Allen Tullos, March 25, 1980, H-0258, Southern Oral History Program Collection #4007, Wilson Library, Southern Historical Collection, University of North Carolina at Chapel Hill.

77. "Influenza," *Journal of the South Carolina Medical Association* 14, no. 10 (October 1918): 247.

78. Partridge and Towell, *Transformation,* 39. The authors quote from J. Decherd Guess, *A Medical History of Greenville County, South Carolina.* 1959.

79. Partridge and Towell, *Transformation,* 40.

80. "Wanted," *Greenville Daily News,* October 8, 1918.

81. Patterson, "Black Nurses in the Great War," 549.

82. Stimson, *Medical Department of the United States Army,* 288–89; Telford, "American Nursing Shortage during World War I," 92.

83. Bristow, *American Pandemic,* 134.

84. C. L. Williams, *Torchbearers of Democracy,* 101; Brown, *Private Politics and Public Voices,* 71.

85. Thoms, *Pathfinders,* 159–67; Budreau and Prior, *Answering the Call,* 65.

86. Thoms, *Pathfinders,* 166–67.

87. Patterson, "Black Nurses in the Great War," 547; Gavin, *American Women in World War I,* 59–60. For more on these women, and the short-term and long-term legacies of their work during World War I, see Jones and Saines, "Eighteen of 1918–1919."

88. Sheldon, "Brief History of Black Women in the Military"; E. J. Scott, *Scott's Official History of the American Negro in the World War,* 376–79.

89. Hine, *Black Women in White,* xviii.

90. Thoms, *Pathfinders,* 165–67.

91. Bristow, *American Pandemic,* 135.

92. Threat, *Nursing Civil Rights,* 24.

93. "List of Cases of Influenza, and of Deaths Caused by Pneumonia Following That Disease Reported to the State Health Officer during October, 1918," *Thirty-ninth Annual Report of the State Board of Health of South Carolina for the Fiscal Year 1918 to the Legislature of South Carolina,* 39.

94. "Tale about Swan White."

95. Bainbridge, *Academy and College,* 156.

96. "Out of Quarantine," *Greenville Daily News,* November 22, 1918.

97. Erwin [last name unknown] to Benjamin Draeger, November 10, 1918, in the author's possession.

98. "Furman Boys in Army Write Fine Letters," *Furman Hornet,* November 8, 1918.

99. "Epidemic Influenza: Prevalence in the United States," *Public Health Reports* Volume 34, No. 1 (January 3, 1919), 1–2. United States National Library of Medicine, National Institutes of Health. Accessed January 6, 2021: https://www.ncbi.nlm.nih.gov/. "In addition the Charleston Sanitary District listed 1,427 cases, Camp Gordon in Georgia had 1,660, and Camp Taylor in Kentucky and Indiana (the extra-cantonment zone covered parts of both states) had 13,285.

100. Keene, "Americans as Warriors," 17.

101. Sayres (born December 15, 1878) served as assistant superintendent from 1918 to 1935. She died on January 1, 1948, at the age of sixty-nine and was buried in Arlington National Cemetery. Feller and Moore, *Highlights in the History of the Army Nurse Corps,* 10, 70; "Sayres, Louise Milliken," Wall of Valor Project; Helsley, *Hidden History of Greenville County,* 95.

102. "Health Officials Check Epidemic," *Greenville News,* January 6, 1924.

103. US Army Center of Military History, *Organizations and Activities,* 472.

104. Helsley, *Hidden History of Greenville County,* 97.

105. Katie Youndgdahl, "The 1918–19 Spanish Influenza Pandemic and Vaccine Development," The History of Vaccines: An Educational Resource by the College of Physicians of Philadelphia (September 26, 2018). Accessed January 7, 2021: https://www.historyofvaccines.org/.

106. Barry, *Great Influenza,* 403; Arnold, *Pandemic 1918,* 1–17.

Chapter 9: "Grow with Greenville"

1. "Nation Rejoices at War's End; City Is Jubilant," *New York Times,* November 12, 1918; "Many County Towns Join in Parades," *Los Angeles Times,* November 12, 1918; "City Wild with Joy," *Washington Post,* November 12, 1918; Charleston Museum, "The Centennial of Armistice Day." https://www.charlestonmuseum.org/.

2. "Peace!" *Greenville Piedmont,* November 11, 1918.

3. "Great Demonstration Here Yesterday after Good News Was Heard," *Greenville Daily News,* November 12, 1918.

4. "Parade of Students," *Furman Hornet,* November 15, 1918.

5. "Great Demonstration Here Yesterday after Good News Was Heard"; "First Baptist Church," *Greenville Daily News,* November 16, 1918. On Sunday, November 17, the First Baptist Church observed "Peace Sunday." Pastor George W. Quick's sermon during the morning service was titled "The Armistice of Grace," while his evening sermon, "The Sword or Justice? Shall Germany Be Punished?" weighed diplomatic approaches to Germany's defeat.

6. Daniel, *Century of Progress,* 85; "A Call for a Great National Liberty Sing," *Greenville Daily News,* November 22, 1918. The Great National Patriotic Sing was led by the women's committee of the National Council of Defense and was chaired nationally by Dr. Anna Howard Shaw.

7. Willie Gray Martin (Mrs. C.B. Martin), "Greenville in the Making," 1927, South Carolina Room, Greenville County Library. The Martins lived at 307 Crescent Avenue. Willie Gray's husband, Ben, was a real-estate agent.

8. Henry E. Stradley, "The Greenville Spirit," *Greenville Civic and Commercial Journal* 1, no. 1 (September 1921): 12. South Carolina Room, Greenville County Library.

9. Judith T. Bainbridge, "Richard F. Watson." *Greenville News,* December 29, 2016.

10. "'Grow with Greenville' Slogan of Public-Spirited Citizens and Firms Planning for the Future," *Greenville Daily News,* September 7, 1918; "All Together Now, Pull!!!," advertisement, *Greenville Daily News,* November 15, 1918.

11. Huff, *Greenville,* 421. Huff cites US Census data for City of Greenville population statistics. In 1900 the city population was 11,860; in 1910 it was 15,741; in 1920 it grew to 23,127; and in 1930 it was 29,154. The population of Greenville County grew from 68,000 to 88,000, or 29.4 percent, from 1910 to 1920.

12. Community Council of Greenville, *Everybody's Business,* 4.

13. William B. Scott and Peter M. Rutkoff, "Great Migration," in Edgar, *South Carolina Encyclopedia,* 393–94; Capace, *Encyclopedia of South Carolina,* 49.

14. Edgar, *South Carolina: A History,"* 481.

15. Walter White to John Shillady, October 26, 1918.

16. C. L. Williams, "Vanguards of the New Negro," 349; DuBois, "Returning Soldiers," Crisis XVIII (May 1919) 13.

17. Hudson, Entangled by White Supremacy, 212.

18. White, *Too Heavy a Load,* 114–15.

19. Damon Fordham, "Charleston Riot (1919)," in Edgar, *South Carolina Encyclopedia,* 157.

Notes to Pages 180–184   273

20. Ibid.; "Six Men Killed at Race Battle in Charleston," *Atlanta Constitution,* May 11, 1919; National Archives, "Red Summer 1919." https://www.archives.gov/calendar/event/red-summer-1919 -commemorating-the-past-confronting-its-presence.

21. "Negroes League Organized Here," *Greenville Daily News,* October 27, 1919; "Spoke to Negroes at Mass Meeting," *Greenville Daily News,* November 11, 1919.

22. Telegram from John R. Shillady to Thomas R. Marshall, National Archives, Records of the US Senate. Shillady sent the telegram to the vice president, who was essentially functioning as president while Wilson was in Europe. Wilson returned from France on July 8, 1919.

23. Blee, "Evidence, Empathy, and Ethics," 601, 606.

24. Gordon, *Second Coming of the KKK,* 2–3.

25. Huff, *Greenville,* 323–25; Edgar, *South Carolina: A Historya,* 484. The Black Business District included the blocks surrounding the Working Benevolent Temple and John Wesley Church, at the contemporary intersections of Broad and Falls and East Court Streets.

26. Szymanski, "Beyond Parochialism," 122.

27. Edgar, *South Carolina: A History,* 468.

28. Edgar, *South Carolina: A History,* 483.

29. These bootleggers attempted to alter their cars to make them as fast as possibleSee Thompson, *Driving with the Devil,* and Pierce, *Real NASCAR.*

30. Green, *Southern Strategies,* 27; Sidney R. Bland, "Eulalie Chafee Salley," in Edgar, *South Carolina Encyclopedia,* 831.

31. Editorial, *Bamberg Herald,* February 27, 1919.

32. "Lunatic Women Injure Cause," *Watchman and Southron,* February 22, 1919.

33. Hudson, *Entangled by White Supremacy,* 211; "Will Women Vote in Next Primary in South Carolina? Nice Legal Points Involved," *Greenville Daily News,* March 28, 1920; Taylor, "South Carolina and the Enfranchisement of Women," 306–9.

34. "Senator Blease Strikes Back against Critics of Record," *Greenville News,* August 10, 1930.

35. Woodward, *Origins of the New South,* 369.

36. Mary Bryan, *Proud Heritage: A History of the League of Women Voters of South Carolina (Columbia: League of Women Voters of South Carolina, 1978),* 7, South Carolina Room, Greenville County Library.

37. "State Suffrage Group to Pass Out," *Orangeburg Times and Democrat,* June 26, 1920.

38. Shankman, "Jury of Her Peers."

39. "Representative Crowd Hears Candidates at Courthouse," *Greenville News,* August 15, 1922. When the state of South Carolina opened the bar exam to women in 1918, Perry became the first woman admitted to the SC Bar and eventually the first woman to become a partner with a law firm in the state. Five years after she broke the legal profession's gender barrier, Greenvillians Julia David Charles and Anna McCants Beaty joined the first all-female law practice in the state. For more information on Jim Perry, see Huff, *Greenville,* 264, and Judith T. Bainbridge, "James Margrave Perry," in Edgar, *South Carolina Encyclopedia,* 713.

40. Judith T. Bainbridge, "Who Was Mary Camilla Judson, Namesake of Judson Booksellers?" *Greenville News,* August 22, 2019.

41. "Women's Aim in Politics Told by State Head," *Greenville News,* July 1, 1922; "Important Bills Favored by Women's State Council," *Greenville News,* December 3, 1922; "Platform for the South Carolina League of Women Voters," *Edgefield Advertiser,* December 1, 1920.

42. A. F. McKissick, "Greenville County's State Income Tax Record," *Greenville Civic and Commercial Journal,* 2, no. 4 (February 1923): 1.

43. "Says Everybody Favors Campaign," *Greenville News,* April 14, 1922; Cleveland Foundation, "How Goff's Idea Has Enriched the World's Social Capital." https://www.clevelandfoundation

274 Notes to Pages 184–190

100.org/. The movement was begun by Cleveland Banker Fred Goff, who established the Cleveland Foundation in 1914.

44. "Community Fund to Start Tomorrow," *Greenville News,* April 23, 1922. The trust evolved into the Community Chest of Greater Greenville, the United Fund of Greenville County, and the United Way. Eighty-two thousand dollars in 1922 is the equivalent of approximately $1.3 million in 2022. The goal for the African American campaign was less than 10 percent of the White campaign. Rhoda Livingston Haynsworth was Mrs. Harry J. Haynsworth.

45. W. P. Conyers, "A Personal Word from the Retiring President," *Greenville Civic and Commercial Journal* 3, no. 12 (November 1924): 1.

46. Judith Bainbridge, "Bill Timmons Led Chamber of Commerce during Its Glory Days," *Greenville News,* July 30, 2017. Bill Timmons graduated from Furman in 1912 and served in the US Army during the war.

47. *Ladies Home Journal* quoted in Jensen, *Mobilizing Minerva,* 222.

48. Huff, *Greenville,* 264; Gullick, "Greenville County," 64–65.

49. "The Woman's Bureau of the Greenville Chamber of Commerce," SC Pam,box 66, Woman's Bureau of the Greenville Chamber of Commerce folder, South Carolina Room, Greenville County Library.

50. "Woman's Bureau Here Attracting Wide Attention," *Greenville News,* August 20, 1922; Link, *Paradox of Southern Progressivism,* 185; Gullick, "Greenville County," 64–65. May Belle McGlothlin was Mrs. W. J. McGlothlin.

51. Hutchison, "Cure for Domestic Neglect," 168.

52. "Letter to Marshall Moore from Administrative Assistant, Better Homes in America," May 17, 1924, Better Homes in America Records, box 16, folder 8, First Savings Bank, Hoover Institution Library and Archives, Greenville; Bainbridge, "Richard F. Watson."

53. In 1928 the Phillis Wheatley Center coordinated with the Woman's Bureau to involve African American women in Better Homes Week. In 1929 Delphinia Wilkinson led African American women's efforts.

54. "10,000 Visit Model Homes during Better Homes Week," *Greenville News,* April 28, 1929; "Greenville Winner of First Prize in Better Homes Week," *Greenville News,* July 1, 1929. The president of the Woman's Bureau in 1929 was Willie Gray Martin. The chairperson of the Better Homes committee was Hessie T. Morrah. Minnie Quinn Gassaway (Mrs. W. L.) led efforts to present the community garden festival and also served as state chairperson of the Better Homes movement.

55. "The Auto Tags," *Greenville Civic and Commercial Journal* 1, no. 3 (November 1921): 32.

56. "Many Rotarians Here to Attend Big Convention," *Greenville News,* March 15, 1920; "Another Million Dollar Industry for Greenville," *Greenville News,* March 25, 1920; "Brevard Plans Great Welcome," *Greenville News,* June 18, 1922; "Saluda Party Given Warm Welcome by Greenville Folk," *Greenville News,* July 13, 1922.

57. Huff, *Greenville,* 306.

58. "Mill Town Miracle: Extension of Remarks of Hon. Joseph R. Bryson of South Carolina," *Appendix to the Congressional Record: Proceedings and Debates of the 77th Congress,* A4199; "Druggists to Visit Greenville," *Greenville Civic and Commercial Journal* 2, no. 8 (June 1923): 8; "The Southeastern Congress of Optometry," *Greenville Civic and Commercial Journal* 3, no. 8 (June 1924): 7; "Greenville, a Foremost Food Supply Center," *Greenville Civic and Commercial Journal* 2, no. 7 (May 1923): 5.

59. Huff, *Greenville,* 310. Within one year of its establishment, in 1923, Greenville's new Civitan Club brought the Boy Scout movement to the city.

60. Huff, *Greenville,* 307. Frances Sullivan McDavid was Mrs. P. A. McDavid.

61. Judith T. Bainbridge, "Beacham and LeGrand," in Edgar, *South Carolina Encyclopedia,* 58–59. J. E. Sirrine and Co. cultivated the careers of many of Greenville's notable architects during this period, such as Beacham, LeGrand, and Joseph G. Cunningham.

Notes to Pages 190–196   275

62. "Casual Comments on the Old Home Town," *Greenville Civic and Commercial Journal* 2, no. 9 (July 1923): 9; Dunlap, "Victims of Neglect," 46, 86.

63. "Greenville Only S.C. City to Build over 15 Stories High," *Abbeville Press and Banner,* March 2, 1921.

64. "New Office Building One of Finest in Southland," *Greenville News*, June 17, 1923.

65. Dunlap, "Victims of Neglect," 67–69; "A Landmark of Greenville Progress," *Greenville News,* February 10, 1924; "It Takes an Income to Make Greenville Grow," *Greenville News,* "Greenville, USA" supplement, June 26, 1962; "Woodside Building to Be Formally Turned Over to City Tomorrow; Various Clubs and Organizations Plan to Participate," *Greenville News,* June 17, 1923.

66. Willie Gray Martin (Mrs. C. B. Martin), "Greenville in the Making," 1927, South Carolina Room, Greenville County Library.

67. Bastian, "Tall Office Buildings in Small American Cities; National Register of Historic Places, "South Carolina Inventory Form for Historic Districts and Individual Properties in a Multiple Property Submission: Imperial Hotel." The Imperial Hotel was a seven-story structure when it was built in 1911, and it was commonly referred to as a skyscraper, though technically it was not. The two skyscrapers noted in Bastion's article are the Woodside Building and the Chamber of Commerce building.

68. Living Places, "Colonel Elias Earle Historic District"; Kimberley Collier, "Augusta Road Area, Not Just a 'Place' but More 'a Way of Life,'" *Greenville Journal*, October 1, 2019, https://greenvillejournal.com/homes/places-augusta-road-area-not-just-a-place-but-more-a-way-of-life/. Rooted by Earle Town House, built in 1810, and Whitehall, a majestic home built in 1813, the area had been subdivided in the early 1900s, and subsequently lots had become available for purchase.

69. "Greenville Roads Attract Everyone," *Greenville Daily News*, September 14, 1917.

70. "Roads and highways."

71. "Facts: When You Talk of Greenville, Talk Facts," *Greenville Civic and Commercial Journal* 1, no. 1 (September 1921): 22.

72. "Greenville an Auto Center," *Greenville Civic and Commercial Journal* 1, no. 6 (February 1922): 16.

73. Huff, *Greenville*, 310; Grady et al. *v. City of Greenville et al*, 129 S.C. 89 (SC 1924); Judith T. Bainbridge, "Moving the Confederate Monument Was Controversial in 1922," *Greenville News,* June 19, 2017; "Hold Conference on New Location for Monument," *Greenville News,* June 17, 1924; "Would Place Monument on Plot at Cemetery Entrance," *Greenville News,* June 19, 1924; "Discusses City Monument Case," *Greenville News,* June 20, 1924; "Man of the Monument Takes Post atop Column Once More," *Greenville News,* July 20, 1924.

74. Aheron, *Greenville*, 104.

75. "Greenville Carriers Name Negro Delegate," *Southern Indicator* (Columbia, SC), July 16, 1921. In 1921 Holloway's White colleagues elected him as their delegate to the National Association of Letter Carriers annual meeting in Saint Louis that September. For more on Holloway, see Huff, *Greenville,* 313–15. For an excerpt from a prepared statement Holloway gave on WFBC radio on February 15, 1940, for National Negro History Week, see Drake, "Negro in Greenville, South Carolina," 172–73.

76. Judith T. Bainbridge, "Greenville's Spinners Were the City's Baseball Team for Decades," *Greenville News,* November 27, 2017.

77. Judith T. Bainbridge, "Ex-mayor a Major Success in All Trades," *Greenville News,* January 5, 2017.

78. Greenville Water, "History." https://www.greenvillewater.com/history/; Judith Bainbridge, "Paris Mountain State Park Has Been a Greenville Favorite for Decades," *Greenville News,* August 22, 2017.

79. "Set May 24 as Tentative Date for Dedication of New City Reservoir," *Greenville News,* April 21, 1928.

276 Notes to Pages 196–199

80. Greenville Water, "History."

81. Bainbridge quotes from the November 18, 1926 issue of the *Greenville News* in Bainbridge, *Attorneys and Law in Greenville County*.

82. Bainbridge, "Beacham and LeGrand"; "South Carolina," *Modern Hospital* 16, no. 4 (April 1921): 82; "Hospitals and Homes of the Salvation Army," *Modern Hospital* 17, no. 1 (July 1921): 24. In 1931 Dr. Charles Wyatt requested that management of the hospital move from the Salvation Army to the Catholic Church. The next year the Franciscan Sisters of the Poor purchased the hospital at a cost of fifty-five thousand dollars and renovated the hospital to include sixty beds and eight bassinets. The dedication ceremony of the new St. Francis Infirmary, which drew six thousand people, took place on July 14, 1932, with the first patient admitted four days later.

83. Huff, *Greenville*, 317–18; Davis, "Coming to Greenville."

84. The Shriners organization dates to 1872. The first Shriners Hospital for Crippled Children opened in Shreveport, Louisiana, in 1922 with the purpose of providing free orthopedic care to children under the age of eighteen. W. W. Burgess created an endowment of $1.25 million for the expansion of Greenville's real estate. The nonprofit hospital opened in 1927 on Pleasantburg Drive.

85. Beardsley, *A History of Neglect*, 14.

86. "Begin Work on Sanitarium for the Tubercular," *Greenville Daily News*, April 28, 1915; E. B. Holloway, "Worthy Causes for Our Colored Citizens," *Greenville Daily News*, September 8, 1919; "Hopewell Holds Drive to Erase Ill in Negroes," *Greenville News*, March 23, 1937; "Mrs. M. P. Gridley Started Hopewell Unit Years Ago," *Greenville News*, October 7, 1938; South Carolina Department of Health and Environmental Control, "History of Tuberculosis in South Carolina."

87. "Colored Citizens Aid in Health Work," *Greenville News*, December 7, 1924.

88. "Mrs. M. P. Gridley to Head Her 22nd Annual Seal Sale," *Greenville Daily News*, November 22, 1938. Gridley celebrated her eighty-eighth birthday in September 1938 with her first airplane ride. Several months later she became ill and began limiting her activities. She died in December 1939.

89. "Subbing for Santa," *American Legion Weekly*, December 15, 1922, 11; "Uncle Sam's Insurance," *American Legion Weekly*, July 25, 1919, 28.

90. B. Scott, *History Happened Here*, 295.

91. The hospital functioned until 1948.

92. Judith T. Bainbridge, "Dr. W. C. Black Came to Greenville in 1889 as Well Prepared as a Young Physician Could Be," *Greenville News*, October 18, 2016.

93. "Forty Nurses Qualify for Tusk. Hospital," *Baltimore Afro-American*, May 11, 1923; "National Association of Colored Graduate Nurses," 21.

94. Beardsley, *History of Neglect*, 16, 18.

95. *Reports and Resolutions of South Carolina to the General Assembly 1920;* "New Temple Is Formally Opened by Negro Lodge," *Greenville News*, August 10, 1922; National Register of Historic Places, "Working Benevolent Temple and Professional Building." In January 1919 James A. Tolbert and E. W. Biggs led efforts to establish the Working Benevolent Realty Company. The formal dedication of the building included comments from African American leaders Biggs and Gandy and White leaders W. C. Beacham and Mayor Harvley. The building, located at the corner of Broad and Fall Streets, later served as a center for African Americans during the civil rights movement in the 1960s.

96. Huff, *Greenville*, 296.

97. Thomas Parker, "Some Educational and Legislative Needs of South Carolina's Mill Villages," 14–15.

98. Lerda, "Southern Progressivism in Historical Perspective," 74.

99. James A. Dunlap, III, "Mill Schools," in Edgar, *South Carolina Encyclopedia*, 632–33.

100. Huff, *Greenville*, 296; Virginia B. Bartels, "The History of South Carolina Schools." (Center for Educator Recruitment, Retention, and Advancement, 2010) 15. www.teachercadets.com/media /documents/2010/8/; 15; Oral History with Ellen Perry, by Verena Bryson and Gretchen Robinson,

Notes to Pages 199–203 277

Greenville County Foundation and Greenville County Library, November 30, 1979, Ellen Perry Folder, South Carolina Room, Greenville County Library. Ellen Perry was instrumental in assisting Parker and Hollis.

101. Carlton, *Mill and Town in South Carolina*, 264; Rulinda Price, "The Pathfinder: Thomas Parker's Influence Spread from Monaghan Mill to the Greenville Library System," *Greenville Journal*, November 11, 2016. Price describes Monaghan as a "model of progressive management."

102. "Mill Town Miracle," *Appendix to the Congressional Record: Proceedings and Debates of the 77th Congress*, A4199.

103. Edgar, *South Carolina: A History*, 462.

104. "Mill Town Miracle," A4199.

105. Mack Duncan, interview with Allen Tullos, June 7 and August 30, 1979, H-0242, Southern Oral History Program Collection #4007, Southern Historical Collection, Wilson Library, University of North Carolina at Chapel Hill, 54–55; Carlton, *Mill and Town in South Carolina*, 113–14; Kohn, *Cotton Mills of South Carolina*, 128.

106. Huff, *Greenville*, 246.

107. Geddes E. Dodson, interview with Allen Tullos, May 26, 1980, H-0239, Southern Oral History Program Collection #4007, Southern Historical Collection, Wilson Library, University of North Carolina at Chapel Hill, 10.

108. Myrtle Cleveland, interview with Allen Tullos, October 22, 1979, H-0238, Southern Oral History Program Collection #4007, Southern Historical Collection, Wilson Library, University of North Carolina at Chapel Hill, 16–17; Naomi Sizemore Trammell, interview with Allen Tullos, March 25, 1980, H-0258, Southern Oral History Program Collection #4007, Southern Historical Collection, Wilson Library, University of North Carolina at Chapel Hill, 24–25.

109. "Mill Town Miracle"; Huff, *Greenville*, 298.

110. Huff, *Greenville*, 296–98; Bainbridge, *Historic Greenville*, 60; Shi, "'Dr. Pete' Changed Greenville Community." Shi, "Dr. Pete Changed Greendille Community," *Greenville News*, November 27, 2004. In 1949 Hollis was named one of the one hundred "outstanding educators" by *Look* magazine, a biweekly competitor to *Life* magazine. After retiring at the age of sixty-eight, he did not stop in his efforts to better the community: he worked to integrate schools in South Carolina, believing in equitable race relations and equal educational opportunities. Later in his life, Pete Hollis received honorary doctoral degrees from Furman and the University of South Carolina and had elementary and middle schools named after him in Greenville. He was a revered and loved man when in 1978 he died at the age of ninety-five.

111. Shi, "'Dr. Pete' Changed Greenville Community"; Price, "Pathfinder," 21.

112. Mary Mac Ogden Motley, "Wil Lou Gray," in Edgar *South Carolina Encyclopedia*, 392.

113. Ogden, *Wil Lou Gray*, 76, 78.

114. Ogden Motley, "Wil Lou Gray," 63.

115. This school ultimately became the Wil Lou Gray Opportunity School and eventually included men and other races.

116. Ogden, *Wil Lou Gray*, 91; "Wil Lou Gray," in Edgar, *South Carolina Encyclopedia*.

117. Ogden, *Wil Lou Gray*, 56, 76, 80; Fink, *Progressive Intellectuals and the Dilemmas of Democratic Commitment*, 260. Gray was also an early advocate for integration. In 1931 she performed an experiment by offering two literacy camps: one for White students at Clemson College and one for African Americans at the Seneca Institute, a segregated Baptist junior college nearby. With assistance from the Carnegie Corporation and scholars from the University of Chicago and Yale, the experiment found similar learning abilities between Black and White students, which prompted Gray to advocate for integrated adult schools.

118. *Fifty-second Annual Report of the State Superintendent of Education of the State of South Carolina 1920* (Columbia, SC: Gonzales & Bryan, State Printers, 1921), 12, 25. The report details

278 Notes to Pages 203–205

further breakdown of each dollar: salaries for White teachers represented 0.578, while salaries for African American teachers represented 0.097, with White schools allocated the remaining 30.7 percent and African Americans schools the final 1.8 percent. In the 1919–20 school year, 17,615 (70.2 percent) of the county's 25,085 students were White, and 7,470 (29.7 percent) were African American.

119. Gullick, "Greenville County," 64–65.

120. Work et al., "Some Negro Members of Reconstruction Conventions and Legislatures and of Congress," 79–80; Eric Connor, "3 Years after Historical Allen School Torn Down, Townhomes Coming to East Stone Avenue Land," *Greenville News,* June 17, 2019. The Allen School first used rooms in the Goodlett Hotel at the corner of Washington and Main Streets. It moved from Laurens Street to Elford Street and eventually to East Stone Avenue.

121. National Register of Historic Places, "Richland Cemetery." The school burned in 1941 and was relocated and rebuilt just north of Richland Cemetery on Cemetery Street, near today's East Stone Avenue and North Church Street. The Allen School closed in 1970 when Greenville County schools integrated.

122. National Register of Historic Places, "Rosenwald School Building Fund and Associated Buildings (1913–1937)." In Alabama, communities gave children boxes to fill with coins, while teens and adults picked cotton in the summer heat, and sometimes even cut lumber to build the Rosenwald school trademark one-room schoolhouse.

123. National Register of Historic Places, "Rosenwald School Building Program in South Carolina (1917–1932)." Rosenwald schools were built throughout Greenville until the early 1930s.

124. Anderson, *Education of Blacks in the South,* 226; South Carolina Department of Archives and History, "Rosenwald Schools, Greenville County."

125. "Rosenwald School Building Program in South Carolina (1917–1932)," 7–8.

126. Ellen Perry, *Free Reading for Everybody* (1973), Greenville County Library, South Carolina Reading Room, 3–5; Woods, "Summary of Address of C. A. Woods at a Dinner Given to Promote the Building of a Public Library in the City of Greenville, South Carolina," 1913–1921, South Carolina Historical Society Archives, Addlestone Library, College of Charleston; "City Should Have $100,000 Library," *Greenville Daily News,* August 19, 1919; "Greenville Library Association Formed and Quarter Secured as Nucleus for Public Library Here," *Greenville News,* May 4, 1921. Woods said to the assembled group of three hundred, "As an incident of the great war, wealth has flowed into the hands of the Southern people in an abundance. . . . This sudden coming of prosperity has increased, it is true, the spirit of enterprise and acquisition; but it has also released the spirit of altruism and generosity. . . . In this thinking the first consideration should be the relief of men and women suffering from disease and hunger in all lands. After that should be the elevation of our own people from the blight of darkness and ignorance to spiritual and intellectual vitality and power. In our times these are the chief trusts attached to the possession of wealth." Founding board members included H. C. Harvley, Fred W. Symmes, Mrs. W. H. Earle, J. W. Norwood, Mrs. H. H. Harris, Thomas F. Parker, and Mary P. Gridley.

127. Dredge, "Contradictions of Corporate Benevolence."

128. Oral History with Ellen Perry, by Verena Bryson and Gretchen Robinson, Greenville County Foundation and Greenville County Library, November 30, 1979, 7, Ellen Perry Folder, South Carolina Room, Greenville County Library.

129. Dredge, "Contradictions of Corporate Benevolence," 319. Ellen Perry and Annie Porter drove the bookmobile to mill schools and elsewhere. Oral History with Ellen Perry, 3.

130. "City Institution Has Had Unusual Growth during Last 3 Years," *Greenville News,* December 30, 1923.

131. Bainbridge, *Historic Greenville,* 61.

132. "Ella Mae Logan: A Passion for Service, *Greenville News,* May 27, 1982.

Notes to Pages 206–210   279

133. Hunter, *Nickel and a Prayer*; White, *Too Heavy a Load*, 102. A new and annotated edition of *A Nickel and a Prayer*, edited by Rhondda Robinson Thompson of Clemson University, was published in 2011 by West Virginia University Press.

134. E. B. Holloway, "Worthy Causes for Our Colored Citizens," *Greenville Daily News*, September 8, 1919.

135. Henri, *Bitter Victory*, 8.

136. Thomas F. Parker, "The Phillis Wheatley Center, Greenville, SC," *Southern Workman*, November 1, 1925, 497.

137. Ibid. "Colored Community Center Dedicated Here Yesterday," *Greenville News*, December 8, 1924. Some of the White charter members included Rion McKissick, L. P. Hollis, Thomas F. Parker, B. H. Peace, H. C. Harvley, Bennette E. Geer, Dr. J. L. Mann, Mrs. J. E. Daniel, Rhoda Livingston Haynsworth (Mrs. H. J. Haynsworth), and Gridley. African American members of the arrangements committee included Rev. C. F. Gandy, E. B. Holloway, and Charles D. Brier.

138. "A Visit to Remember," South Carolina Room, Greenville County Library System, Biog.–G; Aslean Madison, "She Shared Her Home with Those in Need," *Greenville News*, March 12, 1982.

139. Parker, "The Phillis Wheatley Center, Greenville, SC," 498.

140. White, *Too Heavy a Load*, 102.

141. "Phillis Wheatley Ass'n Memoranda," December 31, 1925, South Carolina Room, Greenville County Library.

142. Graham, *Right to Read*, 167; McPheeters, *Library Service in Black and White*, 104.

143. Greenville County Library System, "Service for All," *Library Now: A Publication of the Greenville Library System*, Spring 2021, https://issuu.com/greenvillelibrary/docs/springmag21_issuu /s/11928490. In 1933 the library employed Annie L. Watters (McPheeters), a young African American librarian who had previously taught at Saint Albans County Training School in Simpsonville. She drove a Greenville County Library bookmobile through rural areas of the county to expand the library's reach to African Americans. In 1934 she moved to Atlanta and began a career as one of the first African American librarians in the Atlanta library system, where she influenced African American children in the city, such as a young Martin Luther King Jr., for decades. Her career and experiences as a civil rights activist are chronicled in her autobiography, *Library Service in Black and White*.

144. Letter from E. B. Holloway to J. E. Springarn, September 27, 1929, I:G-197, Records of the National Association for the Advancement of Colored People, Manuscript Division, Library of Congress, Washington, DC.

145. Letter from J. E. Springarn to E. B. Holloway, October 31, 1929, I:G-197, Records of the National Association for the Advancement of Colored People, Manuscript Division, Library of Congress, Washington, DC.

146. Lau, *Democracy Rising*, 96–98.

147. Wilhelmina Jackson, "Greenville Notes, S.C," 5–7, Ralph Bunche Papers, Carnegie-Myrdal, Greenville interviews, Sc MG 290, Carnegie-Myrdal Study of the Negro in America research memoranda collection, 1935–1948, box 36, folder 3, Schomburg Center for Research in Black Culture, Manuscripts, Archives and Rare Books Division, New York Public Library.

148. Huff, *Greenville*, 257.

149. Judith T. Bainbridge, "William Wilson Cook," in Edgar, *South Carolina Encyclopedia*, 223; "Prominent S.C. Couple Die in Dual Slaying," *Chicago Defender*, May 11, 1940; "Another in Greenville Kills Paramour and Self," *Negro Star*, June 14, 1940; "Architect Kills Teacher and Self in Lovers' Quarrel," *Pittsburgh Courier*, May 11, 1940; "Double Killing at Greenville." *Times and Democrat*, May 1, 1940.

150. Gilmore, *Gender and Jim Crow*.

280 Notes to Pages 210–218

151. "Benefit Program to Be Held by Negroes," *Greenville Daily News,* February 28, 1928; "Armistice Day Is Kept by Negroes," *Greenville Daily News,* November 12, 1928; "$1000 Is Reported by Center Drive Workers," *Greenville Daily News,* March 21, 1922; Ella Mae Logan: A Passion for Service, *Greenville News,* May 27, 1982, 45; Hudson, *Entangled by White Supremacy,* 108; Johnson, *Southern Women, New Ladies,* 76, 78, 168–69, 181–201.

152. "40th Anniversary South Carolina Federation of Colored Women's Clubs, 1909–1949," South Caroliniana Library, University of South Carolina; "Fiftieth Anniversary of the South Carolina Federation of Colored Women's Clubs, 1909–1959," Septima P. Clark Papers, ca. 1910–1990, AMN 1000 box 11 folder 02, Avery Research Center at the College of Charleston; Johnson, *Southern Women, New Ladies,* 249n20. It is not known if the Will Do Club and the Sunshine Club were members of the SCFCWC.

153. Hudson, "The Great War and Expanded Equality?" 156–57.

154. Huff, *Greenville,* 312.

155. Letter from Arthur [last name unknown] to F. E. Livingood, November 24, 1918, in the author's possession.

156. McKoy, *Greenville, S.C.,* 36.

157. US Bureau of the Census, *Census of Religious Bodies, 1916,* 306; US Bureau of the Census, *Census of Religious Bodies, 1926,* 670–71.

158. Huff, *Greenville,* 267.

159. US Bureau of the Census, *Census of Religious Bodies, 1916,* 306; US Bureau of the Census, *Census of Religious Bodies, 1926,* 670–71. The 1916 religious census listed 324 Roman Catholics. The 1926 listed 544.

160. "Drive Begins for St. Mary's School," *Greenville Daily News,* April 5, 1920.

161. Randall M. Miller, "Catholics," in Edgar, *South Carolina Encyclopedia,* 140–141; Saint Mary's Catholic School, "History of St. Mary's"; Huff, *Greenville,* 317. Monsignor Andrew Keene Gwynn pastored from 1900 to 1952.

162. David E. Shi, "Furman Law School Short-Lived but Influential," *Greenville News,* October 9, 2005; Judith T. Bainbridge, "Furman Law School Lasted about a Decade," *Greenville News,* September 6, 2017; "Will Require Certificates," *Greenville Daily News,* August 23, 1919.

163. Katz, *History of Compulsory Education Laws,* 18.

164. Reid, *Furman University,* 50.

165. Bainbridge, *Attorneys and Law in Greenville County,* 90.

166. Reid, *Furman University,* 33; Henderson, "'Building Intelligent and Active Public Minds,'" 39–40; Neumann, "'We Cannot Expect to Rebuild the World Overnight,'" 127; Miranda Flowers, "William Joseph McGlothlin: An Administration of Accomplishments," Furmaniana, Special Collections and University Archives, Duke Library, Furman University. One aspect of the university's vision during the McGlothlin and Geer administrations included the use of Furman faculty, staff, and students for public benefit, through leadership in the Greenville County Council for Community Development locally, and regionally through McGlothlin's service on the Southern Commission on the Study of Lynching.

167. Huff, *Greenville,* 316–17. The city installed the Donaldson Air Force Base during World War II.

Epilogue: Memorialization of the Great War

1. "Barbeque, Parade, and Dance Be Features of Soldiers' Celebration," *Greenville Daily News,* April 24, 1919.

2. "Thousands Cheer Returned Heroes in Great Parade," *Greenville Daily News,* May 11, 1919.

3. "Gov. Cooper and Major Workman Laud Heroism Veterans of Two Wars," *Greenville Daily News,* May 11, 1919.

Notes to Pages 218–224 281

4. "Legion Drive to Be Started Today," *Greenville Daily News*, January 28, 1920. For more information on the establishment of the American Legion and its role as "custodians" of the popular memory of World War I, see Trout, *On the Battlefield of Memory*, 42–106.

5. "Headquarters of Legion Opened," *Greenville Daily News*, August 5, 1919; "Men of 30th Want Reunion Here, Is Workman's Belief," *Greenville Daily News*, April 6, 1919; Trout, *On the Battlefield of Memory*, 89–91; Keene, "A Comparative Study of White and Black American Soldiers During the First World War," 71–90 According to Keene, "only four of the twelve states which made up the "Solid South" (North Carolina, Tennessee, Kentucky, and Virginia) would even consider applications for black posts."

6. For more on the development, meaning, and legacy of Confederate culture, see Cox, *Dixie's Daughters*.

7. "Men of 30th Want Reunion Here, Is Workman's Belief"; "Thousands Cheer Returned Heroes in Great Parade."

8. "Reward Holloway with Basket Fruit," *Greenville Daily News*, September 27, 1919; "Furman Student Serve as Guards," *Greenville Daily News*, September 27, 1919. For a preserved silent recording of the reunion, see "1919 Reunion of the 30th Division," South Carolina Room, Greenville County Library Asheville, North Carolina, hosted the Thirtieth Division's second reunion in September 1920; in 1924 the reunion was held in Charleston. North Carolina Department of Natural and Cultural Resources, "Military Collection, XI. World War I Papers, 1903–1933, Military Organizations."

9. "Armistice Signed Year Ago Today," *Greenville Daily News*, November 11, 1918.

10. Trout, *On the Battlefield of Memory*, 110.

11. Wingate, "Over the Top," 31.

12. "In Honor of Furman Men, 'Spirit of the American Doughboy' Be Unveiled June 7," *Greenville News*, May 15, 1921. Viquesney marketed his doughboy as the one officially embraced by the American Legion and selected for the Centralia statue, and articles in newspapers across the country frequently mentioned this. However, Centralia's doughboy, placed in 1924, was sculpted not by Viquesney but by Alonzo Victor Lewis. Earl D. Smith, "The Spirit of the American Doughboy," https://doughboysearcher.weebly.com/.

13. Fletcher, "Lest We Forget," *Bulletin of Furman University*, July 9, 1921, 22–25.

14. Fletcher, 22–25. The first doughboy to be fabricated stands in Nashville, Georgia. It was submitted for the Centralia competition and was subsequently displayed nearby in an Americus, Georgia, theater and hotel lobby to encourage sales.

15. In scholarly debates about the attributes and liabilities of memorialization efforts soon after and well beyond the event being memorialized, scholars often reference the difference just twenty years would have made in memorials that commemorated the "War to End All Wars." The bulk of Civil War memorialization occurred from 1890 to 1915, twenty-five to fifty years after the conflict, whereas the commemorative impulse toward the Great War occurred immediately after the Armistice. Perhaps this was due in part to the fact that fighting did not occur domestically, thus there was no rebuilding of infrastructure and serious economic devastation. Undoubtedly the heretofore unseen trauma of World War I, combined with the fact that it was contested at no expense to American infrastructure, that it actually boosted much of the US economy, and that it ended amid the increased civic involvement of the Progressive Era, propelled a desire to honor and honor fast.

16. Wingate, *Sculpting Doughboys*, 5.

17. Wingate, "Adeline Adams," 27; Wingate, "Over the Top," 44.

18. Wingate cites Adams in "Over the Top," 27.

19. Wingate, 28.

20. In 1919 the American Legion advocated for programs that aided in veteran reassimilation. During and after the war, countries of the British Empire and many states in the United States considered soldier settlement programs. The General Assembly of South Carolina debated the South

282 Notes to Pages 224–227

Carolina Soldier Settlement Act in 1919 to "provide useful employment and rural homes" for veterans not only of World War I but of other wars as well. Debate continued into the 1920 session, where the last documentation of it suggests it was sent to "Other Proceedings." However, on March 5, 1920, the General Assembly ratified Senate Bill 1238/House Bill 689 to provide for free tuition for former soldiers. Several other states provided free tuition for up to four years as well. In 1921 the American Legion commissioned a study and publicized the lack of care given to sick veterans of the Great War. *Journal of the Senate of the General Assembly of the State of South Carolina 1919*, 536; *Journal of the Senate of SC 1920*, 878; "Farms for Soldiers–Deferred," *American Legion Weekly*, August 29, 1919, 12.

21. "A Live Bunch," *Greenville Civic and Commercial Journal* 1, no. 1 (September 1921): 19.

22. Others who participated in the 1927 American Legion meeting in Paris included Reid Elkins of the veterans bureau in Greenville; Mr. and Mrs. Frank Kennedy and Mrs. Kennedy's mother, Mrs. K. D. Eckman; R. N. Nezille; and Dr. and Mrs. Theodore C. Stone. "Local Residents to Attend Paris Meet," *Greenville News*, August 6, 1927.

23. "On to Paris," *American Legion* 3, no. 3 (September 1927): 53.

24. "On to Paris," *American Legion* 3, no. 3 (September 1927): 53–56; American Legion, "Legion to Congress: Preserve Pershing Hall History, Artifacts," *The American Legion*, December 16. 2015, https://www.legion.org/honor/230681/. In 1991 the legion relinquished Pershing Hall to the Department of Veterans Affairs, who subsequently leased it to a company that developed it as a luxury hotel, also named Pershing Hall.

25. "Legion Memorial Work Is Approved," *Greenville Daily News*, October 8, 1927; "Greenville Legion Post Dedicates Memorial Highway," *Greenville Daily News*, November 12, 1927; "Legion Memorial Highway Funds Increased Nearly $150 By Schools," *Greenville Daily News*, October 30, 1927.

26. "Lawyers Start Move to Raise $100,000 for Memorial Library Here," *Greenville Daily News*, December 4, 1919; "Urges Memorial City Building to Stand over River," *Greenville Daily News*, November 13, 1927.

27. South Carolina General Assembly, *The Official Roster of South Carolina Soldiers, Sailors, and Marines in the World War, 1917–18*; Megginson, "Black South Carolinians in World War I," 153–54.

28. For more on the effort to create state histories of World War I, see Lamay Licursi, *Remembering World War I in America*, 1–42.

29. Wingate, *Sculpting Doughboys*, 20.

30. *The Official Roster of South Carolina Soldiers, Sailors, and Marines in the World War, 1917–18*, vol. 1, pt. 3, 816.

31. F. H. Payne, assistant secretary of war, to Mrs. M. E. Mallette, president, Keith Home Improvement Association, n.d., file "Colored Mothers and Widows," Pilgrimage, Gold Star, Record Group 92, National Archives.

32. Potter, "World War I Gold Star Mothers Pilgrimages."

33. American Battle Monuments Commission, "Women and World War I Commemoration: The Gold Star Mothers and Widows Pilgrimages, 1930–33," https://www.abmc.gov/news-events/news/; Plant and Clarke, "Crowning Insult," 406.

34. Ancestry, Willie Wise's WWI Registration Card, Local Board for the County of Newberry, State of South Carolina, February 25, 1918, sheet No. 1; Ancestry, Passenger List of Organizations, USS *Leviathan*, Company K, 371st Infantry, from Brest to Hoboken, February 3, 1919. Discrepancies exist in his birth date as well, with 1896; August 15, 1897; and February 1899 listed in different sources available on Ancestry.com.

35. Rosanna Schumfort to War Department, February 21, 1931, provided to the author from the Willie Wise file, Aisne-Marne Cemetery. Records indicate discrepancies in Wise's mother's name, yet

Notes to Pages 227–232   283

the sentiments of the letter are undoubtedly representative of many rural and especially African American mothers. Records indicate that Private Wise listed an aunt, Mrs. Delan Dominick of Prosperity, as his emergency contact. Twelfth Census of the United States, Newberry County, South Carolina, National Archives. I thank Marian Strobel for bringing this to my attention.

36. "Raise Memorials to Gallant Sons," *Columbia State*, May 18, 1919.

37. "Roach Stewart," *Greenville News*, May 31, 1935; Matthews, "From Memory to Honor."

38. Judith T. Bainbridge, "Greenville's Downtown Rotary Club Is Celebrating Its Centennial in Style," *Greenville News*, June 16, 2016.

39. "Mother of Boys Lays Rose Spray in Remembrance," *Greenville News*, May 21, 1934. The tablet is located at the intersection of West Lee and Pine Knoll roads.

40. "War Department Records Show Glory of the 30th," *Greenville News*, September 29, 1937.

41. "Greenville Again Hostess to Men of Old Hickory," *Greenville News*, September 29, 1937.

42. "Marker Will be Dedicated Later," *Greenville News*, November 8, 1938; "Mark Camp Sevier," *Greenville News*, May 17, 1939; "The Rounded Hills of Tennessee," *Greenville News*, December 3, 1939. The exact date of the dedication is unknown.

43. "Busy America Honors Dead," *Greenville News*, November 12, 1943.

44. Loewen, *Lies Across America*, 44–45.

45. "'Wildcat' Division to Hold Reunion," *Albertville (AL) Herald*, September 27, 1956. "'Wildcat' Veterans Check In," *Greenville News*, October 13, 1956. The marker was later moved to a small park adjacent to Springwood Cemetery, where it stands near the Confederate statue. Below the granite marker to the Wildcat Division is a bronze plaque memorializing the achievements of the Thirtieth Division. The date of its dedication is unknown.

46. "How Barbara Tuchman's *The Guns of August* Influenced Decision Making during the Cuban Missile Crisis," *Reader's Almanac* (the official blog of the Library of America), March 19, 2012. https://www.loa.org/.

47. "Doughboy Suit," *Greenville News*, August 4, 1966

48. "Time Fails to Dim Their Memories," *Greenville News*, July 30, 1967.

49. "In 50 Years, Bloodied Argonne Becomes Lush," *Greenville News*, November 10, 1968.

50. "Giving New Veterans a Chance," *Greenville News*, November 11, 1968.

51. "Lest We Forget," *Furman Magazine*, Summer 1970, 1–3.

52. The fact that forty-nine African Americans were awarded the Medal of Honor in the Civil War, the Native American campaigns, and the Spanish-American War and none received a Medal of Honor from World War I and World War II until 1991 is indicative of a decline in the quality of race relations commensurate with an increase in White vulnerability and opposition to changes in the status quo. This includes four men from the Black Seminoles, a group of Seminole Indians of African descent. One African American Medal of Honor recipient from the Civil War, Andrew Jackson Smith, was not awarded until 2001. The overwhelming majority were awarded in the years immediately following the war in which the recipient served. Staff, "WFW Honors African-American Medal of Honor Recipients," February 7, 2020, https://www.vfw.org/; Glenn Allen Knoblock, "A History of Black Medal of Honor Winners," Oxford African American Studies Center, accessed July 14, 2020, https://oxfordaasc.com/page; Staff, "Valor 24," U.S. Army, accessed July 14, 2020, https://www.army.mil/.

53. Eisenstadt, *Encyclopedia of New York State*, 824. The investigation that resulted in Stowers's Medal of Honor sparked further studies, which revealed that in addition to African Americans, Jewish Americans, Hispanic Americans, and Japanese Americans had also been subject to racial discrimination and had not received the medals for which they had qualified. Beginnings in the 1990s, dozens of men received long-overdue medals. One of the men was Pvt. Henry Johnson of the 369th. Although born in North Carolina, Johnson had lived in New York since his teenage years, and it was there that he returned, injured, after the battle in the Ardennes. His injuries were so severe that they

interfered with his ability to maintain a job, yet he received no medical benefits because his discharge papers included no mention of injuries. His personal life suffered, and he died in 1929 at the age of thirty-two. Johnson's son Herman, one of the famed Tuskegee Airmen in World War II, had long lobbied for additional distinctions for his father in cooperation with the 369th Veterans Association. In 1991 the city of Albany, New York, where Johnson had worked as a railroad porter before entering the service, honored him by naming part of a major boulevard for him. They also subsequently erected a memorial featuring a bronze bust of Johnson in Washington Park. President Clinton awarded him a Purple Heart in 1996, and seven years later he received the Distinguished Service Cross in a ceremony at the Pentagon. Meanwhile research continued on Johnson's case. In 2001 paperwork revealed that he had been buried with military honors at Arlington National Cemetery, not in an unmarked pauper's grave, as his son had long believed. In 2011 an aide in the office of New York senator Chuck Schumer discovered a memo authored by General Pershing on May 20, 1918, five days after the German attack on Johnson and Roberts: "Reports in hand show notable instance of bravery and devotion shown by 2 soldiers of American colored regiment operating in French sector. . . . Before day light on May 15, Private Henry Johnson and Private Roberts, while on sentry duty at some distance from one another, were attacked by German raiding party estimated at 20 men, who advanced in 2 groups attacking at once from flank and rear. Both men fought bravely in hand-to-hand encounters, one resorting to use of bolo knife after rifle jammed and further fighting with bayonet and butt became impossible. Evidence that at least one and probably second German was severely cut. Third known to have been shot. Attention drawn to fact that the 2 colored sentries first attacked continued fighting after receiving wounds, and despite of use of grenades by superior force, and should be given credit for preventing by their bravery the taking prisoner of our men." "General Pershing's Official Reports," in *Army-Navy Register* 63, no. 1975 (1918): 659. Senator Schumer's office joined the movement to have the Medal of Honor bestowed upon Johnson.

54. Emily Masters, "Veteran Who Fought for Henry Johnson Honored by City of Albany," *Albany (NY) Times-Union,* June 5, 2017. Henry Johnson was born in Winston-Salem, North Carolina but moved to Albany, New York, as a teenager. In 2017, one hundred years to the day after he registered with the Selective Service drive, the city of Albany deemed June 5, 2017, Henry Johnson Day and awarded the inaugural Henry Johnson Award for Distinguished Community Service.

55. "Lawsuit Challenges SC Heritage Act Over Monuments," *Columbia State,* July 25, 2015.

56. Ibid.

57. "Ward: Moral Imperative Drove Me to Challenge Heritage Act," *Greenwood Index-Journal,* July 7, 2018.

58. Larry Luxner, "Bosnia, Cradle of World War I, Still Struggles with Ethnic Divisions," *Washington Diplomat,* August 2014, 15.

59. Das et al., "Global Perspectives on World War I."

60. As quoted by Adam Hochschild on the back cover of Richard Rubin's book, *The Last of the Doughboys.*

61. Capozzola et al., "Interchange," 474.

62. Peck, "Why Don't We Celebrate the Doughboys as the 'Greatest Generation'?," National Interest, March 1, 2020, https://nationalinterest.org/blog/buzz/.

63. Das et al., "Global Perspectives on World War I." The centennial of the war has occurred concurrently with the centennials of the Spanish influenza epidemic and the last several years of the fight for women's suffrage. Anniversaries prompt a resurgence in scholarship as well as popular interest in events from the past, and apparently pandemics do too. Though the increasing historiographical emphasis on the war within a global context in advance of the centennial aided scholarship on the pandemic of 1918, COVID-19 has prompted increased popular interest in the virus patterns, means of coping, freedom of movement restrictions, and methods of recovery during and after the Spanish influenza. Just as the 1918–19 pandemic affected the ongoing fight for women's suffrage, so too did

Notes to Pages 235–238   285

the COVID-19 pandemic affect efforts to celebrate the centennial of the Nineteenth Amendment in August 2020. The fight for women's suffrage creatively and powerfully overcame its obstacles, however, as has the effort to commemorate it. The centennial has focused on increasingly diversifying the narrative of the movement by incorporating women of color, non-elite women, and male supporters. Through an effort by the National Votes for Women Trail, it has also honored the fight for women's suffrage by adding hundreds of markers on the public landscape throughout the country.

64. "State Memorial Building to War Vets Dedicated," *Greenville News,* March 24, 1937.

65. "Proposed SC Statehouse Statue to Black WWI Regiment Faces Stiff Law," *Charleston Post and Courier,* January 19, 2019. According to Sonya Grantham, one of the strongest proponents for the memorial, supporters are hoping to erect a statue on the grounds of Fort Jackson. In December 2019 the Gateway to the Army Association approved the inclusion of the 371st memorial in a five-acre Centennial Park they are planning to develop at Fort Jackson. 371st Monument, "The 371st Infantry Regiment WWI Monument" June 28, 2018. https://www.carolinapanorama.com/news/local/; CISION PR Newswire, "Monument to Southern African-American Heroes Approved for Fort Jackson's Centennial Park." December 2, 2019. https://www.prnewswire.com/news-releases/. The limits of the act with regard to privately owned monuments was placed into relief by the removal of the John C. Calhoun statue in Charleston's Marion Square in 2020.

66. 371st Monument, "371st Infantry Regiment WWI Monument."

67. Orwell, *1984,* 44.

68. Oliphant, *New Simms History of South Carolina,* 253–54. Oliphant was the granddaughter of the nineteenth-century novelist William Gilmore Simms.

69. Mary C. Simms Oliphant, *South Carolina from the Mountains to the Sea.* The quote was taken from Reynolds, *Reconstruction in South Carolina, 1865–1877.*

70. Foner, "Why Reconstruction Matters," *New York Times,* March 18, 2015.

71. Domby, *False Cause,* 165; Keeanga-Yamahtta Taylor, "American Racism and the Buffalo Shooting," *New Yorker,* May 15, 2022.

72. Jennifer Schuessler, "Taking Another Look at the Reconstruction Era," *New York Times,* August 24, 2015.

73. Established by President Obama as a US national monument in 2017 and later named as a national historical park in 2019, the park is the first national monument or park dedicated to the Reconstruction era.

74. "Schuessler, "Taking Another Look at the Reconstruction Era"; White, *Too Heavy a Load,* 118–19. White asserts that early efforts to revise scholarship regarding Reconstruction began as part of the New Negro movement in the mid-1920s.

75. "Greenville Dedicates Unity Park Plaza to the Late Community Activist Lila Mae Brock," *Greenville Business Magazine,* April 19, 2022; "Unity Park Opening Draws Large Crowd, Some Protesters," *Greenville News,* May 19, 2022.

Bibliography

Manuscript Collections

Atlanta Federal Penitentiary Case Files, National Archives and Records Administration, Atlanta.

Ben P. Gulledge Papers. Southern Historical Collection, University of North Carolina at Chapel Hill.

City of Greenville Archives.

Fulton Bag and Cotton Mill Records, Georgia Tech Special Collections.

Special Collection and University Archives. Duke Library. Furman University, Greenville, SC.

Greenville County Historical Society.

Henry Bacon McKoy Papers. Greenville County Historical Society.

Henry Bacon McKoy Scrapbook Collection. Special Collections and Archives. Furman University, Greenville, SC.

Hoover Institution Library & Archives. Stanford University.

Hutchison Family Papers. South Caroliniana Collection. University of South Carolina.

Ida Salley Reamer Papers. Manuscripts Division. University of South Carolina.

John Hope Franklin Papers. David M. Rubenstein Rare Book and Manuscript Library, Duke University, Durham, NC.

Military Collection, State Archives of North Carolina, Raleigh.

Papers of the German Friendly Society. South Carolina Historical Society. College of Charleston, Charleston, SC.

Paul Eliot Green Papers. Southern Historical Collection. University of North Carolina at Chapel Hill.

Records of the National Association for the Advancement of Colored People. Manuscript Division. Library of Congress. Washington, DC.

Schomburg Center. Manuscripts, Archives, and Rare Books Division, New York Public Library.

Schomburg Center. Photographs and Prints, New York Public Library.

Sophia Smith Collection of Women's History. Smith College, Northampton, MA.

South Carolina Historical Society. Addlestone Library. College of Charleston, Charleston, SC.

South Carolina Room. Greenville County Library.

Southern Oral History Program Collection. Southern Historical Collection, Wilson Library, University of North Carolina at Chapel Hill.

Special Collections. Georgia Tech University Library, Atlanta.

Suffragists Oral History Project. Regional Oral History Office. Bancroft Library. University of California at Berkeley.

Archives and Special Collections. University of South Carolina-Upstate Library. University of South Carolina-Upstate.

Webb Papers. Southern Historical Collection. University of North Carolina at Chapel Hill.

Newspapers and Periodicals

The Abbeville (SC) Medium
Abbeville (SC) Press and Banner
Albany (NY) Times-Union

288 Bibliography

Albertville (AL) Herald
American Legion Weekly
Anderson (SC) Intelligencer
Annual of the Southern Baptist Convention
Army-Navy Register
Atlanta Constitution
Atlanta Georgian
The Atlantic
The Arena
Baltimore Afro-American
The Bamberg (SC) Herald
Baptist Courier
Baptist World
Birmingham News
Boston Globe
Bristol (TN) Herald Courier
Bulletin of the American Association of University Professors
Bulletin of the Catholic Laymen's Association of Georgia
Bulletin of Furman University
Charleston Evening Post
Charleston News and Courier/Post and Courier
Charlotte News
Charlotte Observer
Chattanooga News
Chicago Defender
The Chronicle of Higher Education
Clarksville (TN) Leaf-Chronicle
Concord Times
The Crisis
Daily Intelligencer (Wheeling, WV)
Daily Press
Edgefield (SC) Advertiser
Furman Bulletin
Furman Magazine
Gaffney Ledger
Greenville Civic and Commercial Journal
Greenville Daily News/Greenville News
Greenville Daily Piedmont/Greenville Piedmont
Greenville Enterprise
Greenville Journal
Greenville Mountaineer
Greenville News City People
Greenville Republican
Greenville Semi-weekly News
Greenwood Index-Journal
Harper's New Monthly Magazine
Hollywood Reporter
The Hornet/Furman Hornet
Isaqueena (Greenville, SC)

The Joymaker (Greenville, SC)
Keowee Courier
Knoxville Sunday Journal and Tribune
Los Angeles Times
The Messenger
Modern Hospital
Montgomery Advertiser
Monthly Review of the U.S. Bureau of Labor Statistics
The National Interest
Negro Star
New York Times
New Yorker
Newberry Weekly Herald
Orangeburg Times and Democrat
The Outlook
Pickens Sentinel
The Piedmont
Pittsburgh Courier
Post and Courier
Progressive Greenville
Rochester (NY) North Star
San Francisco Chronicle
Southern Enterprise
The Southern Indicator
The Southern Workman
The State (Columbia, SC)
The Suffragist
Sumter Watchman and Southron
The Textile Worker
Town (Greenville, SC)
The Tradesman
Trench and Camp
Upstate Business Journal
Washington Bee
Washington Diplomat
Washington Post
Wheeling (WV) Daily Intelligencer
Wofford College Journal
The Woman Citizen

Government Documents

Fifty-Second Annual Report of the State Superintendent of Education of the State of South Carolina 1920. Columbia, SC: Gonzales and Bryan, State Printers, 1921.

Library of Congress. *Lynchings by States and Counties in the United States, 1900 to 1931: Data from Research Department, Tuskegee Institute.* New York: American Map Company, 1931

"List of Cases of Influenza, and of Deaths Caused by Pneumonia Following that Disease Reported to the State Health Officer during October, 1918," *Thirty-Ninth Annual Report of the State Board of Health of South Carolina for the Fiscal Year 1918 to the Legislature of South Carolina.* Columbia, SC: Gonzales & Bryan, State Printers, 1919.

290   Bibliography

Reports and Resolutions of South Carolina to the General Assembly. Columbia, SC: Gonzales & Bryan, State Printers, 1920.

Snyder, Thomas D. *120 Years of American Education: A Statistical Portrait*. Washington, DC: National Center for Education Statistics, 1993.

South Carolina Commissioner of Agriculture, Commerce, and Industries. "Labor Division Cotton Report," *Seventh Annual Report*. Columbia, SC: Gonzales & Bryan State Printers, 1915.

South Carolina General Assembly. *Acts and Joint Resolutions, 1891*. Columbia, SC: James H. Woodrow, State Printer, 1891.

———. *Acts and Joint Resolutions, 1915*. Columbia, SC: Gonzales & Bryan State Printers, 1915–1916.

———. *Journal of the Senate of the General Assembly of the State of South Carolina, 1919*. Columbia, SC: Gonzales & Bryan State Printers, 1918–1919.

———. *Journal of the Senate of South Carolina, 1920*. Columbia, SC: Gonzales & Bryan State Printers, 1920.

———. *The Official Roster of South Carolina Soldiers, Sailors, and Marines in the World War, 1917–18*. Columbia: South Carolina State Library, 1929.

South Carolina State Council of Defense. *The South Carolina Handbook of the War*. Columbia, SC: The State Co., 1917.

Student Army Training Corps: Descriptive Circular. October 14, 1918.

United States. "World War I Draft Registration Cards, 1917–1918." Ancestry.com.

U.S. Army Center of Military History. *Organizations and Activities of the War Department*, vol. 3, pt 1 of *Order of Battle of the United States Land Forces in the World War, Zone of the Interior* (Washington, DC: Government Printing Office, 1931–49, rpt., 1988).

———. *Territorial Departments Tactical Division Organized in 1918 Posts, Camps, and Stations* vol. 3, pt 2 of *Order of Battle of the United States Land Forces in the World War, Zone of the Interior* (Washington, DC: Government Printing Office, 1931–1949, reprinted 1988).

U.S. Congress. "Donaldson Air Force Base." *Congressional Record, Proceedings and Debates of the 82nd Congress, First Session, Appendix,* Vol. 97, Part 12, March 15, 1951–May 21, 1951. (Washington, DC: Government Printing Office, 1951).

U.S. Congress. "Mill Town Miracle." *Congressional Record Proceedings and Debates Of The 77th Congress, Second Session, Appendix* Volume 88 Part 10, July 27, 1942-December 6, 1942. (Washington, DC: Government Printing Office, 1942).

U.S. Department of Commerce, Bureau of the Census. *Census of Religious Bodies, 1916, pt. 1, Summary and General Tables*. Washington, DC: Government Printing Office, 1919.

———. *Census of Religious Bodies, 1926*, vol. 1, *Summary and Detailed Tables*. (Washington, DC: Government Printing Office, 1930).

———. *Fourteenth Census of the United States Taken in the Year 1920: Vol. 3, Composition and Characteristics of the Population by States*. (Washington, DC: Government Printing Office, 1922).

U.S. Department of Health and Human Services. "The Great Pandemic: The United States in 1918–1919." Last modified March 5, 2009. https://cybercemetery.unt.edu/archive/allcollections/2009 0305010427/.

U.S. Office of the Surgeon General. *Public Health Bulletin No. 94: Rural Sanitation: A Report on Special Studies Made in 15 Counties in 1914, 1915, 1915, and 1916*. L. L. Lumsden. (Washington, DC: Government Printing Office, 1918).

U.S. War Department. *Annual Reports of the War Department: 1918*, Vol. 1. (Washington, DC: Government Printing Office, 1919).

U.S. War Department. *Final Report of the Provost Marshall General to the Secretary of War on the Operations of the Selective Service Systems to July 15, 1919*. (Washington, DC: Government Printing Office, 1920).

Bibliography 291

Secondary Works

Aheron, Piper Peters. *Greenville*. Mount Pleasant, SC: Arcadia, 2003.

Anderson, James D. *The Education of Blacks in the South, 1860–1935*. Columbia: University of South Carolina Press, 2010.

Arnold, Catherine. *Pandemic 1918: Eyewitness Accounts from the Greatest Medical Holocaust in Modern History*. New York: St. Martin's, 2018.

Bainbridge, Judith T. *Academy and College: The History of the Woman's College of Furman University*. Macon, GA: Mercer University Press, 2001.

———. *Attorneys and Law in Greenville County: A History*. Charleston, SC: The History Press, 2015.

———. *Greenville Communities: The Judson Community*. Self-published, 1999.

———. *Historic Greenville: The Story of Greenville and Greenville County*. San Antonio, TX: Historical Publishing Network, 2008.

Barbeau, Arthur E., and Florette Henri. *The Unknown Soldiers: Black American Troops in World War I*. Philadelphia: Temple University Press, 1974.

Barry, John M. *The Great Influenza: The Story of the Deadliest Pandemic in History*. New York: Penguin, 2005.

Bartels, Virginia B. "The History of South Carolina Schools." *Center for Educator Recruitment, Retention, and Advancement*.

Bass, Jack, and W. Scott Poole. *The Palmetto State: The Making of South Carolina*. Columbia: University of South Carolina Press, 2009.

Bastian, Robert W. "Tall Office Buildings in Small American Cities, 1923–1931." *Geografiska Annaler, Series B, Human Geography* 75, no. 1 (1993): 33–39.

Batson, Mann. *Early Travel and Accommodations Along the Roads of the Upper Part of Greenville County, South Carolina and Surrounding Areas*. Taylors, SC: Faith, 1995.

———. *A History of the Upper Part of Greenville County South Carolina*. Taylors, SC: Faith, 1993.

Beardsley, Edward H. "Allied Against Sin: American and British Responses to Venereal Disease in World War I." *Medical History* 20 (1976): 189–202.

———. *A History of Neglect: Healthcare for Blacks and Mill Workers in the Twentieth-Century South*. Knoxville: University of Tennessee Press, 1990.

Belcher, Ray. *Greenville County, South Carolina: From Cotton Fields to Textile Center of the World*. Charleston, SC: The History Press, 2006.

Belcher, Ray, and Joada P. Hiatt. *Greer: From Cotton Town to Industrial Center*. Charleston, SC: Arcadia, 2003.

Bernstein, David E. *Only One Place of Redress: African Americans, Labor Organizations, and the Court from Reconstruction to the New Deal*. Durham, NC: Duke University Press, 2001.

Black, Jeremy. *The Great War and the Making of the Modern World*. New York: Continuum, 2011.

Bland, Sidney R. "Fighting the Odds: Militant Suffragists in South Carolina." *South Carolina Historical Magazine* 82, no.1 (January 1981): 32–43

Blee, Kathleen. "Evidence, Empathy, and Ethics: Lessons from Oral Histories with the Klan." *Journal of American History* 80, no. 2 (September 1993): 596–606.

Blight, David. *Race and Reunion: The Civil War in American Memory*. Cambridge, SC: Harvard University Press, 2001.

Blue, Rupert. "Conserving the Nation's Man Power: How the Government is Sanitating the Civil Zones Around Cantonment Areas." *National Geographic* 32, no. 3 (September 1917): 255–78.

Blum, Edward J. *Reforging the White Republic: Race, Religion, and American Nationalism, 1865–1898*. Baton Rouge: Louisiana State University Press, 2015.

292 Bibliography

Bollet, Albert Jay. *Plagues and Poxes: The Impact of Human History on Epidemic Disease*. New York: Demos, 2004.

Bradshaw, Sidney E. *History of Furman University: An Outline*. Self-published, 1921.

Brickman, William W. "American Higher Education in Historical Perspective." *Annals of the American Academy of Political and Social Science* 404 (November 1972): 31–43.

Bristow, Nancy K. *American Pandemic: The Lost Worlds of the 1918 Influenza Epidemic*. New York: Oxford University Press, 2012.

———. *Making Men Moral: Social Engineering During the Great War*. New York: New York University Press, 1996.

Brown, Nikki. *Private Politics and Public Voices: Black Women's Activism from World War I to the New Deal*. Bloomington: Indiana University Press, 2006.

Bryan, Jami L. "Fighting for Respect: African Americans in World War I." *On Point: The Journal of Army History* 8, no. 4 (Winter 2002): 11–14.

Buchanan, John G. "War Legislation Against Alcoholic Liquor and Prostitution." *Journal of Criminal Law and Criminology* 9, no. 4 (May 1918–February 1919): 520–29.

Budreau, Lisa M. *Bodies of War: World War I and the Politics of Commemoration in America, 1919–1933*. New York: New York University Press, 2011.

Budreau Lisa M., and Richard M. Prior, eds. *Answering the Call: The U.S. Army Nurse Corps, 1917–1919*. Washington, DC: Government Printing Office, 2008.

Burke, W. Lewis. *All for Civil Rights: African American Lawyers in South Carolina, 1868–1968*. Athens: University of Georgia Press, 2017.

Byerley, Carol R. "The U.S. Military and the Influenza Pandemic of 1918–1919." *Public Health Reports* 125, supplement no. 3, (2010): 82–91.

Caldwell, AB. *History of the American Negro: South Carolina Edition*. Atlanta: A.B. Caldwell Pub. Co, 1919.

Capace, Nancy. *Encyclopedia of South Carolina*. St. Clair Shores: Somerset, 2000.

Capozzola, Christopher. *Uncle Sam Wants You: World War I and the Making of the Modern American Citizen*. Oxford: Oxford University Press, 2008.

———. "The United States Empire." In *Empires at War, 1911–1923*, edited by Robert Gerwarth and Erez Manela, 235–53. Oxford: Oxford University Press, 2014.

Capozzola, Christopher, Andrew Huebner, Julia Irwin, Jennifer D. Keene, Ross Kennedy, Michael Neiberg, Stephen R. Ortiz, Chad Williams, and Jay Winter. "Interchange: World War I." *Journal of American History* 102, no. 2 (September 2015): 463–99. https://doi.org/10.1093/jahist/jav474.

Carolina Stories: Over Here: The Homefront During WWI. 2007. Columbia: South Carolina Educational Television, 2017. PBS Video.

Carlton, David L. *Mill and Town in South Carolina 1880–1920*. Baton Rouge: Louisiana State University Press, 1982.

Carnegie, M. Elizabeth. *The Path We Tread: Black Nursing Worldwide, 1854–1994*. Sudbury, MA: Jones & Bartlett, 1999.

Cash, W. J. *The Mind of the South*. New York: Knopf, 1941.

Chafe, William H., Raymond Gavins, and Robert Korstad. *Remembering Jim Crow: African Americans Tell About Life in the Segregated South*. New York: New Press, 2001.

Clark, Daniel. "United Textile Workers." In *Encyclopedia of U.S. Labor and Working-class History*, Vol. 1, edited by Eric Arnesen, 1457–59. New York: Routledge, 2007.

Community Council of Greenville. *Everybody's Business: A Self-Survey of Conditions Affecting the Negro Population of the Greenville Area*. Greenville, SC: Community Council of Greenville County, 1950.

Conwill, Kinshasha Holman. *We Return Fighting: World War I and the Shaping of Modern Black Identity*. Washington, DC: Smithsonian Books, 2019.

Bibliography   293

Conyers, James L., ed. *Charles H. Houston: An Interdisciplinary Study of Civil Rights Leadership*. Lanham, MD: Lexington Books, 2012.

Conyers, W. P. "A Personal Word from the Retiring President." *Greenville Civic and Commercial Journal* 3, no. 12 (November 1924): 1.

Cooley, Angela Jill. "Food Soldiers: Rural Southerners and Food Regulation during World War I." In *The American South and the Great War, 1914–1924* edited by M. Downs & R. Floyd, 89–115. Baton Rouge: Louisiana State University Press, 2018.

Cooper, Nancy Vance Ashmore. *Greenville: Woven from the Past*. Sun Valley, CA: American Historical Press, 2000.

Cox, Annette. "Cotton Chaotic Home Front: The First World War and the Southern Textile Industry." In *The American South and the Great War, 1914–1924*, edited by Matthew L. Downs and M. Ryan Floyd, 181–206. Baton Rouge: Louisiana State University Press, 2018.

Cox, Karen L. *Dixie's Daughters: The United Daughters of the Confederacy and the Preservation of Confederate Culture*. Gainesville: University Press of Florida, 2003.

Daniel, Robert Norman. *A Century of Progress: Being the History of the First Baptist Church, Greenville, South Carolina*. Greenville, SC: First Baptist Church, 1957.

Das, Santanu, Gerhard Hirschfeld, Heather Jones, Jennifer Keene, Boris Kolonitskii, and Jay Winter. "Global Perspectives on World War I: A Roundtable Discussion." *Zeithistorische Forschungen Studies in Contemporary History* 1 (2014): 92–119. https://doi.org/10.14765/zzf.dok-1493.

Davis, David A. *World War I and Southern Modernism*. Jackson: University Press of Mississippi, 2017.

Degler, Carl N. "Thesis, Antithesis, Synthesis: The South, the North, and the Nation." *Journal of Southern History* 53 (February 1987): 3–18.

Doenecke, Justus D. *Nothing Less Than War: A New History of America's Entry into World War I*. Lexington: University Press of Kentucky, 2011.

Domby, Adam H. *The False Cause: Fraud, Fabrication, and White Supremacy in Confederate Memory*. Charlottesville: University of Virginia Press, 2020.

Douglas, George H. *The Golden Age of the Newspaper*. Westport, CT: Greenwood, 1999.

Doyle, Don H. *New Men, New Cities, New South: Atlanta, Nashville, Charleston, Mobile, 1860–1910*. Chapel Hill: University of North Carolina Press, 1990.

Drake, Joseph Turpin. *The Negro in Greenville, South Carolina*. Chapel Hill: University of North Carolina Press, 1940.

Dredge, Bart. "Contradictions of Corporate Benevolence: Industrial Libraries in the Southern Textile Industry, 1920–1945." *Libraries and the Cultural Record* 43, no. 3 (2008): 308–26.

Du Bois, W. E. B. *Darkwater: Voices from Within the Veil*. New York: Harcourt, Brace and Howe, 1920.

Dumenil, Lynn. *The Second Line of Defense: American Women and World War I*. Chapel Hill: University of North Carolina Press, 2017.

Duren, Robert Franklin. *Lasting Legacy to the Carolinas: The Duke Endowment, 1924–1997*. Durham, NC: Duke University Press, 1998.

Edgar, Walter B. *South Carolina: A History*. Columbia: University of South Carolina Press, 1998.

———. *South Carolina in the Modern Age*. Columbia: University of South Carolina Press, 1992.

———, ed. *The South Carolina Encyclopedia*. Columbia: University of South Carolina Press, 2006.

Edwards, Rebecca. "Politics, Social Movements, and the Periodization of U.S. History." *Journal of the Gilded Age and Progressive Era* 8, no. 4 (October 2009): 463–73.

Eisenstadt, ed., Peter. *The Encyclopedia of New York State*. Syracuse: Syracuse University Press, 2005.

Ellis, Mark. *Race, War, and Surveillance: African Americans and the United States Government During World War I*. Bloomington: Indiana University Press, 2001.

———. "W. E. B. Du Bois and the Formation of Black Opinion in World War I: A Commentary on 'The Damnable Dilemma.'" *Journal of American History* 81, no. 4 (1995): 1584–1590.

"Epidemic Influenza: Prevalence in the United States." *Public Health Reports* (1896–1970) 34, no. 1 (1919): 1–2.

Ewing, Adam. *The Age of Garvey: How a Jamaican Activist Created a Mass Movement and Changed Global Black Politics.* Princeton, NJ: Princeton University Press, 2014.

Feller, Carolyn M., and Constance J. Moore, eds. *Highlights in the History of the Army Nurse Corps.* Washington: US Army Center of Military History, 1995. https://history.army.mil/html/books/085/.

Field, Kendra. "Introduction: African American Migration and Mobility after the Civil War, 1865–1915." *Journal of American History* 102, no. 4 (2017): 421–26.

Filene, Peter G. "An Obituary for 'The Progressive Movement.'" *American Quarterly* 22, no 1 (Spring 1970): 20–34.

Fink, Leon. *Progressive Intellectuals and the Dilemmas of Democratic Commitment.* Cambridge, MA: Harvard University Press, 1997.

Flanagan, Maureen A. *America Reformed: Progressives and Progressivisms, 1890s-1920s.* Oxford: Oxford University Press, 2006.

Fletcher, A. L. *History of the 113th Field Artillery 30th Division.* Raleigh, NC: The History Committee of 113th F. A., 1920

Floyd, M. Ryan. "'A Diarrhea of Plans and Constipation of Action': The Influence of Alabama Cotton Farmers, Merchants, and Brokers on Anglo-American Diplomacy during the First World War, 1914–1915." In *The American South and the Great War, 1914–1924,* edited by Matthew L. Downs and M. Ryan Floyd, 181–206. Baton Rouge: Louisiana State University Press, 2018.

Ford, Nancy Gentile. *Americans All! Foreign-Born Soldiers in World War I.* College Station: Texas A&M University Press, 2001.

Fortescue, Granville. "Training the New Armies of Liberty: Camp Lee, Virginia's Home for the National Army." *National Geographic* 32, nos. 5 and 6 (November-December 1917): 421–38.

Foster, Gaines. *Ghosts of the Confederacy: Defeat, the Lost Cause, and the Emergence of the New South, 1865–1913.* Oxford: Oxford University Press, 1988.

Gallagher, Gary W., Myra McPherson, and Alan T. Nolan, eds. *The Myth of the Lost Cause and Civil War History.* Bloomington: Indiana University Press, 2000.

Gaston, Paul. *New South Creed: A Study in Southern Mythmaking.* Athens: University of Georgia Press, 2011.

Gatewood, Willard B. "The Rollin Sisters: Black Women in Reconstruction South Carolina." In *South Carolina Women: Their Lives and Times-Volume 2,* edited by Marjorie Julian Spruill, Valinda W. Littlefield, and Joan Marie Johnson, 50–67. Athens: University of Georgia Press, 2010.

Gaughan, Anthony. "Woodrow Wilson and the Rise of Militant Interventionism in the South." *Journal of Southern History* 65, no. 4 (1999): 771–808.

Gavin, Lettie. *American Women in World War I: They Also Served.* Boulder: University Press of Colorado, 2006.

Gentile Ford, Nancy. *Americans All!: Foreign-born Soldiers in World War I.* College Station: Texas A&M University Press, 2001.

Gergel, Belinda F. "Irene Goldsmith Kohn." In *South Carolina Women: Their Lives and Times-Volume 2,* edited by Marjorie Julian Spruill, Valinda W. Littlefield, and Joan Marie Johnson, 105–127. Athens: University of Georgia Press, 2010.

Gerwarth and Manela. *Empires at War: 1911–1923.* Oxford: Oxford University Press, 2015.

Gilmore, Glenda. *Gender and Jim Crow: Women and the Politics of White Supremacy in North Carolina, 1896–1920.* Chapel Hill: University of North Carolina Press, 1996.

Gordon, Linda. *The Second Coming of the KKK: The Ku Klux Klan of the 1920s and the American Political Tradition.* New York: Liveright, 2017.

Bibliography 295

Graham, Patterson Toby. *A Right to Read: Segregation and Civil Rights in Alabama's Libraries, 1900–1965.* Tuscaloosa: University of Alabama Press, 2002.

Green, Elna C. *Southern Strategies: Southern Women and the Woman Suffrage Question.* Chapel Hill: University of North Carolina Press, 1997.

Guess, J. Decherd. *A Medical History of Greenville County, South Carolina.* Greenville, SC: Greenville County Medical Society, 1959.

Gullick, Guy A. *Greenville County, Economic and Social.* Greenville: University of South Carolina, 1921.

Hale, Grace Elizabeth. *Making Whiteness: The Culture of Segregation in the South, 1890–1940.* New York: Pantheon Books, 1998.

Hall, James. "Manhood, Duty, and Service: Conscription in North Carolina during the First World War," in *The American South and the Great War, 1914–1924,* ed. Matthew L. Downs and M. Ryan Floyd, 41–60. Baton Rouge: Louisiana State University, 2018.

Hamer, Fritz. *Forward Together: South Carolinians in the Great War.* Charleston, SC: History Press, 2007.

———. "World War I and South Carolina's Council on Defense: Its Campaign to Root out Disloyalty, 1917–1918." In *The American South and the Great War, 1914–1924,* ed. Matthew L. Downs and M. Ryan Floyd, 61–88. Baton Rouge: Louisiana State University, 2018.

Hamilton, John Maxwell. *Manipulating the Masses: Woodrow Wilson and the Birth of American Propaganda.* Baton Rouge: Louisiana State University Press, 2020.

Harper, Ida Husted. *The History of Woman Suffrage, Vol. 4.* Indianapolis: Hollenbeck, 1902.

Harrison, Robert. *Congress, Progressive Reform, and the New American State.* Cambridge: Cambridge University Press, 2004.

Helling, Thomas. *The Great War and the Birth of Modern Medicine.* New York: Pegasus Books, 2022.

Helsley, Alexia Jones. *Hidden History of Greenville County.* Charleston, SC: History Press, 2009.

Hemmingway, Theodore. "Prelude to Change: Black Carolinians in the War Years, 1914–1920." *Journal of Negro History* 65, no. 3 (Summer, 1980): 212–27.

Henderson, A. Scott. "'Building Intelligent and Active Public Minds': Education and Social Reform in Greenville County During the 1930s." *South Carolina Historical Society Magazine* 106, no. 1 (January 2005): 34–58.

Henri, Florette. *Bitter Victory: A History of Black Soldiers in World War I.* New York: Doubleday, 1970.

Herbermann, Charles. *The Catholic Encyclopedia: An International Work of Reference on the Doctrine, Discipline, and History of the Catholic Church, Vol. 17.* New York: Encyclopedia Press, 1922.

Hickel, K. Walter. "War, Region, and Social Welfare: Federal Aid to Servicemen's Dependents in the South, 1917–1921." *Journal of American History* 87, no. 4 (March 2001): 1362–91.

Hine, Darlene Clark. *Black Women in White: Racial Conflict and Cooperation in the Nursing Profession, 1890–1950.* Bloomington: Indiana University Press, 1989.

Hudson, Janet G. *Entangled by White Supremacy: Reform in World War I-Era South Carolina.* Lexington: University Press of Kentucky, 2009.

———. "The Great War and Expanded Equality?: Black Carolinians Test Boundaries." In *The American South and the Great War, 1914–1924,* ed. Matthew L. Downs and M. Ryan Floyd, 140–61. Baton Rouge: Louisiana State University, 2018.

Huff, Archie Vernon. *Greenville: The History of the City and County in the South Carolina Piedmont.* Columbia: University of South Carolina Press, 1995.

Hunter, Jane Edna. *A Nickel and a Prayer.* Morgantown: West Virginia University Press, 2011.

Hunter, Tera W. *To 'Joy My Freedom: Southern Black Women's Lives and Labors After the Civil War.* Cambridge, MA: Harvard University Press, 1997.

Hutchison, Janet. "The Cure for Domestic Neglect: Better Homes in America, 1922–1935." *Perspectives in Vernacular Architecture*, Vol. 2 (1986): 168–78.

Ingram, Tammy. *Dixie Highway: Road Building and the Making of the Modern South, 1900–1930.* Chapel Hill: University of North Carolina Press, 2016.

Iowa PBS. "Black Officers at Fort Des Moines in World War I." https://www.iowapbs.org/iowapathways/mypath/2514/.

Jackson, David H, Jr. "Booker T. Washington in South Carolina, March 1909." *South Carolina Historical Magazine* 113, no. 3 (July 2012): 192–220.

Jensen, Kimberly. *Mobilizing Minerva: American Women in the First World War.* Champaign: University of Illinois Press, 2008

Johnson, Joan Marie. "Louisa B. Poppenheim and Marion B. Wilkinson: The Parallel Lives of Black and White Clubwomen." In *South Carolina Women: Their Lives and Times-Volume 2*, edited by Marjorie Julian Spruill, Valinda W. Littlefield, and Joan Marie Johnson, 105–27. Athens: University of Georgia Press, 2010.

———. *Southern Ladies, New Women: Race, Region, and Clubwomen in South Carolina, 1890–1930.* Gainesville: University Press of Florida, 2004.

Johnson, Marianne. "Learning the Fighting Game: Black Americans and the First World War." *Gettysburg Historical Journal* 14 (2015): 27–42.

Johnston, Robert D. "One . . . Two . . . Many Progressivisms," review of Maureen Flanagan, *American Reformed: Progressives and Progressivisms, 1890s-1920s. Journal of the Gilded Age and Progressive Era* 11 (April 2012): 305–8.

Jones, Marian Moser, and Matilda Saines. "The Eighteen of 1918–1919: Black Nurses and the Great Flu Pandemic in the United States." *American Journal of Public Health* 109, no. 6 (June 2019): 877–84.

Kantrowitz, Stephen. *Ben Tillman and the Reconstruction of White Supremacy.* Chapel Hill: University of North Carolina Press, 2000.

Katz, Michael. "A History of Compulsory Education Laws." Bloomington: Phi Delta Kappa, 1976. https://files.eric.ed.gov/.

Keene, Jennifer D. "Americans as Warriors: 'Doughboys' in Battle During the First World War." *OAH Magazine of History* 17, no.1 (October 2002): 15–18.

———. "A Comparative Study of White and Black Soldiers During the First World War." *Annales de Demographie Historique* 1, no. 103 (2002): 71–90.

———. *Doughboys, the Great War, and the Remaking of America.* Baltimore: Johns Hopkins University Press, 2001.

———. *The United States and the First World War.* London: Routledge, 2014.

———. *World War I: The American Soldier Experience.* Lincoln: University of Nebraska Press, 2011.

Keith, Jeanette. "The Politics of Southern Draft Resistance, 1917–1918: Class, Race, and Conscription in the Rural South." *Journal of American History* 87, no. 4 (March 2001): 1335–65.

———. *Rich Man's War, Poor Man's Fight: Race, Class, and Power in the Rural South during the First World War.* Chapel Hill: University of North Carolina Press, 2004.

Kelsey and Guild. *Beautifying and Improving Greenville, South Carolina: Report to the Municipal League, Greenville, South Carolina.* Boston: Kelsey and Guild, 1907.

Kennedy, David M. *Over Here: The First World War and American Society.* Oxford: Oxford University Press, 2004.

Kinley, David. *The Autobiography of David Kinley.* Urbana: University of Illinois Press, 1920.

Kohn, August. *The Cotton Mills of South Carolina, 1907: Letters Written to the News and Courier.* Columbia, SC: Daggett, 1907.

Korzeniewski, Kryzstof. "Sexually Transmitted Infections Among Army Personnel in the Military Environment." In *Sexually Transmitted Infections,* edited by Nancy Malla, 165–82. London: InTech, 2012.

Bibliography 297

Kuhlman, Erika A. *Reconstructing Patriarchy after the Great War: Women, Gender, and Postwar Reconciliation between Nations.* New York: Palgrave Macmillan, 2008.

Kuhn, Clifford. *Contesting the New South Order: The 1914–1915 Strike at Atlanta's Fulton Mills.* Chapel Hill: University of North Carolina Press, 2001.

Kytle, Ethan J., and Blain Roberts. *Denmark Vesey's Garden: Slavery and Memory in the Cradle of the Confederacy.* New York: The New Press, 2019.

Lamay Licursi, Kimberly J. *Remembering World War I in America.* Lincoln: University of Nebraska Press, 2018.

Lane, Jack C. *Armed Progressive: General Leonard Wood.* Lincoln: University of Nebraska Press, 2009.

Lau, Peter F. *Democracy Rising: South Carolina and the Fight for Black Equality Since 1865.* Lexington: University Press of Kentucky, 2006.

Leatherwood, Jeffrey M. *The Quest for Streetcar Unionism in the Carolina Piedmont, 1919–1922.* Newcastle: Cambridge Scholars, 2017.

Lentz-Smith, Adriane. *Freedom Struggles: African Americans and World War I.* Cambridge, MA: Harvard University Press, 2011.

Lerda, Valeria Gennaro. "Southern Progressivism in Historical Perspective: The 1890s and the 1990s." *RSA Journal* 11 (2000): 71–84.

Levine, David O. *The American College and the Culture of Aspiration, 1915–1940.* Ithaca, NY: Cornell University Press, 1987.

Link, William. *The Paradox of Southern Progressivism, 1880–1930.* Chapel Hill: University of North Carolina Press, 1992.

Litwack, Leon. *Been in the Storm So Long: The Aftermath of Slavery.* New York: Knopf, 1979.

———. *How Free is Free? The Long Death of Jim Crow.* Cambridge, MA: Harvard University Press, 2009.

———. *Trouble in Mind: Black Southerners in the Age of Jim Crow.* New York: Knopf, 1998.

Loewen, James. *Lies Across America: What Our Sites Get Wrong.* New York: New Press, 1999.

Logan, Rayford. *The Betrayal of the Negro from Rutherford B. Hayes to Woodrow Wilson.* New York: Collier Books, 1965.

———. *The Negro in American Life and Thought: The Nadir, 1877–1901.* New York: Dial Press, 1954.

Marriott, A. E. *Suggested Athletics for Army Camps.* New York: Association Press, 1918.

McCallum, Jack. *Leonard Wood: Rough Rider, Surgeon Architect of American Imperialism.* New York: New York University Press, 2006.

McCartin, Joseph A. *Labor's Great War: The Struggle for Industrial Democracy and the Origins of Modern American Labor Relations, 1912–1921.* Chapel Hill: University of North Carolina Press, 1998.

McGlothlin, William J. *Baptist Beginnings in Education: A History of Furman University.* Nashville: Sunday School Board of the Southern Baptist Convention, 1926.

———. "The Christian, the War, and the Future." An Address Delivered by Prof. W. J. McGlothlin at the Southern Baptist Convention, Hot Springs, Ark., May 13, 1918.

McKoy, Henry Bacon. *Greenville, S.C. As Seen Through the Eyes of Henry Bacon McKoy: Facts and Memories.* Self-published, 1989.

McPheeters, Annie L. *Library Service in Black and White: Some Personal Recollections, 1921–1980.* Lanham, MD: Scarecrow Press, 1988.

Megginson, W. J. *African American Life in South Carolina's Upper Piedmont, 1780–1900.* Columbia: University of South Carolina Press, 2006.

———. *Black Soldiers in World War I: Anderson, Pickens, and Oconee Counties, South Carolina.* Seneca: Oconee County Historical Society, 1994.

298 Bibliography

————. "Black South Carolinians in World War I: The Official Roster as a Resource for Local History Mobility and African American History." *South Carolina Historical Magazine* 96, no. 2 (April 1995): 153–73.

Miller, Kelly. "The Disgrace of Democracy." Self-published. 1917.

————. *Kelly Miller's History of the World War for Human Rights.* Austin Jenkins, 1919.

Mills, Cynthia, and Pamela H. Simpson, eds. *Monuments to the Lost Cause: Women, Art, and the Landscapes of Southern Memory.* Knoxville: University of Tennessee Press, 2003.

Mitchell, George Sinclair. *Textile Unionism and the South.* Chapel Hill: University of North Carolina Press, 1931.

Mjagkij, Nina. *Loyalty in a Time of Trial: The African American Experience in World War I.* Lanham: Rowman & Littlefield, 2011.

Moore, John Hammond. "Charleston in World War I: Seeds of Change." *South Carolina Historical Magazine* 86, no.1 (January 1985): 39–49.

Moseley, A. M. *The Buncombe Street Methodist Story.* Self-published, 1965.

"National Association of Colored Graduate Nurses." In *Women of 1924 International,* edited by Ida Clyde Clarke. New York: Women's News Service, 1924: 20–21.

Murphy, Elmer A., and Robert S. Thomas. *The Thirtieth Division in the World War.* Lepanto, AR: Old Hickory Publishing Company, 1936.

Neiberg, Michael S. *The Path to War: How the First World War Created Modern America.* Oxford: Oxford University Press, 2016.

Neumann, Brian. "'We Cannot Expect to Rebuild the World Overnight': Race, Reform, and Reaction at Furman University, 1933–1955." *South Carolina Historical Magazine* 116, no. 2 (April 2015): 122–41.

Newby, Idus A. *Black Carolinians: A History of Blacks in South Carolina from 1895 to 1968.* South Carolina Tricentennial Commission, 1973.

Nolan, Cathal J. *The Allure of Battle: A History of How Wars Have Been Won and Lost.* Oxford: Oxford University Press, 2017.

Ogden, Mary Macdonald. *Wil Lou Gray: The Making of a Southern Progressive from New South to New Deal.* Columbia: University of South Carolina Press, 2015.

Ogden Motley, Mary Mac. "Wil Lou Gray." In *Palmetto Profiles: The South Carolina Encyclopedia Guide to the South Carolina Hall of Fame,* edited by Eric W. Emerson, 62–63. Columbia: University of South Carolina Press, 2013.

Oliphant, Mary C. Simms. *The New Simms History of South Carolina, Centennial Edition 1840–1940.* Columbia: The State Company, 1941.

————. *South Carolina from the Mountains to the Sea.* Columbia, SC: The State Company, 1964.

Opdycke, Sandra. *The Flu Epidemic of 1918: America's Experience in the Global Health Crisis.* New York: Routledge, 2014.

Orr, Mary, and William A. Foran. "The Weimar Letters of Mary Orr." *South Carolina Historical Magazine* 56, no. 2 (April 1955): 77–84.

Ortiz, Paul. *Emancipation Betrayed: The Hidden History of Black Organizing and White Violence in Florida from Reconstruction to the Bloody Election of 1920.* Berkeley: University of California Press, 2006.

Orwell, George. *1984.* London: Secker & Warburg, 1949.

Owens, Loulie Latimer. *The Thursday Club, Greenville, S.C., 1889–1989.* Greenville, SC: Graphics Now, 1988.

Parker, Thomas F. *Some educational and legislative needs of South Carolina mill villages.* Columbia: University of South Carolina, 1911.

Partridge, Dave, and Fay Towell. *Transformation: The Story of Greenville Hospital System University Medical Center, 1912–2012.* Spartanburg, SC: Reprint Company, 2012.

Bibliography 299

Patterson, Andrea. "Black Nurses in the Great War: Fighting for and with the American Military in the Struggle for Civil Rights." *Canadian Journal of History* 40, no. 7 (Winter 2012): 545–66.

Perry, Elizabeth Israels. "Men Are From the Gilded Age, Women Are From the Progressive Era." *Journal of the Gilded Age and Progressive Era* 1, no.1 (January 2002): 25–48.

Pierce, Daniel S. *Real NASCAR: White Lightning, Red Clay and Big Bill France.* Chapel Hill: University of North Carolina Press, 2010.

Plant, Rebecca Jo, and Frances M. Clarke. "The Crowning Insult: Federal Segregation and the Gold Star Mother and Widow Pilgrimages of the Early 1930s." *Journal of American History* 102, no. 2 (September 2015): 406–32.

Poole, W. Scott. *Never Surrender: Confederate Memory and Conservatism in the South Carolina Upcountry.* Athens: University of Georgia Press, 2004.

Potter, Constance. "World War I Gold Star Mothers' Pilgrimages: Part I." *Prologue: Quarterly of the National Archives and Records Administration* 31, no.2 (Summer 1999): 140–45.

Power, Garrett. "Apartheid Baltimore Style: The Residential Segregation Ordinances of 1910–1913." *Maryland Law Review* 42 (1983): 289–328.

Preston, Howard L. *Dirt Roads to Dixie: Accessibility and Modernization in the South, 1885–1935.* Knoxville: University of Tennessee Press, 1991.

Proctor, Tammy M. *Civilians in a World at War, 1914–1918.* New York: New York University Press, 2010.

Quinn, Adam. "Reforming History: Contemporary Scholarship on the Progressive Era." *The H-Net Book Channel,* March 28, 2017.

Quigley, Paul. "Independence Day Dilemmas in the American South, 1848–1865." *Journal of Southern History* 75, no. 2 (May 2009): 235–66.

Rammelkamp, Charles H. *Illinois College: A Centennial History 1829–1929.* New Haven, CT: Yale University Press, 1928.

Ramsay, David Marshall. "An Old Man Answers His Daughter." *North American Review* 235 (February 1933): 172–77.

Reid, Alfred S. *Furman University: Toward a New Identity, 1925–1975.* Durham, NC: Duke University Press, 1976.

"Report of Committee U on Patriotic Service." *Bulletin of the America Association of University Professors* 5, no. 3 (March 1919): 31–34.

Reynolds, John S. *Reconstruction in South Carolina, 1865–1877.* London: Forgotten Books, 2012.

Richardson, James M. *History of Greenville County South Carolina.* Greenville, SC: Southern Historical Press, 1993.

Robertson, Ben. *Red Hills and Cotton.* New York: Alfred A. Knopf, 1942.

Rogers, Charles R. *History of the 119th Infantry, 60th Brigade, 30th Division.* Wilmington, NC: Wilmington Chamber of Commerce, 1920.

Rubin, Richard. *The Last of the Doughboys: The Forgotten Generation and Their Forgotten World War.* Boston: Houghton Mifflin Harcourt, 2013.

Salem, Dorothy C. *To Better Our World: Black women in organized reform, 1890–1920.* Brooklyn, NY: Carlson Pub., 1990.

Sawyer, Richard D. *Greetings From Camp Sevier: Greenville, SC 1917–1919.* Self-published, 1996.

Scott, Anne Firor. "After Suffrage: Southern Women in the Twenties." *Journal of Southern History* 30, no. 3 (August 1964): 298–318.

Scott, Brian. *History Happened Here: South Carolina's Roadside Historical Markers.* Self-published, 2015.

Scott, Emmett J. "More Letters of Negro Migrants of 1916–1918." *Journal of Negro History* 4, no. 4 (October 1919): 412–65.

———. *Scott's Official History of the American Negro in the World War.* Chicago: Homewood Press, 1919.

300 Bibliography

Shah, Courtney Q. "'Against Their Own Weakness:' Policing Sexuality and Women in San Antonio During World War I." *Journal of the History of Sexuality* 19, no. 3 (September 2010): 458–82.

Shankman, Arnold. "A Jury of Her Peers: The South Carolina Woman and Her Campaign for Jury Service." *South Carolina Historical Magazine* 81, no. 2 (April 1980): 102–21.

Shearer, Benjamin F. "An Experiment in Military and Civilian Education: The Students' Army Training Corps at the University of Illinois." *Journal of Illinois State Historical Society* 72, no. 3 (August 1979): 213–24.

Sheldon, Kathryn. "A Brief History of Black Women in the Military." *Minerva's Bulletin Board*, vol. III, no. 4, 1995.

Showalter, William Joseph. "America's New Soldier Cities." *National Geographic* 32, nos. 5–6 (November–December 1917): 439–76.

Siegler, Robert S. *A Guide to Confederate Monuments in South Carolina: Passing the Silent Cup.* Columbia: University of South Carolina Press, 1997.

Silver, Christopher. "The Racial Origins of Zoning in American Cities." In *Urban Planning and the African American Community: In the Shadows,* edited by June Manning Thomas and Marsha Ritzdorf, 23–42. Thousand Oaks, CA: Sage, 1997.

Simon, Bryant. *A Fabric of Defeat: The Politics of South Carolina Millhands, 1910–1948.* Chapel Hill: University of North Carolina Press, 2000.

Smith, Steven D., and James A. Zeidler, eds. *A Historic Context for the African American Military Experience.* Springfield: US Army Construction Engineering Research Laboratories, 1998.

Snead, David L. "South Carolina Engineers in the 42nd (Rainbow) Division in World War I." In *Proceedings of the South Carolina Historical Association,* edited by Stephen Lowe, 49–62. Columbia: South Carolina Historical Association, South Carolina Department of Archives and History, 2003.

Snyder, Henry Nelson. *An Educational Odyssey.* New York: Abingdon-Cokesbury, 1947.

Southern Baptist Convention. *Annual of the Southern Baptist Convention, 1917.* Nashville: Marshall & Bruce, 1917.

Stephenson, Gilbert T. "The Segregation of the White and Negro Races in Cities by Legislation." *National Municipal Review* 3 (July 1914): 496–504.

Stevenson, Ana. *The Woman as Slave in Nineteenth-Century American Social Movements.* London: Palgrave Macmillan, 2020.

Stimson, Julia. *Medical Department of the United States Army During World War I,* vol. 8, pt.2: *The Army Nurse Corps.* Washington, DC: Government Printing Office, 1927.

Stokes, Barbara. *Myrtle Beach: A History, 1900–1980.* Columbia: University of South Carolina Press, 2007.

Stowers Jackson, Tonnie. *Corporal Freddie Stowers: A Memoir, Familial Past and Present.* Pendleton: Sancho Educational Group, 2019.

Strickland, Jeffery. "How the Germans Became White Southerners: German Immigrants and African Americans in Charleston, South Carolina, 1860–1880." *Journal of Ethnic History* 28, no. 1 (Fall 2008): 52–69.

Strobel, Marian Elizabeth. "Eudora Ramsay Richardson." In *101 Women Who Shaped South Carolina,* edited by Valinda Littlefield, 113. Columbia: University of South Carolina Press, 2020.

Sumners, Bill. "Joseph Judson Taylor: A Baptist Pacifist." *Baptist Peacemaker* 4 (October 1985): 12.

Sundquist, Eric J., ed., *The Oxford W. E. B. Du Bois Reader.* New York: Oxford University Press, 1996.

Sutherland, Jonathan. *African Americans at War: An Encyclopedia, Vol. 2.* Santa Barbara, CA: ABC-CLIO, 2003.

Szymanski, Ann-Marie. "Beyond Parochialism: Southern Progressivism, Prohibition, and State-Building." *Journal of Southern History* 69, no. 1 (February 2003): 107–36.

Bibliography 30?

Taylor, Antoinette Elizabeth. "South Carolina and the Enfranchisement of Women: The Later Years." *South Carolina Historical Magazine* 80, no. 4 (October 1979): 298–310.

Telford, Jennifer Casavant. "The American Nursing Shortage During World War I: The Debate Over the Use of Nurses' Aids." *Canadian Bulletin of Medical History* 27, no. 1 (2010): 85–99.

Terborg-Penn, Rosalyn. *African American Women in the Struggle for the Vote, 1850–1920*. Bloomington: Indiana University Press, 1998.

Tetzlaff, Monica Maria. *Cultivating a New South: Abbie Holmes Christensen and the Politics of Race and Gender, 1852–1938*. Columbia: University of South Carolina Press, 2002.

Thomas, Rhondda Robinson and Susanna Ashton, eds. *The South Carolina Roots of African American Thought: A Reader*. Columbia: University of South Carolina Press, 2014.

Thompson, Neal. *Driving with the Devil: Southern Moonshine, Detroit Wheels and the Birth of NASCAR*. New York: Three Rivers, 2006.

Thoms, Adah B. Pathfinders: *A History of the Progress of Colored Graduate Nurses*. New York: Garland, 1985.

Threat, Charissa J. *Nursing Civil Rights: Gender and Race in the Army Nurse Corps*. Urbana: University of Illinois Press, 2015.

Tindall, George B. *Emergence of the New South, 1913–1945*. Baton Rouge: Louisiana State University Press, 1967.

Tolnay, Stewart Emory, and E. M. Beck. *A Festival of Violence: An Analysis of Southern Lynchings, 1882–1930*. Urbana: University of Illinois Press, 1995.

Tooze, Adam. *The Deluge: The Great War, America and the Remaking of the Global Order, 1916–1931*. New York: Penguin Books, 2014.

Trout, Steven. *On the Battlefield of Memory: The First World War and American Remembrance, 1919–1941*. Tuscaloosa: University of Alabama Press, 2010.

Tuchman, Barbara W. *The Guns of August*. New York: Presidio, 2004.

Tucker, Susan. *Telling Memories Among Southern Women: Domestic Workers and Their Employers in the Segregated South*. Baton Rouge: Louisiana State University Press, 2002.

Vuic, Kara Dixon. *The Girls Next Door: Bringing the Home Front to the Front Lines*. Cambridge, MA: Harvard University Press, 2019.

Walker, Melissa. *All We Knew Was to Farm: Rural Women in the Upcountry South, 1919–1941*. Baltimore: Johns Hopkins University Press, 2000.

West, Elizabeth. "The University of South Carolina in the Great War: Confronting Problems While Contributing to the War Effort." In *Forward Together: South Carolinians in the Great War* edited by Fritz P. Hamer, 71–91. Charleston, SC: The History Press, 2007.

West, Stephen A. "'A Hot Municipal Contest': Prohibition and Black Politics in Greenville, South Carolina, after Reconstruction." *Journal of the Gilded Age and Progressive Era* 11, no. 4 (October 2012): 519–51.

———. *From Yeoman to Redneck in the South Carolina Upcountry, 1850–1915*. Charlottesville: University of Virginia Press, 2008.

Weyeneth, Robert R. "The Architecture of Racial Segregation: The Challenges of Preserving the Problematic Past." *Public Historian* 27, no. 4 (Fall 2005): 11–44.

"Whiskey in Influenza and Pneumonia." *Journal of the South Carolina Medical Association* 14, no. 10 (November 1918): 277–80.

White, Deborah Gray. *Too Heavy a Load: Black Women in Defense of Themselves, 1894–1994*. New York: W. W. Norton & Company, 1999.

Wieters, Rebecca. "Ethnicity, Politics, and Society in the New South: Examining German Immigrant Communities in Early Twentieth-Century Charleston." *History Matters: An Undergraduate Journal of Historical Research* 3 (April 2005): 56–63.

302 Bibliography

Williams, Chad L. *Torchbearers of Democracy: African American Soldiers in the WWI Era.* Chapel Hill: University of North Carolina Press, 2010.

———. "Vanguards of the New Negro: African American Veterans and Post-World War I Racial Militancy." *Journal of African American History* 92, no. 3 (Summer 2007): 347–70.

Williams, Charles H. *Sidelights on Negro Soldiers.* Boston: B. J. Brimmer Company, 1923.

Willis, Jeffrey R., and the Greenville County Historical Society. *Remembering Greenville: Photographs from the Coxe Collection.* Charleston, SC: Arcadia Publishing, 2003.

Wilson, Adam P. *African American Army Officers of World War I: A Vanguard of Equality in War and Beyond.* Jefferson, NC: McFarland, 2015.

Wilson, Charles Reagan. *Baptized in Blood: The Religion of the Lost Cause, 1865–1920.* Athens: University of Georgia Press, 2011.

Wilson, William H. *The City Beautiful Movement.* Baltimore: Johns Hopkins University Press, 1994.

Wingate, Jennifer. "Adeline Adams." In *The Grove Encyclopedia of American Art,* Vol. 1, edited by Joan M. Marter, 27–28. Oxford: Oxford University Press, 2011.

———. "Over the Top: The Doughboy in World War I Memorials and Visual Culture." *American Art* 19, no. 2 (2005): 26–47.

———. *Sculpting Doughboys: Memory, Gender, and Taste in America's World War I Memorials.* Abingdon, England: Taylor & Francis, 2017.

Wood, Eric Fisher. *Leonard Wood: Conservator of Americanism.* Ann Arbor: University of Michigan Press, 1920.

Woodward, C. Vann. *Origins of the New South, 1877–1913.* Baton Rouge: Louisiana State University Press, 1971.

Work, Monroe N., ed. *Negro Year Book: An Annual Encyclopedia of the Negro 1918–1919.* Tuskegee: Negro Year Book Company, 1919.

Work, Monroe N., Thomas S. Staples, H. A. Wallace, Kelly Miller, Whitefield McKinlay, Samuel E. Lacy, R. L. Smith, and H. R. McIlwaine. "Some Negro Members of Reconstruction Conventions and Legislatures and of Congress." *Journal of Negro History* 5, no. 1 (January 1920): 63–119.

Wright, Jennifer. *Get Well Soon: History's Worst Plagues and the Heroes Who Fought Them.* New York: Holt, 2017.

Youngdgahl, Katie. "The 1918–19 Spanish Influenza Pandemic and Vaccine Development." *The History of Vaccines: An Educational Resource by the College of Physicians of Philadelphia.* September 26, 2018.

Zieger, Robert. *America's Great War: World War I and the American Experience.* Lanham: Rowman & Littlefield, 2000.

Zonderman, David. "Yet Another Look at Progressives." Review of *American Reformers 1870–1920* by Steven Piott. *H-SHGAPE, H-Net Reviews,* July 2009.

Dissertations, Theses, and Unpublished Manuscripts

Barker, Andrew. "'A Sane Sense of Loyalty to Nation in Peace and War': Military Education and Patriotism at Wofford College, 1917–45." MA thesis, Clemson University, 2012. https://tigerprints.clemson.edu/all_theses/1387.

Davis, Jessie. "Coming to Greenville: The Salvation Army's History and Continuing Impact on Grenville, South Carolina." Unpublished manuscript, 2007.

Doward, Oscar W., Jr. "Determining If the Actions of African American Combat Forces during World War I Positively Affected the Employment of African American Combat Soldiers during World War II." MA thesis, University of South Florida, 2006.

Dunlap, James A., III. "Victims of Neglect: The Career and Creations of John T. Woodside, 1865–1986." MA thesis, University of South Carolina, 1986.

Gallivan, Gene. "Henry Thompson Mills." Unpublished paper, 2016.

Bibliography 303

Herndon, Eliza. "Woman Suffrage in South Carolina: 1872–1920." MA thesis, University of South Carolina, 1953.

Kuntz, Anna T. "German-American Identity in Charleston During World War I: A Study of Six Members of the German Friendly Society." MA thesis, University of South Carolina, 2006.

Langston, Stan. "Anti-Unionism in Greenville Textiles." Unpublished manuscript, February 27, 1984. Greenville Public Library.

———. "Greenville, Unionism, and the General Strike in the Textile Industry, 1934." Unpublished manuscript, 1974. Greenville Public Library.

Matthews, Amy. "From Memory to Honor: Stories of South Carolina's World War Monuments." Master's thesis, Clemson University, 2008. https://tigerprints.clemson.edu/all_theses/413.

McLeod, Julia Poindexter. "Home/Economics: Enterprise, Property, and Money in Women's Domestic Fiction, 1860–1930." PhD diss., University of Tennessee, 2015.

Richardson, James M. "Scion of the Flatwoods." Unpublished manuscript, 1941. Special Collections and University Archives, James B. Duke Library, Furman University.

Stathakis, Paula Maria. "Almost White: Greek and Lebanese-Syrian Immigrants in North and South Carolina, 1900–1940." PhD diss., University of South Carolina, 1996.

Thacker, Marta Leslie. "Working for the City Beautiful: Civic Improvement in Three South Carolina Communities." MA thesis, University of South Carolina 1999.

Ulmer, Barbara Bellows. "Virginia Durant Young: New South Suffragist." MA thesis, University of South Carolina, 1979.

Wilkinson, Carl. "The Life and Work of William Joseph McGlothlin." PhD diss., The Southern Baptist Theological Seminary, 1980.

Williams, Daniel T. *Amid the Gathering Multitude: The Story of Lynching in America. A Classified Listing.* Unpublished manuscript, 1968.

Index

Abbott, Robert, 107

Act to Compel a Separation of the Races Laboring in Textile Manufactories (1915), 48–49

Adler, Heinrich, 73

African American clubwomen, 23, 89, 189, 197, 210, 255n42, 280n152

African American college graduates, 140–41

African American economic power, 29, 120, 181, 273n25

African American entrepreneurs, 9, 110–11, 119, 198, 261n39, 276n95

African American majorities, 3, 21, 44, 116, 179

African American ministers, 10, 20–21, 32, 105–6, 111, 118–19, 122, 126, 180, 210, 244n82, 260–61n34

African American nurses, 170–72, 197

African American soldiers: governmental policies, 126, 129; home support for, 111, 113; memorialization of, 218, 235–36; training, 69, 134; White fear of/hostility toward, 125, 131–32, 134, 179; see also Camp Sevier: African American soldiers; Community Club for Negro Soldiers; World War I: African American soldiers

African American State Council of Defense, 116

African American–owned newspapers, 5, 107, 139

African Americans: 1, 3, 5, 18, 21, 34, 111, 116, 178, 185, 195, 221; agricultural work, 104, 110, 125; civil rights activism, 115–16, 118–19, 123, 140–41, 179, 206, 209–11, 230, 276n95; economic exclusion/advancement, 14, 20, 32, 39, 48–49, 104, 107–9, 120; education exclusion/opportunities, 39, 149–50, 203–4, 277n117, 277–78n118; in Greenville, 4, 32, 54, 102, 110, 120–21, 178–79, 207–8, 214–15; healthcare, 113, 185, 197–98, 261n35, 273n25; patriotism,

120–21, 124; professionals, 22, 32, 198, 209, 279n143; Progressive movement, 8–9; voting disenfranchise/rights, 21, 27, 104, 124, 179, 242n40; wages, 48, 116, 118, 120, 124; White people's fears of, 30, 48, 125, 127, 129, 135–36, 139, 141–42, 182; work or fight law, 97, 116–17; see also Charleston: African Americans; Columbia: African Americans; lynching; race riots; racial violence; racism; segregation; World War I: African American Greenville soldiers

African Americans: labor coercion resistance, 118, 127

African American women, 5, 18, 27, 82, 89, 111, 114, 116–19, 127–28, 179, 189, 205, 226, 274n53

Allen School, 113, 203, 278n120, 121

Allen Temple AME Church, 209, 260n33

Allen, James M., 203

Allen, James O., 10, 111

Allen, Jim "Lefty," 76

Allen, Robert, 101, 119

Allison, A. P., 9, 110, 119, 261n39, 262n71

altruism, 7, 278n126

American Association of University Professors (AAUP), 148

American Battlefield Monuments Commission, 225–26

American Council on Education (ACE), 148, 155

American Legion, 5, 197, 220, 218, 221–22, 224, 228–29, 232–33, 281n12, 281–82n20, 282n22,24

American Nurses Association, 170

American Spinning Mill, 35

American Woman Suffrage Association, 22

Americanism, 153–54, 180–81, 221

Americanness, 99

Anderson (city), 48, 114, 243n66

Anderson County, 48, 92

Index

Anderson, Rudolf, 91, 256n58
Anderson University, 102, 232
Anthony Amendment, 182
Anthony, Susan B., 26–27
Anti-Saloon League, 8
Armistice Day, 190, 210, 220, 225, 228–29, 232
Army Nurses Corps, 163, 170–74, 269n39
Arrington, J. W. (Mrs.), 187
Arrington, J. W., 112, 184–85
Associate Reformed Presbyterian Church, 94
Association of American Universities Professors (AAUP), 143, 155
Austin, Mose, 110
automobiles, 51, 192–93

Bailey, Daisy P., 26
Bainbridge, Judith T., 4, 13, 19, 165, 184, 242–43n47, 255n39, 276n82, 277n110
Baker, Emma P., 26
Baker, Newton D., 63, 86, 116, 123, 129–31
Baley, C. L., 18
Ballou, Charles C., 132–34
Bankhead Highway, 52
Bankhead, John, 52
Bankhead, Louise, 52
Bankhead, Tallulah, 52
Baptists, 23
Barry, John M., 160
Baruch, Bernard, 96
Bastion, Robert, 192
Batchelor, Howard B., 97, 257–58n85
Bates, Mary J., 111
Batesville Mill, 24
Beacham and LeGrand, 190, 192, 196, 198, 207, 212
Beacham, James Douthit, 190
Beacham, W. C., 190, 192, 196, 198, 207, 212, 276n95
Beard, William P., 20
Beattie, Frances "Fanny" Perry, 23
Beattie, William, 13
Beaty, Anna M., 187, 213, 273n39
Belmont, Alva F., 57
Better Homes movement, 188–89, 274n53, 54
Biggs, Edgar W., 9, 110, 111, 112, 119, 198, 261n39, 276n95
Birth of a Nation, The (Griffith), 105–6, 115, 126
Blackwell, Henry B., 27

Blackwell, Lucy Stone, 27
Bland, Sidney R., 85, 254n15, 255n27
Blease, Cole, 47–48, 183
Blee, Kathleen, 180
Blight, David, 15
Bliss, Tasker H., 129–30
Blue, Rupert, 161, 166
Blythe, E. M., 82, 93
Board of Trade and Cotton Exchange. See also Greenville Chamber of Commerce
Bolshevism, 156
Bon Secours St. Francis Hospital, 3
Bostick, Hagood, 155
Bradshaw, Sidney E., 147, 151–52, 154–55, 177, 267n62
Brandon Mill, 35, 168
Brier, Charles D., 9, 105, 111–12, 119, 122, 180, 206, 240n30, 261n39, 279n137
Brier, James A., 9, 111, 113–14, 118, 122, 209, 240n30, 261n44
Bristow, Nancy K., 88
Brogan Mill, 48
Brown, John W., 101
Bryan, Jami L., 124
Buncombe Street United Methodist Church, 22, 90, 91, 167
Buncombe Street United Methodist Episcopal Church. See Buncombe Street United Methodist Church
Burgess, W. W., 196
Burke, Allen R., 10, 111–12, 119, 180, 260–61n34
Burnett, E. M., 216
Burnett, Jessie Stokely, 7, 58, 187, 249n86
Burns, Lucy, 182
Business and Professional Women's Club, 187
Byrd, William, 126
Byrnes, James F., 179

Caldabaugh, Harry E., 17–18
Cambria, Joseph, 195
Camp Jackson, 64, 69, 112, 130–31, 133, 135, 137, 156, 161, 165, 173, 226, 232, 268n68, 269n39
Camp Moore (Camp Styx), 147
Camp Sevier: 2, 4–5, 7, 63, 64, 64, 65, 65–67, 68, 68–80, 211, 228, 249n4, 250n12,13, 251n37,47; African American nurses/soldiers, 112–13, 119, 130–33, 171–72; cold

weather, 76–79, 159–60, 168; deserters, 101; disease, 77–78, 151, 159, 161–63, *164*, 165, 167, 173, 175, 197, 226, 268–69n8; effects on Greenville, 87–88, 90–94, 96, 98, 177, 184, 190, 192, 195, 197, 220, 229, 253n90, 254n11; *see also* Furman University: Camp Sevier

Camp Wadsworth, 64, 75, 78, 90, 130, 133–34, 165, 173, 225

Camp Wetherill, 17, 19, 62

Camperdown Mill, 24, 35

Capozzola, Christopher, 129, 133, 239n9

Carlton, David L., 46–47, 72

Carroll, Richard, 32, 105–6, 115

Carter, Jessie Lee, 168

Cary, Mary, 93

Cash, W. J., 48, 266n8

Catholicism, 181

Catt, Carrie Chapman, 58, 83

Central Baptist Church, 94

Charleston Race Riot, 180

Charleston: 28, 196–97, 199, 285n65; African Americans, 3, 32, 109–10, 116, 209, 233, 237, 244–45n83; Civil War/Civil War memory, 3, 15, 99; immigration, 42–44, 246n8; Spanish influenza, 161, 165–66, 271n99; woman suffrage movement, 26, 57, 59, 84, 182, 255n27, 281n8; World War I, 43–44, 62, 87, 92, 93, 176, 266n35; *see also* race riots

Chick Springs Hotel, 75

child labor, 10, 58, 85

Christ Church Episcopal, 90–91

Christian Science Room, 90

City Beautiful movement, 28, 185, 237

Civil War memorialization, 223–24, 281n15

Clark, David, 82

Clay, Laura, 27

Clemson College, 149, 162, 233

Cleveland Park, 3, 181, 195

Cleveland, Alice B., 187

Cleveland, William Choice, 195

Coker, David R., 106

Coleman, Hannah Hemphill, 31, 57

Columbia: 28, 178, 212, 236; African Americans, 3, 32, 110, 115–16, 131, 209, 244–45n83; Civil War/Civil War memory, *15*, 16; Spanish influenza, 165; woman suffrage movement, 22, 26, 57, 182; World War I, 62, 64, 87; *see also* Camp Jackson; University of South Carolina

Commission on Training Camp Activities (CTCA), 73, 86–88

Committee for the Organization of the Scientific Resources of the Country for National Service. *see* National Research Council

Committee on Education and Special Training (US War Department), 152

Committee on Public Information (CPI), 81, 97–99

communism, 221, 224, 237

Community Club for Negro Soldiers, 90, 114

Community Fund, 7, 184, 206, 274n44

Confederate Memorial Day, 16, 99, 216–18

Confederate memorials, 2–3, 16, 19, 193–94, *194*, 237

Congressional Union (CU), 59

Conyers, Marie Gower, 7, 88

Conyers, William P., 7, 180, 185, 206

Cooke, Wilson, 20

Coolidge, Calvin, 188, 226

Cooper, Robert A., 191, 216

cotton market/production, 34–35, 37, 42, 45, 50, 52–53, 60, 79, 110

Council on National Defense (CND), 81, 99–100

COVID-19 pandemic, 2, 235, 284–85n63

Cox, Karen, 15

Creel, George, 98

Crescent Community, 3, 188, 206, 256–57n62

Crocker "Fate," 108

Cunningham, Beulah, 167

Cunningham, Frank, 167, 192

Cunningham, Joseph G., 167, 192

Daniel, James E., 91, 169

Daniel, Robert E. (Mrs.), 187

Darrach, S. A., 168

David, C. A., 78

Davis, Jefferson, 15, 99

Davisor, Emily, 58

Daylight Savings Time (War Time), 94

De Forest, John William, 12–13

Degler, Carl N., 99

Democratic Party, 6, 53

Dill, Flora Putnam, 7, 23, 26, 167, 242n46

Dillingham Commission, 153

Dixie Highway Association, 51

Dixon, Thomas, 105

Dodson, Geddes E., 169

308 Index

Domby, Adam H., 15
Donaldson, John O. W., 155
Doyle, Alex C., 64–65
Drake, H. R., 148
Du Bois, W. E. B., 126, 130, 141, 179
Duckett, Hattie Logan, 8–9, 111, 118–19, 122, 198, 205–206, 209–10, *211*
Duke, Eugenia, 83
Duke, James B., 196
Duke's Sandwich Company, 83
Dumenil, Lynn, 83, 254n17
Dunean Mill, 35, *38*

Edgar, Walter B., 4, 9, 181
education: 39, 87, 153, 198, 201, 231; and African Americans, 9, 20, 104–5, 109, 203–204, 206–8, 210, 277n110; federal involvement, 154–57; improved opportunities, 7, 36, 39, 58, 71, 178, 185, 202; and mill workers, 10, 72, 199, 201; and soldiers, 72, 151, 159; and women, 23, 88, 184; *see also* higher education
Edwards, Rebecca, 6
Edwards, W. A., 71
Eighteenth Amendment, 181
Eldridge, Rube, 76
electric sign, 56–57, *186*
Elks, 90
Ellenburg, John R., 20
Eller, Grace, 87
Elsas, Jacob, 47
Elsas, Oscar, 46–47
Emergency Council on Education. American Council on Education (ACE), 148
Emery, James A., 46
Equal Suffrage Club (Greenville), 58
Espionage Act, 96–97
Ettor, Joseph James, 46
Europe, James R., 133
Evans, Bill, 76
Evans, Emily Plume, 57
Evans, Hiram Wesley, 181
Executive Order 9981, 140, 263n18

Farmer, Roy, 70
Federal Aid Road Act, 52
Federal Fuel Administration, 94
Ferdinand, Franz, 41, 234
Fifteenth Amendment, 21–22

Filene, Peter G., 6
First Baptist Church, 90–91, 94
First Presbyterian Church, 90, 225, 261n64
Flagler, Henry, 14
Flanagan, Maureen A., 6–8, 240n19
Fletcher, A. L., 65–66, 77
Fletcher, Eva E., 5, 7, 92, 112, 221–23, 231, 256n61, 281n14
Fletcher, O. O., 152, 222
Flexner, Abraham, 160
Fogg, Newton H., 103
Ford, Lacy K., 4
Fort Jackson: 232, 236, 285n65; *see also* Camp Jackson
Fortescue, Granville R., 70–72
Fosdick, Raymond, 86
Foster, Gaines, 15
Foster, Guy, 17, 19
Fountain Inn, 54, 204
Four Minute Men, 98–99
Fourth Liberty Loan campaign, 165
Fourth of July, 15–16, 99–100
Franklin Mill, 196
Franklin, John Hope, 139, 265n80
Freedman's Bureau, 12
Freeze, David, 47–48
Frost, Susan Pringle, 59, 84
Furman University: 1, 5, 144–46; Camp Sevier, 151, 153–54, 162; Christianity, 156–57; male student body, 144, 148, 150; Montague Hall Military Company, 144–45, 147; Spanish influenza, 165, 172, *174;* Student Army Training Corps (SATC), 150–52, *153,* 153–56, 172, 177; Whiteness, 144, 150
Furman, Alester G., 7, 17, 28, 33, 58, 227
Furman, Eleanor, 23, 58
Furman, James C., 58

Gallivan Building Company, 55, 64–65
Gallivan, James F., 65
Gandy, Charles F., 10, 111–12, 119, 122, 206, 209, 260–61n34, 276n95, 279n137
Gassaway, Minnie Quinn, 187, 274n54
Gaston, Paul, 14
Gaughan, Anthony, 100
Geer, Bennette E., 7, 47, 50, 185, 196, 206, 267n62, 279n137, 280n166
General Federation of Women's Clubs (GFWC), 24, 57

Index 309

Gilmore, Glenda, 8, 210, 239n15
Gilreath, Perry, 20
Goldsmith, William, 192
Goodyear, Eva T., 7, 86, 92, 254n20
Gordon, Linda, 181
Gorgas, William C., 159, 162
Grace, John P., 43
Grady et al v. City of Greenville, 193
Grady, Henry W., 14
Graham, Allen J., 185, 206
Graham, Edward K., 148
Gray, Wil Lou, 198, 202–203, 277n117
Great Migration: 110, 118, 139, 178, 206; labor
    agents' roles, 107–8
Green, Gladys, 78
Green, John F., 10, 111, 118–19, 260–61n34
Green, Mary, 78
Green, Paul, 67, 71, 74, 159, 161, 251n48
Greenville Baptist Female College (GBFC),
    22–23; *see also* Greenville Woman's College
    (GWC)
Greenville Chamber of Commerce: 33, 187,
    220, 256n45; establishment of, 3, 13; progres-
    sivism, 57, 82, 103, 178, 184–85; sanitation
    promotion, 53–54, 56; World War I, 62–63,
    82, 89–90, 250n14
Greenville City Council, 29, 30, 117, *194*
Greenville City Hospital, 170, 196
Greenville Country Club, 192
Greenville County Library, 3, 202, 208; *see also*
    Phillis Wheatley Center
Greenville Light Infantry, 21
Greenville Spirit, 10, 103, 178, 214
Greenville Water Works, 79
Greenville Woman's Club, 28, 54
Greenville Woman's College (GWC): 58, 75–76,
    144–45, 147, 151–52, 165–66, 168–69,
    172–73, 177; *see also* Greenville Baptist
    Female College (GBFC)
Greenwood: African Americans, 108–9; public
    memorials, 231–34, 236
Greer, 54, 181, 204, 225
Gregory, Julia, 111
Gridley, Mary Putnam, 7, 10, 26, 184, *187,* 187,
    206, 242n46, 276n88, 278n126, 279n137;
    healthcare activism, 88, 185, 197; temperance
    activism, 22–23; suffrage activism, 24–27, 58,
    254n20, 255n27
Griffin, W. E.: 88

Griffith, D. W.: 105; *see also Birth of a Nation,
    The*
Guerry, Bob, 76
Guess, J. Decherd, 170
Gulledge, Ben P., 77
Gullick, Guy, 218

Hall, George F., 13
Hall, J. K., 97, 257–58n85
Hall, James, 101
Hamilton, John Maxwell, 98, 258n90
Harlem Hellfighters, 134
Harrison, Robert, 6
Harvley, Hanny Clyde, 7, 96, 98, 116, 118, 180,
    216, 255n27, 276n95, 278n126, 279n137
Hawkins, J. B., 21
Haynsworth, Rhoda Livingston, 7, 185, 197,
    206, 274n44, 279n137
Hayward, William, 135
healthcare, 3, 5, 7, 9, 39, 178, 196, 198
Hemmingway, Theodore, 104, 115
Hemphill, Robert R., 26–27, 31, 183
Heritage Act, 233, 236
higher education, 143–44, 147–49, 152, 157,
    212–13, 265n1; *see also* Furman University;
    Wofford College
highways, 36–37, 51–52, 63, 79–80, 192–93,
    219, 225
Hill, Elsie, 84
Hine, Darlene Clark, 172
Historically Black Colleges and Universities,
    149, 266n35
Hollis, Lawrence Peter "Pete," 7, 8, 10, 98, 190,
    199–202, 204, 206, 277n110, 279n137
Holloway, Elias B., 9, 122, 180, 195, 205–6, 209,
    219, 219, 237, 275n75, 279n137
Hood, John O., 91
Hoover, Herbert, 93, 188
Howard, E. H., 88
Howland, Helen G., 57
Hudson, Janet G., 4, 31, 104, 115–16, 118, 182,
    239n15, 244n82, 244–45n83, 255n23,42
Hudson, W. Austin, 98
Huff, A. V., 4, 34, 240n1, 272n11
Huguenot Mill, 35
Hunt, William C., 5
Hunter, Jane Edna, 205, 207, 279n133
Huntington and Guerry, 64–65
Hutchison, Anne, 77–78

Hutchison, Hiram, 78
Hyde, Tristram T., 176

immigration/immigrants: 43–44, 102, 224; *see also* Charleston: immigration
Imperial Hotel, 96, 192
imperialism, 156, 228
industrialization, 1, 10–12, 14, 39, 71
infrastructure, 3, 7, 10, 35–37, 39, 51, 64, 98, 178, 192–93, 196, 213–14, 281n15
Ingram, Tammy, 52
International Workers of the World (IWW), 46–47, 50
isolationism, 60, 79, 155, 181, 224

J. E. Sirrine and Company, 36, 50, 190, 196, 274n61
Jackson, "Shoeless Joe," 35, 245n97
Jackson, Andrew, 64, 68, 100, 227
Jackson, Marion, 46–47
Janhz, Julius H., 43
Jensen, Kimberly, 83
Jewish Welfare Board, 86
Johnson, Ira, 21
Johnson, J. Monroe, 235
Johnson, James Weldon, 226
Johnson, Joan Marie, 31–32, 39, 83
Johnson, William Henry, 135, 232, 283–84n53, 284n54
Johnstone, Alan, 88–89
Jones, Marie, 87
Jordan, Louise A., 84
Judson Literary Society, 23
Judson Mill, 35, 47
Judson, Charles C., 23
Judson, Mary Camilla, 23, 184
Juvenile Protective Bureau, 88, 118

Keene, Jennifer D., 2, 73, 140, 234, 263n22, 265n84, 281n5
Keith, Jeanette, 100
Keith, Tom, 21
Kelsey, Harlan P., 28–29, 200, 237
Kennedy, David, 99, 126
Kennedy, John F., 230
Kennedy, Robert H., 20
Kenney, John A., 172
Kerr, J. W., 56

Kilgore, Benjamin, 52
Kinley, David, 154
Kiwanis Club, 3, 194
Knights of Columbus, 87
Kohlrus, C. F., 16
Kuhlman, Erika, 83
Ku Klux Klan, 105–106, 125, 179, 180–82, 209

labor rights movement: 46–48; *see also* International Workers of the World (IWW); United Textile Workers (UTW)
Ladies Auxiliary of the YMCA, 94, 256n46
Ladies' Memorial Associations, 15–16, 193
La Follette, Robert, 6
Lansing, Isaac J., 113
Lau, Peter, 32
Laval, W. L., 162
Lawton, T. O., 98
League of Women Voters, 3, 31, 183–84
Lee, Robert E., 15, 155
LeGrand, Leon, 190
Lehlbach, Frederick, 106
Lerda, Valeria Gennaro, 22, 239n15, 240n16, 240n24
Levine, David O., 143, 147–48
Liberty Bonds, 93, 257–58n85
Liebenfels, 43
Linard, J. L. A., 138
Lindley, E. H., 147
Link, Arthur, 6
Link, William, 6, 8, 239n15, 240n22
lintheads. See mill culture
literacy: 7, 27, 71–72, 98, 128, 178, 198–99, 202–4, 277n117; *see also* South Carolina Illiteracy Commission
Litwack, Leon, 139
localism, 8–10
Loewen, James, 229, 235–36
Logan, Ella Mae, 9, 210
Logan, Rayford, 121–22, 125, 139
Lost Cause mythology, 2, 14–15, 16–17, 32, 39, 85, 100, 102, 120–21, 183, 193, 194, 216, 217, 218, 227, 228, 237–38
Loving, Walter Howard, 133
Lynch, Harriet Powe, 183
lynching, 20–21, 125–26, 130, 133, 180, 220
Lyon, C. J., 73
Lyon, Thomas J., 222

Index 311

MacArthur, Douglas, 69

Maclaurin, Richard, 151

Maddox, J. B., 108

mail service, 36, 43, 219

Mallon, Eunice, 161

Manning, Richard, 48, 52, 72, 93, 97, 106, 116,
125, 128, 130, 169, 227, 257n66, 263n17

Mann, J. L., 98, 166

Mansion House (hotel), 18, 96, 192

March, Peyton, 164

Marshall, John, 62

Marshall, Thomas R., 180

Martin, B. F., 98

Martin, John C., 119

Martin, Willie Gray, 187, 192

Masons, 90

Mayberry Park, 195, 237

Mayes, Charles, 94

Mayes, F. Louise, 7, 28, 93–95, 95, 102,
256n46

McAfee, Thomas, 167

McDavid, Frances Sullivan, 190

McGlothlin, Mary Belle, 187

McGlothlin, William J., 155–57, 212–13,
221–22, 267n62, 280n166

McKinley, William, 17

McKinney, James P. "Jim," 136

McKissick, E. S. (Mrs.), 187

McKissick, J. Rion, 7, 100, 102–3, 279n137

McKissick, Margaret Adger Smyth, 5, 7, 31,
31, 184, 187, 224, 242n46, 244n79

McKoy, Henry Bacon, 5, 63, 65, 68, 77, 212,
250n12

McPherson, John A., 194

McSwain, J. J., 178

Meadowbrook Park, 195

measles, 77, 159–60, 165, 174, 268–69n8

Medal of Honor, 231–32, 283n52, 283–84n53

Men and Religion Forward Movement, 47

meningitis, 159, 165, 256–57n62

Middleton, Henry, 18

militarism, 81, 100

mill villages: 7, 10, 13, 20, 181; children, 10, 56,
201; labor movement, 47–49; public education, 72, 98, 199; quality of life, 14, 35, 40,
200, 202; sanitation, 54–55, 175; Whiteness,
20–21, 104

Miller, Kelly, 129–30, 139

Milliken, Sayres Louise, 87, 163, 171–72, 173–74

Mills Mill, 35, 55

Mills, A. L., 62, 112

Mills, Henry T., 118, 219, 261–62n64

Mills, Robert, 190, 204

Miner, Maude, 87

Molina, Juan Benito, 209

Monaghan Mill, 28, 35, 46

moonshine, 182

Moore, Ernest, 5

Moore, Tack, 20–21

Moore, Walter B., 55

Morgan, J. P., 14, 42

Morrah, Hessie T., 187

Moseley, A. M., 91

Mother Emanuel African Methodist Episcopal
(AME) Church, 223, 237

Mount Zion Colored Baptist Church, 20

mumps, 77, 165

Municipal League of Greenville, 28, 184, 194

municipal services, 2, 10, 185, 194–95

Nathanael Greene Chapter of the Daughters
of the American Revolution (DAR), 95

National American Woman Suffrage Association (NAWSA), 26–27, 57–59, 83–84, 182

National Association for the Advancement of
Colored People (NAACP), 3, 33, 106, 115,
117, 123, 126, 150, 179–80, 209, 244n82,
244–45n83

National Association of Colored Graduate
Nurses, 170

National Association of Colored Women, 210

National Guard, 64, 91, 123–24, 126, 130,
133–34, 147, 263n18

nationalism, 2, 3, 10, 53, 56, 72, 99, 156, 212,
224

National Negro Business League, 105

National Research Council, 144, 148

National Woman's Party (NWP), 59, 84, 182,
254n17, 255n26

Naval Training Camp (Charleston), 161

Navy Nurses Corps, 170

Neblett Free Library, 90, 204, 256n52

Neblett, A. Viola, 7, 22–23, 24, 24, 25, 25–27,
204, 242n46, 243n61

Negro Civic Preparedness Commission, 106

Negro Progressive League, 180

New Era Club, 57
New Negro movement, 179
New South boosterism, 1
New South Creed, 14
New South: and Greenville, 10, 19, 33–34, 189; women, 24, 85–86
Newton, B. R., 56
Nicholls, Samuel J., 106
Nineteenth Amendment, 2, 182–83, 215, 284–85n63
Norwood, John W., 7, 51, 88, 204, 278n126

Okeh Mill, 167
Orr, James Lawrence, 188, 244n78
Orr, Mary, 41
Orth, Albert, 43
Ottoray Hotel, 190, 193–94, 219

Pace, Edward A., 154
Paris Mountain Water Company, 63, 79
Paris Peace Conference, 177
Paris Station, 65
Park and Tree Commission, 28
Parker Cotton Mills, 45
Parker School District/Parker High School, 199, 201–2, 249n89
Parker, Hattie, 111, 210
Parker, Joe, 108
Parker, Lewis Wardlaw, 28, 51, 192
Parker, Margaret Smith, 167, 242n46
Parker, Thomas F., 7, 10, 28, 46–47, 119, 196, 199–202, 205–8, 276–77n100, 279n137
Parkers Mill, 35
paternalism, 14, 123
patriarchy, 183
patriotism, 3, 19, 43, 57, 62, 72–73, 76, 96, 100, 102–3, 114, 118, 120–21, 124, 154, 193–94
Patterson, Andrea Christensen, 7, 23, 58, 187, 188, 242n46, 244n78
Patterson, Lawrence Orr, 188
Patterson, Martha Orr, 7, 23, 31, 242n46, 244n78, 254n20
Paul, Alice, 58–59, 84, 85
Payne, W. E., 9, 105, 111
Pearson, Joseph Anderson, 37
Perrott, J. C., 162–63, 173
Perry, Benjamin F., 13, 23, 52
Perry, Elizabeth, 58, 254n20
Perry, Ellen, 23, 58, 98, 249n89, 276–77n100

Perry, James M. "Miss Jim," 184, 213, 273n39
Perry, William H., 52
Pershing, John "Blackjack," 63, 138, 164
Phillis Wheatley Community Center, 3, 202, 204–6, 208, 208–11, 274n53
Pickens Cotton Mill, 47
Piedmont Mill, 35
Piedmont Shirt Company, 14
Pinson, J. A., 20
Plattsburg Movement, 146, 250n8
Plessy v. Ferguson (1895), 29, 125
Plyler, John L., 71
Pneumonia, 77, 159–61, 163–164, 166, 169, 173–75, 270n41
Poe Mill, 20, 21, 35, 169
Poinsett Club, 89, 105, 256n61
Poinsett Hotel, 192
Poinsett Mill, 35
Pollitzer, Anita, 84, 182
Pollock, William, 85, 255n27
Poole, W. Scott, 4, 15
Pope, Thomas H., 98
Popelin, Jacques, 66–68
Poppenheim, Louisa, 32
Poppenheim, Mary, 32
population growth, 2, 9–10, 13, 27, 35, 39, 110, 178
Populists, 37
Porter, J. W., 100
Prather, D. J., 71
Preston, Howard Lawrence, 36
Pridgen, Joe, 70, 74, 76–77, 79, 268–69n8
Prisma Health, 3
Prison Special (National Woman's Party), 182
Progressive Greenville, 7, 10, 189, 214
Progressive Greenville, 57, 81, 185
Progressive Party, 6
Progressivism: and business, 8, 199; different approaches to, 6, 239n15, 240n27; and education, 213; in Greenville, 7, 9, 28–29, 40, 56–57, 103, 178, 189; and highways, 36–37; historiography, 1, 3, 6, 202; in the South, 6, 8–9, 22, 28–29, 183, 240n19, 240n24,30, 255n23; outside the South, 6, 8, 183–84, 196, 202
Prohibition, 8–9, 37, 169, 177, 181–82
prostitution, 86–89, 181
Putnam, George, 13, 24
Putnam, Mary, 25, 26

Quigley, Paul, 99

race riots: 21, 133, 140, 180; *see also* Charleston Race Riot
racial violence, 20–21, 125, 133, 139–40, 179–80, 233, 236, 242n36; *see also* lynching
racism, 27, 48–49, 109, 127, 129, 140, 171, 179, 180–81, 231, 232–33, 237
railroads, 35, 51–52, 56, 63, 107
Ramsay, David, 75, 152, 169, 249n87
Ramsay, Eudora, 23, 58
Ramsay, Mary, 187, 242n46
Rector, Hendrix, 47, 108, 166, 216, 217
Red Cross: 44, 86, 148, 169, 184, 206, 256n61, 256–57n62, 257–58n85; African Americans, 110–15, 170–71, 210; support for soldiers, 76, 89, 91–93, 159, 161, 168
Red Shirts, 125
Red Summer, 140, 180, 206
Rees, Robert I., 149
regionalism, 10
Reserve Officers Training Corps (ROTC), 149, 154–55
Rice, William F., 10, 111–12, 119, 180
Richards, Pauline, 88
Richardson, James A., 151
Richardson, James F., 17, 50
Richardson, James M., 17, 36, 51, 58, 258n92
Richey, A. V. R., 137–38
Roberts Mill, 35
Roberts, Needham, 135
Robertson, W. F., 62
Rollin, Charlotte "Lottie," 22
Rollin, Frances "Frank," 16, 22
Rollin, Katherine, 22
Roosevelt, Theodore, 63, 73, 125
Rosenwald Fund, 203
Rosenwald, Julius, 203, 247n35, 278n122, 278n123
Rotary Club, 3, 7, 53, 62, 92, 166, 204, 212, 228
Rubenstein, Julius, 73
Rule, Walter S., 91

Saint Mary's Catholic Church, 90, 94, 212
Saint Mary's School, 212
Salley, Eulalie Chafee, 182–83
Saluda Mill, 167
Salvation Army, 3, 27, 89, 97, 196, 243n62, 255n39, 256n61, 276n82

Sampson, Oscar H., 13
Sanders, Stella E., 163–64
sanitation, 3, 9, 24, 28, 53–56, 69–71, 111, 159–60, 175, 188
Santacaterina, Donny, 1, 239n3
Sarratt, Lois, 87–88
Scott, Emmett J., 123, 126, 129, 134, 150, 260n29
Second Presbyterian Church, 90
sectionalism, 17
Sedition Act (1918), 84, 97
segregation: 9, 33, 53, 89, 109, 132, 176, 197, 214, 243n66; *de facto,* 19, 29; *de jure,* 19, 29, 53, 195, 197; of civic organizations, 110, 170, 189; of higher education, 150, 277n117; of the military, 123, 128–30, 133, 140–41, 170–72, 218, 226, 263n18; of mill villages, 40, 49; of neighborhoods, 28–30, 33; of public schools, 198–99, 203; *see also* Act to Compel a Separation of the Races Laboring in Textile Manufactories (1915); World War I: African American soldiers
Selective Service Act (1917): 63, 70, 73, 86, 98, 164, 258–59n104; African Americans, 116–17, 121, 124–25, 127–29, 132, 137, 141, 145–46, 262n16; college students, 145, 147; resistance to, 101, 130, 257–58n85
Sellers, Charles, 78
Sevier, John, 63
sexism, 127, 171
Shaw, Anna Howard, 57–58, 83, 272n6
Shearer, Benjamin F., 154
Shemin, William, 232
Shillady, John R., 117–18, 150, 179–80, 273n22
Simpson, French, 166
Simpsonville, 54, 204
Sims, W. T., 130
Sinclair, Upton, 46
Sires, Edward B., 97
Sires, Elsie V., 97
Sirrine, George W., 7, 180, 250n11
Sirrine, Joseph "Joe" E., 7, 50, 63–65, 93, 185, 250n11,12,14,15
Sirrine, Nana Louise McLeod, 7, 92, 112, 114, 187, 243n62, 256n61, 256–57n6
Sirrine, Sarah "Odie," 7, 22–23, 25, 63, 242n46, 250n11
Sirrine, William G., 63, 98, 250n11
Sissle, Noble, 133
Skinner, Zulieme, 23

Smith, Clarence E., 55
Smith, John B., 138
Smith-Towner Act, 154, 156
Snyder, Henry Nelson, 150, 152–55
Social Gospel, 46
Sons of Temperance, 8, 181
South Carolina Board of Health, 165–68
South Carolina constitutions, 21, 27, 29, 57, 85, 104, 183, 203, 218
South Carolina Equal Rights Association (SCERA), 26–27
South Carolina Equal Suffrage League (SCESL), 31, 57–58, 95, 182–83
South Carolina Federation of Colored Women's Clubs (SCFCWC), 210, 211, 255n42, 260n33, 280n152
South Carolina Federation of Women's Clubs (SCFWC), 24, 32, 39, 72, 95, 198, 242–43n47
South Carolina General Assembly, 13, 225
South Carolina Good Roads Association, 36
South Carolina Illiteracy Commission, 202
South Carolina League of Women Voters, 31, 183
South Carolina Race Conference, 32
South Carolina State Council on Defense, 81
South Carolina Woman's Christian Temperance Union (SCWCTU), 22, 24
South Carolina Woman's Council on Defense (SCCD), 81, 93–95, 110
Southern Baptist Convention, 32, 100, 102
Southern Power Company, 64
Southern Textile Association, 82
Southern Textile Exhibition, 50, 76, 192
Spanish influenza: 2, 5, 151–53, 158–65, 166, 166–70, 172–75, 174, 197, 284–85n63; see also Charleston: Spanish influenza; Columbia: Spanish influenza
Spanish-American War, 10, 17, 50, 62–63, 67, 77, 125, 148, 231, 283n52
Sparks, Joe, 106
Spartanburg-Gaffney-Greenville-Anderson National Highway, 52
Spirit of the American Doughboy, 5, 221–22, 223, 281n12
Springfield Baptist Church, 105, 113
Standard Time Act (1918), 94
states' rights, 85, 181, 183
Stevenson, L. L., 51
Stewart, Rhoda, 88

Story, G. E., 97
Stowers, Freddie, 137–38, 231–32, 283–84n53
Stradley, C. D., 94
Student Army Training Corps (SATC), 143, 149–51, 154–55
suffrage: 2, 215, 254n17, 255n27, 284–85n63; critics of, 84–86, 179, 182–83; in Greenville, 7, 23–24, 26, 39, 57–59, 84, 178, 243n61, 244n78; and Progressivism, 8, 37, 177, 240n22; and White supremacy, 22, 27, 85, 182–83; see also American Woman Suffrage Association; Charleston: woman suffrage movement; Columbia: woman suffrage movement; Equal Suffrage Club; Gridley, Mary Putnam: suffrage activism; National American Woman Suffrage Association (NAWSA); Nineteenth Amendment; South Carolina Equal Suffrage League (SCESL); Vaughan, Helen E.: suffrage activism; Wilson, Woodrow: woman's suffrage
Symmes, Fred W., 184
Szymanski, Ann-Marie, 8, 239n15, 240n19

Table Rock Reservoir, 196
Taylor, Will, 108
Textile Hall, 50–51, 76, 177, 190, 229, 247n50
textile industry: 20, 33–35; patriotism, 57; progressivism, 57; World War 1, 45–46, 50, 52–53; see also Act to Compel a Separation of the Races Laboring in Textile Manufactories (1915); cotton; International Workers of the World (IWW); labor rights movement; Southern Textile Exposition; United Textile Workers (UTW)
Thursday Afternoon Club, 188
Thursday Club, 23–24, 188, 204, 242n46, 242–43n47, 244n78, 248n60
Tigerville, 204
Tillman, Benjamin Ryan "Pitchfork Ben," 21, 27, 84–86, 93, 104, 126, 233
Timmons, William R. "Bill," 184
Tindall, George B., 8–9, 139, 199, 239n15
Tolbert, James A., 9, 111, 119, 240n30, 261n39, 276n95
Townes, H. K., 98
Trammell, Naomi Sizemore, 169
Trinity Lutheran Church, 90, 94, 225
Trout, Steven, 218, 221
Truman, Harry S., 140

tuberculosis, 5, 24, 175, 196–98, 205, 210
Tuchman, Barbara, 230
Turnipseed, R. E., 167
typhoid, 69–70

Union Bleachery, 35
United Confederate Veterans, 193
United Daughters of the Confederacy (UDC): 32, 185; and clubwomen, 31, 244n79; and suffrage, 31, 95, 183; and White supremacy, 15–16
United Textile Workers (UTW), 47–50
United War Work Campaign, 120
United Way, 3, 274n44
University of South Carolina, 145, 155
urbanization, 11, 224
US Bureau of War Risk Insurance (BWRI), 95, 116, 118
US Food Administration, 93–94
US Public Health Service, 53–54, 71, 164, 175

Vardaman, James K., 141
Vaughan, Helen E.: 7, 10, 187; national reconciliation activism, 102, 183; woman's suffrage activism, 58, 84–86, 183, 254n15,20, 255n27
Vaughan, Victor C., 153, 158, 160, 167, 175
venereal disease, 87–89
Veteran's Day, 231
Victor Mill, 35, 196
Villa, Pancho, 86–87
Viquesney, Ernest Moore, 5, 221, 223, 235, 281n12
volunteerism, 9, 121, 125–27, 146

Wadsworth, James S., 64
Walker, M. K., 151
Walker, Melissa, 34
War Camp Community Service (WCCS), 86, 89–92, 95, 102, 114, 256n45
War Risk Insurance Act (1918), 95, 116, 124
Washington, Booker T., 104–5, 129
Wassum, J. W., 93
Watson, Richard F., 7, 178, 190, 193, 195
Watson, Thomas, 36
Webb, Charles S., 52, 62
West Greenville, 35, 54–55, 195
Wetherill, Alexander, 17
Whaley, A. M., 71
White elites, 5, 14, 23, 32, 39–40, 193

White minority control, 38–39, 102, 127, 183, 206
White supremacy: 14–15, 21–22, 27–31, 33, 44, 85, 104–105, 116, 125, 127, 133, 139, 182–83, 255n23
White, Deborah Gray, 139, 180
White, John E., 102
White, Walter, 117, 179
Whitin, George C., 13
Wierse, Paul, 43
Wilburn, D. M., 173
Wilkes, Carl V., 148
Wilkins, Harry, 151
Willard, Frances, 21
Williams, Anna C., 82
Williams, Chad, 1, 140, 171, 179, 262n16
Williams, Charles H., 114–15, 132
Williams, Hattie E., 9, 111, 122, 210, 260n33
Williams, James T., 17
Williams, Robert, 21
Willis, Le Roy, 114
Wilson, Adam Patrick, 127
Wilson, Charles Reagan, 15, 17, 266n8
Wilson, John, 35
Wilson, Margaret, 90
Wilson, Woodrow: 180, 182, 220, 257–58n85, 273n22; Grenville support for, 53, 60–61, 82; isolationism, 60; League of Nations, 59, 156; race relations, 117, 123–24, 126, 129–30, 140–41, 180; transportation reform, 37, 51–52; woman's suffrage, 57, 84, 182; World War I, 59–60, 63, 81, 101, 119, 146, 164, 176–77
Wingate, Jennifer, 223-225
Winter, Jay, 4
Wofford College, 148–50, 153–54, 226–27
Woman's Bureau (Chamber of Commerce), 187–89
Woman's Christian Temperance Union (WCTU), 8, 22–23, 181
Woman's Committee on the Council of National Defense (WCND), 81, 83
women 1, 3, 8; club movement, 7, 22–24; textile industry, 82; war work as precursor for suffrage, 83, 185; World War I, 82–83, 86, 92–96; see also New South: women; Nineteenth Amendment; suffrage
Women's Social and Political Union (WSPU), 58
Wood, Leonard, 62–63, 145, 250n12, 278n126

Woods, Charles A., 204
Woodside Building, 190, *191*, 191–92
Woodside Mill, 35, *36*, 169
Woodside, John T., 35, 190, 192
Woodside, Lou, 167
Woodsmen, 90
Woodward, Baldwin, and Company, 13
Work or Fight laws, 97, 116–17
Working Benevolent Society Hospital, 198
Working Benevolent Society, 113
Working Benevolent Temple and Professional
   Building, 198, 207, 273n25, 276n95
Workman, W. D., 216–18, 222, 256n52
World War I: 1, 2, 35, 44, 73, 86–87, 97, 99, 158,
   176, 212, 215, 230, 258–59n104, 281–82n20;
   Eighty-First Infantry Division, 4, 69, 97, 229,
   251n37; higher education impacts, 143, 147,
   157; historiography, 1–2, 4, 234, 284–85n63;
   impacts on Greenville, 1, 4, 10, 59, 62, 73,
   75–76, 79–80; memorialization of, 5, 217,
   223–24, 226, 230, 232, 234–36, 281n15; One
   Hundred Eighteenth Infantry Division, 5, 66,
77; poison gas use/victims, 5, 197, 224; songs,
72–73, 96, 162; Thirtieth "Old Hickory"
Infantry Division, 3–5, 68, 101, 216–18, *220*,
228, 235, 281n8, 283n45; volunteerism,
145–47, 155; White soldiers, 2, 138; women,
269n39; *see also* African American soldiers;
Charleston: World War I; segregation: and
the military
World War II, 220, 229, 232, 283–84n53
Wright, Juanita, 88

Yates, J. L., 152
Young Men's Christian Association (YMCA),
   3, 25, 58, 64, 74, 86, 89, 90–92, 94, 110, 148,
   162–63, 185, 200, 202, 206, 249n86, 256n52
Young Women's Christian Association (YWCA),
   24, 90–92, 185, 200, 202, 206
Young, Alice, 163–64
Young, Virginia Durant, 24–27, 57

Zieger, Robert, 42, 53, 141
Zimmerman, Arthur, 59